Essays on Transport Economics

Contributions to Economics

www.springer.com/series/1262

Further volumes of this series can be found at our homepage.

Pablo Coto-Millán (Ed.)
Essays on Microeconomics and Industrial Organisation, 2nd Edition
2004. ISBN 3-7908-0104-6

Wendelin Schnedler
The Value of Signals in Hidden Action Models
2004. ISBN 3-7908-0173-9

Carsten Schröder
Variable Income Equivalence Scales
2004. ISBN 3-7908-0183-6

Wilhelm J. Meester
Locational Preferences of Entrepreneurs
2004. ISBN 3-7908-0178-X

Russel Cooper/Gary Madden (Eds.)
Frontiers of Broadband, Electronic and Mobile Commerce
2004. ISBN 3-7908-0087-2

Sardar M. N. Islam
Empirical Finance
2004. ISBN 3-7908-1551-9

Jan-Egbert Sturm/Timo Wollmershäuser (Eds.)
Ifo Survey Data in Business Cycle and Monetary Policy Analysis
2005. ISBN 3-7908-0174-7

Bernard Michael Gilroy/Thomas Gries/Willem A. Naudé (Eds.)
Multinational Enterprises, Foreign Direct Investment and Growth in Africa
2005. ISBN 3-7908-0276-X

Günter S. Heiduk/Kar-yiu Wong (Eds.)
WTO and World Trade
2005. ISBN 3-7908-1579-9

Emilio Colombo/Luca Stanca
Financial Market Imperfections and Corporate Decisions
2006. ISBN 3-7908-1581-0

Birgit Mattil
Pension Systems
2006. ISBN 3-7908-1675-2

Francesco C. Billari/Thomas Fent/Alexia Prskawetz/Jürgen Scheffran (Eds.)
Agent-Based Computational Modelling
2006. ISBN 3-7908-1640-X

Kerstin Press
A Life Cycle for Clusters?
2006. ISBN 3-7908-1710-4

Russel Cooper/Gary Madden/Ashley Lloyd/Michael Schipp (Eds.)
The Economics of Online Markets and ICT Networks
2006. ISBN 3-7908-1706-6

Renato Giannetti/Michelangelo Vasta (Eds.)
Evolution of Italian Enterprises in the 20th Century
2006. ISBN 3-7908-1711-2

Ralph Setzer
The Politics of Exchange Rates in Developing Countries
2006. ISBN 3-7908-1715-5

Dora Borbély
Trade Specialization in the Enlarged European Union
2006. ISBN 3-7908-1704-X

Iris A. Hauswirth
Effective and Efficient Organisations?
2006. ISBN 3-7908-1730-9

Marco Neuhaus
The Impact of FDI on Economic Growth
2006. ISBN 3-7908-1734-1

Nicola Jentzsch
The Economics and Regulation of Financial Privacy
2006. ISBN 3-7908-1737-6

Klaus Winkler
Negotiations with Asymmetrical Distribution of Power
2006. ISBN 3-7908-1743-0

Sasha Tsenkova, Zorica Nedović-Budić (Eds.)
The Urban Mosaic of Post-Socialist Europe
2006. ISBN 3-7908-1726-0

Brigitte Preissl/Jürgen Müller (Eds.)
Governance of Communication Networks
2006. ISBN 3-7908-1745-7

Lei Delsen/Derek Bosworth/Hermann Groß/Rafael Muñoz de Bustillo y Llorente (Eds.)
Operating Hours and Working Times
2006. ISBN 3-7908-1759-7

Pablo Coto-Millán; Vincente Inglada (Eds.)
Essays on Transport Economics
2007. ISBN 3-7908-1764-3

Christian H. Fahrholz
New Political Economy of Exchange Rate Policies and the Enlargement of the Eurozone
2007. ISBN 3-7908-1761-9

Pablo Coto-Millán · Vicente Inglada
(Editors)

Essays on Transport Economics

With 41 Figures and 75 Tables

Physica-Verlag
A Springer Company

Series Editors
Werner A. Müller
Martina Bihn

Editors
Prof. Dr. Pablo Coto-Millán
Department of Economics
Universidad de Cantabria
Avenida de los Castros s/n
39005 Santander
Spain
cotop@unican.es

Prof. Dr. Vicente Inglada
Department of Applied Economics II
Universidad Complutense de Madrid
Campus de Somosaguas
28223 Pozuelo Madrid
Spain
vinglada@ccee.ucm.es

Published with the financial support of the Logistics Technology Center of Cantabria (CTL)

Library of Congress Control Number: 2006937537

ISSN 1431 - 1933
ISBN-10 3-7908-1764-3 Physica-Verlag Heidelberg New York
ISBN-13 978-3-7908-1764-5 Physica-Verlag Heidelberg New York

Physica-Verlag is part of Springer Science+Business Media

springer.com

Production: LE-TeX Jelonek, Schmidt & Vöckler GbR, Leipzig
Cover-design: Erich Kirchner, Heidelberg

SPIN 11825845 88/3100YL - 5 4 3 2 1 0 Printed on acid-free paper

Contents

Introduction

An analysis of the history of economic thought reveals that transport and economics have always gone hand-in-hand. Many methodological developments in economic theory have emerged from the sphere of transport; Jules Dupuit (1849) and Arthur C. Pigou (1912), for example, proposed price setting in transport infrastructures, particularly on congested roads. This issue is referred to in economic literature as optimum price setting and is still the subject of much attention even today. It is difficult to imagine how the transcendental change in economic development brought about by the industrial revolution would have occurred without the invention of the railway. Today's "new economics", which is for some an innovative concept in economic science, is also closely linked to transport.

However, not only is transport present in the entire economic tissue, it is also a key element in individual behaviour, revealed in decisions about work, place of residence and location of companies, among others.

One characteristic of transport is that it is a service that can also be used as an intermediary factor in the production process or form part of final household consumption. Studies on this sector therefore have a number of dimensions.

As it encompasses a number of branches of economic theory, the study of transport from an economic point of view is an ideal test bench for applying the methodological developments of economic science to the real world.

This text includes topics that hold a privileged position in current economic debate, which form part of the most diverse branches of economic science: Microeconomic Analysis, Industrial Organisation, Welfare Economics, General Equilibrium and Input-Output Analysis, Public Economics, Statistics, Econometrics, etc.

In addition to classic issues of economic science on production functions, costs, utility and demand, such as technical and allocative efficiency, other timeless issues are also discussed, such as: New Economics; competition and the effects of deregulation; uses of time; the effects of public investment on the Economy and social welfare, and internalization of externalities through prices.

This book uses the methodological structure of an economics handbook, i.e. research is analysed in accordance with the traditional parts of economics: Utility, Demand, Supply, General Equilibrium and Economic Impact Studies, Failures of market, Evaluation of Infrastructure and Transport Projects and New Economics and Innovation. Each chapter begins with a brief theoretical introduction, written with the utmost scientific rigour. They then turn to look at case studies using the most up-to-date statistical and econometric techniques, such as cointegration, discrete choice and panel analysis, among others.

This book is therefore useful for students and practitioners of the various branches of economics as it helps to clarify and strengthen the ties between economic theory and practice, as well as introducing the latest developments in economic theory.

It will also be of interest for individuals, be they students or practitioners, involved in transport to a greater or lesser degree: engineers, economists, geographers, planners, etc.

The text consists of five parts: Demand, Supply and Efficiency, Market and Economic Impact Study, Valuation of Benefits and Costs and, finally, Transportation Network and Information and Communications Technology.

Section I deals with demand and starts with a paper that develops an alternative approach for analysing the phenomenon of congestion within an urban road network industrial demand. The theoretical approach differs from previous contributions where congestion is usually analysed as an externality rather than in terms of household production using a congested public good. It is illustrated the applicability and feasibility of the approach for a simple network of two parallel links. In chapter 2 after time value theories are reviewed, the value of the time spent by students for travelling in Santander (Spain) is calculated. With this end in view the transport demand function is estimated by means of logit and probit models. To conclude this section, Chapter 3 analyses the Marshallian demand functions with respect to relevant income and price variables for each modes of transport and income and price elasticities are estimated.

Section II deals with supply and efficiency issues. The purpose of the Chapter 4 is to classify urban passenger transportation services with respect to service structure and with respect to type of service. In chapter 5, allocative efficiency is analysed for the case of the RENFE, a public service body which develops its activity as a commercial firm and is the main railway transport provider in Spain. In order to measure properly the allocative efficiency, a Shephard distance function for the input .is estimated that allows to check if the inputs are efficiently used or, otherwise, if there is any kind of inefficiency. In chapter 6 cargo handling activities is analysed through the estimation of a cost function with output described as total volume handled, from which marginal costs, scale economies and policy conclusions are obtained. Then the results are compared against those arising from output described in detail. In chapter 7 cost functions for the passengers railway transport are estimated. The functional form used is the translog and Allen and Morishima elasticities of substitution are also estimated. Chapter 8 studies the economic efficiency of a sample of Spanish civil airports. With this aim, a frontier-cost function is estimated by applying the panel data technology. Finally, Chapter 9 presents an economic study of cargo handling operations in Spain for the period from 1990 to 1998 in order to evaluate the reform process to cargo handling regulation. To do it, a multi-output cost function of the cargo handling operation is estimated.

Section III studies the market and economic impact. Chapter 10 offers a methodological review of port impact studies and their possible applications to policy design. Chapter 11 studies the effects of airport management on airline and airport competition. The methodology used takes as starting point the analysis of the most common airport practices in terms of ownership, finance and airline access policies for the OECD countries. Then, possible types of airport and airline competition, stressing interactions between both agents, are analyzed. Finally, chapter 12 proposes a potential way to avoid one of the structural weaknesses of economic impact studies that rely on the static character of the Leontief Input-Output methodology, by linking the Input-Output methodology to the System dynamics simulation supported on econometric estimations of certain of the model variables.

Section IV deals with Cost-Benefit Analysis and transport externalities issues. Chapter 13 reviews and interpret existing literature, evaluating the economic benefits of bicycle facilities. Then methods and strategies for doing so in future work are suggested. Chapter 14 presents three applications of Stated Choice technique undertaken in Santiago (Chile), to estimate prices that are not revealed by simple market observation and to elicit willingness to pay for improving urban road safety, better air quality and increasing levels of quietness. Finally, chapter 15 compares the results obtained from the application of the different transport policies – price and investment – which pursue the objective of reducing negative external effects.

Section V studies transportation network and information and communications technology. Chapter 16 studies the influence on spatial patterns of activities produced by innovations in transportation systems, analyzing the possible role of ITS in location theory. In the chapter 17 the dynamics of transportation network growth is analyzed, considering the growth of transportation networks as endogenous, in contrast with current transportation planning practice that strives to exogenously direct that growth. Chapter 18 studies the role of transport investment in influencing the location of economic activity. It presents an empirical contribution regarding dynamic location effects of transport infrastructure investment based on data for the Spanish road building programme over the period from 1980 to 2000 and municipality-level manufacturing data. Finally, chapter 19 presents an analysis of relationships between ICT and travel. Firstly it maps the terrain of existing work to date related to ICT and household travel. Then it sheds light on emerging phenomena to help conceptualize future research.

PART I DEMAND

1 A Reassessment of the Characterisation of Congestion on an Urban Road Network – Some Theoretical Suggestions and Illustrative Experiments

Truong P. Truong
School of Economics
University of New South Wales (Australia)

David A. Hensher
Institute of Transport and Logistics Studies
University of Sydney (Australia)

To the memory of Peter J. Hills

1.1 Introduction

When a road user selects a particular part of the network to use, they are in the main buying speed – or its inverse, travel time savings, in return for an outlay of money, the latter including a toll or congestion charge where applicable. To study the phenomenon of buying speed as the indicator of service levels within a particular link, it is important to consider also the issue of interconnections between different links, since speed (and all its related concepts such as travel time, link capacity, and congestion) is to be seen as the outcome, not only of what happens on a particular link, but also of available service levels on other inter-connected links. In this paper, we first establish the framework for analysing the basic activity on one link, and then extend the analysis to consider the interconnection between different links. The purpose of the framework is to establish a foundation on which more comprehensive analysis of a general inter-connected network can be carried out in a routine manner, once the basic building blocks have been created.

We show that the approach can be considered as a modification and/or extension of the traditional approach (e.g., Else 1981, Evans 1992) where the concepts of 'capacity' and 'congestion' have been defined, not explicitly, in terms of the infrastructure capacity of the network or the traffic volume density, but rather in terms of the traffic flow *outcome*, which is the *product* of these two basic variables[1]. We will illustrate that by *separating out* the two basic *components* of this traffic flow variable, we can see the underlying process of interaction between travel demand and capacity supply, or price (travel time, or its inverse, speed) and quantity (traffic density) more clearly as compared to the situation when both of these components are mixed together in a single 'flow' variable.

Having defined the basic concepts of 'price' and 'quantity' in an economic framework describing the underlying travel activity supply and demand, we can then relate these concepts to the empirical data on how prices and quantities (or demand and supply) are related to each other in different empirical situations. These empirical observations often take the form of traffic density-travel time (or speed) curves, which are unique characteristics for each particular link. From these empirical observations, we can deduce an underlying congestion 'index' to represent the equilibrium outcome of the demand-supply interactions in a particular circumstance. We then use these indices as criteria to plan for the future, either in the form of short run 'congestion pricing', to reduce the level of congestion at a particular link, given a fixed capacity, and/or long run investment planning, to expand capacity to cope with expected rising demand. The congestion index is a useful way of summarising the underlying demand-supply interactions, as a guide for policy design.

The paper is organised as follows. Section 2 defines the basic concepts of 'capacity' and 'congestion'. Section 3 establishes the basic economic framework for linking the concepts of capacity and congestion as defined in the context of the basic *individual* travel activity within the transport link, as described by the theory of consumption (or production) of a congested public good. Section 4 then extends the analysis to apply to the case of a heterogenous population of travellers within a given link. Section 5 illustrates how the theoretical approach can be applied, using the example of a simple network of two parallel links with data calibrated on the information obtained from the Sydney road network. Section 6 concludes the paper.

1.2 Defining 'Capacity' and 'Congestion'

Let x be the traffic flow (vehicles per unit time) within a link of a network, and t be the average travel time per unit of trip distance for each level of traffic flow. The product xt is then equal to the total *social* cost[2] of travel (per unit of distance) along this link, while t is the *private* time-cost. If t is an increasing function of x, then $\partial t/\partial x > 0$ and $\partial(tx)/\partial x = t + x\partial t/\partial x > t$. The marginal social cost of travel when

[1] Traffic *flow* being the product of *speed* multiplied by traffic *density*.

[2] We only look at the time cost of travel and ignoring money cost for the moment.

traffic flow increases by one unit is thus greater than the private marginal cost (t)[3]. This is referred to as a situation of 'congestion' where each additional traveller (vehicle) on the link imposes a negative externality on the rest so that the overall social costs increase more than the sum of all the private costs. Congestion (in the traditional approach) is thus defined in terms of the level of traffic flow and average travel time[4]. When traffic flow reaches a maximum level, defined as the situation where $\partial t/\partial x \rightarrow \infty$, we say the (absolute) 'capacity' of the link has been reached.

Defining congestion and capacity of a link in terms of the traffic *flow* has certain practical and intuitive appeals, because the image of 'traffic' always entails an image of 'flow', and traffic flow is an easily measurable quantity. It has certain disadvantages, however. For example, the same level of traffic flow can come about from a situation of low traffic 'demand' (such as characterised by low traffic density) with a high traffic 'supply' (such as characterised by high speed), or from a reverse situation of high traffic demand (density) and a low traffic supply (low speed). This means that using traffic flow to characterise a particular demand or supply interaction can be ambiguous.

The deficiency of using traffic flow as a measure of the demand or supply conditions within a road network has been noted before (Hills 1993, 2001). Hills and Gray (2000), for example, suggest: "*That what people demand are trips not flow (or throughput)*...". A 'trip', however, is an individually-produced commodity, and when aggregated, it gives rise to the traffic density level at a particular point in time and for a particular segment of the road. Despite the fact that density is a 'static variable', it is a more accurate measure of the level of travel demand than traffic flow. This is because, as indicated above, flow consists of density * speed (or density ÷ travel time). While density is unambiguously related to the level of demand, travel time is not, since it is the 'price' rather than quantity variable. Therefore, 'embedding' the price variable with a quantity variable to produce a demand (quantity) signal may not be entirely accurate.

From the travel time – density (or speed-density) curves, as often observed in traffic studies, we can infer an underlying supply-demand interrelationship. For demand, we hypothesise that each individual traveller would regard the travel time across a link as a component of the overall generalised cost of travel across the link. The higher this cost the smaller would be the aggregate number of people wanting to 'demand' the trip (as would be reflected in a lower density level). On the supply side, the larger the quantity of supply (the greater the density of traffic), the higher will be the cost of supply, which includes the traveller's own opportunity cost of travel (i.e., the travel time). The supply curve therefore is reflected in the form of the travel time-density (or speed-density) curve. Demand is given 'exogenously' in the form of the number of people wanting to make the trip at

[3] Average travel time is also equal to the *marginal* private cost, because each individual traveller cannot influence the overall average travel time, and hence must take this as given, therefore, the marginal private cost is a constant and is equal to the average private cost.

[4] See for example, Walters (1961).

various levels of travel time and travel cost, which can be inferred from a study of the distribution of the behavioural value of travel time savings of a population of potential travellers as well as the distribution of money travel costs (Hensher and Greene 2003, Verhoef and Small 2004). For example, let U be the utility of the travel activity across the link. Assume for simplicity that U is the same for all travellers. An individual will decide to cross the link if and only if $U > (c + t.v)$ where c is the money cost and $t.v$ is the time cost, which consists of a travel time component (t) and a value of this travel time (v[5]). Assume also that v is distributed as shown in Figure 2 for a heterogenous population of potential travellers[6]. From the relationship $U > (c + tv)$, the higher the level of t, the lower will have to be the value of v for which the condition can be met (with a given level of U and c). This also means a smaller proportion of the total number of potential travellers will want to make the trip, and therefore, the traffic density on the road will be lower.

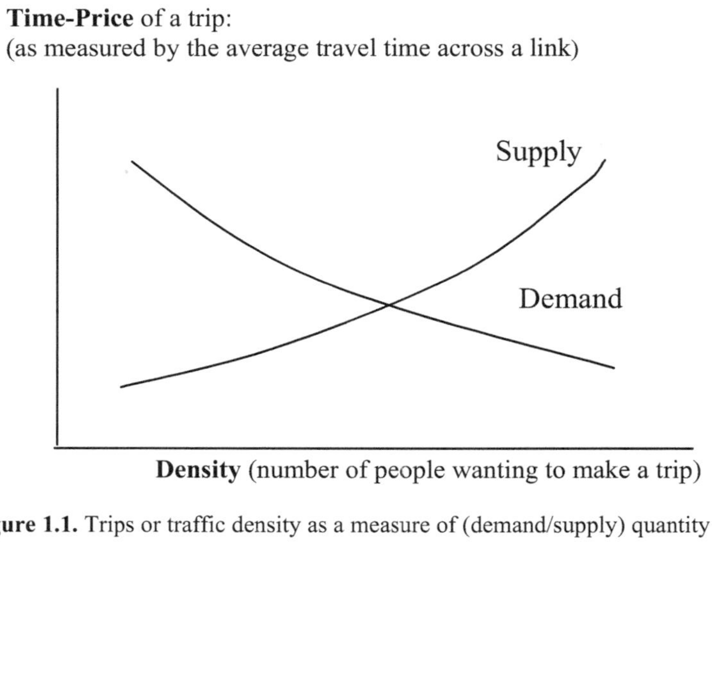

Figure 1.1. Trips or traffic density as a measure of (demand/supply) quantity

[5] We assume that v is the value of travel time *savings* rather than the value of travel time as a resource, to denote the fact that travel time acts both as a resource constraint as well as a commodity to be consumed while crossing the link. This means the value of v will reflect not only the resource opportunity cost of time, but also the value of the *quality* of travel time as determined by factors such as comfort, convenience, etc.

[6] This distribution will be used in section 5.

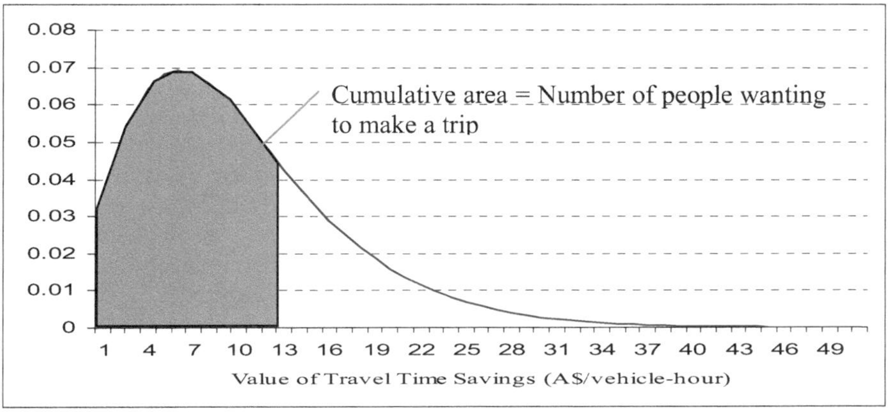

Figure 1.2. Density function of the value of travel time savings for a specific population of potential travellers.

1.3 Linking 'Capacity' and 'Congestion' Concepts to the Basic Individual Travel Activity across a Transport Link

To build up a framework for the analysis of congestion, whether across a specific link, or spreading through the network as a whole, we need to define the basic activity within a particular link. This activity can be regarded as either an (intermediate) production activity, or as a (final) consumption activity. If it is a production activity, then the interconnected network as a whole can be considered as analogous to a multi-sector economy. Trips across different links are production activities in different 'sectors', which may be substitutes (e.g., when links run in parallel) or complements (such as when links run in series). The general equilibrium condition within the network is then influenced by relative economic prices of these sectoral activities. These relative economic prices may in turn be influenced by sector-specific policies (such as the imposition of tolls across certain links), or by the general economic condition (such as the price of fuel relative to values of travel time savings). Viewed in this way, 'congestion' can be regarded both as a short run and/or link-specific phenomenon such as when we consider the equilibrium condition for a particular link with a fixed level of link capacity and fixed level of demand; and also as a long run or network-wide phenomenon, such as when we analyse the equilibrium condition for the entire network with the possibility of demand variation or capacity expansion across all links. The theory which describes the basic *individual* travel activity occurring in the link developed herein is based on the concept of a congested public good[7].

Let $f^i(.)$ be the production function[8] for user i. This production activity uses as inputs: the individual user's travel time and effort[9] t_i, money costs c_i, private capital (vehicle) k_i, and public infrastructure capital ('capacity' of the link) G. The key feature in this activity is the individual user's utilisation of a public capital good (G) which can become congested when the number of users exceeds a certain level. Following Oakland (1987), we note that when public infrastructure capital becomes a 'congested public' good, each individual user's *utilisation* of the public good generates a negative externality on all other users. As a result, the production function for a user i now includes, not only the total capacity level G of the link, but also the *capacity utilisation* levels $G_1, \ldots, G_n$ of all[10] n users:

$$f^i = f^i(t_i, c_i, k_i, G_1, \ldots, G_n, G) \tag{1.1}$$

We have:

$$\partial f^i / \partial G_i > 0; \quad \partial f^i / \partial G_j < 0, \quad \text{for } i \neq j \tag{1.2}$$

which implies that the marginal productivity of public infrastructure capital is positive for each individual user i (the first term in Eq. 1.2), but when the good becomes congested, each user's utilisation of this public capacity creates a negative externality on others (the second inequality in Eq. 1.2). From the economic analysis of public goods:

$$G_i = G, \quad i = 1, \ldots, n \tag{1.3}$$

---

[7] In contrast, it can be said that the traditional approach (such as described in Walters (1961)), defines congestion more in terms of an externality rather than in terms of the use of a congested public good (even though the theories of public good and theories of externalities are closely related).

[8] For convenience, we consider the case when a trip across a link is a 'production' activity. In this case, the output is the number of trips over a given period of time. It can also be considered as a 'consumption' activity, in which case the output is the level of 'utility' generated by that trip. In either case, the individual is maximising an objective function (output, or utility) subject to the link's capacity constraint and the individual's own resource constraints. Mathematically, the treatment will be similar; hence we sometimes use the words 'output' and 'utility' interchangeably.

[9] For the present, we assume that 'effort' is represented in the amount of travel time incurred and the 'value' (or price) of effort is also reflected in the value of travel time savings.

[10] Strictly speaking, we need to include only (n-1) utilisation levels of other users if G is also included in (1). However, to keep the formulation simple, we include all n utilisation levels in addition to G, noting that only (n-1) utilisation levels are independent, given a level of G and level of congestion.

if the good is 'uncongested' (i.e., the congestion level is zero, or the good is regarded as a 'pure' public good). When the good becomes congested, we have[11]:

$$G_i \leq G, \text{but} \sum_{i=1}^{n} G_i \geq G. \tag{1.4}$$

Following Oakland (1987), we also proceed to simplify the production function (Eq. 1.1), by introducing the concept of a 'congestion function' which relates the sum of all utilisation levels of all users to the maximum capacity of the link. A simple congestion function can take the following form:

$$\theta = \theta(\sum_{i=1}^{n} G_i, G). \tag{1.5}$$

Here, it is assumed that the congestion level θ is determined by comparing the sum of all the utilisation levels of all users $\sum_{i=1}^{n} G_i$ to the maximum capacity G. Through this congestion function $\theta(.)$, the specification of the production function (Eq. 1.1) can be simplified to:

$$f^i = f^i(t_i, c_i, k_i, G_i, \theta) \tag{1.6}$$

Next, we proceed to define the variables G_i and G. From an engineering point of view, 'capacity' G and capacity utilisation level G_i can be defined either in terms of the physical characteristics of the good (such as lane-kilometres), or alternatively the maximum number of people who can use the public good at any particular point in time without causing 'congestion'. The former definition is unhelpful from an economic viewpoint because from the theory of public goods, we know that a public good is one which is jointly consumed by all users; and even if a user only uses part of the road to travel (in a multi-lane section), the unit of consumption (or supply) of the good remains constant for all users[12]. Furthermore, it should not matter to a specific individual how many lanes a road link has, because *if* there is no congestion, an individual can travel across the link at the maximum free flow

---

[11] The situation when $\sum_{i=1}^{n} G_i = G$ is referred to as the case of a (pure) private good, the opposite of the case of a pure public good. In this particular case (perhaps when traffic has come to a stand still), any user's utilisation of the road space (capacity) is entirely at the expense of some other users. Hence, capacity is completely 'rival' in this case, similar to the case of a private good.

[12] In a similar manner, a user of a public park or a public beach is assumed (in theory at least) to 'consume' the *whole* integral park or beach rather than only a tiny part of it, even if (in practice) he may not be able to do so. In other words, in the case of a public good, the quantity remains constant, only the marginal willingness to pay varies between individuals.

speed. That is, for a specific individual, the 'capacity' of the road link remains 'constant'. Only when congestion occurs, and the travel speed starts to drop below the free flow level, can we say the user's utilisation level G_i has dropped below 'full capacity', i.e. $G_i.< G$. In other words, *speed*, or its inverse, average *travel time* across the link, can be used as a good proxy for the abstract concepts of 'capacity' and 'capacity utilisation level' *from an individual user's point of view*. The engineering characteristics (such as number of lanes or aggregate *number*[13] of users) are more useful from an aggregate supply or aggregate demand viewpoint, but are not the appropriate variable to be used as 'input' into an individual production function. From an individual user's point of view, capacity G and capacity utilisation level G_i are what a user can 'extract' from the public infrastructure good under various circumstances, and this is seen to manifest in the level of average speed (or its inverse, travel time). As a result, we can say that while t_i is also an input into the individual user's production function, since this travel time is closely and uniquely related to G_i and G, it can therefore be dropped from this function[14].

Using Eq. 1.6 (but without t_i), we can proceed to describe the optimal decision of each individual user i on the link. We note that, since congestion implies each individual user's action has an impact on others, these decisions cannot be considered in isolation, but rather, the equilibrium condition for the link as a whole must be considered. One of the possible equilibrium conditions which we can consider is the traditional Pareto optimality situation, defined as follows:

$$\begin{aligned}
&\text{Max } f^i(c_i, k_i, G_i, \theta) \\
&\text{s.t. } f^j(c_j, k_j, G_j, \theta) \geq U_j, \;\; j \neq i, \;\; j = 1, \ldots, n. \\
&G_j \leq G, \quad j = 1, \ldots, n. \\
&F\Big(\sum_{i=1}^{n} k_i, G\Big) \leq 0.
\end{aligned} \tag{1.7}$$

In this equilibrium condition, no single user's objective function can be improved upon without adversely affecting the utility (or output) level of at least one other user (represented by the constraint level U_j). The third expression in Eq. 1.7 merely re-iterates the 'congested public good' nature of capacity, and the final expression represents the transformation frontier between private and public capital goods, the slope of which represents the 'shadow price' of public capital G.

---

13 Not the aggregate *level of utilisation* i.e. $\sum_{i=1}^{n} G_i$ which may influence individuals' behaviour when there is congestion.

14 Or in fact, implied or represented by G_i. Note also that in terms of the 'cause and effect' relationship, G_i and θ causes a particular level of t_i rather than the reverse. Hence it is more meaningful to drop of t_i rather than G_i out of the production function (6) even though the two variables are highly correlated.

Forming the Lagrangian for the optimisation problem in Eq. 1.7 as:

$$L_i = f^i(t_i, c_i, k_i, G_i, \theta)] + \sum_{j \neq i} \lambda_j [U_j - f^j(t_j, c_j, k_j, G_j, \theta)]$$
$$+ \sum_{j=1}^{n} \gamma_j (G_j - G) + \mu F(\sum_{j=1}^{n} k_j, G); \quad \text{for } i = 1,\dots n. \tag{1.8}$$

Eq. 1.8 specifies the Lagrangian for i = 1,…, n users. However, since the model solves only for the relative rather than absolute prices, we can set an arbitrary level for the price of the 'reference' user. We choose, for convenience, λ_i = -1 and U_i = 0 for the reference user i. We can then re-write Eq. 1.8 in a more general form:

$$L = \sum_{j=1}^{n} \lambda_j [U_j - f^j(t_j, c_j, k_j, G_j, \theta)]$$
$$+ \sum_{j=1}^{n} \gamma_j (G_j - G) + \mu F(\sum_{j=1}^{n} k_j, G); \tag{1.9}$$

Eq. 1.9 applies to *all* users, hence we need to consider the solution for just one arbitrary user i. To derive the first order conditions for Eq. 1.9, we assume for simplicity that $G_i < G$ (i.e., congestion is non-zero), which gives $\gamma_i = 0$ for all i's; and the first order conditions for optimality are then simplified to[15]:

$$\frac{\partial L}{\partial k_i} = -\lambda_i f^i_{k_i} + \mu F_P = 0, \quad \text{for } \forall i \tag{1.10}$$

$$\frac{\partial L}{\partial G_i} = -\lambda_i f^i_{G_i} - \sum_{j=1}^{n} \lambda_j f^j_\theta \theta_1 = 0, \quad \text{for } \forall i \tag{1.11}$$

[15] The convention for notation is as follows: for a *function*, a super-script indicates the user; while a subscript indicates first-order partial derivative of the function with respect to the variable as indicated by the subscript; if the subscript is a number, this indicates the order in which the variable appears in the function, thus '1' represents the total utilization variable, $\sum_{i=1}^{n} G_i$, and '2' represents maximum capacity variable G for the case of the congestion function $\theta(.)$. For a *variable*, however, a subscript indicates the user.

$$\frac{\partial L}{\partial G} = -\sum_{j=1}^{n} \lambda_j f_\theta^j \theta_2 + \mu F_G = 0, \tag{1.12}$$

We note the following definitions for Eqs. 1.10-1.12:

$$f_x^i = \partial f^i / \partial x, \quad x = \{t_i, c_i, k_i, G_i, \theta\},$$
$$\theta_1 = \partial\theta / \partial\left(\sum_{i=1}^{N} G_i\right), \quad \theta_2 = \partial\theta / \partial(G), \tag{1.13}$$
$$F_P = \partial F / \partial\left(\sum_{i=1}^{N} k_i\right), \quad F_G = \partial F / \partial G.$$

Eqs. 1.11 and 1.12 can be combined to give:

$$\lambda_i f_{G_i}^i - (\theta_1 / \theta_2)(\mu F_G) = 0 \tag{1.14}$$

Using Eqs. 1.10 and 1.14, we derive:.

$$(f_{G_i}^i / f_{k_i}^i) = -(\theta_1 / \theta_2)(F_G / F_P) \tag{1.15}$$

The ratio (F_G/F_P) is the 'economy-wide' or general marginal rate of transformation between private and public capital for *all* users, and hence can be referred to as the general shadow price of public capital in terms of private capital foregone and denoted as P_G. The ratio $(f_{G_i}^i / f_{k_i}^i)$ is the marginal rate of substitution between private and public capital for a specific user i and can be referred to as the user-specific shadow price of public capital in terms of private capital.

If we assume that the function $\theta(.)$ is homogeneous of degree zero in its arguments[16] (i.e., increasing the aggregate utilisation rate and the link capacity by the same proportion will leave congestion level unchanged)[17], then we have:

---

[16] That is, as $\theta(kx,ky)=k^0.\theta(x,y)$, for any constant k, which means $d\theta(x,y)=0=(\partial\theta/\partial x)dx + (\partial\theta/\partial y)dy= (\partial\theta/\partial x)x + (\partial\theta/\partial y)y$ (for $dx= (k-1)x$, and $dy= (k-1)y$).

[17] This assumption implies constant returns to scale in capacity *utilization*, which is a reasonable assumption in the case of road capacity: doubling the capacity utilization rates G_i of all users but then also doubling the capacity G will leave the level of congestion unchanged. Note, however, that constant returns to scale in capacity *utilization* does not necessarily mean constant returns to scale in capacity *generation*. For example, doubling the number of lanes may more than doubling the capacity G for a road if passing is made easier. In this case, we can say that either the maximum free flow speed has more than doubled following a doubling in the number of lanes (assuming traffic density level re-

$$\theta_1 \sum_{i=1}^{n} G_i + \theta_2 G = 0. \tag{1.16}$$

This gives:

$$(\theta_1 / \theta_2) = -G / (\sum_{i=1}^{n} G_i) \tag{1.17}$$

Substituting Eq. 1.17 into Eqs. 1.15 and 1.16, we have:

$$(f_{G_i}^i / f_{k_i}^i) = [G / (\sum_{i=1}^{n} G_i)](F_G / F_P) \tag{1.18}$$

Multiplying both sides of Eq. 1.18 by G_i and sum over all i's, we have:

$$\sum_{i=1}^{n} (f_{G_i}^i / f_{k_i}^i) G_i = G(F_G / F_P) = GP_G, \tag{1.19}$$

Let $T_i = (f_{G_i}^i / f_{k_i}^i) G_i$ define for the willingness to pay for capacity by user i[18], which can also be referred to as the Lindahl's price of public capital applied to user *i*. Eq. 1.19 states that the sum of these Lindahl prices equals the system's total capacity cost (GP_G). This is the Samuelson condition for optimal provision of a congested public good[19].

1.4 Equilibrium Condition for a Heterogenous Population of Travellers

Having defined the activity for a single individual, we now consider the aggregation of all individual decisions to arrive at an aggregate level of demand (or traffic

mains the same), or the maximum density at which the old free flow speed can be maintained has more than doubled (see Figure 8, section 5 below). This is quite consistent with the assumption that when G (maximum free flow speed) is more than doubled *at density level* n_0, and all other G_i*'s* are also more than doubled *at density level n*, then the speed density curve simply shifts upwards, and the underlying congestion measure at each particular point *n* of the speed-density curve remains the same.

[18] This willingness to pay is the product of the marginal willingness to pay and the effective level of capacity utilisation by user *i*.

[19] See Oakland (1987).

density) across a link. For each individual i to make a trip across a road link, the following condition must be satisfied:

$$U_i > T_i + v_i t_i + c_i + rk_i \tag{1.20}$$

where U_i is the utility of the trip for user i. The first term on the right hand side of Eq. 1.20 represents the individual user i's shadow cost of capacity utilisation. The second term stands for the total time-cost of travel time, and the third and last terms stand for the total money costs, which consists of an operating costs component c_i and a private capital rental cost component (rk_i) where r is the rental price of private capital.

Assume that individual user i is taken from a sample of a population whose value of travel time savings v_i is distributed according to a probability density function:

$$\pi(v) = av^{\alpha} \exp(-\beta v) \tag{1.21}$$

where $\pi(v)$ is the number of potential users whose value of travel time savings is v, and α and β are parameters. From Eq. 1.20, user i will decide to use the link if and only if:

$$v_i < v_{\max} = -(T_i + c_i + rk_i - U_i)/t_i \tag{1.22}$$

and therefore, the total number of users who will travel along this particular link is given by:

$$n(v_{\max}) = \int_0^{v_{\max}} \pi(v)dv \tag{1.23}$$

Eqs. 1.22 and 1.23 give the equilibrium condition for the number of users who decide to cross the link, given the values of U_i, T_i, c_i, rk_i, and t_i. Assuming, for example, that U_i, c_i, and rk_i remain unchanged for a given level of traffic congestion, the equilibrium value of T_i, t_i, and therefore of n, will then be determined jointly. This is then used to infer, for example, the optimal[20] value for a toll which can be levied on the link (which will be equal to the user's willingness to pay for capacity T_i

[20] 'Optimality' here is defined in terms of the objective of using T_i to achieve a particular level of congestion (as implied by t_i) assuming that density level is n, and given the values of U_i, c_i, and rk_i. Naturally, a more general objective function can be defined which will incorporate not only the congestion or travel time variable t_i but also other welfare measures such as capacity supply costs, etc. A more general welfare analysis is beyond the scope of this paper, because the objective here is mainly to demonstrate the methodology of *economic equilibrium* analysis for a road network, assuming a particular supply or network characteristics (such as given by the speed-density curve), and demand characteristics (such as implied by the density level n and the distribution function (1.21)).

In considering the use of Eqs. 1.22 and 1.23 to examine the impact of a particular pricing policy (such as the levy of a toll) on a specific link, we note that the policy may have spillover effects onto other links. This is because some of the potential travellers for this link, whose conditions 1.20 or 1.22 are not satisfied[21], may decide to travel on a different link. As a result, the equilibrium condition for a particular link cannot be determined in isolation, but rather jointly with other links (as in a general equilibrium model of an economy). We will illustrate this point in the next section.

1.5 Application

To apply the model considered in the previous sections to the case of a particular road network, we must first find an empirical functional specification for the 'congestion function' (Eq. 1.5). The following specification has been found to fit the empirical data well (see Fig. 1.7)[22]:

$$\theta(n,G) = 1 - \frac{1}{\ln n}[\ln(\sum_{i=1}^{n} G_i) - \ln G)] \tag{1.24}$$

or alternatively:

$$n^{1-\theta(n,G)} = (\sum_{i=1}^{n} G_i)/G \tag{1.25}$$

Eqs. 1.24 and 1.25 indicate that when the public good G is uncongested, $G_i = G$, and $\theta = 0$. When the public good G becomes heavily congested we can reach a limiting case, where the good becomes a pure private good. In this case ($\sum_{i=1}^{n} G_i \rightarrow G$) and $\theta \rightarrow 1$. In general, ($G < \sum_{i=1}^{n} G_i < nG$) and $0<\theta<1$, and therefore, the value of θ derived from Eq. 1.25 can be interpreted as a 'congestion index'.

From Eq. 1.25, we can also derive an empirical measure for the shadow price of capacity (as defined by Eqs. 1.17 and 1.18 in section 3):

---

[21] Even when condition 1.23 is satisfied, if there are alternative choices, a user will want to choose a link which has the greater 'surplus' defined in terms of the difference: ($U^i - T^i -$ $-c_i - rk_i - v_i t_i$).

[22] Note that θ is not a constant parameter but rather it is a function of n and G. G_i which appears on the right hand side of equations (24-25) is also a function of n and G.

$$
\begin{aligned}
(\theta_1 / \theta_2) &= [\partial\theta / \partial(\sum_{i=1}^{n} G_i)]/[\partial\theta / \partial(G)] \\
&= -G/(\sum_{i=1}^{n} G_i) \\
&= -(n)^{\theta-1}
\end{aligned}
\tag{1.26}
$$

$$
\begin{aligned}
P_{G_i} &= (\theta_1 / \theta_2)(F_G / F_P) \\
&= (n)^{\theta-1} P_G
\end{aligned}
\tag{1.27}
$$

Substituting Eq. 1.27, into Eq. 1.19, we have:

$$\sum_{i=1}^{n} (n)^{\theta-1} P_G G_i = (n)^{\theta} P_G G_i = P_G G. \tag{1.28}$$

or

$$n^{\theta(n,G)} = (G / G_i) \tag{1.29}$$

Next, following the discussion in Section 3, we noted that we can use *speed* as a proxy variable for G and G_i. For example, let s_F be the maximum free flow speed attainable on a road link, and s_i be the actual speed achieved by a user i. When $s_i = s_F$, we can say $G_i = G$. When $s_i < s_F$, we can say $G_i < G$. Therefore, the ratio (s_i/s_F) can be used to indicate the relative level of capacity utilisation (G_i/G), and from this we can hypothesise a relationship:

$$(G / G_i) = h(s_F / s_i) \tag{1.30}$$

where $h(.)$ is a monotonic increasing function with initial value $h(1)=1$. Combining Eq. 1.29 with 1.30 gives:

$$n^{\theta(n,G)} = h(s_F / s_i) \tag{1.31}$$

Eq. 1.31 can then be 'calibrated' from the empirical speed-density information[23].

[23] Seen in this way, equation (31) is an empirical specification of equation (5) which is estimated or 'calibrated' based on the speed-density relationship. Each point on this speed-density relationship is an equilibrium outcome of the demand-supply interaction.

1.5.1 Application to a Hypothetical Network of Two Parallel Links

To illustrate the application of the model developed, we consider a hypothetical network of two parallel links '*a*' and '*b*' (see Fig. 1.3). Although the analysis of travel activity within two parallel network links has been carried out before (see, for example, Verhoef and Small 2004; Verhoef 1999; Glazier and Niskanen 2000), the purpose of our analysis, however, is to demonstrate our methodology of analysing the equilibrium outcome in a network, rather than focusing on the results per se. Therefore, the choice of this (simplified) network is only a starting point. Once the approach has been demonstrated, it is open to future applications to use more complicated network[24].

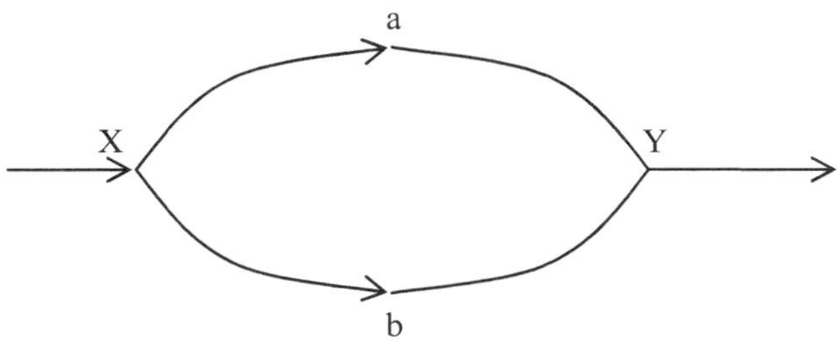

Figure 1.3. Network of two parallel links "a" and "b"

Assume that there is a population of users who have to cross these two alternative links to go from point X to point Y. These users are heterogenous in terms of their valuations of travel time savings, and the density function for this circumstance is given by Eq. 1.22. Let the utility associated with crossing the links to go from point X to point Y be the same for all users, i.e., $U_i=U$, and also, assume for simplicity that the value of capital used to cross the link are the same for all users, i.e., $rk_i = rk$ for all i's. Assume that link a is subject to a toll T_a but link b is not. Each user is now facing a choice between using link a and paying a toll, but the speed may be faster (i.e, the congestion level is lower), and the alternative of using link b which has no toll, but the user may have to 'pay' in terms of lower speed (and hence longer travel time). At equilibrium, if a user decided to use link a, we must have[25]:

$$(U - T_a - v_a t_a - rk) > (U - v_a t_b - rk) \tag{1.32}$$

or

[24] In the same manner, an analysis of the equilibrium supply-demand outcome in a simplified two sector economy can be generalised into a multi-sector economy.

[25] For simplicity, we drop the user script 'i', but replace this with a sub-script 'a' (or 'b') to denote a user who crosses link a (or link b).

$$T_a < v_a(t_b - t_a) \quad (1.33)$$

where v_a, v_b are the values of time savings of users who decided to cross link a and link b respectively and t_a, t_b are the average travel times across these links. Similarly, for a user who decided to cross link b, we must have:

$$(U - T_a - v_b t_a - rk) < (U - v_b t_b - rk) \quad (1.34)$$

or

$$T_a > v_b(t_b - t_a) \quad (1.35)$$

Assume that the toll T_a is related to the speed achievable by the user in link a, i.e., $T_a = \tau_a s_a$ where s_a is the speed along link a and τ_a is the toll rate (expressed as dollars per unit of speed achievable within link a). Eqs. 1.33 and 1.35 can be rewritten as:

$$\tau_a s_a < l v_a(1/s_b - 1/s_a) \quad \text{or} \quad v_a > [(\tau_a/l)(s_a)^2(s_b)]/(s_a - s_b) \quad (1.36a)$$

$$\tau_a s_a > l v_b(1/s_b - 1/s_a) \quad \text{or} \quad v_b < [(\tau_a/l)(s_a)^2(s_b)]/(s_a - s_b) \quad (1.36b)$$

where l is the length of the links (assumed to be the same). Given the distribution of users according to their values of time savings v as given by Eq. 1.21, and the speed-density relationships as defined by Eq. 1.31, we can define the problem of 'equilibrium assignment' of traffic flow between links a and link b as follows: find a marginal (or equilibrium) value of travel time savings v^* such that[26]:

$$v_b \le v^* = [(\tau_a/l)(s_a)^2(s_b)]/(s_a - s_b) \le v_a \quad (1.37)$$

with the values of s_a and s_b - and hence the corresponding values of n_a and n_b determined via Eq. 1.31 - such that we will have

$$n_a = \int_{v^*}^{\infty} \pi(v)dv \quad (1.38a)$$

$$n_b = \int_0^{v^*} \pi(v)dv \quad (1.38b)$$

[26] See for example, Verhoef and Small (2004).

The solution to the problem defined by Eqs. 1.37-1.38 will give the equilibrium[27] value for the toll rate τ_a given existing capacities of the links (as defined implicitly by Eq. 1.31[28] and the existing level of 'demand' (as reflected in the distribution function (1.21), repeated in (1.38a,b)).

1.5.2 An Illustrative Experiment Using Empirical Data from Some Sydney Road Links

To illustrate the applicability of the model, we compiled data for a sample of 3,730 different road links in the Sydney Metropolitan Area in 2001[29] by link type (arterial, highway, expressway, freeway, etc.), link length (kms), number of lanes, vehicle density (vehicles per lane per km), travel time and speed, for different time periods of day (AM, Mid-day, PM, and night time),. From this data we plot the information on vehicle speed versus traffic density for each link type (Fig. 1.4). We choose link types 4 (arterial undivided) and 11 (freeway) for an illustrative experiment.

First, we estimate an empirical speed-density relationship for the AM time period for these links. The best-fit relationship is of the following form:

$$\begin{aligned} s &= 83.6 && \text{for } n \le n_0 = 3.816, \\ s &= 83.6\exp(-0.015[n-n_0]) && \text{for } 3.816 < n \le 25.77; \quad R^2 = 0.87, \\ s &= 58.8\exp(-0.009[n-n_0]) && \text{for } n > 25.77; \quad R^2 = 0.98. \end{aligned} \qquad (1.39)$$

for a freeway, and

$$\begin{aligned} s &= 65.0 && \text{for } n \le n_0 = 0.011, \\ s &= 65\exp(-0.0133[n-n_0]) && \text{for } n > n_0 = 0.011; \quad R^2 = 0.97. \end{aligned} \qquad (1.39b)$$

for an arterial road, where s is speed in kilometre per hour (km/h) and n is density in vehicles per lane per kilometre (vehicles/lane/km). These are shown in Figs. 1.5 and 1.6.

Eqs. 1.39a,b implies a congestion relationship of the following form:

$$\ln(s_F / s_i) = A(n - n_0) \qquad (1.40a)$$

---

[27] The equilibrium condition can be varied depending on whether we want to equilibrate traffic densities (i.e. $n_a = n_b$), or congestion level (i.e. $\theta_a = \theta_b$), see Table 1.1 in the next section.

[28] As the capacities of the links expand, the empirical relationship 1.31 will also change. See the Illustrative Experiment below.

[29] Data was purchased from the Transport Data Centre (within the New South Wales Department of Transport).

Combining this with Eq. 1.31, and assuming that $h(.) = \ln(.)$, we have:

$$n^{\theta(n,G)} = A(n - n_0) \quad (1.40b)$$

where A is a constant as defined in equation (1.39a,b). The value of θ is then estimated for each value of n (assuming an implicit and constant value for G). The values of θ are shown in Fig. 1.7.

Next, to describe the behavioural characteristics of the population of travellers, we assume that the distribution of their values of time savings is given by the following empirical density function (based on a previous study on Sydney travellers).

$$\pi(v) = 0.008v^2 \exp(-0.25v) \quad (1.41)$$

This is shown in Fig. 1.2 based on an empirical model in Hensher and Greene (2003).

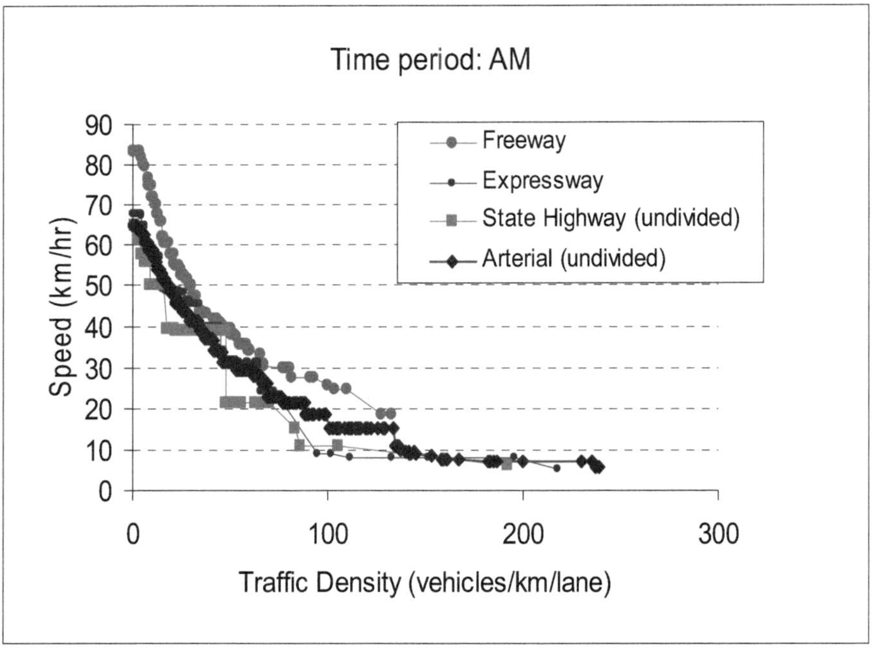

Figure 1.4. Maximum speed versus traffic density

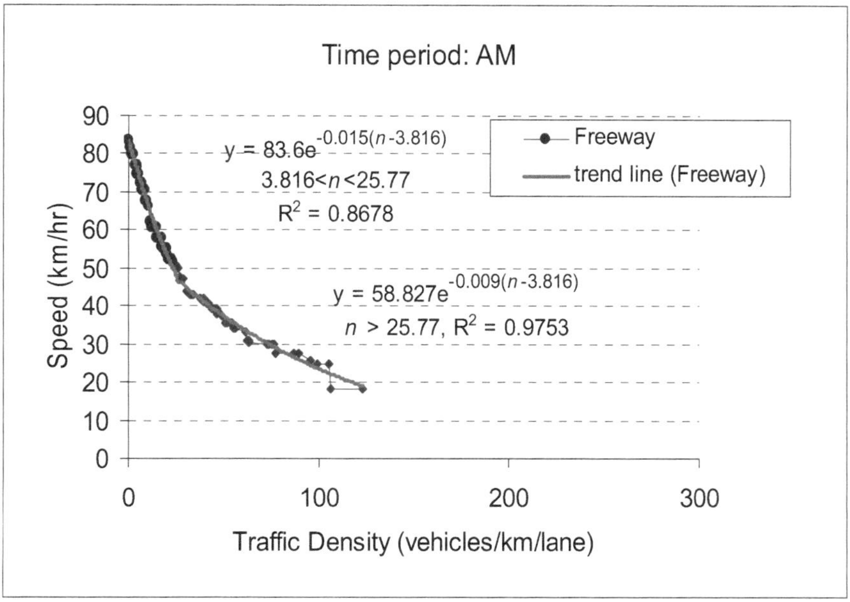

Figure 1.5. Speed-Density curve for Freeway

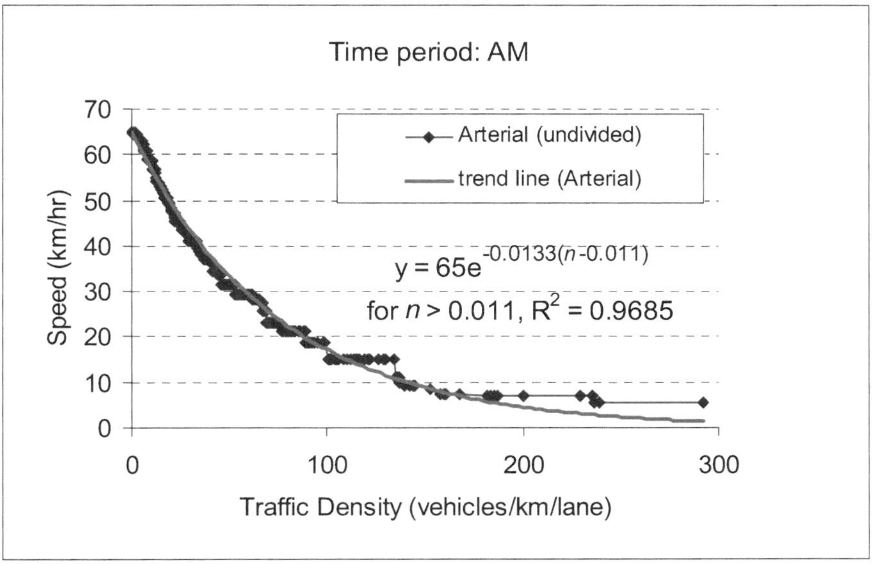

Figure 1.6. Speed-Density curve for Arterial link

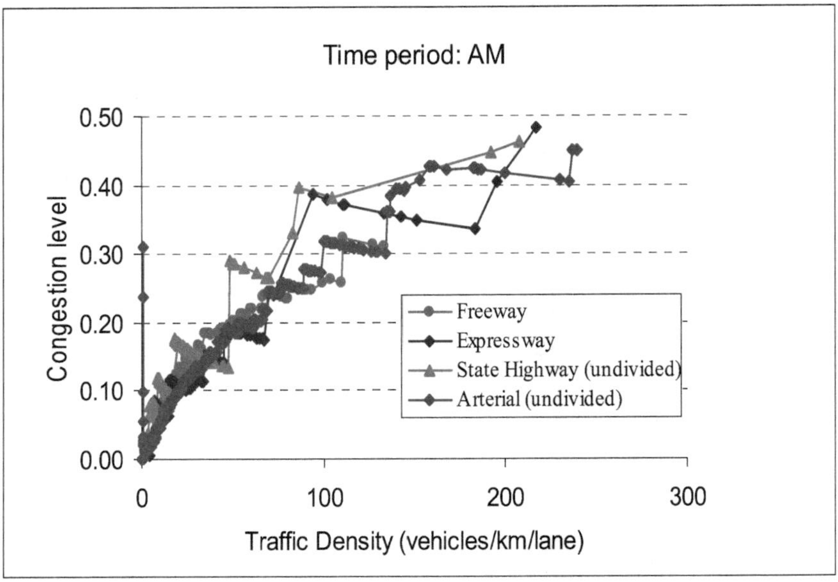

Figure 1.7. Congestion level versus traffic density

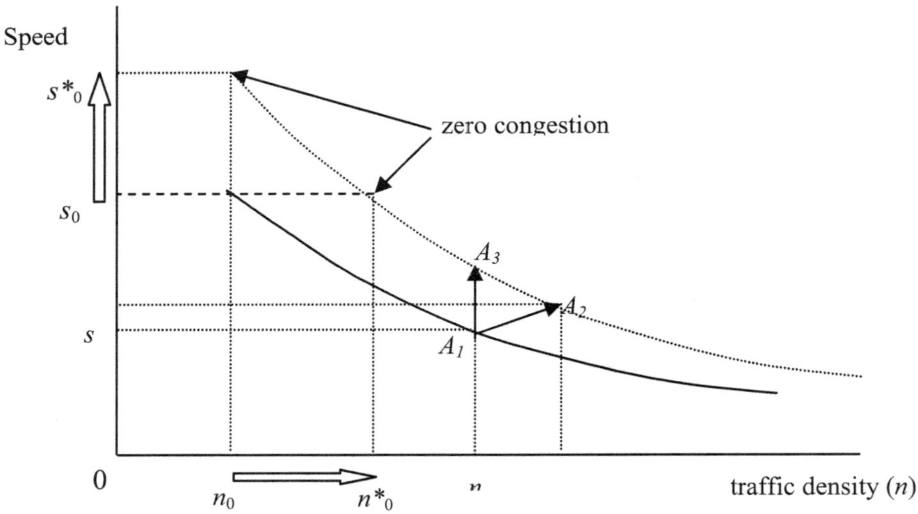

Figure 1.8. Effect of an increase in the *physical* capacity of road link

Short run analysis: For the purpose of an illustrative experiment, we assume that link *a* in Fig. 1.3 is a freeway and link *b* is an arterial road, and therefore, their speed-density relationships will be determined by equations (39a-b). For short-run analysis, we assume these relationships to remain fixed (i.e., capacities of the links remain fixed). We now conduct an experiment where we assume link *a* is subject to a speed-based toll of (τ_a/l) Australian dollars per km/h per km of road link ($A/(km/h)/km)[30], and link *b* is toll-free. To simplify the analysis, we assume a constant speed within each link, i.e., we are concerned only with equilibrium conditions in both links. Let *N* be the total level of demand (total number of vehicles per kilometre per lane) to be assigned to these two links. Initially, when there is no toll, we assume (following the principle of equilibrium traffic assignment) that the speed in the two links will be equalised. The congestion levels on these links, however, are not necessarily the same because the capacities as well as actual traffic density levels on these links are not necessarily the same. When a speed-toll profile is loaded onto link *a*, this will dislodge some of the traffic on link *a* towards link *b*. Congestion on link *b* will therefore increase, while that on link *a* will decrease. Table 1 shows how congestion levels respond to different levels of the speed and toll, as well as the level of demand (number of travellers *N*) travelling on both links.

From Table 1.1, it can be seen that if a toll is imposed on link *a*, it can release some of the congestion level on this link, but this will be at the expense of increased congestion for link *b*. For example, when N = 100 (vehicles/lane/km), congestion on link *a* will be 0.17, and congestion on link *b* will be 0.13, if the average speed on both links are the same at 41.01 km/h (row 1 of Table 1) [31]. If a toll of 0.001119[32] is levied on link *a*, then traffic density on this link will now be re-

[30] Because the length of the road link can vary, to facilitate comparison of the toll between different links, the speed based toll is also expressed as dollar per unit of speed as well as per unit of road length. Thus a toll of 0.005 (A$/km/h/km) implies a vehicle travelling at 100 km/h for 10 km of this road link will pay a total toll of A$5. If the road length is 20 km, the total toll will be A$10.

[31] At first sight, it may seem strange that congestion level in Freeway is higher than that in an Arterial link even though the speeds in both links are the same. On closer examination, however, this makes sense. This is because 'congestion' as a *general* concept is hardly useful because different links have different capacities, and different speed limits which will have different effects on the observed traffic flow. In other words, congestion should be *context-based* and a useful index of congestion for comparison across different types of links (different contexts) should also take this into account. An analogy is the 'poverty' index. Since poverty is relative to the environment in which a person lives, an index of poverty should take into account. In our case, a freeway has higher speed limit and also higher capacity. Therefore, when the actual speed in a freeway is reduced to the same absolute level as that in an arterial link this should not necessarily imply that congestion in the two links are now equal. In fact, it is reasonable to expect that when average speeds are the same in both link types, congestion will be greater in a freeway as compared to an arterial road (which is as shown in Table 1.1).

[32] In Australian dollars per km/h per km of road length. This translates into a toll of about 0.001119*44.46*10= A$0.50 for a vehicle travelling at the speed of 44.46 km/h and over a link length of 10 km. Note that this toll is an equilibrium toll, calculated based on the

duced to 55.51 while that on link *b* will increase to 43.49 (vehicles/lane/km). Congestion on link *a* is now reduced to 0.16 with a speed of 44.61 km/h, while congestion on link *b* is now increased to 0.16 with a speed of 36.14/hr. When the toll is raised to 0.002013[33], then half of the traffic will travel on link *a* and half will travel on link *b*. Congestion on link *a* is now reduced to 0.15 with a speed of 47.3 km/h, while congestion on link *b* is now increased to 0.17 with a speed of 33.1 km/h. The value of travel time savings of the marginal user who is indifferent between the two links in this case is now increased to $10.5/hour (from previous $9.51/hr). That is, individuals with values of travel time savings greater than or equal to $10.5/hr will be travelling on link *a* while the rest will be using link *b*. If the toll is raised even higher to 0.010617[34], then traffic density on link *a* will be reduced to 9.22 while that in link *b* will increase to 90.78 (vehicles/lane/km). Congestion on link *a* is now reduced to 0.05 with a speed of 75.0 km/h, while congestion on link *b* is now increased to 0.27 with a speed of just 19.06/hr.

When the total level of traffic density increases from 100 to 200 (vehicles/lane/km), the value of the toll required to equalise traffic between the two links now increases, from 0.002013 to 0.009114, even though the actual level of congestion on both links is now increased. The use of a toll to reduce congestion (even on one link only) is now hampered by the fact that the total capacities of the two links are limited, and therefore, there is a limit as to how 'local' congestion (on link a) can be shifted to another link (link *b*). This is the case when *long run* investment to expand capacity of either link *a* alone, or of both links is to be considered.

Long-run analysis: When extra capacity is called for, a question arises: where should the extra capacity be added, and how much more? The investment in extra capacity involves supply side questions - how much does it cost to add *physical* - and hence economic - capacity to the link? How can economic capacity be measured? - and demand side question - what is the *return* to such investment?

To answer the supply side question, we need to define the *economic* capacity of a link. As explained in previous sections, the economic capacity of a link is an abstract concept, unlike physical capacity. However, it can be deduced via the many economic/traffic variables which we can measure; for example, the combination

---

objective of equalisation of the congestion levels across the two links. Different objective functions will result in different types of 'optimal' tolls as seen in Table 1. Since the purpose of our analysis here is to demonstrate the ability of the model to calculate an *equilibrium* toll given any objective function, rather than to conduct a comprehensive welfare analysis of congestion pricing (which is the future step in the application of the methodology suggested in this paper) therefore, we have not considered the issue of supply costs or consumer and producer surplus. See also footnote 22.

33 Or 0.002013*47.30*10= A$0.95 for a vehicle travelling at the maximum speed of 47.3 km/h and over a link length of 10 km. Again this toll has been estimated as an *equilibrium* toll when the objective is to equalise traffic densities across the links.

34 Or 0.010617*75*10= A$7.96 for a vehicle travelling at the maximum speed of 75.00 km/h and over a link length of 10 km.

(n_0, s_0) where n_0 is the 'maximum'[35] traffic density at which free flow speed s_0 can still be observed. When traffic density exceeds this level, speed will fall below the free flow level and by definition, congestion starts to occur. The combination (n_0, s_0), thus, can be used to define the 'economic capacity' of the link. When the *physical* capacity of the link is expanded, this combination can also be expanded. If s_0 is to remain constant (e.g., by traffic regulation), any increase in the physical capacity of the link will be reflected in an increase n_0 and therefore, n_0 can be regarded as the economic capacity of the link at a given level of s_0. 'Capacity' in this case is defined as the ability to hold a certain level of demand (n_0) without the capacity - being defined as a public good – which becomes a congested good. If s_0 is also allowed to increase when the physical capacity of the link is increased, then n_0 alone will not be sufficient to describe the economic capacity of the link. In this case, both n_0 and s_0 will be increased. The other limiting case is when n_0 is to remain constant, then, any increase in the physical capacity of the link will be reflected in an increase in the free flow speed. In this case, 'capacity' can be viewed (from an individual user's point of view) as the ability to supply 'speed'[36]. In general, when $n > n_0$ and $s < s_0$, an increase in the physical capacity of the link will be reflected partly as an increase in n and partly as an increase in s (a movement from point A_1 to point A_2 in Fig. 1.8[37]). The *change* in capacity in this case can be identified via the change in the parameters of the speed-density function (1.39). For example, assuming a parallel shift of this function to the right, following an improvement in the physical capacity link *a* in Figure 1.3, Eq. 1.39 a now becomes:

$$\begin{aligned} s &= 83.6 && \text{for } n \le n_0 = 3.816 + \Delta n_0, \\ s &= 83.6\exp(-0.015[n - n_0]) && \text{for } 3.816 + \Delta n_0 < n \le 25.77 + \Delta n_0; \\ s &= 58.8\exp(-0.009[n - n_0]) && \text{for } n > 25.77 + \Delta n_0; \end{aligned} \tag{1.42}$$

for $\Delta n_0 = 10$. If there is no toll imposed on either link *a* or *b* before and after the change, then some traffic on link *b* will overflow to link *a* after the expansion in capacity of link *a*. This is shown in Table 1.1, row 9 (compared to row 1). In row 10, we show how a toll can be imposed on link *a* (or if a toll has already been imposed, how it can be increased) after the expansion in capacity in link *a*, so as to prevent traffic from link *b* overflowing to link a (if this is the objective). The value of this toll can then be used to estimate the return to investment in capacity expan-

35 'Maximum' in the sense of free flow condition, because traffic density can still exceed this level.

36 After all, what an *individual* user demands from the link is speed, and does not care so much about the level of traffic flow or density, so long as this speed is achieved.

37 It is an empirical question whether the *shape* of the speed-density curve will also change as the curve moves to the right. An investigation of this issue goes beyond the scope of this paper. In this paper, we assume for simplicity that the shape does not change. This may apply, for example, to a case when the physical dimensions of the link are changed but drivers' driving habits, and the dimensions as well as driving qualities of the vehicles remain unchanged.

sion on link *a*. For example, assuming that the equilibrium density on the link before investment was 50 vehicles/lane/km and the equilibrium speed was 47.3km/h.; after investment in capacity expansion, the speed is increased to 51.76 km/h (for the same level of traffic density). Assume that there are m lanes on link *a*; the length of the link is l km, and there are x number of crossings over the link per year. Total annual return to the investment is R = (0.002209*51.76-0.002013*47.30)*50*m*l*x. For illustrative purposes, let l=10km, m=4, x=400,000, then R = A$15,298,352.

Table 1.1. The relationship between the value of the speed-toll (τ/l) and congestion levels in link *a* (with toll) and link *b* (without toll).

	Toll (per unit of speed per link length) (A$/(km/h)/km)	Total Demand (traffic density) (vehicles/lane/km)	Link *a* (with toll) Density (vehicles lane/km)	Speed (km/h)	Congestion level	Link *b* (without toll) Density (vehicles /lane/km)	Speed (km/h)	Congestion level	Value of travel time savings of marginal user
	τ/l	N	n_a	s_a	θ_a	n_b	s_b	θ_b	v*
1	0	100	65.87	41.01	0.17	34.13	41.01	0.13	8.14
2	0.0011	100	55.51	44.61	0.16	43.49	36.14	0.16	9.51
3	0.0020	100	50.00	47.30	0.15	50.00	33.10	0.17	10.50
4	0.0106	100	9.22	75.00	0.05	90.78	19.06	0.27	20.49
5	0	200	125.87	23.90	0.26	74.13	23.90	0.23	8.57
6	0.0023	200	118.94	37.89	0.25	81.06	25.43	0.25	9.07
7	0.0091	200	100.0	30.16	0.22	100.0	16.85	0.29	10.50
8	0.0440	200	23.96	65.00	0.08	176.04	6.01	0.46	19.20
			Capacity of link *a* is expanded by: $\Delta n_0 = 10$			Capacity of link *b* remains the same			
9	0	100	69.87	43.28	0.15	30.13	43.28	0.12	7.56
10	0.0022	100	50.00	51.76	0.12	50.00	33.10	0.17	10.50

1.6 Conclusions

In this paper we have developed an alternative approach for analysing the phenomenon of congestion within an urban road network. The framework differs from the traditional approach in that it separates out the speed and the density components in the flow variable and uses these to define the 'price' and 'quantity' levels of travel demand and supply on a particular link. Having separated out the price and quantity components in demand and supply, we set out a theoretical model to represent the individual demand behaviour for travel activity across a link, based on the concept of a household production function, using a (*congested*) *public* infrastructure good (road capacity).

The theoretical approach differs from previous contributions where congestion is usually analysed as an externality rather than in terms of household production using a congested public good. Even though the concept of externality and public goods are closely related, the analysis based on the former concept allows us to see more clearly the role of public infrastructure pricing and investment decisions than mere externality analysis.

The proposed approach lays down the basic foundations for extending the analysis into a more complex road network structure, drawing on economic equilibrium analysis (analogous to the concept of general equilibrium in conventional economic analysis). We have illustrated the applicability and feasibility of the approach for a simple network of two parallel links.

References

Else PK (1981) A reformulation of the theory of optimal congestion taxes. Journal of Transport Economics and Policy 15: 217-232.

Evans AW (1992) Road congestion: The diagrammatic analysis. Journal of Political Economy 100(1): 211-217.

Hensher DA, Greene WH (2003) Mixed logit models: state of practice. Transportation 30 (2): 133-176.

Hills P (1993) Road Congestion Pricing: When is it a good policy? A comment. Journal of Transport Economics and Policy: 91-99.

Hills P (2001) Supply curves for urban road networks: A Comment. Journal of Transport Economics and Policy 35(2): 343-348.

Hills P, Gray P (2000) Characterisation of Congestion on an Urban Road Network Subject to Road-Use Pricing – A Fundamental Review. Paper presented at the_IATBR 2000, the 9th International Association For Travel Behaviour Conference at Gold Coast, Queensland, Australia, 2 - 6 July.

Oakland WH (1987) Theory of Public Goods. In: A. J. Auerbach and M. Feldstein (eds) Handbook of Public Economics, Volume 2. North Holland, Amsterdam.

Verhoef ET (1999) Time, speeds, flows and densities in static models of road traffic congestion and congestion pricing. Regional Science and Urban Economics 29: 341-369.

Verhoef ET, Small KA (2004), Product Differentiation on Roads: Constrained Congestion Pricing with Heterogeneous Users. Journal of Transport Economics and Policy 38(1): 127-156.

Walters AA (1961) The Theory and Measurement of Private and Social Cost of Highway Congestion. Econometrica 29(4) October: 676-99.

2 Estimation of the Economic Value of Student Urban Travel Time

Pablo Coto-Millán
Department of Economics
University of Cantabria (Spain)

Vicente Inglada
Department of Economics
University Carlos III of Madrid (Spain)

Miguel A. Pesquera
Department of Transports
University of Cantabria (Spain)

Rubén Sainz
Department of Economics
University of Cantabria (Spain)

Nuria Sánchez
Department of Economics
University of Cantabria (Spain)

2.1 Introduction

Value models of individuals' travel time are based on Hicks (1932 and 1939) and Becker's (1965) assumptions for continuous goods, and on Train and McFadden's (1978) for continuous and discrete goods.

Considering the model by Jara Díaz and Farah (1987) – that differentiates from the model by Train-McFadden in the fact that income is exogenous - we have made a study about the subjective value of Santander students' travel time.

In order to study travel time value, it is necessary to have a database containing the diverse travels and to know the different means of transport, time, cost and socio-economic variables of travellers.

Our model will be based on discrete choice models, particularly the one by Jara-Díaz and Farah (1987), which allows us to easily obtain subjective travel time value. The data used to estimate the model are based on a home survey campaign carried out in Santander, which enables us to specify travellers' behaviour with respect to their choice of transportation means.

The purpose of this paper is to determine the value of students' travel time in Santander. With this in mind, we have estimated the transport demand function using logit and probit models. Section 2.2 offers a review of time value theories. Section 2.3 presents a description of the survey and an explanation of the used variables. In Section 2.4 we present the estimations and comment the results and finalise with the conclusions obtained.

2.2 Overview of Time Value Theories

Travel Choice Microeconomics consider time value from two different points of view:

1 Consumer choice models, by introducing time directly in the utility function (Becker, Johnson, Oort, Deserpa, Evans).
2 Discrete choice models, which are based on the choice of goods from an alternatives array (travelling or not, means of transport to use). (Train and McFadden (1978), Jara Díaz and Farah (1987)).

One of this theory's basic assumption is that individuals choose the time allocation that maximizes personal utility, this being subject to the characteristics of time: it cannot be stored, like money and therefore must be necessarily spent in other activities.

Becker tried to introduce the variable time cost in decisions about activities that are not work, in particular by analyzing the use of time in education, apprenticeship and other forms of human capital. Becker's work shows that time is another scarce resource, and therefore, during the decision making process economic agents will also take into account the value of the time used instead of prices only.

Becker (1965) is the first to introduce time in the classic theory of consumer behaviour. Becker states that individuals' utility – that are both consumers and producers – is provided by "Final Goods" (Z). These "final goods" will be composed by the quantities of consumed goods and the time needed to consume them, the individual will then have the following utility function:

$$U[Z(X,T)]$$

According to the classic theory of consumer choice, the individual faces an income restriction and will spend the total income he/she receives. Moreover, Becker points out that the individual also has a time restriction, a day is 24 hours long and his life is finite. Thus, the problem faced by the individual will be:

$$\underset{Z}{Max}\, U[Z(X,T)]$$
$$subject\ to:$$
$$\sum X_i P_i = wW$$
$$\sum T_i + W = \tau$$

Becker also describes that:

$$T_i = a_i Z_i$$
$$X_i = b_i Z_i$$

where a_i and b_i are the coefficients which transform final goods into time and goods respectively. From the restrictions we can observe that time can be transformed into goods, it will only be necessary to reduce consumption time and work more.

We can see that, from time and income restrictions, and taking into account coefficients a_i and b_i, we can obtain one single restriction:

$$\sum X_i P_i = w\left(\tau - \sum T_i\right) \Rightarrow \sum b_i Z_i P_i + w \sum a_i Z_i = w\tau \Rightarrow$$

$$\left(\sum b_i P_i + \sum a_i w\right) Z_i = w\tau$$

Becker defined the parts of the equation as follows:

Full Price: left side of the equation. The cost of the final goods in time (estimated by the wage rate) and in goods (estimated by the market prices); and Full Income: right side of the equation. The income we would obtain if we dedicated all time available to work obtaining a wage rate w.

The basic idea of this approach is that time re-allocation involves a parallel re-allocation of goods and utilities. Some of the critics made to this model were that Becker's assumption of time being transformed into utilities can only be sustained if work hours are freely chosen by individuals and if work hours are not included in the utility function.

Johnson, Oort, DeSerpa or Evans were among the critics of this model. It was probably DeSerpa the one who had a higher impact on posterior studies about time value.

Time value obtained by Becker is equal to wage rate because all the time used to consume, in this case to travel, is valued by its opportunity cost, which is the wage.

DeSerpa's model main characteristics (1971) are:

1 Utility is not only a function of goods, but also of the time allocated the consumption of such goods.
2 Individuals' decisions are subject to two restrictions, one related to income and the other to time.

3 The decision to consume a particular quantity of a good requires to allocate a minimum quantity of time to that good, but the individual can spend more time than the minimum if he/she so desires (technological restriction).

DeSerpa's great contribution is the third characteristic. He understood something that seems to be obvious: in order to consume a particular good, a minimum consumption of time is necessary.

Thus, DeSerpa considers that consumers face the utility function:

$$U(X_1,\ldots\ldots,X_n,T_1,\ldots\ldots\ldots,T_n)$$

where X represents the quantities of goods and T consumption times allocated. We assume that individual's preferences are represented by a continuous utility function. At first sight, we could criticise DeSerpa the same way as Becker since work time does not seem to be included in the utility function. However, DeSerpa takes into account a type of goods denominated "Pure time goods", estimated in time only , work will be included among these goods. Regular restrictions are time and income. DeSerpa's great contribution - the allocation of minimum times for goods consumption - introduces a third restriction, as stated below:

$$T_i \geq a_i X_i \qquad \forall i = 1,\ldots\ldots,n$$

where a_i is the minimum time needed by the individual to consume one unit $X_{i,}$ known with certainty. For example, we dedicate minimum 6 hours to sleep and 20 to lunch. Individuals allocate the least possible time to undesirable activities; for example, they allocate a minimum of 40 minutes to travel to the workplace. However, we allocate more time than the minimum required to other activities. For example, individuals allocate one more hour to sleep or half an hour more to lunch (compared with the minimum necessary); because their willingness to pay for sleeping more time or for spending more time over lunch, is a little higher. In nay case, willingness to pay has to be equal for each activities' last unit.

We face the following consumer utility maximization problem:

$$\underset{X,T}{Max} \quad U(X_1,\ldots\ldots\ldots,X_n,T_1,\ldots\ldots\ldots,T_n)$$

$$subject\ to:$$

$$\sum X_i P_i = Y \qquad (\lambda)$$

$$\sum T_i = \tau \qquad (\mu)$$

$$T_i \geq a_i X_i \qquad (\kappa_i)$$

where μ and λ, and κ_i are Lagrange multipliers for each restriction. μ and λ account for time and income marginal utilities respectively and κ_i, is the marginal utility of time saving.

We operate and obtain:

$$\frac{\kappa_i}{\lambda} = \frac{\mu}{\lambda} - \frac{\partial U / \partial T_i}{\lambda}$$

We can define the parts of this equation as:

$\frac{\kappa_i}{\lambda}$ is the value of time saving and we can observe that, if we dedicated more time than the minimum required to carry out an activity, this quotient would be zero because the Lagrange multiplier would be zero. This allows us to define for the first time leisure activities as those to which we allocate more time than the minimum necessary. If they were not leisure, we would allocate the minimum.

$\frac{\mu}{\lambda}$ is the value of time as a resource, it is equal to leisure time value. The consumer will not be willing to pay to reduce his/her leisure time since utility would not be increased.

Finally, we have $\frac{\partial U / \partial T_i}{\lambda}$, which is the value of the time allocated to a specific activity: travel, in our case.

The value of time as a resource: always expressed in terms of substitution marginal relations. It will be the value of time (for example, if the day lasted one minute less, what value would we award to that minute?)

The value of the time allocated to a specific activity: how much we value reducing consumption of goods one minute (travelling to workplace), taking into account that the reduction of that minute can make us work more, but can as well decrease safety and comfort.

The value of time saving: Since each restriction of time consumption represents the need of spending time consuming certain goods, releasing the i-th consumption restriction is equal to saving time in the i-th consumption activity. As we have already seen, K_i must be interpreted as the marginal utility of time saving and ratio K_i/λ as the value of time saving. By giving a positive value to time saving in consumption of a certain good, we infer that the time saved in the consumption of that good can be used consuming other goods with a higher value. Since because of a technological restriction, we have an amount of time to spend on that good and, in the event of a technological improvement that would make us to spend less time consuming that good, the time saved could be spent in other goods that are highly valued. The time saved in the consumption of a good will be expressed as the difference between the value of time as a resource minus the value of the time spent in the consumption of a good:

$$\frac{K_i}{\lambda} = \frac{\mu}{\lambda} - \frac{\partial U / \partial T_i}{\lambda}$$

From DeSerpa's point of view, and taking into account that travel is not a desired activity, the individual must spend more time than he/she wishes to its consumption because of the restriction minimum consumption of time. The individual could increase his/her utility by using part of the time dedicated to the undesired activity on a leisure activity. Therefore, K_i/λ would represent the monetary value of the time saved in the undesired activity and transferred to the leisure activity: "value of time". Consequently, if transport infrastructures were improved, the individual could spend less time travelling and dedicate more time to another activity that will provide him/her more utility.

The main difference between this model and others included in value of time literature (such as Hicks (1932), Hicks (1939), Becker(1965), Johnson (1966), Oort (1969), Juster (1970), Lancaster(1971), Evans (1972), McFadden (1973), McFadden (1974), Domencich and McFadden(1975), Train y McFadden (1978), McFadden (1981), Amemiya (1981), Gronau (1986),Winston (1987), Truong y Hensher (1985), Bates (1987), Jara-Díaz et al.(1994), Coto-Millán et al. (1997), Jara-Díaz (1998), Coto-Millán et al. (1999); Baños-Pino et al.(2003) Coto-Millán et al. (2005a) and Coto-Millán et al. (2005b)), is the technological restriction. The technological restriction indicates that allocating time to an activity is the individual's choice, but also a need. This restriction shows that if time allocation is a need, we have a limited minimum of time to carry out activities. If it is not a need, this restriction will not be operative.

Evans (1972) proposed the following: if journeys are a par of what individuals do and utility depends on the activities resulting from time and money allocation, then the travel decisions must be studied, modeled and understood in the context of human activities.

Evans' contribution to the study of time value is the distinction he made between the value of increasing total time available for the consumer and the value of the time employed in a particular use. Evans proposed a model in which he measured all the activities in time units, thus the only argument of the utility function was the time destined to different activities $U(t_i)$; t_i accounts for the number of time units used in activity i (Evans uses a_i for time units, we use t_i for convenience), the individual will choose the best combination of activities, taking into account income and time restrictions.

$$T = \sum_i t_i \qquad (\mu)$$

$$\sum r_i t_i = 0 \qquad (\lambda)$$

where the cost per hour r_i may be positive (if the individual pays for the activity) or negative (if he/she receives money. During work, for example); and, naturally, it will be zero if the activity is free of charge. The cost per hour r_i in certain activities can be the addition of different costs.

If we maximise the function subject to the restrictions, we obtain:

$$U_i = \mu + \lambda r_i \qquad (i = 1,2,\ldots,n)$$

Thus, the time spent on each activity depends on the utility or disutility derived from its use, as well as on the price the individual pays/receives to perform it.

The equation shows that if an individual allocates time to different activities optimally, a small increase of the time used in one activity counting with equivalent decreases of time used in another, would not make a difference for him/her. If r_i is negative, the payment received by the consumer compensates the time used in that activity, and, if r_i is positive, the time used by the consumer, compensates the spent amount. Therefore, a decrease in travel time used by the individual should not improve or worsen his/her situation. However, empirical evidence shows that decreasing travel time is an improvement for the individual. The explanation given by Evans to this controversy between the theory and the empirical evidence is that the assumption is that the individual is free to allocate his/her time to the activities he/she chooses. The time he/she decides to use travelling is assumed to be totally independent from the amount of time he/she decides to use in any other activity. In fact, most of the trips are made not for the travel itself but for the activities that it allows to develop. In other words, the wish of the consumer might not be to travel but he/she must do it to carry out other activity. In this case there is a difference between the amount of time spent travelling and the amount he/she would like to spend. In the event of having to spend more time travelling than wished, his/her situation would improve reducing travel time and would be willing to pay for that reduction and the value awarded to travel time would not be the same as the trip's financial cost.

2.2.1 Train-McFadden's Synthesis Model (Compromise Model between Goods and Leisure Activities)

Train-McFadden's Model (1978), uses the following variables with the introduction of McFadden (1981) assumptions: G represents consumed goods by their prices, in other words, it is a scalar that synthesizes all goods in monetary units; variable L represents leisure, in other words, the time not dedicated to work or to get to the workplace; c_i is the price of the transport chosen i; t_i is the travel time used by i; W, the work time in hours; w, the wage rate; τ, the total time available; M, the array of discrete choices of a good that is not included in G; and finally, E are incomes other than wages.

Train and McFadden proposed the model hereunder in 1978:

$$\max_{G,L} \quad U(G,L)$$

$$\textit{subject to}:$$

$$G + c_i \le wW$$

$$W + L + t_i = \tau$$

$$i \in M$$

The abovementioned problem is solved as follows:

We assume that i is the chosen mode of transport and we maximize the utility function with respect to work hours (W) obtaining the conditioned demand function of W (W*), and by substituting it in the utility generic function we obtain the Conditional Indirect Utility Function (CIUF).

$$\underset{W}{Max}\, U = U[(wW - c_i),(\tau - W - t_i)] \Rightarrow W^*(w, t_i, c_i)$$

the first-order condition is:

$$\frac{dU}{dW} = \frac{\partial U}{\partial G} w - \frac{\partial U}{\partial L} = 0 \Rightarrow \frac{\partial U/\partial L}{\partial U/G} = w$$

from which we obtain the optimal amount of work:

$$W^* = W^*[c_i; w; (\tau - t_i)]$$

This result shows that the individual will choose the amount of the good denominated work in such manner that leisure's marginal utility is equal to work's marginal utility.

In the second stage, we take the optimal continuous variable "quantity of work", W*, and substitute it in the direct utility function and we obtain the conditioned indirect utility function, in other words:

$$U[(wW^* - c_i);(\tau - W^* - t_i)] = V_i(c_i; w; \tau - t_i)$$

From here we obtain the subjective value work travel time VS_t,

$$VSt = \frac{\partial V_i/\partial t_i}{\partial V_i/\partial c_i}$$

$$\frac{\partial V_i}{\partial t_i} = \left(\frac{\partial U}{\partial G} w - \frac{\partial U}{\partial L}\right)\frac{\partial W^*}{\partial t_i} - \frac{\partial U}{\partial L} = -\frac{\partial U}{\partial L}$$

$$\frac{\partial V_i}{\partial c_i} = \left(\frac{\partial U}{\partial G} w - \frac{\partial U}{\partial L}\right)\frac{\partial W^*}{\partial c_i} - \frac{\partial U}{\partial G} = -\frac{\partial U}{\partial G}$$

subsequently,

$$VSt = \frac{\partial U/\partial L}{\partial U/\partial G} = w$$

That is to say, in Train and McFadden's model with endogenous income, the subjective value of time is equal to the wage rate. To simplify things, Train and McFadden assume a Cobb-Douglas-type function. The model is:

$$\underset{G,L}{Max}\, U = AG^{1-\beta}L^{\beta}$$

$$subject\ to:$$

$$\mathrm{G} + \mathrm{Bc_i} = wW$$

$$\mathrm{L} + \mathrm{W} + \mathrm{Bt_i} = \tau$$

$$\mathrm{i} \in \mathrm{M}$$

substituting,

$$U = A(wW - Bc_i)^{1-\beta}(\tau - W - Bt_i)^{\beta}$$

$$V_i = V[(wW - Bc_i); w; (\tau - Bt_i)]$$

where the subjective value of time is:

$$VSt = \frac{\partial V_i / \partial t_i}{\partial V_i / \partial c_i} = w$$

Observe that the modal choice only depends on variables (t_i, c_i, w), time, time cost and wage.

2.2.2 Jara-Díaz and Farah Model (1987)

We will use a Jara Díaz and Farah Model (1987) to make our estimates. Its optimization program, considering a Cobb-Douglas-type utility function, is:

$$\underset{G,L}{Max}\, \mathrm{U}(\mathrm{G},\mathrm{L}) = KG^{1-\beta}L^{B}$$

$$subject\ to:$$

$$G = I - Bc_i$$

$$L = T - W - Bt_i$$

where external income E has been omitted to simplify the process. In this case, U_i is easily obtained as $K(I - Bc_i)^{1-\beta}(T - W - Bt_i)^{\beta}$.

Thus, by solving the discrete optimization of the possible (c_i,t_i) alternatives, the result is a general indirect utility function such as:

$$U^*(ci, t_i, I) = K(I - Bc_i)^{1-\beta}(T - W - Bt_i)^{\beta}$$

$$V_i = V[(I - Bc_i); (T - W - Bt_i)]$$

Where travel time value will be:

$$VSt = \frac{\partial V_i / \partial t_i}{\partial V_i / \partial c_i} = \frac{\beta}{(1-\beta)} \frac{(I - Bci)}{(T - W - Bti)} = \frac{\beta}{(1-\beta)} \frac{G}{L}$$

This result shows that the subjective value of travel time decreases with travel cost and increases with time and it depends directly on $I/(T-W)$ quotient, that is defined by Jara Díaz and Farah (1987) as the expense rate, total income per available time unit.

2.3 Time Value in Journeys to Study Locations in Santander

Since choice is discrete (the alternative is selected or not, there are no intermediate options), the models used to perform the modelling of transport selection are discrete.

Discrete choice models describe the individual's behaviour with respect to the remaining possible choices, by using probability choice systems. In other words, in a situation of choice from a finite, exhaustive set of choices whose alternatives exclude one another, qualitative choice models determine the expression of the probability (P_{ij}) of chooser i (identified by a vector of characteristics) selecting j, that is characterized by a series of features.

The discrete choice models used in practice are the logit and probit models. These are models that modelize the problems associated with decision-making when the economic agents face a selection process, in this case binary. The selection criterion depends on the probability associated with each one of the individual's alternatives.

In order to characterize travellers' behaviour when choosing a means of transport in Santander, we have implemented a binary disaggregated choice model (therefore with two options: private vehicle and bus).

To specify the binary choice model, the theory of random utility maximization, Manski (1977) is appropriated. This theory establishes that each individual chooses the option which provides him/her higher utility - which is random - and this leads us to present the choice in probabilistic terms.

We present two options (Option 1 and Option 2) to formalise the model specification, whose random utilities are:

$$U_1 = V_1 + \varepsilon_1 \qquad \text{Option 1}$$

$$U_2 = V_2 + \varepsilon_2 \qquad \text{Option 2}$$

V_1 and V_2 are the systematic components that account for the part that can be measured by the analyst (available data), while ε_1 and ε_2 are the random components representing all the uncertainty associated with the knowledge of the real utility of each option. We assume that these random components behave in accordance with the distribution of joint probability. Considering an extreme value type-I probability distribution (usually, Gumbel G(η, φ)), we obtain the logit model, whilst, if distribution is normal we obtain the probit model.

- Logit Model (logistic probability unit): This model is associated with a logistic distribution function, it is convenient because of its simplicity.

$$\Pr ob(Y_i = 1) = \Lambda(X_i \beta) = \Lambda(Z_i) = \frac{e^{Z_i}}{1 + e^{Z_i}}$$

- Probit Model (probability unit): The specified equation is the distribution function.

$$\Pr ob(Y_i = 1) = \Phi(X_i \beta) = \Phi(Z_i) = \int_{-\infty}^{Z_i} \phi(S) ds$$

2.3.1 The Data

The information used in our study was obtained by means of a home survey campaign carried out in Santander every Tuesday, from March 25 to April 15, 2003. These surveys provided information about 2,793 journeys, nevertheless we have only used journeys with study purposes. The total of study-related journeys in Santander was 252.

The survey, as well as providing necessary information to describe discrete choice models, offers additional information, for example: age, gender, etc.., which are used as proxy variables of the availability of private vehicle.

The explicative variables used were:

1 Supply variables:
  1.1 Variable "time" is considered as the difference between travel time used in a private vehicle and by bus.
  1.2 Variable "cost", considered in differences; cost by private vehicle minus cost by bus.
2 Socio-economic variables:
  2-1 Travellers' age
  2.2 Variable "gender" takes value 1 if the traveller is a man and 0 if it is a woman.

Table 2.1 shows the results of the comparison between the type of mobility (compulsory or not) and the modes of transport chosen, where. The totals reflected in the columns and rows confirm the above statements.

Table 2.1. Mobility distribution in accordance with the means and purpose of travel

Concept	Mandatory	Not mandatory	TOTAL
On foot	582	577	1159
Private vehicle	915	366	1281
Bus	196	120	316
Other	18	19	37
TOTAL	1711	1082	2793

Source: Authors' own elaboration

2.3.2 Empirical Specifications

Implementing the model by Jara Díaz and Farah (1987), characterized by the fact that income is exogenously determined and variables will be affected by a expense rate g, which accounts for the total income per available time unit. By using a Cobb-Douglas-type utility function $U = \kappa G^{1-\alpha} L^{\alpha}$, we can determine the indirect utility function as:

$$V_i = \beta_c g^{-\alpha} p_i + \beta_t g^{1-\alpha} t_i$$

If a set of socio-economic variables is introduced, we can obtain the following functional form:

$$V_i = \beta_0 + \beta_t g^{1-\alpha} t_i + \beta_c g^{-\alpha} c_i + \beta_p p_i + \beta_e e_i + \beta_s s_i$$

We can observe that parameter α is used to calculate the behaviour in the exchange between leisure time and goods (low values of α indicate small preference for leisure), and the expense rate will affect means of transport choice.

Travel time saving value will be obtained proportionally to the expense rate, defined as the total income per available time unit.

We will now consider the study of the probability of the average user choosing to travel either by private vehicle or by bus. We can model this selection as follows:

$$V_1 = \beta_{01} + \beta_t g^{1-\alpha} t_1 + \beta_c g^{-\alpha} c_1 + \beta_p p_1 + \beta_e e_1 + \beta_s s_1$$

$$V_2 = \beta_t g^{1-\alpha} t_2 + \beta_c g^{-\alpha} c_2$$

and the time value is $Vstv = \dfrac{\partial V_i / \partial t_i}{\partial V_i / \partial p_i} g = \dfrac{\beta_t}{\beta_p} g$, where g is travellers' average expense rate.

As formerly stated, parameter α is used to estimate the individual's behaviour in the exchange between leisure activities and goods. This is the reason why we have made the estimates taking into account three values of α: value 0, 1 and 0.5.

2.3.3 Empirical Results

If we make the estimate people's travels by private vehicle or by bus, using the econometric program LIMDEP 8.0, we obtain the following results.

We should point out that we prefer estimations by the probit model since they count with better characteristics than the logit model: their value for the probability function is higher and the values for Akaike's criterion are lower.

Table 2.2. Results of the adjustment of the binary probit model ($\alpha=0$) for study journeys

Variable	Coefficient	Standard error	T-Statistic
Constant	0.279	0.330	0.844
Time	-0.002	0.001	-1.481
Cost	-0.317	0.157	-2.024
Age	-0.015	0.013	-1.162
Sex	0.509	0.176	2.888
Surveys analyzed	252		
Log (L)	-150.487		
Rest.Log (L)	-162.401		

Source: Authors' own elaboration

Table 2.3. Results of the adjustment of the binary probit model ($\alpha=0.5$) for study journeys

Variable	Coefficient	Standard error	T-Statistic
Constant	0.320	0.331	0.965
Time	-0.005	0.004	-1.204
Cost	-0.976	0.401	-2.431
Age	-0.015	0.013	-1.154
Sex	0.489	0.177	2.751
Surveys analyzed	252		
Log (L)	-150.185		
Rest.Log (L)	-162.401		

Source: Authors' own elaboration

The value of time saving is, as already mentioned, proportional to the expense rate g.

$$Vstv = \frac{\beta_t}{\beta_c} g = \frac{\beta_t}{\beta_c} \frac{Y}{\tau - W}$$

In this case, Y is the individual's total daily income, τ are the number of hours/day and W the hours of study. In our case, the expense rate denominator will be a fixed value of 16 hours, assumed to be the available time for all to spend, excluding study hours, which will be always 8h/day.

The subjective value of travel time will be the quotient obtained from dividing the estimated coefficient of time by the estimated coefficient of cost multiplied by travellers' average expense rate.

Table 2.4. Results of the adjustment of the binary probit model (α=1) for study journeys

Variable	Coefficient	Standard error	T-Statistic
Constant	0.384	0.332	1.154
Time	-0.008	0.011	-0.755
Cost	-2.707	0.964	-2.808
Age	-0.015	0.013	-1.118
Sex	0.478	0.179	2.661
Surveys analyzed	252		
Log (L)	-149.781		
Rest.Log (L)	-162.401		

Source: Authors' own elaboration

Table 2.5. Travel time subjective value

alfa	Studies
α=0	3.0456
α=0.5	2.2612
α=1	1.3505

Source: Authors' own elaboration

2.4 Summary and Conclusions

The values of saving in the time spent in journeys to study locations range from 3.04 €/hour for students with low preference for leisure (α=0), to 1.35 €/hour for students with very high preference for leisure.

The estimated coefficients of supply variables are affected by negative signs, results which are intuitively appropriate and show us that an increase in variable private vehicle times and costs difference with respect to bus will decrease the probability to travel by private vehicle. On the other hand, the socio-economic variables reveal that younger men have more probability to travel by private car than women and older people. The annex shows that, statistics improve if we eliminate socio-economic, age and sex variables from our model. .

References

Amemiya T (1981) Qualitative Response Models. Journal of Economic Literature 19: 1481-1536.

Baños-Pino J, Coto-Millán P, Inglada V (2003) Passenger's Choice of Air Transport under Road Competition: The Use of the Cointegration Techniques. In: Coto-Millán, P. (Ed.) Essays on Microeconomics and Industrial Organisation. Physica-Verlag. 2nd edition, Springer, pp 10-27.

Becker G (1965) A Theory of the Allocation of Time. The Economic Journal 75: 493-517.

Coto-Millán P, Baños-Pino J, Inglada V (1997) Marshallian Demands of Intercity Passenger Transport in Spain: 1980-1992. Transportation Research-E 33, 2: 79-96.

Coto-Millán P, Baños-Pino J, Inglada V (1999) Railway Inter-urban Passenger Transport in Spain: A Cointegration Analysis. World Transport Research. (Selected Papers). Transport Modelling/Assessment Vol. 3: 161-170. Pergamon.

Coto-Millán P, Carrera-Gomez G, Inglada V, Pesquera MA (2005) Promoting Competence in Regulates Market: The Case of Spanish Transports. The Annals of Regional Science 39, 1: 73-84.

Coto-Millán, P, Inglada, V, Rey, B (2006) Effects of Network Economies in High Speed Rail: The Spanish Case. The Annals of Regional Science (forthcoming).

DeSerpa A (1971) A Theory of the Economics of Time. The Economic Journal 81: 828-846.

Domencich T, McFadden D (1975) Urban Travel Demand: a Behavioral Analysis. Amsterdam, Holland, North-Holland.

Evans A (1972) On the Theory of the Valuation and Allocation of Time. Scottish Journal of Political Economy Febr:1-17.

Gronau R (1986) Home Production, a Survey. In: Ashenfelter, O., Layard, R. (eds.) Handbook of Labor Economics, vol 1. North-Holland, pp 273-304.

Hicks J (1932) The Theory of Wages. MacMillan.

Hicks J (1939) Value and Capital. Clarendon Press, Oxford.

Jara-Díaz SR (1998) Time and Income in Travel Demand: towards a Microeconomic Activity Framework. In: Garling, T., Laitia, T., Westin, K. (eds.) Theoretical Foundations of Travel Choice Modelling. Elsevier.

Jara-Díaz SR, Farah M (1987) Transport Demand and User's Benefit with Fixed Income: the Goods/Leisure Trade-Off Revisited. Transportation Research 21B: 165-170.

Jara-Díaz SR, Martínez F, Zurita I (1994) A Microeconomic Framework to Understand Residential Location. 2nd European Transport Forum, Proceedings Seminar H, pp 115-128.

Jara-Díaz SR, Guevara CA (2003) Behind the Subjective value of travel time savings: the perception of work, leisure and travel from a joint mode Choice-activity model. Journal of Transport Economic and Policy 37: 29-46 (2003).

Johnson B (1966) Travel Time and the Price of Leisure. Western Economic Journal, Spring: 135-145.

Juster FT (1970): Rethinking Utility Theory. Journal of Behavioral Economics 19: 155-179.

Lancaster K (1971) Consumer Demand: a New Approach. New York, Columbia University Press

McFadden D (1973) Conditional Logit Analysis of Qualitative Choice Behavior. In: Zarembka, P. (ed.) Frontiers in Econometrics. NY & London, Academic Press, 1973.

McFadden D (1974) The Measurement of Urban Travel Demand. Journal of Public Economics: 303-328.

McFadden D (1981) Econometric Models of Probabilistic Choice, en Structural Analysis of Discrete Data with Econometric Applications. Manski, C.F. y McFadden, D. (Eds.). MIT Press: 198-272.

Oort, C (1969) The Evaluation of Travelling Time. Journal of Transport Economics and Policy September: 279-286.

Train K, McFadden D (1978) The Goods/Leisure Trade-Off and Disaggregate Work Trip Mode Choice Models. Transportation Research 12: 349-353.

Winston GC (1987) Activity Choice: a New Approach to Economic Behavior. Journal of Economic Behavior and Organization 8: 567-585.

Annex

Table 2.6. Results of the adjustment of the binary probit model ($\alpha=0$) for study journeys

Variable	Coefficient	Standard error	T-Statistic
Constant	0.179	0.138	1.296
Time	-0.002	0.001	-1.639
Cost	-0.428	0.152	-2.818
Surveys analyzed	252		
Log (L)	-156.448		
Rest.Log (L)	-162.401		

Source: Authors' own elaboration

Table 2.7. Results of the adjustment of the binary probit model ($\alpha=0.5$) for study journeys

Variable	Coefficient	Standard error	T-Statistic
Constant	0.206	0.143	1.437
Time	-0.006	0.004	-1.425
Cost	-1.267	0.388	-3.265
Surveys analyzed	252		
Log (L)	-155.725		
Rest.Log (L)	-162.401		

Source: Authors' own elaboration

Table 2.8. Results of the adjustment of the binary probit model ($\alpha=1$) for study journeys

Variable	Coefficient	Standard error	T-Statistic
Constant	0.265	0.144	1.833
Time	-0.011	0.011	-1.062
Cost	-3.423	0.931	-3.675
Surveys analyzed	252		
Log (L)	-155.038		
Rest.Log (L)	-162.401		

Source: Authors' own elaboration

Table 2.9. Travel time Subjective value of

Alfa	Studies
α=0	2.454
α=0.5	2.011
α=1	1.456

Source: Authors' own elaboration

3 Price and Income Elasticities for Intercity Public Transport in Spain

Pablo Coto-Millán
Department of Economics
University of Cantabria (Spain)

Jose Baños-Pino
Department of Economics
University of Oviedo (Spain)

Gema Carrera-Gómez
Department of Economics
University of Cantabria (Spain)

Juan Castanedo-Galán
Department of Transports
University of Cantabria (Spain)

Miguel A. Pesquera
Department of Transports
University of Cantabria (Spain)

Vicente Inglada
Department of Economics
University Carlos III of Madrid (Spain)

Rubén Sainz
Department of Economics
University of Cantabria (Spain)

3.1 Introduction

Research on the passengers transport demand, has been focused so far, on getting to know the parameters which determine the user's behaviour. It is of particular interest here to gain knowledge of the various price and income elasticities of each mode of transport. Such information can also be used for the analysis of the effects caused by the different tariff policies.

In empirical literature, the demand for public transport falls into two categories. The first one is known as aggregated modal fractioning models, which attempts to determine the quantity of journeys in a. given range of modes of transport with respect to two countries, towns or regions. Through these models, we explain the passenger demand flow variable for each means of transport from a series of explicative variables, such as the price for each mode of transport. Also, the relative duration of the journey for each mode of transport together with the particular generally socioeconomic characteristics of the passenger, can be explained. They are essentially non-conductist studies with cross section data. The research made by Quandt and Baumol (1966) and Levin (1978) can be considered from this point of view.

The second type of demand models are those which assume that passengers optimize a utility function. Such models are based upon the theories of human behaviour postulated under conventional microeconomics. These models display some observations as regards the time series of passengers/km for each regional or national mode of transport, and economic series of income and prices. The major works concerned with this are those of McFadden (1973, 1974) which, in accordance to this, have contributed greatly towards desintegrated modelization. The microeconomics of the second type of model are, for obvious reasons, of great interest. They lie on the assumption of discrete choice of a particular mode of transport from the passenger. It is also assumed that the means of transport chosen by the passenger, optimizes the random utility function, i.e.:

$$U_t^i = U\left(X_t^i, Y_t; \alpha_t\right) + \beta\left(X_t^i, Y_t\right) \text{ with } i = 1, 2, ..., \text{k}$$

where U_t^i represents the utility given to each mode of transport i (with k mode of transport); X_t^i represents the factors assignated to each mode of transport (mainly demand, price and time); Y_t is an income variable which represents the socioeconomic characteristics of the passengers (specially income); and finally β represents the factor which has not been observed and is assumed to represent other variables non included, such as the taste and preference of the user.

Passengers now choose the means of transport i as long as $U_t^i > U_t^j$, $i \neq j$. Moreover, since we have assumed a utility random model, passengers will have a certain probability for the different utilities which satisfy them more in an instant t, as it is shown:

$$P_t^i = Prob(U_t^i > U_t^j, i \neq j)$$

In order to provide the above equation with a functional specification, it is necessary to assume certain types of behaviour in the distribution of the errors. One of the models commonly used in practice is the multinomial logit:

$$P_t^i = exp\{(X_t^i, Y_t; \alpha_t)\} / \sum_{j=1}^{J} exp\{U(X_t^j, Y_t; \alpha_t)\} \tag{3.1}$$

More technical details of Eq 3.1 can be found in Fienberg (1977). Such multinomial logit has been used by McFadden (1973), Train (1980) and Lave (1980). If, on the contrary, it is assumed that errors in expression (4.1) are normally distributed, we obtain a multinominal probit model, which has been studied by Hausmen and Wise (1978).

A more recent research has been made as regards joint choice passengers transport demand models. The passenger joint choice assumption, means that this research takes into account a discrete choice, such as the mode of transport, and a second choice such as the arrival place or a continuous choice of use of the vehicle. The joint choice explains the transport chosen related to other means of transport and activities. For the passenger joint choice, Winston (1985) proposes an indirect utility function as follows:

$$U_t^i = U\left(X_t^i, Y_t, P_t^i, \vec{P}_t^j, S_t \right); \text{ i} = 1, 2, ..., \text{n mode of transport}$$

where U_t^i represents the discrete choice utility in the period of time t; X_t^i is the variable which represents the demand for each means of transport; Y_t represents the passenger's income; P_t^j represents the price of each mode of transport; $\vec{P}_t^j$ is a price vector which represents the prices of the alternative transports and S_t is a variable which represents the socioeconomic characteristics of the passenger. Under Roy's theorem it is possible to write:

$$X_t^i\left(\vec{P}_t^i, Y_t\right) = -\frac{\partial U(\vec{P}_t^j, Y_t) / \partial P_t^i}{\partial U(\vec{P}_t^j, Y_t) / \partial Y_t}$$

Therefore, Marshallian demand functions can be obtained from each of the respective transport, and its generic function is:

$$X_t^i = X(Y_t, P_t^i, \vec{P}_t^j) \tag{3.2}$$

where Eq. 3.2 satisfies the essential assumptions of integrability and optimization.

3.2 Theoretical Model

The following theoretical model is based upon Winston's work (1985). The passengers transport demand of group i transport in the period of time t, X_t^i corresponds to the following modes of transport: talgo, long distance railway, road and air transport. The transport services which have been analyzed correspond to Spanish intercity distances of regular railway service, regular and "charter" air service, and regular and discretional road transport service. The demand will be assessed considering the number of passengers/km, as long as the statistical sources available allow to.

Assume an indirect utility function:

$$U_t = U\left(X_t^i, Y_t, P_t^i, \vec{P}_t^j, S_t \right)$$

where the variables have the same meaning as previously. Assume that each individual has a certain amount of income fixed to face one's intercity journey. That is to say, for each instant t, given an income Y_t the representative individual has a budget restriction:

$$Y_t = \sum_{i=1}^{n} P_t^i X_t^i$$

Besides, it is assumed that each consumer has different combinations to use a group of intercity transport services, that is to say, a consumption system containing only the combinations of use of transport services between different Spanish cities. Assume that this system is close and convex, for this reason, sea transport service has been excluded. This is because such services are only relevant within the peninsula.

It is also assumed that consumers are able to put their preferences in order. As long as the user of the transport services do so under the rationality assumption, the consumer will chose the combination which is first in one's list of preferences. The demand functions of each transport service can be deduced from the mentioned assumptions as optimal combinations of each service which are subject to budget restriction. It must be added that the aggregation of the individual demands, does not mean that all the consumer's particular function properties are verified. That is to say, a certain aggregate behaviour can be represented by the demand functions deduced from the following assumption: distribution of the preferences is under a representative average utility function. Under such an assumption, the transport services aggregate demand can be represented by Marshallian demand curves plus certain random error. It is not necessary to impose Slutsky's equation restrictions, that is to say, symmetry property, and so on., since the preferences can widely vary depending on the agents.

The development of the mentioned model leads the service users to maximize their utility function subject to budget restriction, or to minimize their spending subject to a utility level. That is to say:

$$max\,imize\ U_t = U(X_t^i, Y_t, P_t^i, \vec{P}_t^j, S_t)$$

$$subject \text{ to } Y_t = \sum_{i=1}^{n} P_t^i X_t^i$$

or

$$\text{minimize } Y_t = \sum_{i=1}^{n} P_t^i X_t^i$$

$$\text{subject to } U_t = U(X_t^i, Y_t, P_t^i, \vec{P}_t^j, S_t)$$

It is possible to obtain Marshallian demand functions from the optimization process:

$$X_t^i = X(Y_t, P_t^i, \vec{P}_t^j, S_t)$$

where we must expect:

$$\frac{\partial X_t^i}{\partial Y_t} > 0; \quad \frac{\partial X_t^i}{\partial P_t^i} < 0; \quad \frac{\partial X_t^i}{\partial P_t^j} > 0 \text{ if the service “j” is substitute of “i”.}$$

$$\frac{\partial X_t^i}{\partial P_t^j} < 0 \text{ if the service “j” is complementary of “i”.}$$

With respect to $\partial X_t^i / \partial S_t$, we can find any sign, depending on the included socioeconomic variable. The estimation of the model must face two problems. The first is the identification, and it arises considering that not only the supply, but also the demand evolves simultaneously through time, as an answer to variables of similar features. As far as railway and long distance transport are concerned, the supply is determined by the policy of the company which has the monopoly of the sector, and therefore, it can be considered to be influenced by external factors. In air transport, there are similar conclusions during the research, taking into account that regular national air transport is managed by the companies appointed by the government. Again, the passenger transport fluctuations are particularly due to demand variables, and to a lesser extent, to the supply which can be considered inflexible as regards short term price, and externally controlled during the whole research. In road transport, the market works more flexibly. However, the government has restricted the supply of road passenger transport. Regular lines are granted in public tender with the right of "testing" from the railway lines, a right very often exercised by the national railway company, which has again led to a supply controlled by external factors.

There is a second type of problem related to regulation. The Spanish government has regulated the different modes of transport. Not only the restrictions and limits to participate in transport system, and the levels of service explained before representing the type of state implication, but the regulation has also been carried out through the fixation of prices. As far as this is concerned, Rus (1992) presents a summary of the different kinds of state implication.

This has given rise to the use of regulated prices in the different transport services estimated.

3.3 Empirical Evidence

For the empirical considerations we have taken monthly data from January 1980 to December 1988 (108 observations). The variables from Inglada (1992), used in the analysis are: passenger railway transport price (PF), passenger air transport (PA), evolution of passenger railway transport in millions of passengers per kilometer (QFL), evolution of TALGO passenger transport in millions of passengers per kilometer (QFT), and national passenger air transport in Spain in thousands of passengers (QA).

Since monthly data of the Gross Domestic Product (GDP) were not available as income proxy variable, we have used as proxy of this, the consumption of electric power (CENER), and the Index of Industrial Production (IIP). Both variables have been obtained from the statistics and economic reports published by Banco de España.

Finally, in order to finish the model, we have needed monthly data of the passenger road transport and of their corresponding prices. Since it was impossible to obtain this, we decided to use two approximate variables such as the petrol and gas-oil consumption (QGAS) and a weighted average of the different fuel prices (QGAS). This data has been given by the Instituto Logístico de Hidrocarburos (Logistic Institute of Hydrocarbon (ILHC) and REPSOL,S.A.

Once all the variables have been defined, we have deflated the nominal prices in order to turn them into reality. This has been done from the monthly data of the Consumer Price Index brought out by the Instituto Nacional de Estadística.

Subsequently, all the variables have been seasonally fitted in order to avoid fluctuations arising from the transport demand during summer, Christmas time and Easter.

Finally, in order to obtain price and income elasticities and draw a series of economic conclusions, we have taken logs in all the variables.

As regards long distance passenger railway transport (Table 3.1), and before analyzing the results of the fit, we should comment on the two control variables introduced in order to explain two particular and significant facts. The first one accounts for the strike of the railway staff which taking place in February 1981 (D8102), and the second strike of the interurban transport service, occurred in March 1988 (D88O3).

Table 3.1. Models fitted from the different means of transport

	LSQFL	LSQFT	LSQGAS	LSQA
constant	4,58 (3,84)	-5,96 (-4,11)	10.59 (21,19)	-
LSCENER	0,27 (2,16)	1,21 (7,90)	-	-
LSDPF	-1,01 (-5,84)	-1,33 (-6,32)	-	-
LSDPGAS	0,26 (6,05)	0,21 (4,09)	-0,34. (-11,14)	-0,11 (-3,76)
D88.03	0,17 (3,32)	-	-	-
D81.02	-0,21 (-4,20)	-0,31 (-5,07)	-	-
LSIPI	-	-	0,46 (4,44)	-
LSIPK-12)	-	-	-	1,61 (56.55)
LSDPA	-	-	0,17 (2,20)	-
LSDPA(-12)	-	-	-	-0,52 (-2,81)
Sample	80(01) a 88(12)	80(01) a 88(12)	80(01) a 88(12)'	81(01) a 88(12)
$\overline{R}^2$	0,54	0,84	0,88	0,62
σ	0,05	0,06	0,03	0,06
SSE	0,252	0,379	0,106	0,326
DW	2,10	' 1,80	2,13	1,48
Q(24)	17,47	18,35	52,92	71,08
JB	15,10	1.71	5,45	3,25

Statistic t within brakets. Q represents the statistic Ljung-Box and JB represents the statistic Bera Jarque in order to compare normality. Log variables are preceded by letter L, letter S means that the variable is destationalised, and letter D means that the variable is deflated.

As regards the results of the estimations we can remark on the theoretical interpretation of the positive sign of the income proxy variable. As it was expected, long distance railway transport is a normal good. The railway service price variable has negative sign, as it was predicted, and it has a price elasticity of -1,01. In the American case, Winston (1985) they estimated price elasticities ranging from -1,58 to -1,20 for interurban railway. McFadden (1974) also estimated price elasticities for city passenger railway in San Francisco Bay with values ranging from -0,86 to -0,60. (see Table 3.2).

Table 3.2. Price-demand elasticities for passenger railway transport

Authors	Type of Model	Price Elasticity	Mode of Transport
Winston (1985)	Multinomial Logit	-1,58 to -1,20	Railway passenger intercity
McFadden (1974)	Multinomial Logit	-0,86 to -0,60	Railway urban passenger
Proposed Model	Log-Linear	-1,01	Railway passenger
Proposed Model	Log-Linear	-1,33	TALGO railway passenger

In the analysis of passenger railway transport at a more disintegrated level, such as TALGO, (Table 3.1, second model presented), all the explicative variables of the previous fit are implicated, except for the control variable D8803, with no incidence in this case.

As far as the explicative variables of the fit are concerned, we must remark on the elasticity higher than the unit in the income variable, which means that an increase in the income leads to a more than proportional increase in TALGO demand, something which did not happen in the first model.

Moreover, price elasticity is again higher than the unit in absolute value. The explanation of this is that TALGO transport service is open to price changes. The higher elasticity states that TALGO transport is a normal good and has better facilities. It is undoubtedly the best railway service nowadays in Spain. In fact, this price elasticity of -1,33 is one of the least estimated by Winston, from -1,58 to -1,20. What proves to be a more elastic demand than that corresponding to long distance railway, as it -was expected.

The fact that TALGO transport has positive elasticity with respect to the road transport service price, means that it behaves as an entail. The strike that occurred in February 1981 had a negative influence on TALGO demand.

For the fit of the road transport demand (third model, Table 3.1), we have taken fuel price and air transport as significant variables and the approximation provided by the Index of Industrial Production (IIP), as variable income.

The elasticities we have obtained, function as expected, therefore, we can state that road transport services are normal goods and an entail for air transport. In the American case, McFadden (1974) and Winston (1985) provide price elasticities ranging from -0,22 to -0,47. Besides, Rus (1990) offers estimations for urban transport price elasticities, ranging from -0,4 to -0,2. Therefore, value -0,34 here estimated is consistent with that obtained in other works (see Table 3.3). Observing the values of the statistics, we can deduce the consistency of the demand function presented.

Table 3.3. Price-demand elasticities for passenger road transport

Authors	Type of Model	Price Elasticity	Mode of Transport
McFadden (1974)	Logit Multinomial	-0,22	Road passenger
Winston (1985)	Logit Multinomial	-0,47	Road passenger
Rus (1992)	Lineal and Log-Linear dynamic	-0,4 to -0,2	Interurban public road passenger
Proposed Model	Log-Linear	-0,34	Road passenger

The modelization of air transport is slightly different from the case previously mentioned (fourth model in Table 3.1). As regards to this, it has been necessary to include a year's delay, since the economic agents can make decisions a year in advance, when aggregate national air transport is considered.

Unfortunately, the high grade of air transport demand does not make any difference in its use due to work or leisure reasons. This could be due to the high regulation of the sector. The fixation of prices has been controlled, for this reason, the economic agents could know the prices well in advance. Another reason could be the great air transport demand existing during the year due to holidays.

Moreover, income elasticity is positive and higher than the unit for normal goods, as expected. We have to mention that the price elasticity for such services estimated by Perez (1992) ranges from -0,5 to -0,03. Price elasticity has a reasonable behaviour, and provides information about an inelastic demand. Winston (1985) has estimated a price elasticity for air transport of -0,38 for intercity holiday journeys in the United States. Taking into account that we include here journeys for work reasons, it is not surprisingly a more elastic demand such as that provided by value -0,52 (see Table 3.4). Finally, the negative sign of the road transport price proxy, shows the complementary character of national air transport service. In many cases, national air transport services imply higher use of road transport.

Table 3.4. Price-demand elasticities for passenger air transport

Authors	Type of Model	Price Elasticity	Mode of Transport
Winston (1985)	Multinomial Logit	-0.38	Air passenger
Perez (1992)	Simultaneous equations	-0,5 to -0,03	Air passenger
Proposed Model	Dynamic Log-Linear	-0,52	Air passenger

3.4 Fitted Time Series Models

With the aim to complement the previous demand analysis we have estimated ARIMA models for the QFL, QFT, QA and QGAS series, presented in Table 3.5. The first of tie series corresponds to the "airlines" classical model, that is to say, series with an outstanding seasonal and trend component, this being approximately lineal, joint under a multiplicative scheme. We must remark that the QFL series behavior is more stationary than the QFL series as far as the seasonal component is concerned. Taking into account passenger air transport, we can observe the stationary component is steadier. The model for the QGAS series is similar to that fitted by Peña (1978) for the period 1966.01-1977.08.

Table 3.5. Time series models for passenger transport series (t statistics within brackets)

RAILWAY PASSENGER INTERCITY TRANSPORT:

$$\nabla\nabla_{12} \ln QFL = \underset{(12{,}66)}{(1-0{,}79B)}\underset{(7{,}61)}{(1-0{,}61B^{12})}a_t$$

$\sigma_e = 0{,}05$; SEE $= 0{,}33$; $Q(24) = 13{,}42$

TALGO RAILWAY PASSENGER TRANSPORT;

$$\nabla\nabla_{12} \ln QFT = \underset{(12{,}33)}{(1-0{,}79B)}\underset{(5{,}54)}{(1-0{,}47B^{12})}a_t$$

$\sigma_e = 0{,}06$; SEE $= 0{,}42$; $Q(24) = 15{,}25$

AIR PASSENGER TRANSPORT:

$$\nabla\nabla_{12} \ln LQA = \underset{(4{,}95)}{(1-0{,}42B)}\underset{(16{,}72)}{(1-0{,}76B^{12})}a_t$$

$\sigma_e = 0{,}06$; SEE $= 0{,}42$; $Q(24) = 15{,}25$

ROAD PASSENGER TRANSPORT (PETROL CONSUMPTION):

$$\underset{(-3{,}38)}{(1+0{,}18B)}\nabla\nabla_{12} \ln LQGAS = \underset{(9{,}17)}{(1-0{,}68B)}\underset{(17{,}75)}{(1-0{,}75B^{12})}a_t$$

$\sigma_e = 0{,}03$; SEE $= 0{,}13$; $Q(24) = 21{,}53$

3.5 Conclusions

The previous models, based on the conventional demand theory, provide us with empirical evidence for road, railway and air transport in Spain from 1980 to 1988. We obtain the Marshallian demand functions with respect to relevant income and price variables for each modes of transport analyzed. In this work we offer income and price elasticities estimations as well as exchange of data aggregated to interurban passengers transport in Spain. It is necessary to be cautious when interpreting data, due to the high variable aggregation. Some research could be made in the future on this type of model from the desagregation of transport service demand into different lines.

References

Boletín Estadístico del Banco de España. Several issues.

Boletín Económico del Banco de Espana. Several issues.

CAMPSA. Precios de Gasolinas: 1980.01-1988.12.

Centro de Estudios de la Compañía Logística de Hidrocarburos.

Fienberg SE (1977) The Analysis of Cross-Classified Data. MIT Press, Cambridge, MA.

Inglada V (1992) Intermodalidad y elasticidades precio en el transporte interurbano de viajeros. Revista de Transporte y Comunicaciones (MOPT): 543-14.

Lave C (1980) The Demand for Urban Mass Transit. Review of Economic and Statistics, 52: 320-323.

Levin RC (1978) Allocation in Surface Freight Transportation: Does Rete Regulation Matter?. Bell Journal of Economics: 18-45.

Hausman L, Wise D (1978) A Conditional Probit Model for Qualitative Choice. Econometrica 46: 403-426.

McFadden D (1973) Conditional Logit Analysis of Qualitative Choice Behavior, In: Frontiers in Econometrics, Ed. P. Zarembra, Academic Press, New York, pp 105-142.

McFadden D (1974) The Measurement of Urban Travel Demand. Journal of Public Economic 3: 303-328.

Peña D (1978) La metodología de Box-Jenkins: una aplicación a la previsión del consumo de gasolina en España. Información Comercial Española 542: 135-15.

Pérez, NR (1992) Análisis Económico de los Servicios de Transporte Aéreo Regular en España.

Quandt R, Baumol W (1966) The Demand for Abstract Transport Modes: Theory and Measurement. Journal of Regional Science 6 (2): 13-26.

Rus G (1990) Public Transport Demand Elasticities in Spain. Journal of Transport Economics and Policy 24: 189-201.

Rus G (1992) Economía y Política del Transporte: España y Europa. Editorial Civitas, Madrid.

Train K (1980) A Structured Logit Model of Auto Ownership and Mode Choice. Review of Economic Studies, 47: 357-370.

Winston C (1985) Conceptual Developments in the Economics of Transportation: An interpretative survey. Journal of Economic Literature 23 (2): 57-94.

PART II SUPPLY AND EFFICIENCY

4 Classifying Urban Passenger Transportation Services

Wayne K. Talley
Department of Economics
Old Dominion University (Virginia, USA)

4.1 Introduction

Urban areas are under constant change from changes in their economic, political, social, environmental and transportation systems. The urban area's transportation system is interrelated with these other systems and its expansion promotes urban economic development by increasing the spatial and time accessibility of economic activities. Transportation expansion also contributes to the transformation of centralized, high-density urban areas into decentralized, lower density (but larger) urban areas. As a consequence, workers and firms are more likely to take jobs further from home and to move to new locations, respectively. However, the expansion may also result in such negative urban environmental impacts as air and noise pollution.

The purpose of this chapter is to classify urban passenger transportation services. That is to say, services are classified with respect to service structure – i.e., whether their: (1) service times are scheduled or nonscheduled, (2) service routes are fixed or variable, (3) providers are for-hire or private and (4) passengers share or do not share services. Further, they will be classified with respect to type of service – i.e., whether they are transit, private or paratransit services. These classification schemes provide the urban transportation planner with the means for distinguishing among all (actual and potential) urban passenger transportation services. The schemes should also be useful to urban policymakers in making transportation investment decisions for promoting urban economic development.

In the next section, the service structure and type of urban passenger transportation services are discussed. In the following sections, discussions of specific types of urban passenger transportation services - transit, private and paratransit - are presented. Then, a discussion of the historical development of U. S. street railway and motorbus transit services is presented. Finally, a summary of the discussions is presented.

4.2 Service Structure and Type

Urban passenger transportation service may be classified according to service time and route characteristics (see Figure 4.1). Service may be scheduled (or fixed-time) service or nonscheduled (or variable-time) service. Furthermore, the service may be provided over a fixed route or over a variable route. Transit service is fixed-route, scheduled service. Private transportation service is variable-route, nonscheduled service. Paratransit service may include any combination of the above time and route service characteristics other than the fixed-route, scheduled service as provided by transit.

Routes		Times: Scheduled	Times: Nonscheduled
	Fixed	Transit	Demand-Responsive Paratransit (Jitney)
	Variable	Commuter Paratransit (Carpool, vanpool, subscription bus)	Private (Pedestrian, private automobile, private bicycle, private motorcycle) Demand-Responsive Paratransit (Dial-a-ride, exclusive-ride taxi, automobile rental)
		Scheduled	Nonscheduled
		Times	

Fig. 4.1. Urban passenger transportation services: routes and times

Urban passenger transportation services may be provided by for-hire as well as by private providers (see Figure 4.2). For-hire providers are transportation firms such as transit firms that provide transportation service for others. Private providers provide transportation service for themselves (e.g., an individual operating his own automobile).

Occupancy		Provision: Private	Provision: For-Hire
Occupancy	Shared	Commuter Paratransit (Carpool, vanpool, subscription bus)	Transit Commuter Paratransit (Vanpool, subscription bus) Demand-Responsive Paratransit (Dial-a-ride, jitney)
Occupancy	Non-shared	Private (Pedestrian, private automobile, private bicycle, private motorcycle)	Demand-Responsive Paratransit (Exclusive-ride taxi, automobile rental)

Fig. 4.2. Urban passenger transportation services: occupancy and provision

Urban passenger transportation service may further be classified as either shared or non-shared service, i.e., whether the service is shared with another passenger or passengers (see Figure 4.2). Transit service is shared service; private transportation is non-shared service; and paratransit service may be shared or non-shared.

Based upon the above discussion, transit service may be formally defined as for-hire, shared urban passenger transportation service that is fixed-route and scheduled. Private urban passenger transportation service may be defined as privately provided, non-shared urban passenger transportation service that is variable-route and nonscheduled. Paratransit service is any urban passenger transportation service other than transit and private services. As a shared service, paratransit service may be defined as either privately provided (e.g., car pool) or for-hire (e.g., jitney) urban passenger transportation service that includes any combination of fixed-variable-route and scheduled-nonscheduled services other than fixed-route, scheduled service. As a non-shared service, paratransit service may be defined as for-hire urban passenger transportation service that is variable-route and nonscheduled (e.g., exclusive-ride taxi service).

4.3 Transit Services

Transit services have been classified by the U.S. American Public Transit Association as: (1) motorbus, (2) heavy rail, (3) light rail, (4) trolley bus, (5) commuter railroad, (6) urban ferryboat, (7) inclined plane, (8) cable car, (9) aerial tramway, (10) automated guideway and (11) monorail transit services. Motorbus service is provided by vehicles that are rubber-tired, self-propelled, manually steered with their fuel supply carried aboard. In the U. S., motorbus transit passenger trips represent the largest percentage of total transit trips (see Table 2.1); further, most U.S. urban transit firms provide motorbus service.

Table 4.1. U. S. urban transit passenger trips (millions)

Year	Motorbus	Heavy Rail	Light Rail	Trolley Bus	Commuter Rail	Other
1990	5,677	2,346	175	126	328	79
1991	5,624	2,172	184	125	318	81
1992	5,517	2,207	188	126	314	77
1993	5,381	2,046	188	121	322	78
1994	4,871	2,169	284	118	339	80
1995	4,848	2,033	251	119	344	80
1996	4,887	2,157	261	117	352	81
1997	5,013	2,430	262	121	357	92
1998	5,399	2,393	276	117	381	89
1999	5,648	2,521	292	120	396	91
2000	5,678	2,632	320	122	413	93
2001	5,849	2,728	336	119	419	97
2002	5,868	2,688	337	116	414	97

Source: American Public Transportation Association: http://www.apta.com.

Heavy rail is a subway-type railway, electrically powered and constructed on an exclusive private right-of-way with high-level platform stations. Heavy rail service is also referred to as rapid rail, subway, elevated railway or metropolitan railway service. In the U.S., heavy rail passenger trips are second in number to that of motorbus transit trips (see Table 4.1). Light rail service describes what is also referred to as street railway service - typically electrically powered and operating on fixed rails constructed on city streets or on semiprivate or exclusive private rights-of-way. Trolley bus service is provided by rubber-tired transit vehicles, manually steered and propelled by electric motors - that draw electric current (normally from overhead wires) from a central power source not on board the vehicle.

Commuter rail transit service is that portion of the operations (currently or formerly) of intercity rail passenger carriers that encompasses urban passenger train service for local short-distance travel (between a central city and adjacent suburbs). This service is provided by both locomotive-hauled and self-propelled railroad passenger cars and is also referred to as regional rail or suburban rail service. In the U.S., the percentage of commuter railroad transit passenger trips ranks third behind the percentages of motorbus and heavy rail passenger trips (see Table 4.1).

Urban ferryboat service is provided by passenger-carrying marine vessels - over a scheduled, fixed water-route between two or more points. Ferry vessels are generally steam or diesel-powered conventional ferry vessels, but also may be hovercraft, hydrofoil or other high-speed vessels. The service is usually provided between two points where a bridge does not exist or where the width of the body of water would make a bridge impractical. The urban ferryboat is the largest transit vehicle.

Inclined plane transit service utilizes vehicles operating up and down slopes on rails over a private rights-of-way and propelled by moving cables attached to the vehicles and powered from a central location (i.e., by not-on-board engines or motors). In the U.S., cable car transit service is found only in San Francisco. The service is provided in mixed-street traffic by rail passenger vehicles. Cable cars are individually controlled, propelled by moving cables located below the street surface and powered by engines or motors from a central location. Aerial tramway transit service is provided by a system of aerial cables with suspended unpowered passenger vehicles, propelled by moving cables and powered from a central location. Automated guideway transit service utilizes guided vehicles operating over a fully automated system (i.e., by vehicles operating without vehicle operators or other crewpersons on-board). Monorail transit service utilizes guided vehicles operating on or suspended from a single rail, beam or tube.

4.4 Private Services

Examples of private urban passenger transportation include pedestrian, private automobile, private bicycle and private motorcycle transportation. Pedestrian transportation is upright human locomotion or walking. Although we are not accustomed to thinking of walking as a mode of transportation (possibly because it does not employ a vehicle), it was the predominant mode of urban passenger transportation for thousands of years. Even today, it remains a principal means of transportation in cities. It provides a linkage to and among other urban passenger transportation services that would be difficult to duplicate. Improvements in urban pedestrian transportation have generally been in the form of mechanical aids to pedestrians (such as escalators and moving side-walks) and separation of pedestrians from motor vehicular traffic by either space (such as separate pedestrian ways built above or below street level) or time (such as WALK and DON'T WALK traffic signals).

Private automobile transportation is the operation of privately-owned automobiles for personal use. It is the most personalized and accessible urban passenger transportation service that utilizes a vehicle. It has a comparative advantage over transit services with respect to comfort, personal security and accessibility. It also has a speed advantage except when highway congestion exists. In many U.S. cities it is the dominant vehicular mode of urban passenger transportation.

Bicycle transportation is the operation of a light two-wheeled vehicle that is human powered. Private bicycle transportation is the operation of a bicycle by its owner for personal use. Bicycle transportation has a comparative speed advantage over walking but remains a relatively slow mode, primarily suitable for trips of very short distance. For such trips, it has been promoted as an alternative to the automobile for reducing automobile pollution and congestion in urban areas. Its acceptability as an urban passenger mode varies throughout the world; in the Netherlands, it is a primary means of passenger transportation in some urban areas.

Motorcycle transportation is the operation of a self-propelled bicycle (i.e., powered by a motor). Private motorcycle transportation is the operation of a motorcycle by its owner for personal use. Motorcycle transportation is competitive with automobile transportation with respect to speed (and thus has a comparative speed advantage over the bicycle) but has the same comfort and safety problems as the bicycle.

4.5 Paratransit Services

Paratransit services that are shared but privately provided include carpool, vanpool and subscription bus services and are often referred to as commuter (or ridesharing) paratransit services, since they are primarily used for commuter or work trips (see Figure 4.2). Carpools are pre-arranged ridesharing passenger transportation services where privately-owned automobiles are used and the driver does not receive a fee. Carpoolers typically take turns driving their own automobiles. After participants in a carpool are determined, a fixed pickup-and-delivery time schedule is set for each passenger, but the routing to reach the final (or work) destination may vary (see Figure 4.1).

Vanpools are pre-arranged ridesharing passenger transportation services similar to carpools except that one person is assigned as the driver. Vanpool drivers typically receive a fee for the service, ranging from personal use of the van to a free ride to work as well as profits from passenger fees. The seating capacity of the van is greater than that of a standard automobile, but generally does not exceed fifteen seats.

If the driver owns the van, then the vanpool service is privately provided. However, if the driver enters into a rental agreement with an employer or a third party to provide the van, the vanpool service becomes a for-hire service. In the U.S., 3M Company in Minneapolis was the first company in April, 1973 to start an employee, commuter vanpool program - making vans available to its employees. In the U.S, third parties are generally transit firms that receive government demonstration project funds for purchasing vans and making these available to the general public for vanpool programs. Vanpools are more difficult to organize than carpools because of the additional issues of driver compensation, insurance costs and regulations.

Subscription bus service is a pre-arranged ridesharing passenger transportation service similar to vanpool service, except that a bus rather than a van is used. Such service is appropriate for work trips if enough employees live on or near a narrow route to justify the use of a large vehicle. If the driver owns the vehicle, the service is a privately provided service. If the bus is rented, the service is for-hire (see Figure 4.2).

The remaining paratransit services have been labeled demand-responsive paratransit services - flexible in time (or nonscheduled) in meeting passenger demand. For-hire, shared demand-responsive paratransit services include the variable-route service, dial-a-ride, and the fixed-route service, jitney (see Figure 4.2). Dial-a-ride service utilizes a shared vehicle for providing door-to-door service on demand to a number of travelers with different origins and destinations. The customary method of requesting such a service is by telephone. Upon receiving requests, a dispatcher will dispatch vehicles to collect and distribute passengers to and from similarly requested origin-destination points. Taxi service where vehicles are shared (i.e., shared-ride taxi service) is a dial-a-ride service. Unlike dial-a-ride service, jitney service adheres to a relatively fixed route. Jitney service is a shared vehicle such as a automobile, van or minibus operating along a fixed or a semi-fixed route or routes, where passengers hail the jitney vehicle as they would hail a taxi.

Demand-responsive paratransit services that are for-hire but non-shared include exclusive-ride taxi and automobile rental (see Figure 4.2). Exclusive-ride taxi refers to taxi service where the passenger has exclusive use of the vehicle. Door-to-door passenger service is provided on demand by the passenger either hailing a taxi by telephone or on the street. Automobile rental involves a passenger hiring an automobile by rental agreement from an automobile rental company for a specified period of time. Since the passenger is also the driver, automobile rental is the paratransit service that is most similar to private automobile transportation[1].

In order to gain further understanding of urban transit services, the following section presents the historical development of the U. S. transit system, focusing on street railway and motorbus transit services[2].

4.6 U. S. Street Railway and Motorbus Transit Services: A Historical Perspective

4.6.1 Street Railways

Technological advances in the generation and transmission of electricity allowed for the electrification of street railways. The first electric street cars in the U. S. were installed in St. Joseph, Missouri in late 1887 and in Richmond, Virginia in early 1888. Electrification allowed railway companies to operate larger vehicles at

[1] Note that privately provided but shared bicycles and motorcycles used in work trips would be classified as commuter paratransit services, but classified as demand-responsive paratransit services if for-hire (i.e., rented) but non-shared.

[2] For further discussion of urban passenger transportation services, see Altshuler and Womack (1979) and Vuchic (1981).

higher speeds over longer routes. The service was void of the inflexibility characterized by the cable car - the inflexibility between the cable and the powerhouse. The typical street railway company was a city-wide monopoly. Local governments seeing the service as a tool for economic development granted franchises that conferred monopoly rights. Street railway companies often sold electricity as well as providing transportation service - in some cases eventually becoming electric utility companies. Fares were regulated at the outset and the franchises often required city-wide transfer privileges as quid pro quo for their issuance. As a consequence, passengers traveling short distances often cross-subsidized passengers traveling longer distances.

In 1907 street railways (or light rail services) were used for 94 percent of vehicular urban passenger trips (Saltzman, 1979, p. 28). However, the perception was that street railways were earning excess profits, subsequently, leading to railway franchise amendments and tax levy reprisals. By 1910, many franchises granted in the 1890s had been revised to include company concessions. Concessions for retaining franchises included (Jones, 1985): (1) wider use of discount ticket books, (2) no charge for the transportation of municipal employees, (3) extension of service into newly urbanized areas, (4) increased frequency of night service and (5) greater vehicle capacity provided during rush hours.

By 1917, a large percentage of street railway systems were owned by consolidated utilities. Unlike street railways, light and power utilities were able to obtain wartime rate increases. Also, new markets (residential and industrial-home appliances and industrial heating) for electricity were on the rise. Consequently, consolidated utilities gave priority to capitalizing electric power operations, allowing investment in street railway operations to decline by default if not by design. Track mileage reached its peak and declined thereafter.

By 1920, the financial difficulties of street railways were compounded further with the significant unionization of its work force. Prior to World War I, street railway workers received lower wages and worked longer hours than their manufacturing coounterparts. These conditions could be sustained with unorganized (i.e., nonunionized) workers and a buyer's market for labor swelled by the heavy immigration of blue-collar workers to the U.S. Wartime inflation, however, precipitated demands for wage adjustments throughout the economy. To avoid work stoppages, President Wilson in 1918 established the National War Labor Board (NWLB) which was empowered to arbitrate labor disputes and set wage guidelines.

The NWLB had a significant impact on the wages and work rules of the street railway industry. Almost every major street railway system in the U.S. was involved in work arbitration; approximately 60 percent of the industry's workforce was affected (Jones, 1985). The NWLB's street railway rulings included: (1) increases in wages that averaged 61 percent, (2) a narrow time schedule for promotions, (3) equalization of the wages of men and women performing the same job and (4) bonus payments for extended work hours (i.e., beyond typical work hours for the industry). The Board's rulings also fostered unionization in the industry. By 1920, street railways ranked among the most heavily unionized U.S. industries, even exceeding that of the manufacturing sector.

With the purchase price of the automobile declining steadily and real personal income rising, automobile ownership was within reach of the majority of U.S. households by the middle of the 1920s. At the same time that the cost of automobile ownership was declining, street railways were seeking fare increases to offset the cost of war-time labor settlements. The fare increases, however, failed to improve the industry's financial condition. In larger cities, off-peak and weekend railway ridership were being lost to the automobile while peak ridership was increasing. Off-peak and weekend ridership were needed to share the high cost of providing sufficient street railway capacity to met peak-hour demand.

In addition to the imbalance problem in load factors (between off-peak and peak service), there were pressures to extend service to the new residential developments in city suburbs. Prosperity following World War I fueled urban growth and new residential development. As a franchise supplier of transportation, street railways were under pressure from local authorities and new residents to extend service. The extension of service to city suburbs was to be financially destructive for street railways. Given that the lower population density of new residential development, the density of potential passenger traffic per mile of track for the route extensions was also lower - resulting in less traffic per railway car mile than for established routes. With flat fares, the average revenue per passenger mile for rail extensions was also less. Further, these extensions added peak service to the system, compounding the imbalance problem between rail off-peak and peak service. The financial condition of the industry deteriorated.

4.6.2 Street Railways and Motorbus Operators

The conflict between street railways and local authorities over service extensions allowed for independent motorbus operators to compete with street railways. The typical U.S. motorbus company in 1920 was a family business with a fleet of only three buses. Motorbus competition was encouraged by local authorities "as a political strategy for disciplining street railways unable or unwilling to afford quality service" (Jones, 1985, p. 54). The growing competition from motorbus operations, however, prompted the acquisition of these operations by street railways. This acquisition provided street railways with an alternative for addressing the conflict with local authorities over service extensions to suburbs - i.e., extending street railway service with motorbus service. However, such extensions frequently incurred operating deficits, thus reducing the profitability of the street railway companies. Motorbus service that was previously profitable (under motorbus operator provision) now became unprofitable, i.e., acquired motorbus operations became subject to the work rules, uniform-fare structure, tax structure and service obligations of the street railway company. Thus, the financial conditions of street railways further deteriorated.

The Great Depression of the 1930s led to the extinction of street railway operations in 250 U.S. cities and accelerated the substitution of motorbus routes for street railway lines as well as the decrease in investment in street railway companies. The loss of ridership precipitated by rising unemployment (due to the depression) resulted in operating losses for many street railway companies - thus further increasing the substitution of motorbus service for street railway service. With the financial condition of street railways deteriorating, companies were forced to find an alternative solution (to that of street railway service) to the loss in ridership. Many street railway companies opted for the short-term solution, substituting bus for rail service, i.e., minimizing short-term costs by purchasing buses at a significantly lower capital expense in order to sustain service until the economy and traffic recovered.

The conversion from rail to bus was further enhanced by the antitrust legislation, the Public Utilities Holding Company Act of 1935. The Act required public utility holding companies to divest themselves of captive electric street railways. This divestment was especially financially damaging to those street railways that had obtained electricity at favorable rates from holding companies.

In the early 1930s, there were two types of bus technologies from which to choose - the gasoline powered motorbus and the electric trolley bus. The electric trolley bus was more economical on more densely traveled routes but required a larger initial investment, more likely to have a system failure and did not have the flexibility of the motorbus for rerouting. By the late 1930s, a third type of bus technology became available - a diesel-powered motorbus that was more reliable, more fuel efficient and required less maintenance than the gasoline-powered motorbus. However, street railway companies were reluctant to purchase this new technology. This situation presented a dilemma to producers of diesel-powered motorbuses, principally General Motors.

General Motors responded by forming the holding company – National City Lines – withStandard Oil of California, Firestone Tire Company and two other suppliers of bus-related products for the purpose of acquiring street railway companies and converting them to diesel bus operations. By 1949, the holding company had acquired over 100 street railway companies in 45 U.S. cities and converted them to diesel-bus operations (Talley, 1983). Street cars were replaced with diesel-powered buses in the cities of New York, Philadelphia, Baltimore, St. Louis,Oakland, Salt Lake City, and Los Angeles. By replacing basically pollution-free streetcars with diesel-powered buses, General Motors' campaign was to subsequently have a negative impact on air pollution in a number of major U.S. cities.

4.6.3 Transit Decline: Post World War II

World War II was to bring a boom in U.S. transit ridership. In 1940, transit passengers totaled approximately 13 billion; by 1945, total ridership was over 23 billion (Lave, 1985). The significant rise in ridership has been attributed to wartime restrictions in the production of new automobiles, the rationing of gasoline and the expansion of wartime factory employment in urban areas. By 1944, bus ridership exceeded streetcar ridership. In 1950, however, total transit passengers had declined to 17 billion. Thereafter the decline in the industry's ridership was precipitous-below 10 billion passengers in 1958, below 8 billion in 1969, and below 7 billion in 1961. The industry's financial situation paralleled its ridership situation, i.e., it deteriorated with declining ridership. Between 1954 and 1963, 194 transit systems went out of business (Lave, 1985).

The initial post-war lost in transit ridership is attributed to: (1) returning to a peacetime economy without automobile production restrictions and gasoline rationing and (2) fare increases which were precipitated by catch-up transit wage settlements. During the war years, inflation outpaced adjustments in wages of transit workers (i.e., real wages declined). Following the war, pressure for catch-up wage settlements lead to an unparalleled number of strikes and work stoppages.

The decline in transit ridership that followed the initial postwar decline is attributed to the competitive erosion of the transit industry (Talley, 1983). This erosion was due to internal (i.e., within the industry) as well as external (i.e., outside the industry) forces. The industry's reaction to the initial postwar decline in ridership and its deteriorating financial situation was to increase fares and reduce service - precipitating further declines in ridership. External forces contributing to the competitive erosion include: (1) growth in personal income and automobile ownership and (2) the pro-automobile (or anti-transit) reorganization of the geographic and temporal structure of urban passenger travel[3].

Rising personal incomes in the postwar economy permitted an increasing percentage of U.S. households to own automobiles. Rising incomes and automobile ownership, in turn, permitted households to move and buy homes in the suburbs. The change in the spatial pattern of urban travel that followed compounded the imbalance problem of peak versus off-peak transit ridership (Talley, 1983). Traffic balance was necessary for profitable operation of transit service. With most of the decline in ridership occurring during off-peak hours, the traffic imbalance of the transit industry worsened.

By the 1950s an increasing number of transit systems were willing to consider public acquisition as a last-ditch strategy for salvaging at least some of their past investments. Today, all transit systems in major U.S. urban areas are owned by local governments and generally subsidized (operating and capital subsidies) by these governments as well as by state and federal governments[4]. (For current U.S. transit passenger statistics for the major transit services, see Table 4.1).

4.7 Summary

Urban passenger transportation services may be classified by service structure: times (scheduled versus nonscheduled), routes (fixed versus variable), provision (for-hire versus private) and occupancy (shared versus non-shared). They may also be classified by service type: transit (for-hire, shared, fixed-route and scheduled), private (privately provided, non-shared, variable-route and nonscheduled) and paratransit (all other services other than transit and private). As a shared ser-

---

[3] For further discussion of the impact of automobiles on transit, see Meyer and Gomez-Ibanez (1981).

[4] Current labor issues in transit and taxi services are discussed in Talley and Schwarz-Miller (1996, 2003).

vice, paratransit may be privately provided or for-hire for any combination of routes and times other than fixed-route and scheduled. As a non-shared service, paratransit is variable-route and nonscheduled.

Transit services include the: (1) motorbus, (2) heavy rail, (3) light rail, (4) trolley bus, (5) commuter railroad, (6) urban ferryboat, (7) inclined plane, (8) cable car, (9) aerial tramway, (10) automated guideway and (11) monorail. Private services include the: (1) pedestrian, (2) private automobile, (3) private bicycle and (4) private motorcycle. Commuter paratransit services that are shared and privately provide include carpool, vanpool and subscription bus services; if shared and for-hire, they include vanpool and subscription bus services. Demand-responsive paratransit services that are shared include the variable-route service, dial-a-ride, and the fixed-route service, jitney. Demand-responsive paratransit services that are non-shared include exclusive-ride taxi and automobile rental.

In the U.S., street railway (or light rail) was the primary urban transit passenger service at the beginning of the 20th century; today, it is the motorbus. Cities granted franchises (and therefore monopoly rights) to street railway companies to promote economic development. In addition to providing transit service, these companies often sold electricity – in some cases becoming electric utility companies. The perception of excess profits led to the franchise amendments of fare and service concessions, lowering the railways' return on investment and the redirection of investments into electric utility operations. The industry's financial condition and ridership declined.

Motorbus service was substituted for street railway service in many cities - especially from the deliberate action of the holding company, National City Lines, in acquiring 100 street railway companies in 45 U.S. cities and their conversion to diesel-bus operation. The significant decline in U.S. transit ridership following World War II has been attributed to the increase in automobile ownership and the pro-automobile (or anti-transit) reorganization of the geographic and temporal structure of urban passenger travel. Given the transit industry's poor financial condition and the concerns of bankruptcy and lost of transit service, transit companies in many localities were purchased by local governments. Today, all transit systems in major U.S. cities are publicly owned and subsidized.

References

Altshuler AA, Womack JP (1979) The Urban Transportation System: Politics and Policy Innovation. Cambridge, Massachusetts, MIT Press.

Lave CA (1985) Urban Transit: The Private Challenge to Public Transportation. Cambridge, Massachusetts, Ballinger Publishing.

Meyer JR, Gomez-Ibanez J A (1981) Autos, Transit and Cities. Cambridge, Massachusetts, Harvard University Press.

Jones DW (1985) Urban Transit Policy: An Economic and Political History. Englewood Cliffs, New Jersey, Prentice-Hall.

Saltzman A (1979) The Decline of Transit. Public Transportation: Planning, Operations and Management. Editors, G. E. Gray and L. A. Hoel, Englewood Cliffs, New Jersey, Prentice-Hall.

Talley WK (1983) Introduction to Transportation. Cincinnati, Ohio, South-Western Publishing Company.

Talley WK, Schwarz-Miller AV (1996) The Relative Bargaining Power of Public Transit Labor. Research in Transportation Economics, Vol. 4, B. McMullen, Editor, Greenwich, Connecticut, JAI Press, 69-85.

Talley WK, Schwarz-Miller AV (2003) Effects of Public Transit Policies on Taxi Driver Wages. Journal of Labor Research 24, 131-142.

Vuchic VR (1981) Urban Public Transportation/Systems and Technology. Englewood Cliffs, New Jersey, Prentice-Hall.

5 Analysis of the Allocative Efficiency in Public Firms: the Case of Railway

Pablo Coto-Millán
Department of Economics
University of Cantabria (Spain)

Jose Baños-Pino
Department of Economics
University of Oviedo (Spain)

Ana Rodríguez-Alvarez
Department of Economics
University of Oviedo (Spain)

5.1 Introduction

The works which study the problem of allocative efficiency in firms are increasingly numerous, especially in regulated sectors, (Atkinson and Halvorsen 1986), and in the public sector (Grosskopf and Hayes 1993, Grosskopf et al. 1995), where the hypothesis of cost minimization is extremely questionable.

Railway transport in Spain is mainly provided by RENFE, a public service body which develops its activity as a commercial firm and under the private law system. RENFE exploits passenger and good transport services on a monopoly basis. The fares of the services are fixed by the Government, which also finances the difference between exploitation costs and income and provides the infrastructure.

The recent history of RENFE is characterized by a progressive loss of traffic to road transport. Thus, its share in national good transport in tons per kilometre, has gone down from 15.64% in 1964 to 5.32% in 1993. Passenger transport has also fallen from a share of 28.11% to 7.1% for the same period of time. This fall is probably explained by the presence of more flexible and better adjusted technologies in road transport, with a quick response to the ever-changing market conditions. The protectionist policy that has regulated railway transport in Spain since the forties has not been able to prevent traffic from using other more competitive transport modes. The rearrangement of the railway policy was not carried out until 1984 when a programme-agreement was developed for the 1984-1986 period. Under this agreement, it is agreed that a structuring policy should be followed including staff reductions, the shutdown of lines with a deficit and financial economic repair. The first line shutdown (882 kilometres) took place in 1985. From 1984 to 1987, RENFE's staff was reduced by 15,000 workers. All these measures were carried out with the aim of reducing capacity surplus and inefficiency, and to improve the firm's productivity (Carbajo and De Rus 1991). Later, the 1988-1991 programme-agreement was approved, and it designed a new fare system with price discrimination based on the development of cross grants rather than on cost differences.

The traditional neo-classic model for the theory of production is based on the assumption of the firm's production at a minimum cost. According to this assumption, it must be satisfied that allocative efficiency exists, i.e.:

$$\frac{w_i}{w_j} = \frac{MP_i}{MP_j} = MRTS_{ij} \tag{5.1}$$

where MP is the marginal product of the input (i, j = 1....n), $MRTS_{ij}$ is the marginal rate of the technical substitution between i and j and w is the market price of inputs i, j.

However, this condition may not be satisfied when the costs are minimized in relation to the shadow prices, rather than the market prices. There are increasingly more recent empirical studies that discuss such an assumption: Eakin and Kniesner (1988), English et al. (1993) or Grosskopf et al (1995) are a few examples. The theoretical outline will attempt to explain the existence of these shadow prices in a public firm such as RENFE and their relationship with the market prices.

The purpose of the paper is to prove the existence of allocative efficiency in RENFE, i.e., wether the ratio of productive inputs chosen by the firm, with a given technology and prices, is the best to minimize costs.

In order to measure properly the allocative efficiency, we estimate a Shephard distance function for the input. This allows us to check if the inputs are efficiently used or, otherwise, if there is any kind of inefficiency, i.e., which inputs are relatively under- or over-used. Moreover, the estimation made allows us to calculate the Allen and Morishima dual elasticities.

5.2 Formalization of the Theoretical Model

The theoretical model is based on the assumption of a utility-maximizing behaviour of the firms' management as an alternative aim to profit maximization. These models have been widely used, mainly in sectors such as public enterprise or regulated firms (Williamson 1963; Atkinson and Halvorsen 1986). Following this assumption, the utility function of the firm's management may be formalized as a function with two variables; profit and amount of inputs:

max. U= U (R, x)

$$\text{s. to} \quad R = P(x) - \sum_{i=1}^{n} w_i x_i \tag{5.2}$$

where

U(.) is the utility function that is assumed to be twice differentiable, continuous and quasi-concave;

x is the input vector;

R is the profits obtained by the firm;

P is the income obtained by the public firm. It is assumed that the income is an output function, in such a way that P = g (y), where y represents the output vector. Also, as y = f (x) it may be said that P = g {f (x)};

w_i is the market price of the i input;

x_i is the amount of input i (y = 1....n);

y_r is the amount of output r (r = 1....m).

It is assumed that $\partial U/\partial R > 0$, and $\partial U \partial x \geq$ or < 0 depending on the specific input. Therefore, there will be inputs that provide a positive utility (i.e. "visible" inputs such as staff, sophisticated equipment, etc.), other inputs that provide a negative utility (i.e. those that imply a greater effort by the manager), and others that are neutral.

The solution to the maximization problem is expressed by the Lagrangian:

$$L(R, x, \lambda) = U(R, x) - \lambda \left[R - P(x) + \sum_i w_i x_i \right] \tag{5.3}$$

Operating, it can be obtained that the value of the marginal product for input i equals to

$$\frac{\partial P}{\partial x_i} = w_i - \frac{\dfrac{\partial U}{\partial x_i}}{\dfrac{\partial U}{\partial R}} = w_i^s \tag{5.4}$$

where w_i^s is the shadow price of input i. Thus, w_i^s is different from w_i due to the effects of the manager's utility maximizing behaviour.

Dividing the value of the marginal product of input i by input j, it is obtained that

$$\frac{\dfrac{\partial P}{\partial x_i}}{\dfrac{\partial P}{\partial x_j}} = \frac{w_i^s}{w_j^s} \tag{5.5}$$

As the income is an output function, from Eq. 5.5 it is obtained

$$\frac{w_i^s}{w_j^s} = \frac{\dfrac{\partial P}{\partial y_r}\dfrac{\partial y_r}{\partial x_i}}{\dfrac{\partial P}{\partial y_r}\dfrac{\partial y_r}{\partial x_j}} = \frac{\dfrac{\partial y_r}{\partial x_i}}{\dfrac{\partial y_r}{\partial x_j}} = \frac{MP_i}{MP_j} = MRTS_{ij} \tag{5.6}$$

where:

MP is the marginal product of input (i, j = 1....n);

$MRTS_{ij}$ is the marginal rate of the technical substitution between i and j.

Unlike Eq. 5.1, the necessary condition of minimum cost may no longer be satisfied when costs are not minimized in relation to market prices. The use of shadow prices is useful to test which ones would be those shadow prices (w^s), for which the first order condition of cost minimization would actually be satisfied, given the chosen input share.

5.3 Conclusions to the Theoretical Model

From the previous analysis, the following conclusions may be inferred:

1 the difference between w and w^s (see Eq. 5.4) will inversely depend on the magnitude of $\partial U/\partial R$, i.e., on the variation of the manager's utility against the budget deviation and, therefore, on the incentives for the fulfilment of such utility. Thus, when $\partial U/\partial R$ is high (low), i.e., when there are more (less) incentives to optimise the budget deviation, there will be a tendency to be more (less) efficient in costs;

2 the difference between w and w^s will also depend (Eq. 5.4) on the magnitude of $\partial U/\partial x_i$ in absolute value;

3 moreover, we can obtain relative comparisons of the inputs. Thus, for example, if $w_i^s > w_i$ y $w_j^s < w_j$, then input i will be under-utilized in relation to input j, and vice versa.

The drawback of this model is that the shadow prices cannot be observed, and a difficult relationship between the shadow and market prices is obtained from equation (5.4), since the utility function is not known. Therefore, it is necessary to introduce a more simplified relationship between the shadow and market prices of the productive inputs, which is obtained from the estimation of a Shepard distance function (Shepard 1953) put forward in the following section.

5.4 The Distance Function

In order to introduce the concept of distance function, assume that there is a technology which determines that output vector $y(y_1, ...y_m)$ may be obtained with input vector $x(x_1,...,x_n)$.. The set of possibilities of production L (y) is the set of feasible x and y values. Assume we have an arbitrary pair of vectors (y^0, x^0) in such a way that amount x^o is more than sufficient to produce y^o. Thus, all the items of x^o may be reduced in the same proportion and continue to produce y^o. Formally, given any two x and y vectors, the Shephard distance function for the input is defined as

$$D_I = (y, x) = \max(\delta \geq 1 : (x/\delta), y \in L(y)) \tag{5.7}$$

where y is the level of output of the firm; x $(x_1, ...x_n)$ is the input vector; $L(y) = (x \in R_n^+ : x \text{ may produce } y \in R_m^+)$.

The distance function for the input may also be defined as the maximum possible proportional increase in the output vector, the input vector, and the technology. Applications of this type of function may be found in English et al (1993) and Grosskopf et al (1995).

In order to explain graphically the distance function, consider (Figure 5.1) a firm which produces only one output y for which it uses two production inputs (x_1 and x_2).

The 0R/0P ratio is the radial measure of Farrel's technical efficiency (TE, Farrel 1957) for the point P and means the maximum proportional reduction which may be carried out in the productive inputs used and which may produce the same amount of output.

Formally:

$$TE(y, x) = \min.(\lambda \in (0,1) : \lambda x \in L(y)) \tag{5.8}$$

The maximum value for this index is the unit, which would mean that the firm operates on the isoquant and, therefore, it would be totally efficient from the technical point of view. A value lower than the unit (as in the previous case) tells us about the grade of technical efficiency reached by the firm.

If we consider the inverse, i.e., 0P/0R, it represents the highest scalar by which we may proportionally divide all inputs and produce the level of output. Thus, following Shepard (1953), the (D_I) distance function for the input may be formally defined as

$$D_I = (y, x) = \max(\delta \geq 1 : (x/\delta) \in L(y)) \tag{5.9}$$

Obviously, $x \in L(y)$, if and only if $D_I(y, x) \geq 1$. As previously, the fact that DI equals the unit again would mean that the firm operates on the isoquant, i.e., it is technically efficient. A value higher than the unit reflects the grade of efficiency reached.

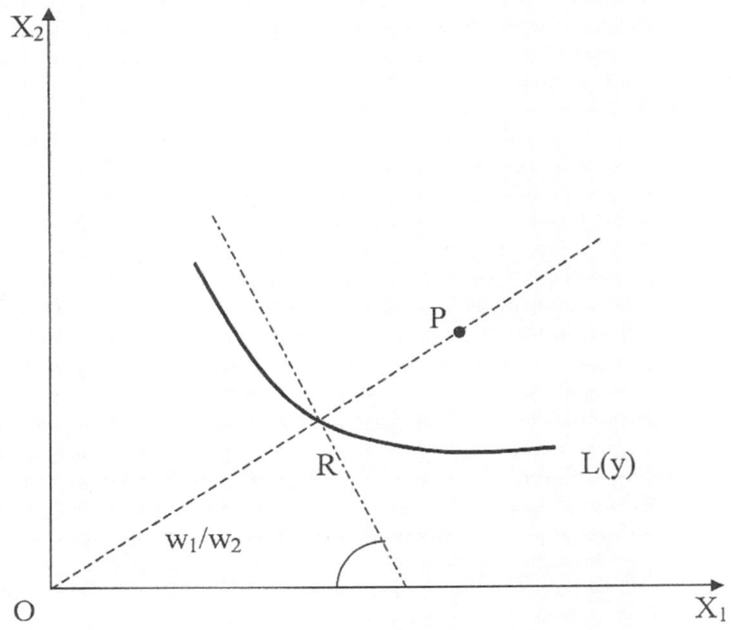

Fig. 5.1. Distance function with two inputs and one output

5.5 Properties of the Distance Function

The distance function is the dual of the cost function and, similarly to the latter, has the advantage that it is valid for multiproduct and multifactor technologies. The Shephard distance function for the input satisfies the regularity conditions (see Cornes 1992) to find a demonstration of these properties).

D_I (y, x) is the dual for the cost function. In order to study this property, we start from the traditional cost function which is expressed as

$$C(y, w) = \min ((w\ x): x \in L(y)) \tag{5.10}$$

We may normalize the input prices in such a way that the maximum cost to produce the desired output equals one, i.e.:

$$C(y, W) = 1 \tag{5.11}$$

where W $(W_1,...,W_n)$ is the normalized input price vector.

Shepard (1953) defines the distance function for the input as the dual of the cost function in the following way:

$$D_I\ (y, x) = \min\ (Wx\ /\ C(y, W) = 1) \tag{5.12}$$

The symmetric expression for the cost function is

$$C(y, W) = \min.\ (W\ x\ /\ D_I\ \ (y, x\ ) = 1) \tag{5.13}$$

The duality between the distance function and the cost function is useful to establish the following property:

$$-\partial\ D_I\ \ (y, x)\ /\ \partial y_i = \partial\ C(W, y)\ /\ \partial y_i\ = \phi_i\ (y, x) \tag{5.14}$$

where f_i (y, x) is the marginal cost of the ith output.

5.6 The Shadow Price Estimation through the Use of a Shephard Distance Function

Initially, the studies which used shadow prices to obtain the allocative or cost efficiency were based on the estimation of a system of equations consisting of a cost function and the expenditure share functions of the different inputs in relation to the total cost (Atkinson and Halvorsen 1986; Eakin and Kniesner 1988).This equation system was able to establish a relationship between the shadow prices and the real market prices through the estimation of the parametric corrections in the input prices necessary for satisfying the minimum cost condition.

Later, Färe and Grosskopf (1990) used an alternative model to get the input shadow prices by the Shephard distance function, thus obtaining an analysis of the firm's cost efficiency. The distance function has a series of advantages in relation to the first method, such as:

1) for the estimation of the distance function, data on the input prices or the assumption that these are exogenous, are not necessary (Lovell 1993, discusses in an application the problems derived from such an assumption);
2) in order to analyse a sample which includes several firms, this method, unlike the former, allows us to obtain the specific shadow prices for each firm.

The method presented by Färe and Grosskopf (1990) is based upon a model which assumes that the firm minimizes the costs with respect to certain shadow prices which may be different to the market prices, so that we may define the shadow cost function (C^s) as

$$C^s\,(y, w^s) = \min\ (w^s\ x : x \in L(y)) = w^s\,x(\ y, w^s) \tag{5.15}$$

where w^s is the shadow price of input i for which the cost minimization condition is satisfied.

If we consider the primal problem of cost minimization as

$$C^s\,(y, w^s) = \min.\ (w^s\ x\!:\ D_I\ (y, x) \geq 1) \tag{5.16}$$

the Lagrangian associated with Eq. 5.16 will be

$$L = w^s x - \lambda (D_I (y, x) - 1) \tag{5.17}$$

From the first order condition we obtain

$$w^s = \lambda (y, x) (\partial D_I (y, x) / \partial x) \tag{5.18}$$

Following Shepard (1953) and Jacobsen (1972), who demonstrate that the following is satisfied in the optimal:

$$C(w^s, y) = \lambda (y, x) \tag{5.19}$$

Combining Eqs. 5.18 and 5.19, the dual of the Shephard Lemma is obtained:

$$w^s / C(y, w^s) = \partial D_I (y, x) / \partial x = W^s (y, x) \tag{5.20}$$

where $W^s (y, x)$ is the normalized shadow price which may be obtained from the distance function.

If we consider any two inputs i, j = 1, 2,...,n, from the Eq. 5.20 we have

$$\frac{\dfrac{\partial D_I(x,y)}{\partial x_i}}{\dfrac{\partial D_I(x,y)}{\partial x_j}} = \frac{W_i^s(y,x)}{W_j^s(y,x)} = \frac{w_i^s(y,x)}{w_j^s(y,x)} \tag{5.21}$$

Thus, we obtain from the distance function, the expression of the normalized shadow prices of the production inputs. Nevertheless, if all the assumptions of cost minimization were satisfied, the relationship between the normalized shadow prices obtained from the distance function must be equal to the quotient of input market prices. However, if inputs are not chosen in the right proportion, i.e., if we incur in allocative inefficiency, the relationships between such prices will be different.

In order to study the significance and sense of such deviation, we will introduce a relationship between the normalized shadow price obtained from the distance function and the real price of input in the market, through a parametric correction of the price (Eakin and Kniesner 1988; Färe and Grosskopf 1990). Therefore,

$$W^s_i (y, x) = k_i \; w_i \tag{5.22}$$

Dividing that expression by that corresponding to input j:

$$\frac{w_i^s(y,x)}{w_j^s(y,x)} = k_{ij} \frac{w_i}{w_j} \tag{5.23}$$

where

$$k_{ij} = k_i / k_j \tag{5.24}$$

Thus, we obtain the degree at which the shadow prices (at which the costs would be minimized given the proportion of inputs chosen) differ from the market prices.

From this expression we may obtain the allocative inefficiency between both inputs, and the sense of such inefficiency in the following way:

- If $k_{ij} > 1$, then input i is being under-utilized in relation to input j;
- If $k_{ij} < 1$, input i is being over-utilized in relation to input j;
- If $k_{ij} = 1$, inputs i and j are being used in the optimal proportions which minimize costs, that is, we are being allocatively efficient.

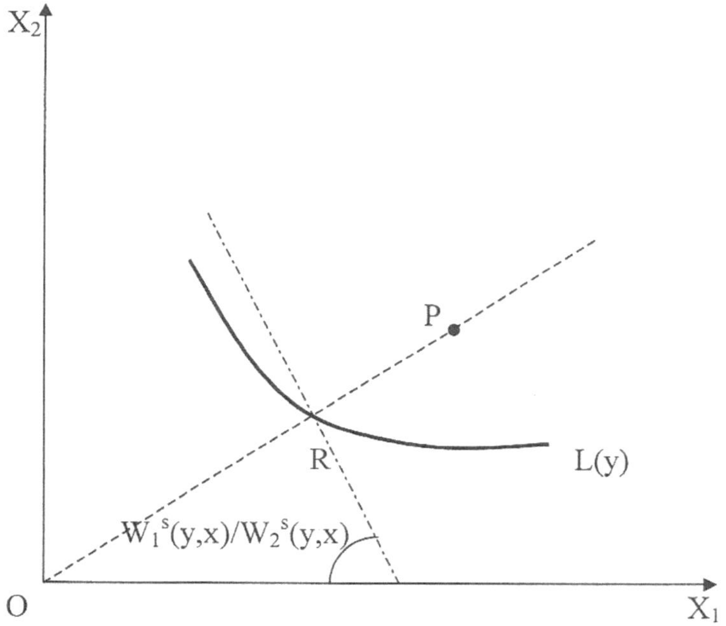

Fig. 5.2. Distance function and isocost line

Thus, the distance function for the input may be used to obtain information referred to the normalized shadow prices of the inputs in a multiproduct and multifactor technology and does not need to use the price of the inputs. As Figure 5.2 shows, the ratio of the normalized shadow price that is obtained from the distance function shows the slope of the isocost which may be obtained if costs were really minimized with the proportion of the inputs chosen. Therefore, the isocost with a slope $W_1^s(y, x) / W_2^s(y, x)$ tells us about at what shadow prices the costs would really be minimized to produce output y, given the technology and the input combination observed. From the paper by Färe and Grosskopf (1990), the studies that use the distance function in order to test the allocative efficiency in production are increasingly numerous, (Grosskopf and Hayes 1993; Grosskopf et al. 1995; English et al. 1993, are some examples).

5.7 The Functional Form

When using a specific functional form, a series of characteristics are being imposed on the technology studied but there is no exact knowledge over the certainty of such properties. For that reason, it is especially convenient to use flexible functional forms that impose the minimum possible restrictions on the technology which is to be described. In this paper, we will use a flexible functional form, more specifically, a multiproduct Translog function. The following are the properties which define this function:

a) it is a second-order approximation in a Taylor series when all variables take the value 1, to the unknown distance function, which we want to model;
b) it is linear in the parameters;
c) it is more flexible than other functional forms (such as the Cobb-Douglas or CES), since it is not necessary to impose the homogeneity and separability condition, and allows us to make a test of these restriction hypotheses;
d) it does not impose restrictions on the elasticities of substitution.

5.8 The Econometric Estimation

Since the aim of this paper is to obtain an estimation of the shadow prices of the productive inputs, we will use a distance function for the input. For this, an econometric method has been chosen. However, the difficulty with using such a method is that the value of D_I (y, x) is not known. To solve this problem the value of the distance function must be equal to one and estimated using ordinary least squares (OLS). This means that the value predicted for the distance function will follow a normal distribution around one. Since the distance function is defined for values equal to one or even higher, the values estimated by OLS must be corrected in order to obtain values equal or higher than one by taking the maximum of $\varepsilon = \mathbf{D}_I(y, x)\text{-}D_I(y, x)$ and adding it to each expected value of the distance function (Greene 1980).

The model developed is based on an stochastic distance function for the following input:

$$1 = D_I\,(y, x) + \varepsilon \tag{5.25}$$

From the parameters estimated in this equation we obtain the normalized shadow prices and the grade of deviation between the shadow prices and the real prices of the production inputs, which is given by the expression k_{ij}.
Moreover, the estimation of the distance function allows us to calculate the Morishima and Allen elasticities of substitution, which are studied in detail in the appendix.

The Shephard distance function for the input will be defined as a Translog of the type

$$\mathrm{Lnl} = \sum_r \alpha_r \ln y_r + \frac{1}{2}\sum_r \sum_s \alpha_{rs} \ln y_r \ln y_s + \sum_i \beta_i \ln x_i +$$

$$+ \frac{1}{2}\sum_i \sum_j \beta_{ij} \ln x_i \ln x_j + \sum_r \sum_i \rho_{ri} \ln y_r \ln x_i + \varepsilon \qquad (5.26)$$

for r, s = 1...m outputs; i, j = 1.....n inputs, and ε being the term for random perturbation.

To this functional form, we impose the homogeneity condition of degree one in the inputs

$$\Sigma\beta_i = 1, \quad \Sigma\beta_{ij} = 0, \quad \Sigma\rho_{ri} = 0 \qquad (5.27)$$

and the symmetry condition

$$\beta_{ij} = \beta_{ji} \qquad (5.28)$$

Such a function may be estimated by restricted square minimums. From this, we may infer the parametric corrections of the prices for each pair of inputs as has been explained in the theoretical model. Thus, from Eqs. 5.21 and 5.24 we may infer k_{ij}:

$$k_{ij} = \frac{\dfrac{w_j}{x_i}\left[\hat{\beta}_i + \sum_j \hat{\beta}_{ij} x_j x_j + \sum_r \hat{\rho}_{ri} y_r\right]}{\dfrac{w_i}{x_j}\left[\hat{\beta}_j + \sum_i \hat{\beta}_{ij} x_i + \sum_r \hat{\rho}_{ri} y_r\right]} \qquad (5.29)$$

5.9 Data

The series of the annual data used cover the 1950-1994 period and come from the official statistics of the Ministry of Transport and from the Annual Reports of RENFE. Bearing in mind that railway activity is multiproduct as regards passenger and goods transport services, origins and destinations, time slots, etc., the output variables have been approximated with two indicators: the kilometres covered by passenger and good vehicles (vehicles-kilometre). Thus, the variable Qkm measures output goods per kilometre and Vkm measures output passengers per kilometre.

The addition of different products (as many as possible origins and destinations in the railway network, and for the different time slots) may obviate the big heterogeneities in the proportion of services. Moreover, this addition is imposed by the data available.

Three inputs have been considered: labour (L) - including the average annual staff, either permanent or hired-, capital (K) - considered as the investment in rolling stock material- and energy (E) -which is the annual consumption of gas oil and electric power measured in K calories-.

5.10 Empirical Results

Table 5.1. Estimated distance function (Sample period 1950-1994)

Variable	Coefficient	Std. Error	t-Statisitc
Log(Qkm)	-0.735403	0.199726	-3.68205
Log(Vkm)	-0.296114	0.170897	-1.73270
Log(L)	0.416440	0.118168	3.52411
Log(E)	0.469200	0.040080	11.70641
Log(K)	0.114359	0.139899	0.81744
Log(Qkm)·Log(Qkm)	0.024593	0.009003	2.73158
Log(Vkm)·Log(Vkm)	0.047606	0.013003	3.66093
Log(Qkm)·Log(Vkm)	-0.014955	0.017262	-0.86636
Log(L)·Log(L)	0.022242	0.004660	4.77291
Log(L)·Log(K)	-0.075384	0.005288	-14.25503
Log(L)·Log(E)	-0.020235	0.008746	-2.31361
Log(E)·Log(K)	-0.003713	0.008382	-0.44296
Log(E)·Log(E)	0.003980	0.001537	2.58978
Log(K)·Log(K)	0.023443	0.003050	7.68411
Log(Qkm)·Log(L)	-0.035832	0.006507	-5.50663
Log(Qkm)·Log(K)	0.078463	0.015967	4.91407
Log(Qkm)·Log(E)	0.022100	0.009585	2.30571
Log(Vkm)·Log(L)	0.021177	0.011811	1.79293
Log(Vkm)·Log(E)	-0.050363	0.011914	-4.22720
Log(Vkm)·Log(K)	-0.035544	0.017572	-2.02274

Method of estimation: OLS
Number of observations: 45
DW=1.93; Q(4)=7.74; Q(8)=15.07; N(2)=2.11.

The estimation of the distance function for the public firm RENFE during the 1950-1994 period has been carried out by the procedure of ordinary square minimums. As the values of the distance function $D_I(y, x)$ are not directly observed, we fix them as equal to the unit, i.e., we would operate in the frontier of technology. Since the dependant variable would be ln (1) = 0, the estimation may be carried out if we impose a linear parameter combination different from zero. Therefore, in order to carry out the square minimum estimation, we apply the conditions required by the theory: homogeneity of degree one in the inputs and symmetry. Moreover, the values resulting from the estimation have been corrected according to Greene (1980).

The results of this estimation are shown in Table 5.1, which shows that the sign of the coefficients coincide with the expected results according to the theoretical.

On the other hand, we have assumed that the outputs are exogenous and that the inputs are endogenous. Then, equation would pose the problem that the inputs and the error would be correlated (the null hypothesis of weak exogeneity for the labor, energy and capital inputs could not be accepted; the value of the Hausman test has been 11.63 for a χ^2 with three degrees of freedom). In order to solve this problem, we have reestimated the distance function equation via instrumental variables. The results of this second estimation are shown in Table 5.2 and it confirms that the coefficients have scarcely changed in relation to the estimation by OLS.

Table 5.2. Estimated distance function (Sample period 1950-1994)

Variable	Coefficient	Std. Error	Statistic-t
Log(Qkm)	-0.971368	0.261860	-3.70949
Log(Vkm)	-0.072595	0.243909	-0.29763
Log(L)	0.420800	0.119950	3.50813
Log(E)	0.504991	0.053796	9.38709
Log(K)	0.074209	0.084449	0.87874
Log(Qkm)·Log(Qkm)	0.022369	0.011979	1.86737
Log(Vkm)·Log(Vkm)	0.060217	0.018774	3.20739
Log(Qkm)·Log(Vkm)	-0.024661	0.028148	-0.87614
Log(L)·Log(L)	0.022887	0.004668	4.90325
Log(L)·Log(K)	-0.071543	0.005091	-14.0526
Log(L)·Log(E)	-0.024869	0.008830	-2.81652
Log(E)·Log(K)	-0.000995	0.008456	-0.11771
Log(E)·Log(E)	0.007083	0.002956	2.39641
Log(K)·Log(K)	0.018729	0.002246	8.33597
Log(Qkm)·Log(L)	-0.043185	0.009682	-4.46044
Log(Qkm)·Log(K)	0.113836	0.027148	4.19307
Log(Qkm)·Log(E)	0.041534	0.018069	2.29866
Log(Vkm)·Log(L)	0.027137	0.013973	1.94205
Log(Vkm)·Log(E)	-0.075082	0.019968	-3.76009
Log(Vkm)·Log(K)	-0.107425	0.051560	-2.08346

Method of estimation: IV

Number of observations: 42

DW=1.98; Q(4)=3.05; Q(8)=7.93; N(2)=1.75

The values of the k_{ij}'s have been obtained from the coefficients estimated for the distance function equation by applying instrumental variables (see equation (5.29)). In order to obtain an arrangement of these proportionality coefficients, we have used a standard bootstrap technique, which consists of selecting a random sample of the of the estimation residues shown in Table 5.2. From here, we have generated "new dependent variables" equal to the randomly selected residues plus the prediction value in the previous equation. This has led us to reestimate 100 new equations of the distance function by the instrumental variable method. In order to obtain the arrangement of the k_{ij}'s, we have calculated the proportion of the k_{ij} estimated which are higher than the unit (Grosskopf et al. 1995).

Table 5.3. Share factors and elasticities of substitution. K_{ij}, M_{ij} and A_{ij} values

	BOOTSTRAP VALUES[a]
$K_{ENERGY,CAPITAL}$	1.095512
$K_{LABOR, CAPITAL}$	0.736148
$K_{LABOR, ENERGY}$	0.858471
$M_{CAPITAL, ENERGY}$	1.015682
$M_{CAPITAL, LABOR}$	0.891055
$M_{LABOR, ENERGY}$	0.892536
$M_{LABOR, CAPITAL}$	1.511427
$M_{ENERGY, CAPITAL}$	0.985323
$M_{ENERGY, LABOR}$	1.066895
$A_{CAPITAL, ENERGY}$	0.103685
$A_{CAPITAL, LABOR}$	-1.352396
$A_{LABOR, ENERGY}$	0.733601

[a] Average values estimated in the sample.

Table 5.3 shows the results of the share factors (k_{ij}) and the Allen and Morishima elasticities of substitution (A_{ij} and M_{ij}) (see Appendix). The estimated proportionality factors are different from one, which leads us to conclude that the productive inputs are not being used in the proportion that would minimize costs. From Table 5.3 it may be inferred that the capital input is being over-utilized with respect to energy, while the labor input is being over-utilized with respect to energy and capital. Figure 5.3 shows the evolution through time of the probability that the k_{ij}'s are higher than the unit. From the sixties, we can observe a tendency to over-utilized capital in relation to energy, while it is also shown that the labor input is being over-utilized in relation to energy and capital.

The estimations of the Allen and Morishima dual elasticities of substitution with a positive sign give us information about the existence of a complementary relationship between inputs and negative values that imply the substitution effect. From the Morishima dual elasticities we may infer a complementary relationship between the different combinations of the inputs, while the Allen dual elasticities suggest complementary relationship between capital and energy, and between labour and energy, detecting a scarce substitution effect between capital and labour.

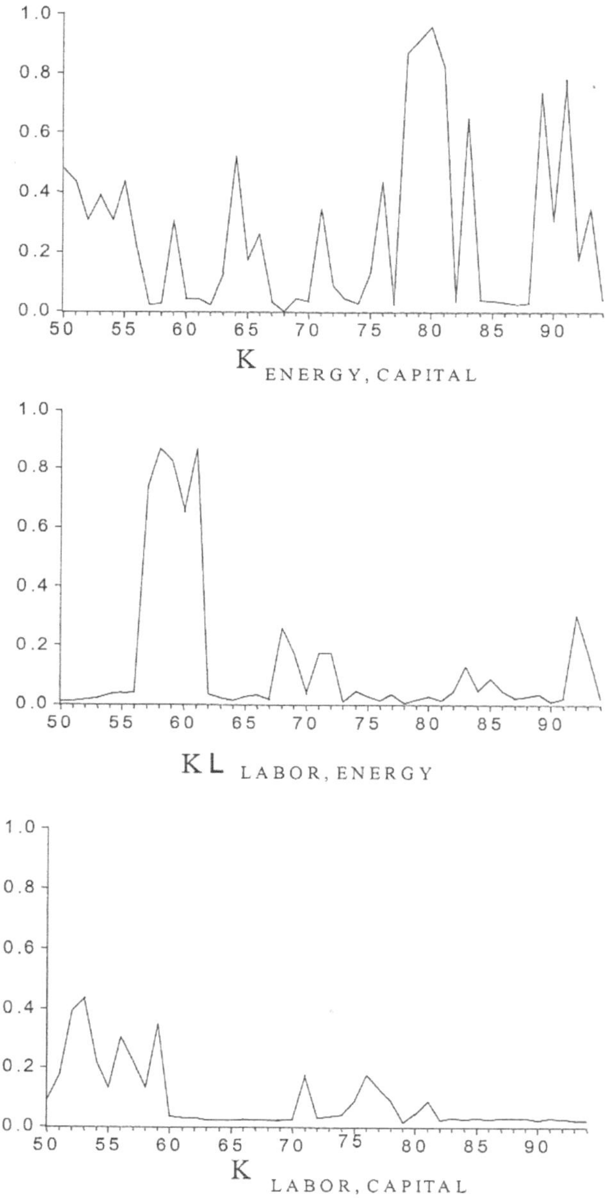

Fig. 5.3. Proportion of $K_{ij} > 1$

5.11 Summary and Conclusions

This paper discusses whether a public firm such as RENFE satisfies the cost minimization condition. Through the estimation of the shadow prices of the production inputs we obtain the grade of the firm's allocative inefficiency and its origin.

The methodology used is based on the estimation of a Shephard distance function for the input, the dual of the cost function, which fully represents the technology and is valid for multiproduct and multifactor firms, with which the shadow prices of the inputs may be obtained making unnecessary the use of their market prices.

From the results obtained in this paper, it may be verified that shadow prices are different to market prices and, therefore, the public firm RENFE does not use the productive inputs in the optimal proportion, that is, it does not minimize costs in relation to the market prices. It may be observed that the capital input is being over-utilized in relation to energy, whereas labour is being over-utilized in relation to the rest of the inputs.

References

Atkinson S, Halvorsen R (1986) The relative efficiency of public and private firms in a regulated environment: the case of U.S. electric utilities. Journal of Public Economics 29: 281-294.

Blackorby C, Russel RR (1989) Will the real elasticity of substitution please stand up? (A comparison of the Allen/Uzawa and Morishima Elasticities). American Economic Review 79: 882-888.

Carbajo JC, De Rus G (1991) Railway Transport Policy in Spain. Journal of Transport Economic and Policy, May: 209-215.

Cornes R (1992) Duality and modern economics. Cambridge University Press.

Eakin BK, Kniesner T (1988) Estimating a non-minimum cost function for hospitals. Southern Economic Journal 54 (3) January: 583-597.

English M, Grosskopf S, Hayes K, Yaisawarng S (1993) Output allocative and technical efficiency of banks. Journal of Banking and Finance 17: 349-366.

Färe R, Grosskopf S (1990) A distance function approach to price efficiency. Journal of Public Economics 43: 123-126.

Farrel MJ (1957) The measurement of productive efficiency. Journal of the Royal Statistical Society A 120: 253-281.

Greene WH (1980) Maximum likelihood estimation of econometric frontier functions. Journal of Econometrics 13: 27-53.

Grosskopf S, Hayes K (1993) Local public sector bureaucrats and their input choices. Journal of Urban Economics 33-2: 151-166.

Grosskopf S, Hayes K, Hirschberg J (1995) Fiscal stress and the production of public safety: a distance function approach. Journal of Public Economics 57: 277-296.

Jacobsen S (1972) On Shepard's duality theorem. Journal of Economic Theory 4-3: 458-464.
Lovell CAK (1993) Discussant's comments on Berger et al and English et al. Journal of Banking and Finance 17: 367-370.
Shepard RW (1963) Cost and Production Functions. Princeton University Press, 1953.
Williamson, O.: Managerial discretion and business behavior. American Economic Review 53: 1032-1057.

Appendix: The Elasticities of Substitution

The elasticity of substitution provides a measure of the extent to which the productive inputs can easily substitute for each other. Since the distance function describes the technology, the grade of substitution between the production inputs, i.e. the curvature of the isoquant, can be studied. This allows the study of the effects of changes in the quantity of the productive inputs. For that purpose, the Morishima (M_{ij}) and Allen (A_{ij}) elasticities of substitution are defined among the productive inputs i, j in relation to the shadow prices such as:

$$\begin{aligned} M_{ij}(y,x) &= -d\left[\ln(D_i(y,x/x_i)/D_j(y,x/x_j\right]/d\ln\left[x_i/x_j\right] = \\ &= x_i D_{ij}(y,x)/D_j(y,x) - x_i D_{ii}(y,x)/D_i(y,x) = \\ &= e_{ij}(y,x) - e_{ii}(y,x) \end{aligned} \tag{5.30}$$

being

D_i the derivative of the distance function in relation to x_i (i=l,..,n).

e_{ij} and e_{ii} are the price elasticities of the input demand (with the output remaining constant). The first term e_{ij} tells us if the pairs of inputs are net substitutes or net complements depending on whether it is lower or higher than zero (unlike the direct elasticities substitution, in which a sign higher than zero indicates net substitution, in this case, the indirect elasticities of substitution are estimated and, therefore, the sign is inverse) and the second term e_{ii} is the demand price elasticity for input i.

The Allen elasticity of substitution may be defined as

$$A_{ij}(y, x) = [D(y, x)D_{ij}(y, x)/D_i(y, x)D_j(y, x)] \tag{5.31}$$

In the presence of only two inputs, the Allen and Morishima elasticities coincide. However, in the presence of more inputs they do not usually coincide, being the Morishima elasticity more representative in the latter case (Blackorby and Russel (1989)).

Using the estimation parameters of the distance function we obtain the value of the Morishima elasticity of substitution according to Eq. 5.30:

$$M_{ij} = \frac{\hat{\beta}_{ij} x_i}{(x_i x_j)\left(\frac{1}{x_j}\right)\left(\hat{\beta} \sum_n \hat{\beta}_{jn} \ln X_n + \sum_r \rho_{ri} \ln y_r\right)}$$

$$-\frac{x_i\left(\hat{\beta}_{ii} - \left(\hat{\beta}_i + \sum_n \hat{\beta}_{in} \ln x_n + \sum_r \rho_{ri} \ln y_r\right)\right)}{(x_i x_i)\left(\frac{1}{x_i}\right)\left(\hat{\beta}_i + \sum_n \hat{\beta}_{in} \ln x_n + \sum_r \rho_{ri} \ln y_r\right)} \tag{5.32}$$

Analogously, the Allen elasticities of substitution are obtained based on Eq. 5.31:

$$A_{ij} = \frac{\hat{\beta}_{ij}}{(x_i x_j) D_i D_j} \tag{5.33}$$

being

$$D_i = \frac{1}{x_i}\left[\hat{\beta}_i + \sum_n \hat{\beta}_{in} \ln x_n + \sum_r \hat{\rho}_{ri} \ln y_r\right] \tag{5.34}$$

6 The Effect of Using Aggregated Output in the Economic Analysis of Cargo Handling Operations

Sergio R. Jara-Díaz
University of Chile

Beatriz Tovar de la Fé
University of Las Palmas de Gran Canaria (Spain)

Lourdes Trujillo
University of Las Palmas de Gran Canaria (Spain)

6.1 Introduction: Cargo Handling in Multipurpose Port Terminals

Starting some decades ago, new technologies for cargo handling and vessel design have been developed such that productivity has increased due to mechanization and work reduction that has translated into shorter stays of the ships at the port. This new technology can be described as "Unitisation", whose general idea is that of repackaging various cargo items of relatively small size into larger units of a standard size that can be moved using specifically designed machines and accommodated into specifically designed ships, speeding up the service.

There are different techniques for unitisation. There are pallets, which can be handled by forklift; wheeled platforms manoeuvred by truck; cargoes that can be "rolled on" the vessel in the loading port, and "rolled off" the vessel in the destination port (e.g. roll-on/roll-off trucks and trailers); containers; and even barges, which are loaded into the LASH vessel[1]. In each of these cases, the cargo handling process is associated with specific machines (cranes and vehicles) making the type of standardized or compact unit used more important than the type of cargo itself. This might cause that the same type of goods can receive different handling treatment depending on the repackaging: bags, pallets, containers, and so on.

The introduction of these new technologies caused the formation of multipurpose port terminals, which are facilities that include infrastructure, equipment and services that take care of loading and unloading of general cargo (both fractioned and unitised) from/to vessels, aiming at an optimal use of labour and equipment.

---

[1] LASH: "Lighter aboard Ship". This means that lash ships carry barges.

Fractioned general cargo has the most complex handling process, from cargo handling within the vessel's hold, movement from ship to shore and then between shore and storage areas, to cargo reception/deliveries. On the other hand, unitised freight includes a variety of forms, most notably containers and rolling stock.

One of the key aspects of cargo unitisation is the inverse correlation between handling capacity and the weight of the standard unit. This is due to the large amount of time that takes the manipulation of small size packages, particularly the process of cargo handling within the vessel's hold. Thus, for a given cargo volume, the larger the standard unit the lower the number of units. The use of containers and rolling units has made it unnecessary the operations of cargo handling on vessel's hold. Moreover, rolling units have the most simple cargo handling process because they do not need to be handled from ship to shore and, sometimes, cargo arrives or is delivered directly without storage. Finally, terminals could differ in how they store and move the containers within the yard. There is no uniform scheme for the terminal storage organization. Basically, we can distinguish among stack with straddle carrier storage, stack with transtainer storage and chassis storage, although most terminals have a mixture of these. The cargo handling process needed in each case affects the provision of basic infrastructure, superstructure, machines and mobile equipment, and labour.

In spite of the heterogeneity of forms in which freight arrives to the port, usual analyses of cargo handling and port activities in general are made using an aggregate description of output like total tons moved or its value, as in Chang (1978), Rekers et al. (1990), Tongzon (1993), Kim and Sachis (1986) and Martínez Budría (1996). In this paper we first analyse cargo handling activities through the estimation of a cost function with output described as total volume handled, from which marginal costs, scale economies and policy conclusions are obtained. Then the results are compared against those arising from output described in detail, showing that the aggregate analysis yields misleading estimates and poorer information for optimal policy design.

6.2 Data and Aggregate Model Formulation

A cost function $C(W, Y)$ represents the minimum expenditure necessary to produce output Y at given input prices W. Accordingly, estimation requires data on expenditure, production and input prices for one or more firms during one or more periods. Our data was collected directly from three private medium size firms operating under concession within the port area of Las Palmas de Gran Canaria, one of the largest of the Spanish system. Figure 6.1 shows the location of the terminals within the port area and Table 6.1 shows their main physical characteristics. Note that firm 3 relocated during the period analysed.

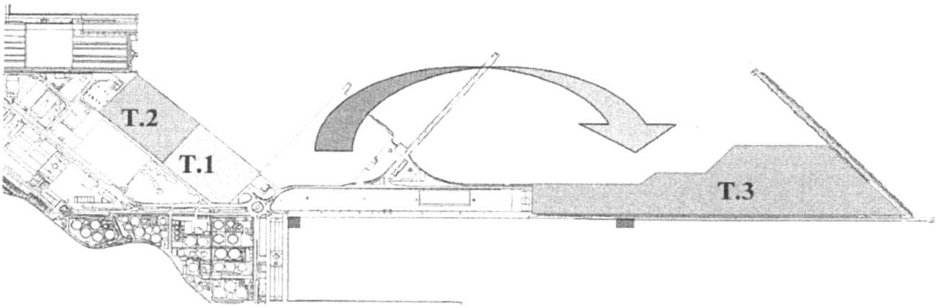

Fig. 6.1. Location of the three firms within the port area

Source: Tovar de la Fé (2002).

Table 6.1. Main physical characteristics of the terminals

	Firm 1		Firm 2	Firm 3 (3)	
Dock length	300 m.(1)		216.5 m.(1)	407.5 m.	866 m.
Drought	11 m.		11 m.	11 m.	11 to 14 m.
Ro-ro ramp	Yes		Yes	Yes	
Area under concession	58,744 m^2	76,489 m^2 (2)	39,713 m^2.	54,080 m^2	65,300 m^2
Mean total area (min / Max)	63,972 m^2 (58,744 / 76,489)		61,527 m^2 (55,113 / 62,613)	64,436 m^2 (50,623 / 126,486)	
Storage Container Capacity	3.350 TEUs.		2.712 TEUs.	4000 TEUs	6.600 TEUs.
Shore cranes in 1999	2 portainer panamax		1 portainer postpanamax 1 portainer panamax	2 portainer super-postpanamax 1 portainer postpanamax 1 portainer panamax	
Other machines in yard	6 various reach stackers 10 tractors		8 various reach stackers 2 tractors	6 trastainers 14 various reach stackers 14 tractors	

(1) The firm can use up to 50 meters of the neighbour dock (see Figure 6.1).
(2) The concession area increases in April 1996.
(3) Re-locates within the port area in October 1997 (see Figure 6.1).
Source: Tovar de la Fé (2002).

The firms deal mainly with containers (87% of total volume), but also operate roll-on/roll-off cargo (ro-ro, 3%) as well as general break-bulk (general) cargo (10%). We gathered 264 monthly observations from 1991 through 1999 (not all years available for all three firms). Table 6.2 shows monthly production and expenditure.

Table 6.2. Monthly production and expenditure

Variable	Mean value	Firm 1 (T1)	Firm 2 (T2)	Firm 3 (T3)
Total monthly expense**	94.8	73.6	81.9	129.4
Containers*	59.2	53.1	33.5	97.4
General cargo *	5.6	0.6	9.9	4.4
Ro-ro cargo*	2.1	1	0.8	4.7
Production-aggregated*	66.8	54.7	44.1	106.5

**Million Pesetas, December 1999.
*Thousand tons.
Source: Tovar de la Fé (2002).

The productive factors have been grouped into four categories: personnel, total area, capital and intermediate inputs. The personnel working in port terminals may be classified in two categories: stevedores or port workers, who handle cargo, and non-port workers, who do not (administrative, executives, maintenance and control personnel, among others). In turn, port workers are divided into two categories: those who are on the payroll (ordinary employment) and those who are not (special employment). These latter can be recruited on a provisional basis by any company to work 6-hour shifts, under the management of the *Sociedad Estatal de Estiba y Destiba* (SEED). Regarding occupied space, each terminal can make use of an area that has been granted under concession, which may be increased by provisionally renting -upon prior request- additional area from the port authority, turning area into a variable factor.

Capital encompasses all the components of tangible assets of the company -i.e. buildings, machines, etc. The monthly cost results from the addition of the accounting depreciation for the period plus the return on the active capital of the period. This rate of return evidences the compensation earned by risk-free capital, which is made up of bank interest plus a risk premium. For the period under analysis the return for both concepts amounts to 8% per annum. Lastly, the rest of the productive factors used by the company that have not been included in any of the three preceding categories, such as office supplies, water, electricity, and the like, have been classified as intermediate consumption.

This analysis shows that firms are in a long run equilibrium, which means that labour, equipment and surface space can be adjusted easily at the margin. This is because firms are able to rent additional area and equipment and to recruit port personnel under special labour relationship. Moreover, the correlation matrix showed that non-port personnel, equipment and total area increase with production.

With this information, a quadratic long run cost function (Eq. 6.1) was estimated along with the input expenses Eqs. 6.2) obtained using Shephard's lemma

$$
\begin{aligned}
CT = {} & A_0 + \alpha(y-\overline{y}) + \sum_{i=1}^{n}\beta_i(p_i-\overline{p_i}) + \phi(T-\overline{T}) \\
& +\frac{1}{2}(y-\overline{y})^2 + \frac{1}{2}\sum_{i=1}^{n}\sum_{j=1}^{n}\gamma_{ij}(p_i-\overline{p_i})(p_j-\overline{p_j}) \\
& +\sum_{j=1}^{n}\rho_j(y-\overline{y})(p_j-\overline{p_j}) + \lambda(y-\overline{y})(T-\overline{T}) + \sum_{i=1}^{n}\mu_i(p_i-\overline{p_i})(T-\overline{T}) \\
& +\pi(T-\overline{T})(T-\overline{T}) + \sum_{i=1}^{N}\vartheta_i D_i
\end{aligned}
\qquad (6.1)
$$

$$
G_i = p_i \cdot x_i = p_i \cdot \left[\beta_i + 2\gamma_{ii}(p_i-\overline{p_i}) + \sum_{j\neq i}^{m}\gamma_{ij}(p_j-\overline{p_j}) + \rho_i(y-\overline{y}) + \mu_i(T-\overline{T})\right] \qquad (6.2)
$$

where y is amount of output, p_i is input i price, n is the number of inputs, D_i are firm specific dummies to capture specific effects, N is the number of firms and T is time trend, included to capture possible technical change. Variables with a horizontal bar are sample means. Table 6.3 shows all the first order coefficients that are relevant for our interpretation of results.

Table 6.3. First order coefficients from the long run aggregated model

Parameter	Estimate	t-statistic
Total cost at the mean (thousand pesetas)	95960.00	120.23
Marginal cost (pesetas/ton)	715.90	33.18
Demand for ordinary workers (worked hours)	1.56	62.86
Demand for special workers (worked hours)	2.33	42.28
Demand for intermediate consumption (thousand pesetas)	981.39	87.59
Demand for total area (m^2)	61755.30	103.51
Demand for capital (thousand pesetas)	575120.00	38.43
Demand for non-port workers (number of men)	0.02	72.55
Trend	83.30	2.55
Dummy T1 (thousand pesetas)	-2227.64	-10.98
Dummy T2 (thousand pesetas)	-2212.13	-8.25

It can be seen that all first order parameters are statistically significant and have the expected signs with the exception of the trend coefficient that has a counterintuitive positive sign indicating that, everything else constant, cost increases with time. The dummy variables are both negative and similarly small, indicating that the smaller firms would exhibit some 2.3% less costs than the larger one if the three produced the mean amount. The single marginal cost estimated at the mean is 715 pesetas/ton and the corresponding value of the degree of economies of scale (the inverse of the cost-product elasticity) is S=1.959, indicating clear increasing returns. These results are fairly compatible with the average cost curve presented in Figure 6.2 based on the aggregated production volume. The curve looks as a traditional long run one, and graphically suggests the presence of economies of scale and, therefore, marginal costs that should fall below the average figures, i.e. less than 750 pesetas/ton, as obtained.

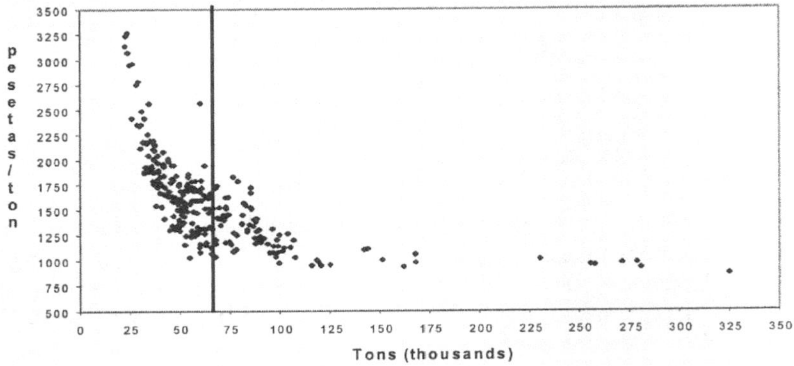

Fig. 6.2. Average cost curve and mean production

Source: Tovar de la Fé (2002).

Marginal cost calculated at the mean production of each firm (terminal) yields little variation (from 706 to 724 pesetas/ton), but scale economies at each mean do vary, yielding 2.38, 3.01 and 1.22 for firms 1, 2 and 3 respectively, monotonically decreasing with average production. According to these results, all three firms should be encouraged to increase production to take advantage of scale economies. As shown in Figure 6.1, all three occupy neighbouring sites. Pushing the three firms to merge and to operate as one could be convenient. If optimal prices were a target, charging marginal cost per ton would require a modest subsidy or, if this is not wanted, a single second best price equal to the average cost in the neighbourhood of 1420 pesetas could be set, accepting a modest social loss. Regulation would play an important role.

6.3 A Cost Function with Distinct Outputs

The preliminary discussion regarding cargo handling suggests that the optimal combination of inputs might differ depending on which outputs are being produced. Following this idea, now we use the same information to estimate a long run cost function where outputs are individually identified, namely, the volume of containers, general cargo and ro-ro. The model specification is just as the previous but three outputs are considered, i.e.

$$CT = A_0 + \sum_{i=1}^{m} \alpha_i(y_i - \overline{y_i}) + \sum_{i=1}^{n} \beta_i(p_i - \overline{p_i}) + \phi(T - \overline{T})$$
$$+\frac{1}{2}\sum_{i=1}^{m}\sum_{j=1}^{m} \delta_{ij}(y_i - \overline{y_i})(y_j - \overline{y_j}) + \frac{1}{2}\sum_{i=1}^{n}\sum_{j=1}^{n} \gamma_{ij}(p_i - \overline{p_i})(p_j - \overline{p_j})$$
$$+\sum_{i=1}^{m}\sum_{j=1}^{n} \rho_{ij}(y_i - \overline{y_i})(p_j - \overline{p_j}) + \sum_{i=1}^{m} \lambda_i(y_i - \overline{y_i})(T - \overline{T}) +$$
$$\sum_{i=1}^{n} \mu_i(p_i - \overline{p_i})(T - \overline{T}) +$$
$$+ \pi(T - \overline{T})(T - \overline{T}) + \sum_{i=1}^{N} \vartheta_i D_i \tag{6.3}$$

$$G_i = p_i \cdot x_i = p_i \cdot \left[\beta_i + 2\gamma_{ii}(p_i - \overline{p_i}) + \sum_{j \neq i}^{m} \gamma_{ij}(p_j - \overline{p_j}) + \sum_{j=1}^{n} \rho_{ij}(y_j - \overline{y_j}) + \mu_i(T - \overline{T}) \right] \tag{6.4}$$

Table 6.4 contains all the relevant coefficients of the long run multioutput cost function. As evident, marginal cost estimates do vary across products and show the expected order: containers exhibit the lowest value, followed by ro-ro cargo and general cargo. As the average cost figure is not useful in this case, these results were compared against maximum tariffs currently applied at the port, grouped by type of cargo. They happen to follow the same relative order and to be always above our marginal costs estimates, which reinforces the quality of the estimation. Note that the marginal costs for both general cargo and ro-ro are definitely larger than the maximum single figure that could be expected from the pseudo average cost curve in Figure 6.2.

The differences among the estimated marginal costs by product are perfectly in accordance with the underlying technical aspects. Handling general cargo presents complicated operations to a degree where machines are less important than labour. Nevertheless, the figures by firm suggest that volume plays a role as well, as the firm that moves a larger quantity (firm 2) exhibits the lowest marginal cost for this output (see Table 6.5 below). On the other hand, the marginal cost estimates for ro-ro (some 40% larger than those of the containers) seem to respond to two effects. In general, operations are simpler than those for containers, making some stages disappear, and they require less equipment. However, space is fundamental for this type of movement and its volume is lower, which seems to influence marginal cost.

The trend variable is negative, as expected, and the firm specific dummies are both small and close to 2,5 % of the cost at the mean. The global degree of scale economies is 1.64 and the product specific degree of returns to scale is practically one for all three outputs. This suggests that economies of scope are present, as these magnify specific scale economies (see Appendix).

Table 6.4. First order coefficients from the long run multioutput cost function

Parameter	Estimate	t-statistic
Total cost at the mean	96680.2	140.02
Marginal cost containers (pesetas/ton)	744.568	28.4829
Marginal cost general cargo (pesetas/ton)	1973.57	14.192
Marginal cost ro-ro cargo (pesetas/ton)	1055.81	2.96036
Demand for ordinary workers (worked hours)	1.57645	69.7386
Demand for special workers (worked hours)	2.33895	45.8603
Demand for intermediate consumption (thousand pesetas)	982.53	87.2994
Demand for total area (m^2)	61592.9	106.851
Demand for capital (thousand pesetas)	583266	40.6078
Demand for non-port workers (number of men)	0.021919	76.6747
Trend	-67.0148	-1.96005
Dummy firm 1(thousand pesetas)	-2460.71	-11.1526
Dummy firm 2 (thousand pesetas)	-2479.14	-7.86803

Source: Jara-Díaz et al. (2005).

The product specific degrees of scale economies are all close to unity, which suggests that the reason for the difference between the global figures on scale are due to the possible presence of economies of scope, which magnifies scale, something impossible to verify with the aggregate approach. If we analyse all possible orthogonal partitions of the product set into two firms, one handling a single output and the other handling the other two, the degree of economies of scope are all close to 0.39. This means that it is better to handle all three cargo types with one firm than to create an additional firm to take care of one output, provided that all three outputs have to be handled. This merits further discussion.

Product specific scale economies close to one means that the incremental cost (cost of the addition of that product to the line) is similar to the marginal variation of total cost (see Appendix), which fits intuition. But it also means that are economies of scope what causes overall economies of scale, due to the presence of common (non operative) costs related to non port personnel and general expenses, plus some complementarities in production provoked by common use of the surface space, labour managed by the firm, shore cranes used for containers and some form of general cargo, and so on.

Finally, scale economies are present for the two smallest firms as the calculated values for S are 2.26 and 2.13. For the largest firm this value is 1.08, reflecting nearly constant returns to scale. These results coupled with those regarding scope suggest that the two small firms could be allowed to merge, as they are located in neighbour sites, keeping competition with the large one.

6.4 Comparisons and Discussion

Comparing the results of the cost functions estimated from the two specifications of product is quite interesting. Let us begin with marginal costs, shown in Table 6.5 by product and firm, along with the degree of economies of scale.

Table 6.5. Marginal costs (MC) and scale economies (ES) by firm for the two models

	Model with aggregated output		Model with disaggregated output	
Terminal 1			MC containers (ptas/ton)	743,866(*)
	MC (ptas/ton)	720,232(*)	MC general cargo (ptas/ton)	1993,92(*)
			MC ro-ro cargo (ptas/ton)	1116,78(*)
	ES	2,38113(*)	ES	2,2577(*)
Terminal 2			MC containers (ptas/ton)	735,383(*)
	MC (ptas/ton)	706,529(*)	MC general cargo (ptas/ton)	1914,77(*)
			MC ro-ro cargo (ptas/ton)	1017,11(*)
	ES	3,00650(*)	ES	2,1259(*)
Terminal 3			MC containers (ptas/ton)	757,006(*)
	MC (ptas/ton)	724,277(*)	MC general cargo (ptas/ton)	2031,77(*)
			MC ro-ro cargo (ptas/ton)	1053,38(*)
	ES	1,21561(*)	ES	1,0752(*)
sample mean	ES	1,95901(*)	ES	1,64416(*)
			ES containers	1,00548(*)
			ES general cargo	1,00147(*)
			ES ro-ro cargo	1,08108(*)

* statistically significant at 5%

The marginal cost estimates for containers are some 4% larger than the corresponding figures obtained from the aggregate model. However, ro-ro marginal costs are between 44% and 55% larger than the single figure for each firm. The most impressive differences are found for general cargo, where marginal costs are more than 170% larger for the disaggregate model than for the original one. Moreover, note that for the disaggregate models the differences in marginal cost estimates among terminals are very small and the order is the same. The similar figures between container marginal costs in the two models seems to be a consequence of the important volume of containers at each terminal, which vary from 76 to 97%.

The firm specific dummies become some 10% more negative than in the aggregate model, keeping a relatively low value regarding the constant, which is an estimate of the cost of the largest firm at the mean. On the other hand, the time coefficient becomes negative, as expected.

Regarding scale economies with multiple outputs (see Appendix), the overall figure of 1.64 is smaller than the 1.96 obtained with the aggregate model. But this hides even larger differences when individual firms are considered, as the three figures drop from 2.38, 3.01 and 1.22 to 2.26, 2.13 and 1.08 respectively when output is correctly specified. This means that the largest terminal has reached constant returns. Therefore, the policy conclusions change dramatically, as the aggregate results suggest that merging could be desirable from a cost viewpoint, charging an optimal price of about 1420 pesetas per ton moved, while the disaggregate model would call for the two smallest firms to join operations, keeping competition with the largest that has already reached constant returns. Different prices should be charged for the movement of one ton moved in a container, as a ro-ro, or as fractioned general cargo, with prices above 760, 1120 and 2040 pesetas/ton respectively, the extra charge depending on the price elasticity of demand.

6.5 Conclusion

Port activities have been usually analysed describing output through some measure of total volume moved. Inputs required to move unitised cargo, however, differ from those required to move fragmented general cargo. Furthermore, input combinations vary within unitised freight depending on the packaging as well. When output is described as a scalar hiding multiple outputs, the observed variation in total output (volume) might be reflecting disproportionate variations in each of the real outputs. This causes various important problems. Evidently, if product specific marginal costs are too different, a single figure will represent a biased estimate of the marginal cost of the bundle mix. Moreover, the impossibility of estimating economies of scope will bias the estimate of scale economies, because potential advantages (or disadvantages) of joint production will not be captured as the presence of economies (or diseconomies) of scope, but as something related to scale.

In this paper we have shown that the analysis of cargo handling activities in ports should consider the various type of outputs moved, where outputs should be defined according to the type of unit being handled. We have compared the results of an estimated cost function using the single output approach for firms operating in a rather large port in Spain, against those obtained with output specified in detail. From this, product specific marginal costs, economies of scale and economies of scope were properly calculated. Our results are quite useful to illustrate the type of problem previously described, as the same type of data has been used in both estimated models that differ only in the output definition (aggregate or disaggregate). We found moderate returns to scale and economies of scope using the multi output approach that can be compared with the strongly increasing returns found when aggregate model is used. Moreover, firm specific returns to scale are lower under the disaggregate output cost model. As scope cannot be revealed in the aggregate model, its presence is spuriously captured through the scale index. This is exactly the type of bias induced when a multioutput activity is looked at as a single output one, as advanced by the results obtained by Jara-Díaz et al (2002) compared with those of Martínez Budría (1996) regarding the services of port infrastructure.

Ultimately what this paper highlights is that the proper approach to analyse port activities is multi-productive, and the consequences of not taken into account this important fact are quite relevant for the adequate regulation in cargo handling port activities. Single output studies could suggest erroneous efficient structures.

Acknowledgements

This research was partially funded with Grant 1050643 from Fondecyt-Chile, the Millenium Nucleus Complex Engineering Systems, and Gobierno Autónomo de Canarias.

References

Baumol W, Panzar J, Willig R (1982) Contestable markets and the theory of industry structure. Harcourt, Bruce and Jovanovich, Inc., New York.

Chang S (1978) Production function and capacity utilization of the port of Mobile. Maritime Policy and Management. Vol. 5: 297-305 .

Jara-Díaz S, Martinez-Budría E, Cortés C, Basso L (2002) A multioutput cost function for the services of Spanish ports' infrastructure. Transportation. 29: 419-437.

Jara-Díaz S, Tovar de la Fé B, Trujillo L (2005) Multioutput analysis of cargo handling firms: An application to a Spanish port. Transportation. 32, 275-291.

Kim M, Sachish A (1986) The structure of production, technical change and productivity in a port. International Journal of Industrial Economics 35: 209-223.

Martínez-Budría E (1996) Un estudio econométrico de los costes del sistema portuario español. Revista Asturiana de Economía 6: 135-149.

Panzar J, Willig R (1977) Economies of scale in multioutput production. Quaterly Journal of Economics 91: 481-494.

Rekers RA, Connell D, Ross DI (1990) The development of a production function for a container terminal in the port of Melbourne. In: Papers of the Australiasian Transport Research Forum, 15: 209-218.

Tongzon JL (1993) The Port of Melbourne Authority's pricing policy: its efficiency and distribution implications. Maritime Policy and Management 20: 197-203.

Tovar de la Fé B (2002) Análisis multiproductivo de los costes de manipulación de mercancías en terminales portuarias. El Puerto de La Luz y de Las Palmas (A multioutput cost analysis for cargo handling services in port terminals. La Luz y de Las Palmas' Port), Ph.D. thesis, Universidad de Las Palmas de Gran Canaria. España.

Appendix: Main Multiproduct Cost Concepts (Baumol et al (1982))

Let C(Y) be the cost function, where factor prices W have been eliminated in order to simplify notation. The degree of global economies of scale S, which is the maximum growth rate that products can reach when factors increase by the same proportion, can be calculated directly from the cost function as (Panzar and Willig (1977)).

$$S = \frac{C(Y)}{Y \ \nabla_y C(Y)}$$

Increasing returns to scale (S>1) implies that a proportional growth of all products induces a less than proportional growth of costs; expanding production has cost advantages. Note that prices equal to marginal costs induce financial losses in this case.

The incremental cost of product i, IC_i is defined as the cost of adding that product to the line of production. This corresponds to

$$IC_i = C(y_1, y_2, ..., y_n) - C(y_1, y_2, ..., y_{i-1}, 0, y_{i+1}, ...y_n)$$

If extended to a subset of products R, the degree of economies of scale specific to R is

$$S_R(Y) = \frac{IC_R(Y)}{\sum_{j\in R} y_j \frac{\partial \ C(Y)}{\partial \ y_i}} = \frac{IC_R(Y)}{\sum_{j\in R} y_i C_i(Y)}$$

The interpretation of $S_R(Y)$ is similar to that of S. S_R >1 implies that the application of prices equal to marginal costs would not cover incremental costs.

Two products are cost complements if the marginal cost of one diminishes as the other increases, which represents some form of advantage in joint production, i.e.

$$C_{ij}(Y) = \frac{\partial^2 C(Y)}{\partial \ y_i y_j} \leq 0,$$

The degree of economies of scope SC_T measures the relative cost increase that would result from the division of product Y into two different production lines. For an orthogonal partition of product vector N into two subsets T and N-T, SC_T is defined as

$$SC_T(Y) = \frac{1}{C(Y)}\left[C(Y_T) + C(Y_{N-T}) - C(Y)\right]$$

If $SC_T(Y)$ >0 economies of scope are said to exist and it would be cheaper to produce vector Y jointly than to produce vectors Y_T and Y_{N-T} separately. In other words, it is not advisable to specialise but to diversify production. It is easy to see that SC should be in the interval (-1, 1). The values of S and SC_T are related by the equation

$$S_N(Y) = \frac{\alpha_T S_T(Y) + (1-\alpha_T) S_{N-T}(Y)}{1 - SC_T(Y)}$$

$$\alpha_T = \frac{\sum_{j \in T} y_j \frac{\partial\ C(Y)}{\partial\ y_j}}{\sum_{j \in N} y_j \frac{\partial\ C(Y)}{\partial\ y_j}}$$

This relation shows that, in the absence of economies of scope (SC=0), S would be a weighted average of the specific economies of scale of each subset. The existence of economies of scope (SC>0) favours the presence of overall economies of scale.

7 Scale Economies, Elasticities of Substitution and Behaviour of the Railway Transport Costs in Spain

Pablo Coto-Millán
Department of Economics
University of Cantabria (Spain)

Gema Carrera-Gómez
Department of Economics
University of Cantabria (Spain)

Vicente Inglada
Department of Economics
University Carlos III of Madrid (Spain)

Ramón Núñez-Sánchez
Department of Economics
University of Cantabria (Spain)

Juan Castanedo
Department of Transports
University of Cantabria (Spain)

Miguel A. Pesquera
Department of Transports
University of Cantabria (Spain)

Rubén Sainz
Department of Economics
University of Cantabria (Spain)

7.1 Introduction

The wish to know the business reaction to the relative prices of production factors, has led to studies of cost and production functions. The elasticity of substitution, formulated by Hicks in 1932 (Ferguson, 1979), is the key concept provided by such a function. In 1938 Allen extended the concept of elasticity of substitution to multiproduct technologies, generating a new concept which carries his name in the economics literature. Subsequently, according to this, there have been some contributions on constant elasticity of substitution production functions, such as the labourby Arrow et al. (1961). However, more recent studies question the accuracy of the Allen elasticity of substitution, since it is a one-factor one-price elasticity and is a derived demand elasticity divided by a share proportion. Thus, other authors state that the Morishima elasticity (Blackorby and Russel 1981) provides some information about economics which is more relevant than Allen's. Blackcorby and Russell (1989) point out the need to assume both of these elasticities of substitution, and warn seriously about the use of the Allen elasticities of substitution when multifactor technologies are being studied.

Railway transport is managed in Spain by a state company, RENFE, which has the monopoly of passengers and goods transport services. Transport prices are fixed by the government which not only finances the differences between the operating costs of the services and the revenues produced by them, but it also provides the infrastructure.

In the present paper, we estimate cost functions for the passengers railway transport by the state company RENFE, from 1964 to 1992. The functional form used is the translog drawn by Christensen, Jorgenson and Lau (1973). We also estimate the Allen and Morishima elasticities of substitution, and we compare and interpret the results as well.

7.2 The Model

The present model is based upon Keeler's (1974) research , and Caves et al. (1981).

It is assumed that the production function has only one output and three inputs. The railway activity is multiproduct as regards passengers and goods services, departures and arrivals, timetables, and so on. For this reason, the production function must strictly have a vector of products. There are also four factors at least. However, the availability of data forces us to consider only three.

It also assumed that production input prices are exogenous.

Due to these two assumptions about product homogeneity and exogeneity of inputs prices, it is possible to represent a transformation surface of combinations of the three production factors in order to obtain the output implicitly:

$$\Phi(Qkm, K, L, F) \tag{7.1}$$

Function Φ in Eq. 7.1 represents the variable Qkm of the output per kilometer, K the capital, L the labour and F the energy.

If Φ meets the conditions of good behaviour (monotonicity, quasi-concavity and grade-one homogeneity), we can apply Shepard's Lemma and obtain the satisfactory combinations of factors and products, from the cost function derivatives with respect to the factor prices.

In other words, there is a dual cost function:

$$C = \Psi(Qkm, m, w, f) \tag{7.2}$$

where m, w, and f are the prices of the respective inputs and C the output production costs.

In order to estimate cost function (Eq. 7.2) we can test several functions, and the most common ones are: Cobb-Douglas, CES, Diewert and translog. Following Okun principle we choose the translog, the function which postulates less number of restrictions and which is the most flexible one. Moreover, through it we can show the particular functions I have mentioned before.

The translog cost specification used is:

$$\begin{aligned} LnC = {} & \alpha_o + \alpha_Q Ln\,Qkm + \frac{1}{2}\alpha_{qq}(Ln\,Qkm)^2 + \beta_L Ln\,w + \beta_K Ln\,m + \\ & + \beta_F Ln\,f + \frac{1}{2}\gamma_{LL}(Ln\,w)^2 + \frac{1}{2}\gamma_{KK}(Ln\,m)^2 + \frac{1}{2}\gamma_{FF}(Ln\,f)^2 + \\ & + \delta_{LK}(Ln\,w)(Ln\,m) + \delta_{LF}(Ln\,w)(Ln\,f) + \delta_{KF}(Ln\,m)(Ln\,f) + \\ & + \rho_{LQ}(Ln\,w)(Ln\,Qkm) + \rho_{KQ}(Ln\,m)(Ln\,Qkm) + \\ & + \rho_{FQ}(Ln\,f)(Ln\,Qkm) \end{aligned} \tag{7.3}$$

In this kind of cost models, Eq. 7.3 is usually estimated along with two share equations, in order to increase the efficiency of the estimation. The equation which is to be excluded is indifferent. Share equations are given by:

$$S_L = \frac{\partial Ln\,C}{\partial Ln\,w} = \beta_L + \gamma_{LL} Ln\,w + \delta_{LK} Ln\,m + \delta_{LF} Ln\,f + \rho_{LQ} Ln\,Qkm$$

$$S_K = \frac{\partial Ln\,C}{\partial Ln\,m} = \beta_K + \gamma_{KK} Ln\,m + \delta_{LK} Ln\,w + \delta_{KF} Ln\,f + \rho_{KQ} Ln\,Qkm$$

$$S_F = \frac{\partial Ln\,C}{\partial Ln\,f} = \beta_F + \gamma_{FF} Ln\,f + \delta_{LF} Ln\,w + \delta_{KF} Ln\,m + \rho_{FQ} Ln\,Qkm$$

The following restrictions guarantee that Eq. (7.3) presents grade one homogeneity in the input prices.

$$\beta_L + \beta_K + \beta_F = 1$$

$$\rho_{LQ} + \rho_{KQ} + \rho_{FQ} = 0$$

$$\gamma_{LL} + \delta_{LF} + \delta_{LK} = 0$$

$$\gamma_{KK} + \delta_{LK} + \delta_{KF} = 0$$

$$\gamma_{FF} + \delta_{LF} + \delta_{KF} = 0$$

The Allen elasticities of substitution. σA_{ij}, between factors are defined as follows (Uzawa (1962)):

$$\sigma A_{ij} = \frac{C\left(\frac{\partial^2 C}{\partial P_i \partial P_j}\right)}{\left(\frac{\partial C}{\partial P_i}\frac{\partial C}{\partial P_j}\right)}$$

where C are the costs and P_i, P_j, are the input prices ($Pi, Pj: m, w, f$).

For the translog cost function, Allen partial elasticities of substitution (Blackorby and Russell 1989) can be estimated as it is shown,

$$\sigma A_{ij} = \frac{\left(\delta_{ij} + S_i S_j\right)}{S_i S_j}; \text{ with i} \neq \text{j}$$

where parameters δ_{ij} refer to the parameters in (7.3): δ_{LK}, δ_{LF} and δ_{KF}. However, variables $S_i.S_j$ account for the different shares: S_L, S_K and S_F.

As regards multiple factors, the Morishima elasticities, σM_{ij}, are defined as follows (Blackorby and Russell 1989):

$$\sigma M_{ij} = \frac{\partial Ln\left(\frac{C_i}{C_j}\right)}{\partial Ln\left(\frac{P_i}{P_j}\right)}$$

where C_i, C_j account for the production costs with the respective factors i and j; and P_i, P_j account for the prices of the factors: m, w and f.

For translog cost function, the Morishima elasticities of substitution can be obtained from the following expressions (Blackorby and Russell 1989):

$$\sigma M_{ij} = \left(\frac{\delta_{ij}}{S_i}\right) - \left(\frac{\gamma_{jj}}{S_j}\right) + 1$$

$$\sigma M_{ji} = \left(\frac{\delta_{ij}}{S_j}\right) - \left(\frac{\gamma_{ii}}{S_i}\right) + 1$$

where $\delta_{ij} = \delta_{ji}$, and $\sigma M_{ij} \neq \sigma M_{ji}$. This means that, unlike the Allen elasticity of substitution, which verifies that $\sigma A_{ij} = \sigma A_{ji}$, the Morishima elasticity is not symmetric, which can be interpreted as follows: the various relative prices of the factors provide different elasticities of substitution, depending on the price (i^{th} or j^{th}) of the modified factor.

7.3 The Data

The set of data used comes from the official statistics of the Ministry of Transport as well as from RENFE Memoranda.

The output variable has been approached by the indicator: Kilometers travelled by the vehicles (vehicles-Km). By adding different products (as many as possible departures and arrivals in the railway network, and for the different timetables) we can observe the great heterogeneities in the amount of services. However, such aggregation depends on the availability of the data.

We have considered four inputs: labour, capital, energy and equipment and services, approaching the input prices. The price of the labour will be represented by (w) of the capital by (m), the price of the energy input will be (e) and the price of the inputs grouped as equipment and services will be represented by (a).

The two last inputs have also been grouped into a single one in order to obtain more efficiency. In this case, the price of energy input and equipment, and services input will be represented by (f).

Finally, the total costs in constant pesetas, C, are made up with the amount of factors used, multiplied by their respective prices, excluding amortization and financial costs, and all costs referring to infrastructure.

7.4 Empirical Results

We have used a translog model with grade-one homogeneity in prices. The results of the estimation are shown in Table 7.1: vehicles-Km, Qtkm-1. In this estimation, energy factors and equipment and services factors have been grouped into one single input (f). The aggregation of four inputs generates an extremely high loss of efficiency. Cost function Qtkm-2 has also been tested, taking into account energy input price (e) and excluding the equipment and services input price (a).

There has been an analysis of the optimal behaviour of the cost function corresponding to function Qtkm-1; the results obtained give evidence of good behaviour since the cost function tested meets the following conditions:

- monotonicity in the factor prices.

- grade-one homogeneity with respect to the factor prices.
- quasi-concavity with respect to the input prices.

The Allen and Morishima elasticities of substitution have been estimated from the coefficient of the Qtkm-1 estimation in Table 7.1. In Table 7.2 we show the elasticities obtained by this procedure.

Table 7.1. Coefficients estimated for translog cost function

Coefficients	Qtkrn-1	Coefficients	Qtkm-2
α_o	21.84	α_o	72.35
	(3.04)[a]		(3.08)
α_Q	-2.66	α_Q	-11.76
	(-2.12)		(-2.86)
α_{QQ}	0.32	α_{QQ}	1.14
	(2.95)		(3.20)
β_L	0.99	β_L	0.99
	(24.95)		(24.75)
B_K	-0.001	B_K	-0.02
	(-194)		(-8.14)
B_F	0.004	B_F	0.0.1
	(3-54)		(8.20)
γ_{LL}	0.30	γ_{LL}	0.20
	(27.27)		(22.22)
γ_{KK}	0.10	γ_{KK}	0.11
	(10.00)		(27.50)
γ_{FF}	0.36	γ_{FF}	0.11
	(7.20)		(12.22)
δ_{LK}	-0.1)26	δ_{LK}	-0.10
	(-3.54)		(-10.44)
δ_{LF}	-0.28	δ_{LF}	-0.1O
	(-11.65)		(-12.18)
δ_{KF}	-0.08	δ_{KF}	-0.01
	(-7.12)		(-1.98)
ρ_{LQ}	-0.04	ρ_{LQ}	-0.05
	(74.07)		(41.66)
ρ_{KQ}	0.02	ρ_{KQ}	0.03
	(36.13)		(18.23)
ρ_{FQ}	0,02	ρ_{FQ}	0.02
	(23 31)		(15.09)
$\overline{R}^2$	0.99	$\overline{R}^2$	0.95
σ_{DV}	0.20	σ_{DV}	0.19
Σ_{SER}	0.008	Σ_{SER}	0.04
SSR	0.001	SSR	0.03
Log likelihood	145.82	Log likelihood	73.70

[a] Statistics *t* in parentheses

Table 7.2. Elasticities of substitution (media calculated)

	Allen Slasticities		Morishima elasticities	
σA_{LK}	0.690		0.040	
	(0.150)	*[a]	(0.500)	
	(0.009)	*[b]	(0.090)	
σA_{KL}	0.690		0.300	
	(0.150)	*	(0.090)	*
	(0.009)	*	(0.060)	*
σA_{FL}	-0.860		-0.670	
	(0.380)	*	(0.250)	*
	(0.039)	*	(0.200)	*
σA_{LF}	-0.860		-0.620	
	(0.380)	*	(0.230)	*
	(0.039)	*	(0.080)	*
σA_{FK}	-0.290		-0.240	
	(0.090)	*	(0.380)	
	(0.028)	*	(0.100)	*
σA_{KF}	-0.290		-0.240	
	(0.090)	*	(0.470)	
	(0.028)	*	(0.230)	

[a] Standard deviations estimated by traditional methods.
[b] Standard deviation estimated by the Pindvck method (1979).
* Statistically significant at the 5% level.

Table 7.3. Scale economies

Year	Scale economies
1964	0.1372
1965	0.1134
1966	0.0897
1967	0.0910
196S	0.0808
1969	0.0826
1970	0.0973
1971	0.0882
1972	0.0878
1973	0.0907
1974	0.0828
1975	0.0850
1976	0.0903
1977	0.0636
1978	0.0589
1979	0.0614
1980	0.0479
1981	0.0110
1982	0.0036
1983	0.0003
1984	0.0038
1985	0.0077
1986	0.0032
1987	-0.0027
1988	-0.0205
1989	-0.0297
1990	.-0.0570
1991	-0.0827
1992	-0.0948

The estimations of the Allen and Morishima elasticities of substitution provide the following results: evidence of substituibility and complementariety between factors.

There is a moderate Allen elasticity of substitution between labour factor and capital factor, while the Morishima elasticities are weak. The results also prove that, with the Allen elasticities, there are complementarieties between labour and energy, and between equipment and services. However, with the Morishima elasticities, complementariety between labour and energy, and between equipment and services is higher than complementariety between energy, equipment and services and labour. Besides, complementarieties are more moderate with the Morishima elasticities than with the Allen eslasticities.

There is a moderate Allen elasticity of substitution between capital factor, and energy, equipment and services factor. Again, Morishima elasticities show differences. When capital is replaced by energy equipment and services input, the elasticity is lower. The comparison between elasticities supports the results of previous works, Blackorby and Russell (1989) and MacMillan et al. (1991): the Allen elasticities overestimate both substituibility and complementariety relationships.

In Table 7.3 we show the Scale Economies obtained. The estimations provide the following result: not existence of scale economies.

7.5 Summary and Conclusions

In this paper, we have studied the behaviour of state company RENFE costs from 1964 to 1992. Translog function with the restriction of grade-one homogeneity in the factor prices, has been analized and acceptable results have been obtained for the vehicles-km output. The cost function estimated has an good behaviour since it meets the conditions of monotonicity, quasi concavity and grade-one homogeneity in the factor prices.

The comparison between elasticities support the results in previous research since it can be observed that the Allen elasticities of substitution with respect to the Morishima elasticities, overestimate both the substituibility and complementariety relationships.

The estimations basically find that the industry is characterized by constant returns to scale.

References

Arrow KJ, Chenery HB, Minhas BS, Solow RW (1961) Capital-Labor Substitution and Economic Efficiency. Review of Economics an Statistics 43: 225-254.

Blackorby C, Russell R (1981) The Morishima Elasticity of Substitution: Symmetry, Constancy, Separability, and Its Relationship to the Hicks and Allen Elasticities. Review of Economic Studies 48: 147-158.

Blackorby C, Russell R (1989) Will the Real Elasticity of Substitution Please Stand Up? (A Comparison of the Allen/Uzawa and Morishima Elasticity of Substitution). American Economic Review 79: 882-888.

Caves D, Christensen L, Swanson J (1981) Productivity Growth, Scale Economies and Capacity Utilization in US Rail-roads 1955 - 1974. American Economic Review 5: 994-1002.

Christensen LR, Jorgenson DW, Lau LJ (1973) Transcendental Logarithmic Production Frontiers. Review of Economics and Statistics 55: 28-45.

Ferguson CE (1979) The Neoclasical Theory of Production & Distribution. Cambridge University Press.

Keeler TE (1974) Railroads Costs, Returns to Scale and Excess Capacity . Review of Economics Statistics 61: 201-208.

McMillan ML, Amoako-Tuffour J (1991) Demands for Local Public Sector Outputs in Rural and Urban Municipalities . American Journal of Agricultural Economics 73: 313-325.

Ministerio de Transportes. Annual reports.

Pindyck RS (1979) Interfuel Substitution and the Industrial Demand for Energy: An International Comparison. Review of Economics and Statistics 61: 169-179.

RENFE Memoranda.

Uzawa H (1962) Production Functions with Constant Elasticities of Substitution. Review of Economic Studies 29: 291-299.

8 Efficiency Stochastic Frontiers: a Panel Data Analysis for Spanish Airports (1992-1994)

Pablo Coto-Millán
Department of Economics
University of Cantabria (Spain)

Gema Carrera-Gómez
Department of Economics
University of Cantabria (Spain)

Juan Castanedo-Galán
Department of Transports
University of Cantabria (Spain)

Miguel A. Pesquera
Department of Transports
University of Cantabria (Spain)

Vicente Inglada
Department of Economics
University Carlos III of Madrid (Spain)

Rubén Sainz
Department of Economics
University of Cantabria (Spain)

Ramón Núñez-Sánchez
Department of Economics
University of Cantabria (Spain)

8.1 Introduction

In this work we analyse and estimate the economic efficiency of a sample of 33 Spanish civil airports in the 1992-1994 period. With this aim, we have estimated a

frontier-cost function by applying the panel data technology, which enables us to classify the different Spanish airports under their economic efficiency.
A frontier cost function represents the minimum cost at which a particular level of output is produced given the technology and the prices of the production factors used. The basic specification of a cost frontier is:

$$C_h = f(w, y; \beta) \exp(U_h), u_h, \geq 0 \tag{8.1}$$

where C is the cost of the h-th firm, w is the price vector of the inputs, f (w, y; β) represents the minimum cost and u_h represents the deviations of the cost effectively achieved by each firm with respect to the minimum cost. Such deviations will be above the cost frontier rather than below it.

A cost frontier can be obtained through the estimation of deterministic or stochastic frontiers. The former assume that the deviations towards the frontier are exclusively due to an economic inefficiency. That is to say, the economic efficiency is defined as (Aigner and Chu 1968):

$$EE = C / f(w, y; \beta) = \exp(u_h) \tag{8.2}$$

On the other hand, the stochastic frontiers take into account the random and uncontrolled factors which may affect the production and costs of a firm - i.e., environmental and weather conditions, problems in the supply of the productive factors, etc. or measurement errors - (Aigner et al. 1997). Therefore, the error term falls now into two categories:

$$C = f(w,y; \beta) \exp(e_h), e_h = v_h + u_h \tag{8.3}$$

where v_h accounts for the random effect and u_h accounts for the economic inefficiency.

The cost frontiers may be parametric (they may impose a particular functional form) or non-parametric. In this research we have used a data panel to estimate the translogarithmic parametric function, for which we have employed an econometric model.

8.2 The Model

With the aim of obtaining the economic efficiency of the different civil airports, we estimate a frontier-cost function. In order to put this model into practice it is necessary to choose a particular functional form. However, this confers a series of characteristics on the technology studied without accurate knowledge of the certainty of such properties. Therefore, it is important to choose flexible functional forms which place the least number of restrictions on the technology. Consequently, we have chosen a flexible functional form: a multiproduct translogarithmic function (Translog). Then, the cost function is specified as follows:

$$CV_h = A + \sum_{r=1}^{m} \alpha_r \ln y_{rht} + \frac{1}{2}\sum_{r=1}^{m}\sum_{s=1}^{m} \alpha_{rs} \ln y_{rht} \ln y_{sht} + \sum_{i=1}^{n} \beta_i \ln w_{iht} +$$
$$+ \frac{1}{2}\sum_{i=1}^{n}\sum_{j=1}^{n} \beta_{ij} \ln w_{iht} \ln w_{jht} + \sum_{r=1}^{m}\sum_{i=1}^{n} \rho_{ri} \ln y_{rht} \ln w_{iht} + \phi_t t + \quad (8.4)$$
$$+ \frac{1}{2}\phi_u t^2 + \sum_{r=1}^{m} \rho_{rt} \ln y_{rht} t + \sum_{i=1}^{n} \beta_{it} \ln w_{iht} t + \varepsilon_{ht}$$

where i, j = 1...n is the price of the different inputs; r, s =1...m is the number of outputs; h = 1...H is the number of civil airports, A is the constant, t is a time trend and ε_{ht} is the random disturbance term. On this function, we have imposed the homogeneity conditions of degree one on the factor prices and the symmetry conditions.

As seen earlier, assume that ε_{ht} has two components: $\varepsilon_{ht} = v_{ht} + u_h$, where v_{ht} accounts for the random disturbance of the usual characteristics [iid, N $(0, \sigma_A)$] and u_h ($\geq$ O) is supposed to capture the inefficiency degree of the h-th firm. This error component follows an unknown distribution iid, D (μ, σ_B).

Schmidt and Sickles (1984) reformulate the model as follows:

$$A^* = A + \mu \quad (8.5)$$

and

$$u_h^* = u_h - \mu \quad (8.6)$$

Therefore, u_h^* is iid with $E(u_h) = 0$. In this sense, both errors have zero as average value, therefore the standard panel data models can be applied (fixed effect model or random effect model). The choice of either model will depend on whether u_h is correlated or not with the explanatory variables recorded:

- The fixed effect model assumes that the individual effects are specific constants for each firm, so that they would take part in the translog functional form.
- The random effect model assumes that the individual effects follow an unknown distribution and therefore would take part in the random disturbance term.

If we assume that the above-mentioned correlation exists, the random effect model would be inconsistent since the explanatory variables would be correlated with the part of random disturbance in correspondence with the individual effect, so that the model of fixed effects must be applied since it lacks this problem and, therefore, the estimators are consistent. On the other hand, if we assume that there is no such correlation, the application of the random effect model is also consistent and more efficient.

With the aim of determining which of these models is suitable in our case, we have applied the Hausman test which identifies any correlation between the fixed effects and the exogenous variables. Therefore, to account for the individual effect (u_h) we have introduced a different dummy variable for each airport in the cost function. This individual effect would be the economic inefficiency. In this sense, the estimated function is a stochastic frontier which isolates the random effects (represented by the error term) thus called economic inefficiency.

8.3 The Data

The data used in the estimation of the cost function have been obtained from a panel of 33 civil airports of national interest observed during the 1992-1994 period. The variable which depends on the model (CV) is the total variable cost - equal to the sum of all the costs: employee costs, depreciation and intermediate consumptions -. The model includes a single production variable obtained when aggregating the airport activity, the total of passengers moved in the airport (the passengers embarked and disembarked). The model also includes three variable inputs: labour (L), capital (K) and intermediate consumptions (E). Prices are obtained as follows: the price of labour (wL) is the quotient obtained by dividing the whole of the employee costs by the total number of workers employed; the price of capital (wK) is obtained dividing the amortization of the period by the number of linear meters of the quays; and the price of the intermediate consumption (wE) is obtained as the quotient of the consumption, external supplies and services costs and other expenses divided by the airport activity measured in passengers.

Table 8.1 shows the statistical aspects of inputs and outputs.

Table 8.1. Summary statistics

	Passengers (thousands)	Labour (Number)	Capital[a] (pesetas)	I. Consumpt. (pesetas)
1992				
Maximum	18,096	818	54,368,078	3,506,631
Minimum	100	37	569,369	23,846
Average	785	142	4,715,669	174,053
Standard Dev.	4,094	183	11,125,006	762,786
1993				
Maximum	17,339	823	60,498,612	3,910,108
Minimum	91	37	650,799	24,869
Average	774	143	5,132,705	195,017
Standard Dev.	4,056	185	12,359,387	830,959
1994				
Maximum	17,786	780	70,650,913	4,589,083
Minimum	93	37	759,989	25,351
Average	786	139	5,991,764	209,403
Standard Dev.	4,173	181	14,431,289	964,753

[a] Aproximated by the amortization estimated in constant pesetas
Source: Memorias Anuales de Aeropuertos Españoles y AENA.

8.4 Econometric Results

Table 8.2 shows the economic efficiency indexes and returns to scale for each civil airport.

Table 8.2. Economic efficiency indexes and returns to scale

Civil Airports	Economic Efficiency Indexes	Returns to Scale
1-Málaga	0.997	<1
2-Las Palmas	0.617	>1
3-Granada	0.468	>1
4-Santiago	0.693	>1
5-Madrid	1	=1
6-Asturias	0.534	>1
7-Bilbao	0.708	>1
8-Vigo	0.547	>1
9-Almería	0.694	>1
10-Alicante	0.937	<1
11-Pamplona	0.470	>1
12-Melilla	0.423	>1
13-San Sebastián	0.390	>1
14-Santander	0.448	>1
15-Barcelona	1	=1
16-Vigo	0.544	>1
17-Zaragoza	0.279	>1
18-Valladolid	0.424	>1
19-Reus	0.589	>1
20-Murcia	0.484	>1
21-Jerez de la Frontera	0.603	>1
22-Ibiza	0.800	>1
23-Valencia	0.681	>1
24-Fuerteventura	0.785	>1
25-Gran Canaria	0.990	>1
26-Hierro	0.295	>1
27-Girona	0.528	>1
28-Tenerife Sur	0.982	>1
29-Tenerife Norte	0.658	>1
30-La Coruña	0.576	>1
31-Palma de Mallorca	1	>1
32-Sevilla	0.631	>1
33-Menorca	0.692	>1

8.5 Conclusions

The most efficient airports are the ones of Madrid, Barcelona, Palma de Mallorca, Malaga, Gran Canaria, Tenerife South, Alicante, Ibiza, Fuerteventura, Menorca and Bilbao.

These airports have the highest traffic of passengers (between 3 million and 19 million).

Airports of medium efficiency are the ones of Tenerife North, Valencia, Seville, Santiago, Almeria, Las Palmas, Asturias, Vigo, Reus, Jerez de la Frontera, Girona and La Coruña. These airports have medium volumes of traffic (between 400 thousand and 3 million).

The airports of Granada, Pamplona, Melilla, San Sebastian, Santander, Zaragoza, Valladolid, Murcia and Hierro have a low efficiency, with volumes of traffic of up to 400 thousand passengers. The airports of Madrid and Barcelona present constant returns to scale because they have extinguished their scale economies as they have achieved their optimum size.

However, the airports of Malaga and Alicante present decreasing returns. A possible reason for this is the strong stationarity in traffics, which requires that airports are big in order to answer to the peaks in demand, while traffics are low the rest of the year.

The remaining airports present increasing returns, as expected. These airports will extinguish their returns to scale economies as they increase the traffic (we have estimated an average increase around 5% during the last 10 years), thus achieving the optimum size.

References

Aigner DJ, Chu SF (1968) On estimating the industry production function. American Economic Review 58: 226-239.

Aigner DJ, Lovell CK, Schmidt P (1997) Formulation and estimation of stochastic frontier production function models. Journal of Econometrics 6: 21-37.

Memorias Anuales de los Aeropuertos Españoles (1992-1994). Dirección General de Aeropuertos, AENA.

Schmidt P, Sickles RC (1984) Production frontiers and panel data. Journal of Business and Economic Statistics 2: 367-374.

9 Multi-Output Analysis of the Costs and Productivity of Cargo Handling in Spanish Ports

Eduardo Martínez-Budría
Instituto Universitario de Desarrollo Regional
Department of Economic Analysis
University of La Laguna (Spain)

Juan José Díaz-Hernández
Instituto Universitario de Desarrollo Regional
Department of Economic Analysis
University of La Laguna (Spain)

9.1 Introduction

An economic study of Spanish ports is important if we consider that the contribution made by Spanish ports to GDP has been estimated at 3% and to the number of jobs generated at 3.3% (Coto Millan and Martinez Budria, 1999). Moreover, ports have always been considered as strategic sites, something that is of special importance with regard to Spanish ports for, at least, the following reasons. First of all, Spain is on the periphery of the European Union, so its dependence on transport is greater than most European countries. Secondly, the Balearic and Canary Island Archipelagos are crucially dependent upon sea transport and the efficiency of port services and infrastructures. Third, 86% of imports and 68% of exports, both measured in tons, go through ports. Synthetically, port services can be divided into two types: services provided by the infrastructure and those related to cargo handling, on which this work focuses.

The cargo handling situation in Spain in 1986 was unsustainable as the labour redundancy was disproportionately high and the technical organisation of the work was completely obsolete. The result was unjustifiably high port costs. For this reason, the reforms started with Royal Decree Law 1/1986 that was followed through with the Framework Agreements of 1986 and 1993, the final intention of which was to make ports more competitive. The result of the reform can be summarised in the following points: a reduction in staff, deregulation of the composition of handling teams and a certain opening up of the business to other companies.

The general objective of this study is to carry out an economic analysis of this process. This has been done by achieving two sub-objectives. First of all, the productive process has been characterised by calculating marginal costs, economies of scale, economies of scope, average incremental costs, specific economies of scale and complementarities between products and factors. This way, it is possible to determine all the relevant aspects of the productive process. Secondly, the changes in total factor productivity have been identified and quantified, dividing these into those attributable to technological change and those that are the consequence of a change in the scale of production. Furthermore, technological change has been separated into its component parts. To attain these two objectives, a long term multi-output cost function has been estimated, using a normalized quadratic functional form.

This work is structured as follows. Section 9.2 describes the cargo handling operation in Spain. In section 9.3, we present the theoretical framework of multi-output theory and productivity. Section 9.4 describes the model to be estimated and presents the estimate made. In section 9.5, the results are analysed and, finally, section 9.6 draws the most relevant conclusions of this work.

9.2 Cargo Handling Operations in Spain

Ports are a set of infrastructural facilities with the main purpose of making it possible to transfer merchandise between the sea and the land. Port activity involves a broad spectrum of agents who provide closely linked, but different, services. To clarify and organise an economic analysis of this range of diverse activities that take place in ports, we can classify port services into three categories:

1 Services provided to ships, including navigation aids, pilot services, tug-boat services, harbour dues, naval repairs supplies, and bunkering.
2 Services provided to the cargo, including cargo handling, storage, transport within the port, etc.
3 General services such as surveillance, inspection of cargo, insurance, sanitary services.

The Spanish ports are organised according to the Law 27/1992 and by the modifications introduced by Law 62/1997, which regulates the activities of the ports that are considered of general interest. Port policy is implemented by the State Harbours Board, which, as part of the Ministry of Public Works, is responsible for establishing economic and financial guidelines and for co-ordinating the activities of the Port Authorities. The Port Authorities, established as independent public bodies, with their own legal standing and budget assets, have the basic mission of planning, building and managing the infrastructure facilities and to regulate all port-related activities.

One of the most important port activities is the cargo handling operation. This encompasses all activities from the moment the cargo is deposited in the port, until it is loaded aboard the ship and vice versa. These activities include stowing and un-stowing, loading and unloading, trans-shipment, receiving and dispatching the cargo. Different factors of production are used in these tasks, depending on how the cargo is packed. In this sense, cranes are used to move the cargo from the ship's holds to the dock and vice versa, while the work done by the stevedores, along with the necessary moving equipment, makes it possible to move the merchandise around within the holds and from the port facilities to wherever it is to be stored, received or delivered.

The need to guarantee availability of professional labour to handle cargo quickly and safely in the ports has meant that these tasks have traditionally been regulated. So cargo handling was reserved exclusively for a class of dock workers (stevedores) that gradually consolidated a monopoly position over cargo handling operations.

In the case of Spain, the management of the stevedores was entrusted to the Port Workers Organisation (OTP from its initials in Spanish), which was an Independent, administrative Body answerable to the Ministry of Work. Under this umbrella, the number of stevedores increased out of all proportion, their salary demands were dealt with without taking into consideration the real productivity of the work done and highly restrictive, and sometimes abusive labour practises became the norm in all their operations (over-sized work teams – feather bedding -, restricted working hours, etc.). This situation led to high rates of inactivity and that port services became excessively expensive, thus reducing the competitiveness of Spanish ports alarmingly.

In the face of this situation, reforms started on the dock work organisation responsible for cargo handling in the mid-eighties. Royal Decree Law 2/1986 of 23 of May, on the public service of cargo handling, and Royal Decree 371/1987 of 13 of March adopting its implementation Regulations, marked the starting point for the legislative reform of the cargo handling industry in Spain, which was subsequently extended by a series of Framework Agreements signed by the Government, cargo handling companies and the unions in 1993 and 1997.

This new legal framework established that, in each and any port that was considered of general interest, a Public Cargo Handling Company (SEED from its initials in Spanish) had to be created. This took the form of a limited company with the State holding over 50% of the share capital, thus guaranteeing government control in the decision-making process for an activity that had been declared an essential public service. Any private companies that want to provide public cargo handling services have to take up the remaining capital in the SEED. Each cargo handling company's stake in the SEED depends on objective criteria like the size of its permanent work force, the investment in mechanical equipment, annual volume of cargo handled and the payments made for the use of port facilities.

Dock workers in cargo-handling related jobs have to be entered in a special register kept by the SEED, which processes the requests for labour received from the cargo handling companies, organising their distribution and allocation on a daily basis using a system of rotations.

Spanish dock workers are divided into two categories, depending on their legal-labour relations. First of all, there are employees with a special labour relation (RLE from the initials in Spanish) that are employed directly by the SEED, rather than by the cargo handling company they work in. If a stevedore company wishes to take on an employee permanently, the employee must give up his status as an RLE worker to become part of the cargo handling company staff covered by a Common Labour Relationship (RLC from the initials in Spanish). If the labour relations between this employee and the cargo handling company are terminated, the employee recovers his status of SEED employee with his RLE. Finally, in exceptional circumstances, if no RLC or RLE employees are available, and having first informed the SEED, the stevedore companies can hire non-dock worker employees to do cargo handling work[1].

The legislative reforms focussed on introducing greater flexibility in deciding the composition of work gangs and their working day for providing their services. The size and composition of the stevedore gangs is no longer regulated nationally, and each company can decide on the composition of these gangs, although they do have to respect minimum safety standards. The working day can be extended too, enabling the cargo handling companies to meet the demand for stevedore services with greater time flexibility, including the possibility of organising night shifts and working on weekends and bank holidays. The salary system, specifically negotiated in each port, takes the form of a collective bargaining agreement that establishes both a minimum wage and a system of incentives.

Together with the dock labour reforms, cargo handling in ports has undergone a substantial technological transformation in recent years that has translated into a unification of cargoes, with Standard packing that makes handling operations faster and easier. In this sense, growing containerisation of cargoes makes transport, transfer between land and sea and storage easier, safer and faster. Apart from containers, the use of pallets for packing has also spread, thus generating compact, though smaller and lighter units than containers, which means that their handling takes longer than containerised cargo.

Closely related to these changes in cargo packing, new mechanical equipment has been introduced that can transfer and move the merchandise faster. In this sense, the increase in port traffic has justified an investment in high-power lifting equipment and dedicated container cranes, making it possible to increase the amount of cargo handled in a given unit of time. Large rail-mounted cranes and wheeled cranes (transtainers) and stackers have also helped to improve cargo transport on land.

In summary, cargo handling in Spain in 1986 was in an unsustainable situation as it was vastly over-manned and the technical organisation of the work was totally obsolete. In consequence, port costs were extremely high. For this reason, re-

[1] For a detailed study of the legal-labour relations in the Spanish cargo handling industry, see Rodríguez Ramos (1997)

forms were started, with the prime purpose of making ports more competitive. The results can be summarised in the following points: down-sizing of manning levels (12,500 dock workers in 1986 compared with 4,100 in 1998), de-regulation of the composition of work gangs and a timid opening up of the industry to other companies.

9.3 The Theoretical Framework

9.3.1 Multi-Output Theory

A micro-economic analysis of the cost function in the port industry requires a different frame of reference from the traditional single output approach. The vectorial nature of the port product makes Multi-output Theory the most appropriate framework for estimating the cost function.

First, we will define the concepts of economies of scale and joint production, following Baumol, Panzar and Willig (1982). If the cost function $C(Q)$ is differentiable from $Q = (q_1,\ldots,q_m)$, the degree of economies of scale will be given by the following equation:

$$S = \frac{C(Q)}{\sum_{j}^{m} q_j Cma_j} = \frac{1}{\sum_{j}^{m} \varepsilon_{C,q_j}} \tag{9.1}$$

where Cma_j is the marginal cost of product j and $\varepsilon_{C,qj}$ the elasticity of costs with respect to product q_j. Thus, economies of scale are (locally) increasing, constant or decreasing, depending on whether S is greater, equal to or less than the unit.

The incremental cost of a product j measures the contribution of this product to the cost of production, and it is given by:

$$CI_j(Q) = C(Q) - C(Q_{-j}) \tag{9.2}$$

where Q_{-j} is a vector of production with output j at zero and with the same values in Q for all other elements. The average incremental cost, CIM_j is given by:

$$CIM_j(Q) = \frac{CI_j}{q_j} \tag{9.3}$$

The degree of specific economies of scale of product j is shown below:

$$S_j = \frac{CIM_j}{CMa_j} \tag{9.4}$$

In multi-output approach, the analysis of scale implies that all products vary in the same proportion. But production can be modified by a different proportion for each product, or new products can even be added to the original supply without having to extend the overall scale of operations. A company's interest in adopting a multi-product supply will be dependent upon some kind of economy that cannot be attained by specialising in a single product.

The key concept for observing the advantage of joint production is the concept of economies of scope. It can be said that there are economies of scope in a set of products *M* if, and only if:

$$C(Q) < \sum_{i=1}^{k} C(Q_{R_i}) \tag{9.5}$$

where R_i is one of *k* orthogonal partitions of *M*.

Economies of scope express the existence of orthogonal subadividity of the cost function, as it is costless to concentrate production of a set of products *M* in a single company, than it is to share production among several companies, each of which would be a specialist in a sub-set of *M*. The degree of economies of scope for orthogonal partition of *M* in *M-R* and *R* is defined as follows:

$$ED_R \equiv \frac{1}{C(Q)}\left[C(Q_R) + C(Q_{M-R}) - C(Q)\right] \tag{9.6}$$

The value of ED_R falls between -1 and 1. If ED_R is zero, the joint production cost of *M* is the same as producing *M-R* and *R* separately. A positive value implies that the company's cost of producing everything is less than the cost of specialised production, and a negative value indicates the opposite, i.e. that joint production is more expensive than specialised production.

Another property of cost function that is related to economies of joint production is cost complementarity. Cost function has this quality if:

$$\frac{\partial^2 C}{\partial q_j \partial q_l} \leq 0 \tag{9.7}$$

That is, the marginal cost of a product does not increase when the volume of production of this, or any of the other products is increased.

9.3.2 Measurement and Decomposition of Productivity

Based on the estimation of the parameters that characterise the cost function, Denny, Fuss and Waverman (1981) propose decomposition of productivity as a function of the effects of technical change and of returns to scale. They get the change in total factor productivity expressed as:

$$\overset{\circ}{TFP} = -\overset{\circ}{T} + \sum_j \varepsilon_{C,qj}\, \overset{\circ}{q_j}\left(\frac{1}{\sum_j \varepsilon_{C,qj}} - 1\right) = -\overset{\circ}{T} + \sum_j \varepsilon_{C,qj}\, \overset{\circ}{q_j}(\mathrm{S}-1) \tag{9.8}$$

Using the next Index for output growth rate:

$$\overset{\circ}{Q} = \frac{\sum_j \varepsilon_{C,qj}\, \overset{\circ}{q_j}}{\sum_j \varepsilon_{C,qj}} \tag{9.9}$$

where:

T is Technical Change evaluated at a point
$\varepsilon_{C,qj}$ the elasticity of costs with regard to output j
q_j is the quantity of output j
S is the degree of economies of scale
Q is an index of outputs

and where a dot over any variable indicates its variation rate

Such decomposition, applied for translog cost functions and adapted to discrete data using the Törnqvist's indices of outputs and inputs, is not applicable to other flexible forms as the quadratic.

Martinez-Budria, Jara-Díaz, and Ramos-Real (2003) extended the application of the Denny *et. al.* model to the quadratic functional form that allow discrete data to be used, obtaining the following expression:

$$\overset{\circ}{TFP} = -\overset{\circ}{D} + \overset{\circ}{M}\left[1 - \frac{1}{2}\sum_{j=1}^{m}\left(\frac{C_{t1}q_{j0}}{C_{t0}q_{j1}}\varepsilon_{C,q_{j1}} + \varepsilon_{C,q_{j0}}\right)\right] \tag{9.10}$$

where:

$$\overset{\circ}{D} = \frac{1}{2C_{t0}}\left[\left(\frac{\partial C}{\partial t}\right)_{t1} + \left(\frac{\partial C}{\partial t}\right)_{t0}\right](t_1 - t_0) = \left[\frac{C_{t1}}{2C_{t0}}\overset{\circ}{T}_{t1} + \frac{1}{2}\overset{\circ}{T}_{t0}\right](t_1 - t_0) \tag{9.11}$$

is the variation rate of technical change between the period t_1 and t_o,

$$\overset{\circ}{T} = \frac{1}{C}\frac{\partial C}{\partial t} \tag{9.12}$$

is the rate of technical change evaluated at one point, and

$$\overset{\circ}{M} = \frac{\sum_{j=1}^{m}\left(\frac{C_{t1}q_{j0}}{C_{t0}q_{j1}}\varepsilon_{C,q_{j1}} + \varepsilon_{C,q_{j0}}\right)\overset{\circ}{q}_j}{\sum_{j=1}^{m}\left(\frac{C_{t1}q_{j0}}{C_{t0}q_{j1}}\varepsilon_{C,q_{j1}} + \varepsilon_{C,q_{j0}}\right)} \tag{9.13}$$

is a specific Index for output growth rate and where:

t_1 and t_0 indicate two consecutive periods
C_{t1}, C_{t0} are cost in t_1 and t_0
q_{j1} and q_{j0} the level of output j in t_1 and t_0
$\varepsilon_{C,qj1}$ and $\varepsilon_{C,qj0}$ the elasticity of costs with regard to product j in t_1 and t_0

We can observe that if radial (proportional) variations of the product vector are considered and the technology exhibits constant returns to scale, then the expression in parenthesis vanish, in which case the productivity index coincides with the index of technical change. Under increasing (decreasing) returns the productivity index is larger (smaller) than the index of technical change (for radial variations of products). These results are equivalent to those derived by Denny, Fuss and Waverman (1981).

9.4 The Model

9.4.1 The Normalized Quadratic Specification of Multi-Output Cost Function

The functional form used should allow the theoretical consistency of the concepts of estimated costs to depend solely on the data analysed and they should not be pre-determined by which functional form is selected. This implies that cost functions cannot, a priori, impose the signs of the first and second derivatives, i.e., it has to be flexible. In this research, we have chosen the normalized quadratic functional form because it is especially suited to the study of economies of scope.

We have included a time trend that is crossed with all the other variables and a dummy variable for each company. The time trend is used as a measure of technological change and, therefore, will explain the variations in productivity that are motivated by variations in time of the cost function itself.

Equation (9.14) presents the normalized quadratic form:

$$C = \alpha_0 + \sum_{j=1}^{m} \alpha_j q_j + \sum_{i=1}^{n-1} \beta_i w_i + \varphi t + \frac{1}{2} \sum_{j=1}^{m} \sum_{l=1}^{m} \delta_{jl}\, q_j q_l + \frac{1}{2} \sum_{i=1}^{n-1} \sum_{s=1}^{n-1} \gamma_{is} w_i w_s + \sum_{j=1}^{m} \sum_{i=1}^{n-1} \rho_{ji}\, q_j w_i + \sum_{j=1}^{m} \lambda_j\, q_j t + \sum_{i=1}^{n-1} \mu_i\, w_i t + \pi\, t^2 \tag{9.14}$$

where:

C is the normalized cost, obtained dividing by the price of input n
m is the number of outputs
n is the number of inputs
w_i is the normalized price of input i
q_j is the quantity of output j
t is the trend

Applying Shephard's lemma to equation (9.14), we get the factor demand equations:

$$x_i = \beta_i + \mu_i t + \sum_{s=1}^{n} \gamma_{is} w_s + \sum_{j=1}^{m} \rho_{ji} q_j \quad i=1,\ldots,n-1 \tag{9.15}$$

9.4.2 The Data

In this section, we will describe the data used, including the source it came from and how they have been processed to define the variables we have used in the study. The data sources are the Annual Reports of the Ports of the State, the Annual Report of each port and a questionnaire that we have drawn up and presented to Sociedades Estatales de Estiba y Desestiba (SEED).

The data from the Annual Reports of the Ports of the State have been used to get the quantities of cargo moved by each port and year included in the sample. The Annual Reports of each port have given us the hours worked by Port Authority cranes. This same source has given us the stock of public and private cranes, their technical specifications, in particular their average performance in normal working conditions, their location and ownership details. Although the information concerning publicly-owned cranes is complete, this is not the case for privately-owned cranes. This has made it necessary to carry out a questionnaire of private crane operators in ports with privately-owned cranes.

The other data source was a questionnaire sent to all SEEDs, which has given us important information on the labour factor, basically concerned with labour costs and hours worked by stevedores.

The products analysed in this study were defined according to how the merchandise is handled, which, in turn, will determine what kind of operation is needed to load or unload it, in short the cost of the operation. Thus, we can distinguish between general container cargo (MGC), non-containerised general cargo (MGNC) and solid bulk cargoes that are handled without special facilities (GSSI).

The costs we will explain encompass the expenditure in labour and the expenditure in capital (cranes) associated with the handling operations for the aforementioned cargo flows. Expenditures are shown in millions of constant 1998 pesetas. To build factor price indicators, we have the total expenditure on each factor and a physical measure of the input used, in this case, the number of hours worked by stevedores and the number of hours of crane use.

Having processed the raw statistical material, the ports included in the study are as follows: Algeciras, Alicante, Almeria, Bilbao, Cadiz, Cartagena, Castellon, Gijon, Huelva, Corunna, Malaga, Majorca, Alcudia, Motril, Pontevedra, Tenerife, La Palma, Santander, Seville, Valencia and Vigo. However, as some SEEDs were created during the study period, the number of observations for each port varies. The above mentioned sources were used to build a data pool with 158 observations for the period from 1990 to 1998.

9.4.3 Estimated Cost Function

We have used the price of capital to normalize cost and price of labour. We then estimated the system of equations consisting of the main cost function equation (Eq. 9.14), together with the demand labour equation (Eq. 9.15), with a multivariant regression system. Zellner's iterative procedure (1962) for equation systems known as Seemingly Unrelated Regressions (SUR) has been used. The statistics package used was LIMDEP version 7.0.

The calculation has been carried out with the variables deviated from the sample mean. The presence of first order autoregressive in the term of disturbance of each of the equations that make up the system has been verified. The procedure used in this case was the procedure proposed by Park (1967). Appendix 1 shows the results of the estimation.

Concerning the parameters associated with the first order variables, we would like to point out that the signs were the ones to be expected, and all of them are statistically significant. Thus, the parameters that estimate marginal costs and input demands in the observation mean are all positive.

The parameter associated with the first order trend is negative and statistically significant, while the parameter related to the square of the trend is positive, suggesting a technical change that tends to diminish over time.

The parameter associated with the second order labour price is negative as expected, and statistically significant. Moreover, the labour demand is positively related to all outputs. The relations between the rest of the variables will be analysed in the next section.

Finally, the estimated cost function is homogeneous of degree one by construction. Monotonicity in factor prices and products was verified for 95% of the observations. The Hessian shows that the function is concave in factor prices. Thus, the estimated cost function fulfills all conditions and can be taken as a good representation of the (dual) underlying technology.

9.5 Analysis of Results

9.5.1 Cost Structure

In this section, we will analyse the results, using the estimation process carried out in the previous section.

Table 9.1 shows marginal costs and cost product elasticities evaluated in the mean of observations. The results indicate the highest value for MGNC, followed by MGC and the minimum marginal cost for GSSI. This generally accepted relative order shows the advantages of grouping cargos in containers over the greater fragmentation of the other port cargo traffic flows.

Table 9.1. Marginal costs and cost-product elasticities

	MGC	MGNC	GSSI
Marginal cost (Ptas./ton)	487.9	592.8	291.8
Cost-product elasticity	0.567	0.026	0.340
Degree of economies of scale		1.071	

The average degree of economies of scale, on the other hand, has been calculated from Eq. 9.1, giving a value of 1.071, which indicates that the average port is not operating an efficient size, as a proportional increase in the outputs vector would generate a fall in the mean Ray cost. From this point of view, the bigger ports would be more competitive. Furthermore, a first order pricing policy, price equals marginal cost, would cause cargo handling companies to make losses and would need financial aid from the public authorities to guarantee their future in cargo handling.

Table 9.2 presents average incremental costs and product specific economies of scale obtained by applying Eqs. 9.3 and 9.4 with Appendix 1 values.

Table 9.2. Average incremental costs and specific economies of scale

	MGC	MGNC	GSSI
Average incremental cost	548.4	575.3	349.8
Degree of specific economies of scale	1.12	0.97	1.19

The average incremental costs per product once again show the same relative order as the one found with the marginal costs, also showing the advantages of containers from the point of view of cargo handling operations. As indicated by the degree of specific economies of scale for the mean port, the individual expansion of MGC and GSSI would cause a reduction in cargo handling average incremental costs. By the contrary, the expansion of MGNC will slightly increase the average incremental cost.

Table 9.3 shows the economies of scope calculated with expression (9.6). The economies of scope for the following orthogonal partitions of the products vector have been obtained:

Table 9.3. Degree of economies of scope

	ED_{MGC}	ED_{MGNC}	ED_{GSSI}
Degree of econ. of scope	0.177	0.329	0.182

ED_{MGC} indicates the degree of economies of scope for a partition MGC vs. MGNC and GSSI.; ED_{MGNC} indicates the degree of economies of scope for a partition MGNC vs. MGC and GSSI while ED_{GSSI} indicates the degree of economies of scope for a partition GSSI vs. MGC and MGNC.

For the three partitions made, the degree of economies of scope gives positive values, which would indicate, on a port-wide level, that specialisation is not advisable from the point of view of cargo handling costs. This fact is especially important for the partition ED_{MGNC} as cargo handling costs are 32.9% lower, in the same port, when containers, MGNC and GSSI are jointly handled. Therefore, from the point of view of cargo handling costs, specialised ports are not justified, a fact that is not contradictory with the existence of specialised terminals within the same port.

Table 9.4 shows complementarities between outputs and inputs, based on estimated second order parameters.

Table 9.4. Relations between outputs and inputs

	PL	MGC	MGNC	GSSI
PL	-44.9	63.7	95.2	39.2
MGC		-0.6	-0.2	0.7
MGNC			0.2	-0.4
GSSI				0.5

First of all, the square input price associated parameter is negative, indicating, as one would expect, that the demand for labour diminishes as its price rises. In Appendix 2 we show a method to obtain the second parameters associated to the price of the normalizer input related to the rest of the inputs. In this case, the parameter associated to PLPK and PKPK are 8.29 and -42.35, respectively. The relations between the capital and the labour is one of substitutability, as is indicated by the positive PLPK sign, which merely corroborates in a long term analysis, that a relative increase in the price of any of the inputs leads cost-minimising port to use the relatively cheaper inputs more intensively.

The relations between outputs and input demands are all positive, that is, increases in product quantity require increments in the quantities of factors demanded. Furthermore, we can see that input demand increases more for increments in MGNC than for the other outputs, which also confirms that this cargo is the most expensive from the point of view of cargo handling. With regard to relations between products, it should be pointed out that their magnitudes are negligible.

9.5.2 Analysis of Productivity and Technical Change

Decomposition of Productivity

In this section, we decompose the interannual variation in *TFP* by applying the Eq. 9.10. For this, first of all the interannual rate of technical change has to be calculated, which has been done in accordance with Eq. 9.11. Moreover, these measures have to be evaluated each year by applying Eq. 9.12, in order to get the period average. Table 9.5 presents the interannual decomposition of the *TFP* variation rate.

Table 9.5. Decomposition of TFP variation rate (%)

Period	Rate of technical change	Scale Effect	TFP variation rate
1990-1991	4.74	0.76	5.50
1991-1992	4.65	-0.69	3.96
1992-1993	4.56	-0.01	4.55
1993-1994	3.85	1.04	4.89
1994-1995	3.74	0.90	4.64
1995-1996	3.12	-0.02	3.10
1996-1997	2.61	0.98	3.59
1997-1998	2.10	0.36	2.46
Annual average 1990-1998	3.66	0.42	4.08

Growth in productivity over the whole period was 37.7%, at an average annual rate of 4.08%. The growth of technical change was 33.39%, which represents 89.7% of TFP variation, and the effect of economies of scale was 10.3%. We can see that technical progress diminishes progressively over time, although present in every year. The effect of economies of scale follows the evolution of cargo traffic flow levels. In this sense, the falls in world economic activity in the early 90s explain the slow down in port activity and its negative impact on productivity. The pronounced increase in port traffic seen after 1993 mades it possible to exploit economies of scale to a greater extent and enhanced its significant importance to productivity.

Decomposition of Technical Change

The rate of technical change, evaluated at one point, is the derivative of the cost function with respect to time dividing by C. In the case of quadratic specification, we get the following expression:

$$\overset{\circ}{T} = \frac{1}{C}\frac{\partial C}{\partial t} = \frac{1}{C}\left[\varphi + \sum_{j}^{m} \lambda_j q_j + \sum_{i}^{n} \mu_i w_i + 2\pi t\right] \tag{9.16}$$

Equation 9.16 shows the decomposition of technical change into its three component parts (Baltagi and Griffin 1988):

Effects due to pure technical change: $-\frac{1}{C}(\varphi + 2\pi t)$

Effects due to non-neutral technical change: $-\frac{1}{C}\sum_{i}^{n} \mu_i w_i$

Effects due to scale–augmenting technical change: $-\frac{1}{C}\sum_{j}^{m} \lambda_j q_j$

Coefficients λ_j and μ_i give an interesting interpretation. λ_j and μ_i are the derivative of the marginal costs of product q_j, and the derivative of the conditioned demand of factor X_i with respect to time respectively, and they suggest that marginal costs and factor demand vary over time at a constant rate of λ_j and μ_i.

Table 9.6 offers the decomposition of technical change into its component parts using the analysis done previously.

Table 9.6. Decomposition of technical change

Year	Pure technical change	Non neutral effect	Scale augmenting effect	Total technical change
1990	4.67	-0.01	-0.03	4.63
1991	4.11	0.27	0.34	4.72
1992	4.07	0.35	0.33	4.76
1993	3.88	0.24	0.17	4.30
1994	3.99	0.09	-0.02	4.06
1995	3.72	-0.27	0.08	3.53
1996	3.40	-0.20	-0.26	2.93
1997	2.85	-0.16	-0.39	2.30
1998	2.01	-0.23	-0.14	1.64
Average 1990-1998	3.63	-0.01	0.01	3.63

From Table 9.6, we can see that technical change for the period 1990-1998 increases at annual average change of 3.63%, practically the same as that of Table 9.5. The difference can be explained by the fact that while the former has been evaluated at a point, the latter is an interannual variation measure.

The composition of technical change shows that, in general, the contribution of the non-neutral effect and of the scale-augmenting effect are inappreciable. Pure technical change is the only effective component in total technical change.

9.6 Summary and Conclusions

In this research, we have carried out an economic study of cargo handling operations in Spain for the period from 1990 to 1998. This period was characterised by major reforms to cargo handling regulation. The final objective was to improve the competitive position of Spanish ports in such a way as to reduce the cost of cargoes passing through ports.

The general goal of this research is to evaluate the aforementioned reform process. To do it, a multi-output cost function of the cargo handling operation has been estimated, which has made it possible to completely characterise the productive process. From the estimated parameters, the measures have been obtained that have made it possible to calculate total factor productivity variation and its decomposition into the contributions to technical change and economies of scale. Technical change has then been decomposed and the contribution of each of its component parts evaluated.

The main conclusions of this work are as follows:

At the sample mean, there is increasing returns to scale, indicating that the minimum efficient size is larger than that of the average company. One immediate consequence of the fact that the degree of economies of scale is larger than the unit, is that a first order pricing policy, that is with prices equal to marginal costs, would cause stevedore companies to make losses.

Economy of scope analysis shows that, for the operation of cargo handling, there are joint production economies, i.e., that port specialisation is not a positive element. In summary, ports should be equipped with specialist terminals for different cargos, but the port itself should not specialise in one particular kind of cargo traffic.

Productivity analysis suggests that there was a 37.7% growth for the whole period, at an average annual rate of 4.08%. The contribution of technical change is the most important component of TFP variation, although gradually diminishing over the years. The contribution of economies of scale followed the characteristic fluctuations of the international economic cycle.

An analysis of the decomposition of technical change shows that the effect of pure technical change is the main component, with an average annual rate of growth of 3.63%. Pure technical change could be attributed to the general organisational change promoted by the structural reform of the operation of cargo handling that has induced an improvement that affects cargo handling services, regardless of factor prices and the composition of the products vector.

Acknowledgements

This research has been funded by Ministerio de Ciencia y Tecnología, Plan Nacional de I+D+I, proyecto TRA1999-0654.

References

Baltagi BH, Griffin JM (1988) A General Index of Technical Change. Journal of Political Economy 96, 1: 20-41.

Baumol WJ, Panzar JC, Willig R (1982) Contestable Markets and the Theory of Industry Structure. In: Harcourt Brace Jovanovich (Ed), New York.

Coto-Millán P, Martinez-Budria E (1999) An approach to the contribution of the Port System in the Spanish economy. In: P. Coto–Millán (ed) Maritime Transport Applied Economics. Civitas Economía y Empresa.

Denny M, Fuss M, Waverman L (1981) The measurement and interpretation of total factor productivity in regulated industries with an application to Canadian telecommunications. In: Cowing T, Stevenson R (eds) Productivity Measurement in Regulated Industries. Academic Press, New York, 1981.

Martínez-Budria E, Jara-Díaz S, Ramos Real F (2003) Adapting productivity theory to the quadratic cost function. An application to the Spanish electric sector. Journal of Productivity Analysis: 213-229.

Park R (1967) Efficient Estimation of a system of regression equations when disturbances are both serially and contemporaneous correlated. Journal of the American Statistical Association 92: 500-509.
Rodríguez-Ramos PT (1997) La relación laboral especial de los estibadores portuarios. Editorial Trotta. Madrid.
Zellner A (1962) An Efficient Method of Estimating Seemingly Unrelated Regressions and Test for Aggregation Bias. Journal of American Statistical Association 57: 585-612.

Appendix 1

Estimated Coefficients

Variable	Parameter	t-student
PL	155.12	19.311
MGC	13.94	28.863
MGNC	16.37	7.005
GSSI	10.10	10.006
T	-1.30	-4.953
PL2	-44.95	-6.861
PLMGC	63.73	30.454
PLMGNC	95.21	8.872
PLGSSI	39.27	7.040
T2	0.08	0.0925
TPL	-7.97	-5.604
TMGC	0.14	1.189
TMGNC	0.26	0.685
TGSSI	-0.61	-4.108
MGCMGNC	-0.21	-1.765
MGCGSSI	0.67	-2.579
MGNCGSSI	-0.40	0.985
MGC2	-0.63	-6.744
MGNC2	0.18	6.506
GSSI2	0.51	5.930
CONSTANT	31.22	22.998

NORMALIZED COST FUNCTION EQUATION		
Mean CTOTN: 0.2647	R square: 0.946	R.square corrected: 0.938
F(20,137)= 121.15	Durbin-Watson Stat.=1.561	Rho used for GLS= 0.584
LABOR DEMAND EQUATION		
Mean QTRAB: 0.0130	R square: 0.951	R.square corrected: 0.949
F(5,152)= 594.03	Durbin-Watson Stat.=1.671	Rho used for GLS= 0.626

Appendix 2

Let be X_i the i input demand *(i=1,...,m-1)*

$$X_i = X_i(W,Q,t) \quad [1a]$$

where:

W is the normalized price vector
Q is the output vector
t is the time trend

Let be W_m the normalizer input price, then:

$$\frac{\partial X_i}{\partial W_k} = \sum_{j \neq k} \frac{\partial X_i}{\partial (W_j/W_k)} \frac{\partial (W_j/W_k)}{\partial W_k} = \sum_{j \neq k} \frac{\partial X_i}{\partial (W_j/W_m)} \left(-\frac{W_j}{W_k^2}\right) = \frac{\partial X_k}{\partial W_i} \quad [2a]$$

and given the i input demand obtained from NQCF by applying Shephard's Lemma

$$X_i(W,Q,t) = \alpha_i + \frac{1}{2}\sum_{j \neq k} \alpha_{ij} W_j + \sum_{r=1}^{n} \alpha_{ir} Q_r + \alpha_{it} t \quad [3a]$$

we obtain:

$$\frac{\partial X_i}{\partial W_k} = -\frac{1}{2W_k^2} \sum_{j \neq k} \alpha_{ij} W_j = \frac{\partial X_k}{\partial W_i} \ (i \neq k) \quad [4a]$$

The Euler's Theorem applied to the m input demand which have to be zero degree homogeneous in input prices lead to the next expression:

$$\sum_{j=1}^{m} \frac{\partial X_k}{\partial W_j} W_j = 0 \quad [5a]$$

Using [5a] and [4a], we get:

$$\frac{\partial X_k}{\partial W_k} = \frac{1}{2W_k^3} \sum_{i \neq k} \sum_{j \neq k} \alpha_{ij} W_i W_j \quad [6a]$$

Thus, we have obtained all the crossed input price parameters of the normalizer input.

PART III MARKET AND ECONOMIC IMPACT STUDIES

10 Economic Impact Study: Application to Ports

Bernard Francou
Université de la Mediterranée (Aix en Provence, France)

Gema Carrera-Gómez
Department of Economics
University of Cantabria (Spain)

Pablo Coto-Millán
Department of Economics
University of Cantabria (Spain)

Juan Castanedo-Galán
Department of Transports
University of Cantabria (Spain)

Miguel A. Pesquera
Department of Transports
University of Cantabria (Spain)

10.1 Introduction

The aim of this work is to carry out a methodological review of port impact studies and their possible applications to policy design. Taking this into account, firstly, the aims and targets of impact studies, are put forward; secondly, the different methodologies used to deal with this issue, are classified and analysed. Not that a simple list of such methodologies is issued, but a systematic classification which allows the evaluation of the availability of the means and the advantages and disadvantages of the possible methodologies, according to the aims. Thirdly, a dynamic view which will undoubtedly be very profitable in the future, is discussed; fourthly, the main criticisms and defences of impact studies, arising from economic literature are offered. Finally, there is a reflection on the possible direction these works may take in the future.

10.2 Aims and Utility

The main aim of these studies is to obtain the economic impact of the operation of a port for a specific year. The economic impact indicators of the stylized results of such studies are the following: added value, jobs, income and taxes. The main aim of some works, such as the U .S. Maritime Administration (1982) and the work by Villaverde Castro and Coto-Millán (1995), is the estimation of the economic impact of ports in U.S.A. and in Spain respectively. Apart from this, there are further aims such as to understand the correlation between port and other local, regional and national industries, as well as to emulate policies of change on ports and assess the effects of the changes on the economic development of the town, area, region or country.

The studies may be useful for Port Authorities and government regulation Agencies which take decisions on port development, whether the port is in operation or a new project of a port is being planned. It may be interesting for legislators, congressmen and for the public in general, since all of them may be concerned with the economic effects of a national port system. It may be also interesting for port users, City Mayors, business and institutions related to port industry.

10.3 Analysis of Different Methodologies

There is no agreement on the opinions about the different methodologies to be applied to port economic impact studies, or on the evaluation of the added value generated by the port. Therefore, an orientative classification of the methodologies applied in the last years is proposed.

In synthetic terms, there are three types of methodologies to be applied to port economic impact.

Methodology I is based upon the cost aggregation of the different economic agents to develop the transport of goods and services related to the port studied.

Methodology II has its grounds on the added value aggregation of two big groups of economic agents (Port Industry and Port Authority) to study the direct economic impact of ports.

Methodology III is based upon the added value of three big groups of economic agents (Port Industry, Port Authority and Users) to study the total economic impact of ports (both direct and indirect).

10.3.1 Methodology I

Methodology I was applied, among others, to the study of the port of Baltimore by Hille et al. (1975). In this study, total economic impacts such as the total amount of the costs of the different economic agents were calculated, not grouped under any criteria, but classified into direct, indirect and induced costs. Such costs were defined as follows:

Direct costs are those supported by shipping companies and their representatives.

Indirect costs are payments to companies which depend on the port, as well as the costs of the Administration.

Induced costs are those derived from the consumption of goods and services in house economies which get their income from the services related to the abovementioned direct and indirect costs.

Direct and indirect costs are estimated in this methodology from more or less detailed surveys. Induced costs are estimated from the multipliers obtained from the input-output tables of the region studied.

In this methodology, direct impact results are estimated for direct jobs, direct cost per ton of general cargo, solid bulk and other goods, and for each of the abovementioned direct cost categories. Indirect impacts are estimated in terms of added value and jobs generated by services contracted from business and institutions, which represent the abovementioned indirect costs. Induced impacts are estimated applying an average multiplier to jobs (service sector), and other nine average multipliers, with the same classification as for the direct costs, from which induced costs are obtained; and finally, four more multipliers to indirect costs according to their own classification. Moreover, an approach to the impact is provided in terms of taxes, according to the estimations of the taxes paid by companies and individuals related to direct costs.

The disadvantage of this methodology is the excessive focus on surveys and the fact that very vague and inaccurate induced multipliers are calculated. It seems that certain induced multipliers are obtained for the input-output table, then, the sectors which are more similar to direct and indirect cost categories, are sought and multipliers are simply applied to them. This methodology is expensive and takes a long time. Its advantage is that it allows to present impact disaggregations per ton of each type of good, such as the total impact of each ton of cars (even of each item), of each ton of goods carried in containers, of each ton of solid bulk,... etc. Furthermore, if the survey is detailed enough, it allows space disaggregations such as the impact for a town, an area and a region.

10.3.2 Methodology II

The Methodology II is based upon the estimation of the added value, and it only estimates direct impacts. Some works which apply this methodology are those realized between 1979 and 1982 by the U.S. Maritime Administration (1982), and those realized in Spain by Fraga and Seijas (1992) and De Rus et al. (1994). In these works, different methods are used to get to estimate the economic impacts of two big groups of economic agents:

1. Port Industry.
2. Port Authority.

In order to estimate the direct economic impacts of these two groups, the following methods or combinations of methods are used:

a) Manual method of impact estimation per ton.
b) Automatic method of the input-output table direct multipliers:
   b.1) Standard multiplier estimation.
   b.2) Multiplier estimation and indicative survey use.
c) Detailed survey method.

The services included in Port Industry and Port Authority, will be described and the application and advantages of every method will be subsequently discussed. In Port Industry, ship assistance services are regarded as the supplies and provisions, repairs, auxiliariy services, docking services such as pilotage, towage, and mooring services-, good shipping and storing services, as well as good handling services. Depending on the type of port referred in the study, this concept will be whether broadened or reduced, including the services provided by fishing ships and other services related to fishing sale. It is also possible, if the study requires so, to include the services provided to cruisers, as well as those services derived from repairs, maintenance and watching of the cruisers. Thus, fishing and cruise industries are included in the work by Braun (1990), since they are economically relevant in the port of Cape Canaveral.

As regards to Port Authority, the costs of this institution, such as staff, supplies and contracts with third parties, are considered. The Port Authority usually provides the widest range of 'facilities and charges a series of tariffs for using them, according to the services. However, it also contracts and pays for the enlargement and improvement of port infrastructures, and port dredging.

The two big groups of economic agents mentioned before, generate direct jobs added value, income and tax, estimated according to the above mentioned methods, and their operative mechanism as well as their advantages and disadvantages, will be analysed below.

The manual method consists of the estimations of the economic impact per ton of a big group of goods (such as: general cargo, solid bulk and oil and its derivatives), calculated through the added value of the port (income obtained from production factors strictly of the port). This approach is made for Broad Brush studies. Such an approach is particularly interesting if the resources available are limited, and its advantage is that it gets short-term results and it can be easily updated. Its main disadvantage is that the magnitudes evaluated may be inaccurate due to particular points of view or prejudices in the sector, which have into topics not verified empirically.

The automatic method consists of the application of the direct multipliers of the region to the services provided by companies, these being considered as a proxy of port industry, and to the application of the direct multipliers of the construction sector to the dredging and construction services contracted by the Port Authority. It requires the availability of the input-output tables for the base period and the region studied. It needs specialists in input-output tables and in port operations. With these means, this method takes little time and, in spite of being more expensive, it is much more efficient than the manual method. It can also be complemented with the previous one and/or with a limited survey.

The detailed survey method takes longer and needs specialists in working with a great deal of data and in surveys, which makes it an extremely expensive method. Nevertheless, it must be said that such a method has been most used in direct impact estimation.

10.3.3 Methodology III

The Methodology III is also based upon the added value aggregation to estimate direct, indirect and induced economic impact of three big groups of economic agents: Port Industry, Port Authority and Users. Both Port Industry and Port Authority are defined as in the above mentioned second methodology. On the contrary, the group of Users is new and needs to be defined. This group accounts for the economic effects generated by the users of port services. With the aim to estimate impacts, several methods or combinations of methods are used according to the type of economic agent dealt with.

a) Methods to estimate Port Industry impacts:
   a.l) Manual method per ton.
   a.2) Multiplier automatic method.
      a.2.1) With standard multiplier values.
      a.2.2) With a discreet survey.
   a.3) Detailed survey method.
b) Method to evaluate Port Authority impact:
   b.l) Method based on construction and dredging business survey.
   b.2) Automatic method of construction sector multipliers.
c) Methods which calculate the User's impact:
   c.l) Limited survey method with manual estimations per ton.
   c.2) Automatic method with multipliers.
      c.2.1) With standard multiplier values.
      c.2.2) With limited survey.
   c.3) Detailed survey method.

Each group of port agents can be estimated with two or three different methods from which different combinations may arise; the choice of a particular combination of methods will be based on the availability of data, the means used in the research and the coherence of the results. The advantages and disadvantages are similar to those described in the second methodology.

Some of the works which used this methodology are: U .S. Maritime Administration (1982), which developed a basic software instrument, the “Tool Kit”, using this methodology in about forty studies on U. S. ports so far (De Salvo (1994)). The works by Conway et al. (1982 and 1989) for the port of Seattle can also be mentioned here, as well as the studies by Opuku (1990) and Pinfold (1991), for the ports of New York & New Jersey and Halifax respectively, the study by Villaverde Castro and Coto-Millán (1995 and 1996) for the port of

Santander (Spain) or the studies of Bernard Francou on the Le Havre container terminal(1997) or the port of Calais (2004).

10.4 A Dynamic View of Port Impact Studies

There is a static and a dynamic point of view related to time, in order to analyse port impacts. From the static point of view the economic impact of a port is studied with respect to a base year, while from a dynamic point of view this impact is studied comparing several years. In order to apply the latter, it is necessary the knowledge of at least two static studies of the same port and under the same methodology. For this reason, the methodologies applied to static port studies have been previously analysed with respect to a base period, therefore, it is necessary to focus on the dynamic aspects of the port.

There is no doubt that an analysis at a certain point in time, provides a limited point of view. However, it is the existence of two or more impact studies of a port, under the same methodology and in different periods, that allows to obtain a richer dynamic view as regards to data, which is therefore, more valuable to interpret certain facts, and to make predictions. In short, it is a true complementary instrument in taking political port decisions. Some of these dynamic estimations have been carried out for ports with certain tradition in impact studies. This is the case of the works by Yochum and Agarwal (1988) and by Warf and Cox (1989). In the former work, the studies made for 1979 and 1984 lead the authors to warn about the possible errors in the predictions made by dynamic port impact studies. The reason for their assumption is that changes in business productivity, regulation and international dollar rate, significantly impact the port traffic tonnage. Nevertheless, these authors (Yochum and Agarwal) state that several port impact studies of a given port, provide important data on the change of port economic structure. Such data can be used for the development of adequate econometric models to predict the :effect of tonnage and other relevant variables which affect port economy.

As regards to the latter work by Warf and Cox (1989), it presents a dynamic interpretation of two studies of the port of New York in 1977 and 1987, providing additional relevant data, reasonably adjusted to reality. However, with the aim to systematically offer the main attacks to port impact studies, as well as the possible responses arising, the following conc1usions have been met.

10.5 Criticisms and Defences of Port Impact Studies

As in all economic studies which adopt a particular methodology or develop a model, it is necessary to make a series of assumptions in port impact studies. The three abovementioned methodologies are based on manual methods, surveys and input-output tables or combinations of these methods. In Methodology II, if a manual method or detailed survey is adopted, since only direct impacts are estimated, the only possible assumption is that the agents are well identified and that the data they provide is reliable.

In Methodologies I and II, and even in the choice between detailed survey and manual method of Methodology II, it is necessary to estimate indirect impacts. If a detailed survey is applied, indirect impacts can be estimated, assuming that the companies from which services are contracted, or which sell products to the port, have production functions of grade-one homogeneity (that is to say, with constant scale output), with a fixed technology and constant elasticity of substitution. With these three assumptions, the total invoicing of each port supplier of goods and services, can fall into two categories: sales and services for business directly related to port activity, and buying and services for other companies. The invoicing level is considered as output divided into port and non-port output. The amounts of inputs that get the port output, are obtained below in constant amounts, so that indirect jobs, income, tax and added value, can be estimated. It would be necessary to assume again that the agents are well identified and that the data provided is reliable.

With the input-output model, it is possible to calculate impact from direct, indirect and induced multipliers. However, in the input-output analysis the following assumptions are included: production functions with constant technology, lack of scale economies and non-input substitution in the process of production.

These assumptions are restrictive and due to this, the main criticisms naturally arise, as in the case of the economic models. The likelihood of such assumptions can be additionally compared in some cases, while they would be accepted «ad hoc» in others.

The input-output analysis has the Leontief production functions, with the particular characteristic that it can only occur with only one constant amount between the productive factors. Moreover, there is no elasticity of substitution between factors in these functions.

In the surveys, a somewhat more complex production function such as the CES (Constant Elasticity of Substitution) is assumed, with grade-one homogeneity (that is to say, constant scale outputs), and constant elasticity of substitution. Furthermore, when this elasticity is both constant and null, the CES function turns into a Leontief function.

Therefore, the assumptions included both in the survey and in the input-output model, are very similar, and the restrictions which imply that such assumptions, have been the main target of the different criticisms.

The work by Waters (1977) is one of the toughest attacks to the economic impact studies. Waters presents a series of criticisms according to the issues below:

1) Data on jobs, income, wages and other costs of service supplying in relation with the port, are not easily available.
2) The role of the port in the economic development of an area, is not available.
3) The price structure and the concept of a port-town without a port, is inconceivable.
4) Import and export impact on local consumption prices is undetermined.

5) The amount of workers, wages and income related to imports and exports, is uncertain and difficult to determine.

These difficulties and the arduous task of estimating the costs of the services provided by companies related to the port, make this a difficult and unfeasible task, and its results become unreliable. Waters (1977) shows this with a table presenting a relation of 64 possible direct costs to be surveyed, which falls into five big groups: ship expenditure in port services, terminal and port service costs, inland transport, ship crew costs and port services. This data is usually complemented with estimations of values of solid bulk and manufactured goods operated through the port itself or a port in the vicinity. Both cost amounts are considered to be exogenous, and a keynesian multiplier is applied to them to determine their effects on income. The result is a regional estimation based on the costs of the port. The method assumes: a) that the price level is considered constant; b) that exports of a region lead to an income growth; c) that cost changes represent exogenous variables which can generate induced changes on the regional income level through the accelerator impact. To the previous assumptions, the lack of a technological change such as the introduction of containerization, should be added, which in the case of maritime transport means to ignore an important gain of quicker and cheaper costs which are more flexible. All these restrictions lead Waters to reject port impact studies and propose cost-benefit analyses based on surveys and completed with input-output models.

Chang (1978) defended port impact studies based upon the fact that their static condition is not a disadvantage but the aim of the study. This is the main focus of the study, a different point of view to analyse the economic effects of a port for a specific year. Moreover, it is important to carry out short term studies (Keynes 1936), long term effects do not have to be estimated. Port impact studies do not aim to measure the effects of the investment made on port facilities, which is a long term issue, but to calculate the costs of such investment for a specific year. In addition, there may not be significant technological changes or considerable price changing during that year. It should be considered that these studies cannot be used for planning, but this is not the aim of port economic impact studies. However, a comparative analysis of different periods, with economic variables referred to a base period, can solve many of the problems arising from the annual analyses. As it was mentioned before, Waters recommended cost-benefit analyses instead of port impact studies. The former may be useful if the study focuses on the setting-up or the enlargement of a specific port. However, the cost-benefit analysis requires the estimation of the benefits obtained from the investment, and due to this, the port impact studies carried out in recent years can be very useful to identify the sources of the benefit and to check the validity of the benefit predictions through a cost-benefit analysis. Chang (1978) is aware of the problems arising from the multiplier, and proposes an econometric model which allows an approach to the dynamic problem which is: the estimation of the use of the future capacity based on the demand predictions, in order to increase the accuracy of port impact analyses. The traffic demand models have been studied by Coto-Millán (1986, 1988a, 1988b, 1993 and 1995). The above mentioned econometric models can be used as complement to the traditional port impact studies, so that they would help to take decisions on the future enlargement of a port, and could partly solve some planning problems.

10.6 New Openings

The dynamic approach was recently also considered from the space point of view by Musso and Haralambides. Indeed, inter-modal supply-chains make the hinterland of ports more and more extended and part of the added-value created by port activities are progressively dispatched all along the itineraries of the land haulage. Some dry ports or logistical platforms are not necessarily installed close to sea ports while their activity is depending on them. Thus, studying the economic impact of ports implies also the definition of borders for the analysis. The objectives of a port Authority is not only to increase tonnage handled in the port facilities but also to maximise the added value in the town or region of the port when cargo is imported or exported through their berths. Measuring the economic impact of ports is also considering the territory of this impact, which may effectively reduce the evaluation of the contribution of port at the local level.

Haezendonck, Coeck and Verbeke(2002) have shown that the usual ranking of European ports by their overall tonnage is distorted by considering the added value they generate (economic impact). They show examples where ports traffic dramatically increased while the added value growth is moderate and the opposite; they paved the way for new research in economic impact of ports. The advantage of this method is to provide the decisions makers a new tool for their strategic orientations.

The European project ECOPORTS (2001 – 2005) points out the environmental impact of ports and open the door for new research on the methods of valuation of such impact; most of the studies on the economic impact show the positive effects on the short term economy but not on the sustainable economy that becomes a major issue for next years.Such consideration is also a major element of the definition of a strategy of development by Ports Authorities.

Such new researches constitute elements that might change the methods of evaluation of economic impacts of ports.

10.7 Final Reflections

The methodologies presented in this paper can be valid and their possible applications allow different combinations in the use of surveys, manual estimations per ton and input-output multipliers. The manual methods per ton and the surveys provide a wide disaggregation into subsectors, which reveal the importance of these subsectors, and even of the companies or group of companies, in economic terms. Such methods particularly disaggregate the port industry impact for ship-

pers, stevedores, services for ship docking (pilotage, towage, mooring,...), storing services and terminals, supplies,...etc.
The automatic methods cannot provide a sectorial distribution of total added value, jobs, wages and taxes, since all the results are presented in too aggregated terms. However, only with this method is it possible to obtain induced multipliers, since the survey would take us too long.

A good procedure is to develop surveys to estimate direct and indirect impacts and to compare the results obtained applying direct and indirect multipliers. If there are significant differences between the results, it is necessary to compare them to additional cross data (such as that from customs statistics, merchant register offices...etc), and therefore, to check the survey reliability and to make the necessary adjustments. If after this process, the differences are insignificant, the induced multipliers can be applied to both types of data (from the survey and from the multipliers), so that total impacts in intervals are obtained, with insignificant differences (less than 15%, as in Coto-Millán (1995) and between 5% and 15% as Villaverde Castro and Coto-Millán (1995)).

There is another reflection with respect to the dynamic view of the studies. Naturally, as studies of a specific port are performed, some errors and omissions of the previous studies are corrected. These corrections must be taken into account when a dynamic analysis is carried out, so that the methodological differences are minimum, and the data provided is reliable. The different studies become more likely from a dynamic view to the extent that a comparative static analysis is rejected, and an analysis of the «stylized facts» as regards to port impact evolution is realised. There is evidence that such an exposure can provide an advantageous discipline to develop a different and deeper analysis framework than that developed so far.

Finally, it must be said that the use of econometric models on the productive capacity, of the port business productivity and cost and of the port service demand, can complement but will never replace port impact studies. Each of these exposures can give interesting but different results as regards to the economic aspects of a port.

The recent focus on the location of added value in ports and environmental impact valuation may also enlarge the scope of the studies and force the searchers to find new tools and methodologies for the evaluation of the economic impact applied to port industry.

References

Chang S (1978) In Defense of Port Economic Impact Studies. Transportation Journal, vol. 17 winter: 79-85.

Coto-Millán P (1986) El transporte marítimo en España: 1974-83. Ph. D. thesis, Dept. of Economic Theory, University of Oviedo.

Coto-Millán P (1988a) Funciones de demanda del transporte marítimo en España. Información Comercial Española 656: 125-141.

Coto-Millán P (1988b) El transporte marítimo en España (1974-1987): Peculiaridades. Información Comercial Española 658: 101-109.
Coto-Millán P, Sarabia JM (1993) Análisis de los servicios de transporte marítimo en España: Demanda, Precios, Renta y Series Temporales. Actas de las IX Jornadas de Economía Industrial, Suplemento: Investigaciones Económicas: 201-213.
De Rus, G. et al (1994) Estimación de la Actividad Económica y Estructura de Costes del Puerto de La Luz y Las Palmas. Civitas y Autoridad Portuaria de Las Palmas.
De Salvo, J (1994) Measuring the Direct Impacts of a Port. Transportation Journal 33: 33-42.
Fraga J, Seijas JA (1992) El Puerto de Ferrol y su influencia en la economía de la comarca. Junta del Puerto y Ría de Ferrol.
Francou B (1997) Port Economics. Informa Maritime and transport- LLP.
Francou B (2004) Les retombées économiques du port de Calais, Chambre de Commerce et d'Industrie de Calais.
Haezendonck E, Coeck C, Verbeke A (2000) The importance of value added to the port sector: development of a pragmatic weighing rule for the assessment of maritime traffic flows in the port of Antwerp. International Journal of Maritime Economics, 2:2.
Haralambides HE (1996) The Economic Impact of Shipping on the National Economy. International Conference on Shipping, Ports and Logistics Services: Solutions for Global Issues. The International Association of Maritime Economists, Vancouver, B.C., Canada.
Hille J et al (1975) The Economic Impact of the Port of Baltimore on Maryland. Division of Transport Business and Public Policy, College of Business and Management, University of Maryland.
Opuku KA (1990) Economic impact of the Port Industry on the New-York and New Yersey Metropolitan Region. Port Authority of New'York and New Jersey.
Pinfold, G.: Port of Halifax. Economic Impact Study. Port of Halifax, 1991.
U. S. Maritime Administration: Port Economic Impact Kit. Office of Port and Intermodal Development, Washington, 1982.
Villaverde Castro J, Coto-Millán P (1995) El impacto del Puerto de Santander en la Economía Cántabra. Autoridad Portuaria de Santander.
Villaverde Castro J, Coto-Millán P (1996) Impacto Económico Portuario: Metodologías para su análisis y aplicación al Puerto de Santander. Autoridad Portuaria de Santander.
Warf B, Cox J (1989) The Changing Economic Impacts of the Port of New York. Maritime Policy and Management 16: 3-11.
Waters RC (1977) Port Economic Impact Studies: Practice and Assessment. Transportation Journal 16: 14-18.
Yochum GR, Agarwal VB (1988) Static and Changing port economic impacts. Maritime Policy Management Vol. 15. No. 2: 157-171.

11 Airport Management and Airline Competition in OECD Markets

Germà Bel
University of Barcelona (Spain)

Xavier Fageda
University of Barcelona (Spain)

11.1 Introduction

Airline liberalization has been followed by an increasing number of countries since United States (US) government deregulate its domestic market in 1978. Although international services are still highly regulated (except in some cases, such as the intra-European routes), it can be said that travellers enjoy currently of a greater choice of alternatives to chose, a higher service frequency and lower prices. There is a consensus that the achievement, maintenance or increase of these benefits in the post-liberalization period depends fundamentally on the existence of an effective competition on the route. In this way, there is a concern related to the scale advantages of major carriers due mainly to airport dominance.

In addition, commercialization (and in many cases privatization) is becoming a general trend in the airport industry in the sense that airports are increasingly run as commercial business and not as public service organizations. This new scenario has brought opportunities for airport competition and so for further efficiency gains.

There is an extensive empirical literature on competition in the airline industry, which refers mostly to the U.S. case[1]. One of the main issues that emerge in this literature refers to the effects of airport dominance on airlines prices. It is generally found that airport dominance, rather than route dominance, explains ability of major airlines to charge higher prices than their competitors charge. However, less

[1] Major contributions refer, among others, to Morrison and Winston (1989), Borenstein (1989), Brander and Zhang (1990), Dresner and Tretheway (1992), Oum et al. (1993), Evans and Kessides (1993), Brueckner and Spiller (1994), Berry et al. (1996) and Dresner et al. (2002). For the EU case, relevant studies are due to Marín (1995), Roller and Sickles (2000) and Lijensen et al. (2001).

attention has been devoted to airport management practices and their role as a potential barrier to air transport competition. Indeed, the particular arrangements between airports and incumbent airlines condition to great extent the opportunities of new entry or expanding services by other firms. Furthermore, airports organized as a group can prevent any form of airport competition.

The objective of this study is to examine the effects of airport management on airline and airport competition. Our methodology takes as starting point the analysis of the most common airport practices in terms of ownership, finance and airline access policies for the OECD countries. Then, we analyze possible types of airport and airline competition, stressing interactions between both agents.

11.2 Airport Management Practices in OECD Countries

In this section, we review airport management practices in OEDC countries. We focus the attention on the European Union (EU) and United States. The diversity of the EU countries has had as a consequence that all possible practices around the rest of OEDC countries (except US) can be found in this geographical area. However, the US case needs a specific analysis due to the large size of its aviation industry and the particularities that characterize airport business. We use as main sources of information reports from the OEDC (1998), the US Federal Aviation Administration (1999), the European Commission (2002a) and ATRS (2004).

11.2.1 European Union

Ownership

Most airports in the (EU) have been traditionally considered as public service organizations. Major international airports were under national government ownership, whereas regional airports were under national, regional or local government control. On the other hand, airports were managed either together as a national group or at an individual level. Airports have not escaped from privatization policies implemented in the last decades. Hence, since 1980s, and particularly in the recent years, a range of different airport ownership types have arisen due to the different historical and political approaches of EU countries so that it is possible to find any type of airport ownership model in this area. This fact makes of great interest to study the EU case, taking into account that airport finance and airline access to airports follow common features all over the world with the important exception of US.

Table 11.1. Airport ownership in European Union countries

Country/Airport	Ownership			Group or individual	Observations
	National Government	Regional/local Government	Private sector		
Austria					
(Vienna)	40%		60%	Individual	
Belgium					Airports (outside Brussels) are operated under management contracts
Brussels	64%		36%	Individual	
Rest of airports		100%		Individual	
Denmark					
(Copenhagen)	34%		66%	Individual	
Finland	100%			Group	
France					Airports (outside Paris) are operated by chambers of commerce and industry
Paris system	100%			Group	
Rest of airports		100%		Individual	
Germany					Privatization plans
(Main airports)					
Berlin system	26%	74%		Group	
Cologne/Bonn	31%	69%		Individual	
Dresden		100%		Individual	
Düsseldorf		50%	50%	Individual	
Frankfurt	18%	53%	29%	Individual	
Munich	26%	74%		Individual	
Nuremberg		100%		Individual	
Greece					Airport revenues (outside Athens) are pooled in a fund for infrastructure development
Athens	55%		45%	Individual	
Rest of airports	100%			Group	
Ireland	100%			Group	Privatization plans
Italy					Privatization plans The secondary airports in Rome and in Milan are too small as to have these systems considered as group management.
(Main airports)					
Milan system		99%	1%	Individual	
Rome system			100%	Individual	
Bergamo		27%	73%	Individual	
Pisa		100%		Individual	
Naples		35%	65%	Individual	
Bologna		100%		Individual	
Venice		67%	33%	Individual	
Netherlands					
(Amsterdam)	76%	24%			
Portugal	100%			Group	Privatization plans. No separation airport management-air traffic control
Spain	100%			Group	No separation airport management-air traffic control
Sweden	100%			Group	
United Kingdom					No separation (generally) ownership land/infrastructure-management
(Main airports)					
London system			100%	Group	
Glasgow			100%	Group	
Edinburgh			100%	Group	
Manchester		100%		Individual	
Birmingham	49%		51%	Individual	
Luton			100%	Individual	
Liverpool			100%	Individual	
Newcastle		51%	49%	Individual	
Belfast system			100%	Individual	

Source: European Commission (2002a)

Before analyzing ownership, it must be said that in Europe there are two causes that explain that airports are mostly been considered as a commercial business, regardless owners belongs to the public or private sector. First, airline liberalization at the beginning of the 1990s has brought competitive forces to the European aviation industry. Second, the need of undertaking capacity expansions along with constrained public budgets has promoted the involvement of private firms and/or a profit-maximizing behavior[2]. As a result, European airport managers are increasingly corporate firms. Regarding airport ownership, Table 11.1 shows its structure across EU countries.

National governments of several countries retain full ownership and control of their airports. In these cases, airports are usually organized jointly as a national network. We can found examples of such airport groups in Spain, Portugal, Greece (outside Athens), Ireland, Finland and Sweden[3], although there are privatization plans in Portugal and Ireland. This is also the case of the new accession countries with the exception of Slovenia, where a private firm partially owns the airport of Ljubljana.

Under this model of management, a state-owned entity controls the relevant features of the airport business (decisions on investments, finance, marketing policies, allocation of new spaces for airlines). It is worth noticing that all these countries but Spain are characterized for having only one large airport and no domestic market for flights. Indeed, Spain is the only EU country with critical size whose airports are managed as a totally integrated network exclusively owned and managed by the State.

Airports not structured as a national network are usually managed on individual bases or as a small group of airports by a public or private authority. In this way, some international airports remain effectively under national government control but have been converted into single corporations. The national government can be the single shareholder entity (this is the case of Aéroports de Paris (ADP) which manages Paris airport system) or the major shareholder. Relevant examples in the latter case are Amsterdam Airport Schipol (AAS), Brussels International Airport Company (BIAC) or Athens Spata airport. Other shareholders in Athens and Brussels come from the private sector, while the national and regional government jointly own Amsterdam[4].

Regional and local governments have full or partial ownership of many European airports, although most of these airports are involved in a gradual process of privatization. Examples of such airports can be found in Germany where the federal government retains often a minority stake in the capital of the airport authority (Frankfurt, Munich, Berlin system, Koln/Bonn and several smaller airports), United Kingdom (Manchester, Newcastle and several smaller airports), Italy (Milan system, Pisa, Venice and several smaller airports) and Belgium (all commercial airports outside Brussels)[5]. A particular case is French airports (outside Paris system) and some Italian airports (as Bolonia) which are managed by local chambers of commerce and industry.

Finally, a substantial number of airports in the EU have been fully or partially privatized. There are different possible privatization models. First, quoted airport

---

[2] The necessity of financing capacity expansions is due to the spectacular growth of air traffic. According to the European Commission (2002b), the annual mean increase of the number of passengers/kilometre moved in EU airports has been 7.4 per cent since 1980.

[3] Airports in Norway are also organised as a public network.

[4] However, in this latter case it is expected a partial privatization in 2004.

[5] This is also the case of the two main Swiss airports (Zurich and Geneva).

groups such as BAA plc [that owns and manages three airports in London, and also those in Glasgow, Edinburgh and Southampton] and Fraport AG (that owns one third of Frankfurt airport shares and manages and/or owns 15 airport companies around the world). Second, airports managed individually with the private sector as the major shareholder (Rome, Naples, Vienna, Copenhagen and several regional airports in UK). Regarding privatization, there is usually a separation between the ownership of the land and the ownership of the company that manages the airport. While ownership of the land remains under public control (except in some airports of the United Kingdom, most notably airports managed by BAA), management is in charge of the private sector through management contracts or operating concessions.

Finance

Network providers are usually self-financed though revenues from aeronautical charges and commercial incomes although they can obtain public grants and loans to finance capital development projects in specific circumstances. In addition, in some countries, such as Ireland (in the case of regional airports) and Sweden, governments have awarded operating subsidies. Given their structure, there is likely to be considerable cross-subsidization between individual airports within the group, with the more profiTable international airports often supporting smaller regional airports.

In general terms, major airports managed on an individual basis are also self-financed through revenues from regular operations and commercial concessions. However, smaller airports require usually operating subsidies from local or national governments. In financing airport capital expenditure, grants and loans from national, regional and local levels of government are made available and have been used in some countries (specially in Germany, France and Italy).

At EU level both grants and loans towards assisting in the funding of airport development projects are also available from a number of institutions. Airports of different size have obtained grants from the European Regional Development Fund (ERDF) and Transport European Networks (TEN) program. Airports have also accessed loans from the European Investment Bank.

Table 11.2 shows the financial profile of a representative sample of major EU airports. It can be seen that air traffic refers to great extent to international destinations. In addition, managing a major airport in Europe seems to be a highly profiTable business although such profitability is lower for airport groups, particularly in the Spanish case[6]. The picture is more diverse with regard to the sources of revenues. In many airports, the weight of aeronautical and non-aeronautical revenues is similar. However, aeronautical revenues are relatively lower in some air-

[6] It must be said that the high fixed costs associated to airport operations explains the existence of a positive relationship, although no necessarily lineal, between airport profitability (and so the amount of investments to self-finance) and airport traffic. However, a recent study of the European Commission (2002a) claims that airports generating traffic of more than 500,000 annual passengers can be profiTable.

ports (Paris system, Dublin, Rome, Munich) and relatively higher in other airports (the Spanish network, Milan system and the smaller airports of the sample]. In any case, the general trend is an increase in the relevance of non-aeronautical revenues for all OECD airports[7].

Table 11.2. Airport profile of selected EU airports (2002)

Airport	Passengers	% International passengers	Total Revenue (Euros million)	% Aeronautical revenues	Profit margin (%)
AENA (Spanish network)	141,239,896	59	1656	67	3
ADP (Paris system)*	73,643,000	96	1453	36	20
London Heathrow	63,012,000	89	1200	48	43
Frankfurt**	48,500,000	68	1800	46	27
Amsterdam	40,700,000	69	747	48	27
London Gatwick	29,519,000	90	416	45	34
SEA (Milan system)*	26,743,000	77	539	71	16.2
Rome Fiumicino	26,288,000	52	506	37	20
Munich	23,160,000	65	542	31	9
Manchester	19,100,000	83	483	52	13
Copenhagen	18,300,000	84	272	52	34
Stockholm	16,431,207	63	553	48	9
Dublin	15,100,000	96	398	21	8
Düsseldorf	14,750,000	87	364	54	18
Brussels	14,446,870	96	245	98	12
Vienna	11,974,000	96	310	73	28
Helsinki	9,609,887	71	191	67	4
Lisbon	9,218,131	76	105	64	35
Hamburg	8,946,505	55	173	65	14
Birmingham	8,000,000	na	152	63	31
Cologne/Bonn	5,466,180	na	191	89	20

Source: ATRS Benchmarking Report (2004)
*Data of international passengers and aeronautical revenues refer to Milan Malpensa and Paris CDG respectively.

Although commercial incomes are becoming increasingly the main source of airports revenues for all OEDC airports, aeronautical charges play an important role in the interaction between airlines and airports. The two main aeronautical charges in European airports are landing fees for aircraft usage of the runway and passenger facility charges for usage of the terminal building. Landing fees are based on a

[7] Zhang and Zhang (1997) show that it is optimal in terms of social welfare that revenues from commercial operations subsidize aeronautical revenues.

unit rate per maximum take-off weight of the aircraft (MTOW)[8]. Generally, the basis of the passenger facility charge is departing passengers with typically a fee paid by the airline (and included in the ticket price) which varies depending on the destination (international and domestic departures).

In the majority of EU member states, the setting of aeronautical charges is usually subject to some form of economic regulation. Economic regulation varies according to the scope of airport activities that are regulated or the method of regulation[9]. Typically, the scope of economic regulation in terms of airport services and functions focuses on aeronautical services. Aeronautical services are regulated within the context of a single-till where the aeronautical charges are set taking into account the non-aeronautical revenues of the airport[10]. Regarding different methods of economic regulation, price-cap regimes[11] are currently applied at Ireland, at the three London BAA airports and Manchester in United Kingdom, at Hamburg in Germany and Vienna. Less formal regimes exist for example in France, Spain and Portugal. In Spain the aeronautical charges are established by national law; they are usually modified when the national budget is passed through the Spanish parliament. In Portugal, the airport operators will submit their proposed set of charges to the regulator who following a consultation period then makes a decision on the proposed level of charges.

Access of Airlines to Airports

Access of airlines to European airports is determined fundamentally on slot allocation rules[12]. Slot allocations are based on Council Regulation (EEC) No 95/93 and IATA-coordinated rules. The basic principles of this procedure are the following: Member States carry out airport capacity surveys and designate congested airports as coordinated or fully coordinated. In each fully coordinated airport, an (inde-

[8] An important exception can be found at the BAA-owned London Heathrow and Gatwick airports. Instead of a unit rate based on MTOW, there exist fixed charges differentiated by peak and off-peak rates. The purpose of this pricing system is to reflect higher costs of operating infrastructure during peak periods and create incentive to airlines to use off-peak schedules.

[9] See Oum et al. (2004) for a recent study that analyses the effects of alternatives methods of economic airport regulation.

[10] However, in the United Kingdom there is an influential debate about reviewing the current regulation regime. The UK's CAA claims that the single-till system should be replaced by a dual-till where aeronautical charges would be set strictly in relation to aeronautical costs. The CAA argues that such a system would deal efficiently with excess demand by setting prices that reflect both the costs and the scarcity of airport facilities.

[11] Price cap regulation effectively forces an airport operator to set charges within limits prescribed in the formula RPI-X or RPI+X with the X factor incorporating and representing the efficiency gains expected of the airport operator and RPI defined as the change in the retail price index

[12] A slot is usually defined as the right to schedule an aircraft arrival or departure by an airline, on a specified day within a specified time frame

pendent) coordinator is in charge of allocating slots in an open, transparent and non-discriminatory way. However, in practice slots allocation is based on historical precedence (or "grandfather rights"); an operator who currently uses a slot can retain the slot each season. In addition, the "use it or lose it" rule applies; an incumbent carrier may loose its grandfather right on a series of slots if it did not use more than 80 per cent of the series. Available slots (non attributed/newly created/withdrawn/given-up) are put in a "pool". In the preliminary coordination phase, the coordinator must propose 50 per cent of the pool to new entrants as defined by Regulation 95/93, and 50 per cent of the pool to incumbent carriers. All carriers with four slots or less during the same day in a given airport are considered as new entrants. Two different carriers may exchange slots on a one for one basis. In addition, carriers can take part in consultations (for example IATA scheduling conferences) to ensure an efficient allocation of slots and coordination of airport schedules.

Finally, scheduled airline services operating on international routes are largely controlled through a system of bilateral air service agreements. These agreements (made by the corresponding governments) have traditionally determined market operations through regulations on the designating airlines, the points to be served in each country and even prices and the frequency of air services. The agreements between U.S and Europe have contained until recently a nationality clause that excluded airlines from other EU state member in a particular bilateral agreement (e.g.; an agreement between US and United Kingdom did not allow French or German airlines to fly from London to US cities). On November 2002, the European Court of Justice rule that the nationality clause violate the freedom of establishment principle contained in Article 43 of the Treaty. It is expected that the removal of this clause will lead to a consolidation process of European flag carriers.

11.2.2 United States

The U.S civil aviation industry is, by far, the largest in the word. In terms of airport traffic data, seventeen of the thirty busiest airports in the world are from this area (Airports Council International, 2004). In terms of airline markets, the number of seats supplied per week in the U.S market is more than 20 millions. The capacity offered in the second airline market, the Japanese market, is less than 3 millions of seats per week (Official Airlines Guide, 2004). In addition, we can remark that U.S airports show important economic and financial differences with respect to the airports of rest of the world. Such differences are due especially to the particular interaction between airports and airlines that determine several management features, such as the access of airlines to the facilities, the price setting of aeronautical charges, decisions on expanding capacity or the sources of finance investment. We explain in the following lines the functioning of airport management in U.S.

Ownership

The Federal Aviation Act of 1958 established that a public owned entity, the Federal Aviation Administration (FAA), would be in charge of the U.S air transport industry. The two broad responsibilities of the FAA relate to the safety and efficiency of civil aviation. In order to tackle these responsibilities, FAA performs a number of tasks, such as licensing and regulating all commercial airports, administering Federal grant programs for the capital improvement of the airports, or developing standards for airport design, development, construction, maintenance, operation, safety and data.

There are approximately 5,300 airports for public use in the United States. Around 10 per cent of them are commercial-service airports[13]. Table 11.3 describes the ownership of public use airports, which cover a variety of organizational forms. In this way, local and regional governments (cities, counties, and states) mostly own commercial airports but they can be managed through commissions, special departments of city or state governments, advisory boards, single-purpose airport authorities or multi-jurisdictional regional authorities. While all airports used by commercial airlines are publicly owned, there are a few small general aviation recreational facilities in the United States that are privately owned[14].

[13] Commercial service airports are legally defined as airports (1) with scheduled passenger service, 2) that annually moves 2,500 passenger or more, and (3) that are publicly controlled, with public ownership of the airfield. Commercial service airports are also categorised by hub size. Large hub airports are airports with at least 1.0 per cent of total national movements. Medium hub airports are airports with less than 1.0 per cent of total national movements, but at least 0.25 per cent. Small hub airports are airports with less than 0.25 per cent of total national movements, but at least 0.05 per cent; non-hub airports are defined as airports with less than 0.05 per cent of total national movements.

[14] In 1997, the FAA introduced an airport privatization pilot scheme with the opportunity for five small commercial airports to be fully privatised. Additionally, some medium hub airports have increased their reliance on private management. For example, Burbank Airport contracts out its daily management to a private company; Indianapolis, a city-owned airport, operates under contract with BAA; and Albany Airport (which has applied an aggressive policy to attract the biggest low cost airline in the world, Southwest) is managed by a private company.

Table 11.3. Ownership of hub and non-hub airports in the United States

Ownership	Percent of total
City	40.2
Regional	22.7
Single County	14.4
State	9.3
Port Authority	4.1
Multi-jurisdictional	6.2
Other (private, etc)	3.1
Total	100.0

Source: Airports Council International-North America, 1998 General survey (Reported in "Airport business practices and their impact on airline competition", FAA/OST Task Force Study, October 1999).

Finance

Major sources of airport funding include user charges (both aeronautical and non-aeronautical), private and public bonds (which are usually tax exempt and with low interest rates for airports), passenger facility charges (fees per-passenger to finance airport expansions) and federal, state and local grants. In contrast to other countries, aeronautical charges depend on the contractual arrangements established with the corresponding airlines. Indeed, it is particularly important to mention the role of the use and lease agreements between airports and signatory airlines. In this way, these agreements specify the financial obligations and other responsibilities that each party assumes with regard to the use of the airport's facilities. Although practices differ greatly among commercial airports, use and lease agreements are usually of three types: residual, compensatory, and hybrid agreements:

1. Residual Use and Lease Agreements: Under residual use and lease agreements, airlines agree to assume the financial risk of running the airport. Airlines guarantee that the airport will break even by paying fees that generate revenues equal to the remaining ("residual") costs of operations when all (or a specified percentage of) non-airline sources of revenue have been considered. The average length of a residual agreement at a large hub airport is approximately 28 years.
2. Compensatory Use and Lease Agreements: Under compensatory use and lease agreements, airlines typically pay only for the facilities and services they actually use, leaving the airport to assume the financial risks and rewards from non-airline facilities. The average length of a compensatory use and lease agreement at large hub airports is approximately 17 years.
3. Hybrid Use and Lease Agreements: A hybrid use and lease agreement is a variation of the two types of agreements discussed above. Hybrid agreements generally take the form of excluding selected non-airline activities from the residual cost pool. A typical example of a hybrid use and lease agreement is one in which only the airfield remains in the residual pool; i.e., through landing fees

signatory air carriers cover the cost of airfield operations that remain after aircraft parking fees and fuel-flowage fees have been collected. The average length of a hybrid use and lease agreement at large hub airports is approximately 20 years.

In the choice of these agreements, airport managers face with a trade-off. Residual agreements transfer the financial risk of operations but limit the airport's control of its sources and uses of funds. In fact, under the residual agreements, airports are often not able to obtain profits to finance investments and so they are very dependent on external financial sources. On the contrary, under compensatory agreements, airports are subject to the cyclical trends of the industry but they have the control of their facilities. A hybrid agreement can be considered a middle point in terms of financial risk and airport control. Table 11.4 shows the distribution of agreement types by hub size for airports that responded to a 1998 Airports Council International-North-America (ACI-NA) survey. It can be seen the great importance of residual and hybrid agreements. In addition, majority-in-interest (MII) clauses frequently accompany these agreements. A traditional MII clause is a contractual provision requiring the airport operator to consult with and seek approval of a prescribed percentage of signatory airlines for a proposed capital project to be developed. Based on the 1998 ACI-NA survey, 84 percent of the residual use and lease agreements have a majority-in-interest (MII) clause, only 20 percent of the compensatory use and lease agreements had an MII provision and 74 percent of airports with hybrid agreements also have MII clauses.

Table 11.4. Airports use and lease arrangements.

Use and lease	Large hubs	Medium hubs	Small hubs
Residual	41%	38%	57%
Compensatory	41%	19%	14%
Hybrid/other	18%	43%	29%
Total	100%	100%	100%

Source: Airports Council International-North America, 1998 Airports gate Availability/PFC Survey (Reported in "Airport business practices and their impact on airline competition, FAA/OST Task Force Study, October 1999).

On the other hand, how airport's facilities in the terminal building (gates, check-in counters, etc) are to be used by airlines depend on whether the contractual agreement specifies either an exclusive, preferential, or a common-use arrangement:

1. Exclusive-Use Contractual Agreements: An exclusive-use arrangement typically assigns to one airline the right to use airport facilities for a specified duration and the right to sublet or assign the facilities, conditioned on the prior written approval of the airport managers. Many airports support long-term, exclusive-use lease arrangements, since they historically relied on a specific airline to finance the construction of new and improved facilities.
2. Preferential-Use Contractual Arrangements: Preferential or shared-use contractual arrangements generally give the tenant airline the primary right to use the

facility when it has operations scheduled. Unlike traditional exclusive-use lease arrangements, preferential-use contracts afford the airport explicit contractual authority to use a tenant's facilities for other airlines in case that the tenant airline does not meet any requirement established, such as a minimum utilization threshold.

3. Common use contractual arrangements. Common-use arrangements describe airport facilities totally under the control of the airport. The airport usually assigns facilities on a short-term basis.

The choice of any of these arrangements determines to great extent the airport dominance of incumbent airlines. Table 11.5 summarizes gate leasing arrangements at large and medium hub airports. The ACI-NA survey results show that exclusively or preferential leased gates were the predominant gate arrangement at 15 large and medium hub airports in 1998. The same trend was expected by 2004, although preferential arrangements are becoming more prevalent than exclusive arrangements in large hubs.

Finally, Table 11.6 shows the financial profile of a representative sample of major US airports. It can be seen the low weight of the international traffic in comparison to EU airports. For a given level of passenger traffic, US airports seem to have a lower capacity of generating revenues than EU airports although there are some exceptions (New York JFK, Miami, Newark). However, profit margins are still relatively high. Aeronautical and non aeronautical revenues have a similar weight although in some airports aeronautical revenues are relatively lower (Las Vegas, Minneapolis, Orlando, Washington-Baltimore, Washington National, Kansas, Indianapolis). As we have said above, the general trend is that commercial revenues are becoming increasingly the main source of airport revenues.

Table 11.5. Summary of Gate Usage Practices of Large and Medium Hub Airports

1998	Number of airports	Exclusive use-gates	Preferential use-gates	Common use gates
Large hubs (percentage)	15	(55.7%)	(32.1%)	(12.2%)
Medium hubs (percentage)	15	(29.3%)	(47.0%)	(23.7%)
2004 (planned)				
Large hubs (percentage)	15	(38.9%)	(46.6%)	(13.6%)
Medium hubs (percentage)	15	(30.1%)	(43.8)	(26.1%)

Source: 1998 ACI-NA survey

Access of Airlines to Airports

Regarding the access of airlines to US airports, it must be taken into account that the issue of airport slot allocation is fundamentally a domestic policy issue in contrast to the EU case, where international organizations have much more to say about slot allocation procedures. This is a consequence of the different role that international traffic play in both airport systems.

In fact, the access to runway capacity in U.S airports is very influenced by the contractual arrangements adopted in the use of terminals to the extent that tenant airlines (under exclusive or preferential use arrangements) can block the entry of new airlines. In any case, slot allocation is based on a first-come first-served basis, although FAA has determined that a carrier may not be denied access to an airport solely based on the non-availability of currently existing facilities and that some arrangements for accommodation must be made if reasonably possible.

It is interesting to point out that the High-Density Rule, which relies on market mechanisms to allocate slots, determines airport access at some of the busiest U.S. airports: Chicago O'Hare, Kennedy and LaGuardia Airports in New York, and Washington National. Indeed, current regulations allow slot holders to sell, trade or lease their domestic slots, after a prescribed minimum period of usage, and permit slots to be held by any party meeting certain FAA qualifications. In Europe, slot swapping (one for one in the same airport) is allowed but without financial transfers. In the US congested airports, slot trades refers to an allocation decision, including a right of access, whereas slot swapping does not involve any new access right but a right for re-timing flight schedules in an airport.

Table 11.6. Airport profile of selected US airports (2002)

Airport	Passengers	% International passengers	Total Revenue (US$ million)	% Aeronautical revenues	Profit margin (%)
Atlanta	76,876,128	8	247	48	36
Chicago O'Hare	66,565,995	13	643	45	4
Los Angeles	56,108,902	26	500	34	19
Dallas-Fort Worth	51,691,588	8	371	39	15
Denver	35,652,084	5	649	46	8
Las Vegas	35,094,986	3	334	31	21
Phoenix	34,244,744	3	257	32	27
Houston	33,809,842	16	261	41	32
Detroit	32,631,463	8	260	43	-2
Minneapolis	32,629,690	5	321	27	28
San Francisco	30,938,182	23	537	58	-15
New York JFK	29,947,152	54	974	52	41
Miami	29,349,913	48	966	27	14
Newark	29,202,654	34	956	40	46
Seattle	26,690,843	8	305	38	25
Orlando	26,653,672	6	316	25	17
Philadelphia	23,471,626	23	234	48	16
Charlotte	23,007,736	18	103	50	15
Boston	22,051,757	17	316	36	21
La Guardia	21,986,679	19	306	58	24
Cincinnati – N. Kentucky	20,812,642	4	278	88	70
Baltimore-	19,181,381	5	171	29	6

Washington Pittsburg	18,027,165	na	187	44	31
Washington Dulles	17,075,965	24	244	50	0
Chicago Midway	16,959,229	1	137	36	14
Washington National	12,871,000	2	337	27	-2
Portland	12,113,869	1	163	48	11
Kansas	10,946,717	na	110	21	13
Cleveland	10,795,270	na	143	37	5
Memphis	8,053,692	3	143	46	15
Indianapolis	6,900,000	na	197	15	23

Source: ATRS Benchmarking Report (2004)

11.2.3 Other Countries

All features regarding ownership models, airport finance and particularly slot allocation rules discussed for the EU case apply also to great extent to the rest of OEDC countries.

In Australia, until 1997 a publicly owned company, the Federal Airports Corporation (FAC), managed the 22 largest airports of Australia. In that period, the Australian government sold to private operators trough long-term leases (50 years with an option to renew for a further 49 years) 17 of the 22 largest airports. The remaining five federal airports - the four Sydney basin airports and Essendon Airport – are currently in process of privatization. Price-cap regulation is also in place at 12 international airports. The most significant particularity of the organizational structure of the main Australian airports refers to the management of the domestic terminals. Since the late 1980s, the two major domestic airlines, Ansett and Qantas Airways, have operated their own domestic terminals under long-term leases negotiated prior to the establishment of the FAC. Under the leases, which usually run to around 2018, airlines are responsible for all operational features at the terminal. In addition, at some airports, including Melbourne and Sydney, airline responsibility extends to providing and maintaining terminal infrastructure, with the airport operator providing only the land for the domestic terminals under the leases. As discussed above, this type of arrangement is also only common in the US.

Until 1994 Transport Canada, a publicly owned entity, had owned and managed as a group 149 Canadian airports, including commercial airports and local airports for private aviation. At that time, the National Airports Policy established a new framework for airport management in Canada. The federal government retained ownership of the 26 commercial airports, which serve more than 90 per cent of all air traffic in Canada, making up a defined national airports system consisting of the airports in the national, provincial and territorial capitals and those that handle at least 200,000 passengers per year. However, it has transferred their management to not-for-profit local airport authorities through long-term leases. Ownership and management of 69 regional and local airports with scheduled traffic below 200,000 passengers per year was offered mainly to provincial and local governments. In addition, it was a created a national fund (based fundamentally on revenues obtained from the 26 main airports) to finance investment and operating losses of the smaller regional and local airports. Aeronautical fees are not based on a detailed formula but charges are required to be competitive and non-discriminatory.

In Mexico and Korea, national governments have been the traditional owners of airports and have managed them on an integrated basis. However, airports in Mexico were privatized at the end of 1990s through operating concessions for companies that manage different geographical groups of airports. Finally, publicly owned airport authorities manage airports in Japan. These authorities are under control of national and/or regional/local governments. There are currently plans for privatizing Tokyo, Osaka and Nagoya airports.

11.3 Competition in the Air Transport Industry: the Interaction between Airports and Airlines

In this section, we analyze different types of airline and airport competition, stressing the interaction between both agents. In this way, we first review the scale advantages that airlines can obtain from a high scale of operations in an airport. Second, we study how the competitive strategies of airlines have affected the way in which airports can compete between each other.

11.3.1 Airline Competition

Competition in the provision of air transport services depends highly on airport access issues. Indeed, prices and service frequency are considered the main determinants of airlines demand, and both features depend on the scale of operations that airlines have in the corresponding airport. In order to understand this fact, it is advisable to tackle some concepts of airline economics.

First, on the supply side the seminal study of Caves et al. (1984) distinguishes between density economies and scale economies. Density economies refer to unit cost variations due to increases of output on the route. Scale economies refer to unit cost variations due to proportional changes both in the size of the route network and in the output on each route of the network. The existence of density economies is commonly accepted, but there is not clear evidence of scale economies [Tretheway and Oum, (1992)]. Density economies along with constant scale economies have an important implication: It is not necessarily cost efficient that just one airline dominates all the main airports of a national network. However, the concentration of services in a few airports has a strong cost reducing effect for airlines.

Second, on the demand side mention must be made of the existence of two different types of travellers. On the one hand, business travellers who are price insensitive but time sensitive. On the other hand, leisure travellers who are time insensitive but price sensitive[15]. Furthermore, air transport is one of the main examples of industries with consumer switching costs (SC). This is due to the use of frequent flier programs (FFP) by airlines in order to create a brand loyalty of the traveller that previously bought their services. Indeed, as long as travellers use the services of different airlines they loose opportunities to obtain points for several advantages, such as free trips. If we consider these two characteristics of the demand, it is easy to see that the demand-side benefits that an airline can obtain from a high airport presence come mainly from offering a high service frequency. A higher service frequency allows a better adjustment to the most preferred flight schedule of travellers, which reduces the waiting time[16]. Along with the preference of business travellers for airlines that offer flexibility in the flight schedule, the demand side advantages that arise from a high service frequency relate also to FFP. Indeed, major carriers offer a greater number of destinations (and so a free trip is more valuable) and a higher service frequency in each airport (and so the accumulation of points is faster) than smaller airlines.

The demand-side advantages of high slot holdings, which relate fundamentally to business passengers, are accompanied by the cost-side advantages (through density economies) that can be exploited particularly on the leisure segment of the market.

The competitive advantages that airlines can obtain from developing a high scale of operations in an airport brings to the question of the inefficiencies that are derived from the slots allocation rules that govern airport access all over the world. This is particularly relevant due to the increasing congestion that bears most of the largest airports. Indeed, grandfathering makes difficult for a new entrant to obtain desirable slots, and even if an airline does obtain slots for new or expanded services at a congested airport, it may still be at a disadvantage (that is, a lower scale of operations and/or more inconvenient schedule time) compared with an incumbent airline. Even under the "use or lose" rules or the new entrant's reservation of the 50 per cent of new slots, there are usually very few slots available in the main (congested) airports. As a means of promoting competition in the slot allocation process, the introduction of market principles, such as slot auctions, higher posted prices or the development of a secondary market for trading slots have been suggested in several studies [Maldom (2003), NERA (2004)]. In the U.S domestic market, the scenario is even worse because many airports have adopted lease and management practices that may effectively yield control over their airport facilities to the incumbent airlines.

It must be taken into account that several studies have shown [Borenstein (1989), Evans and Kessides (1993), Berry et al. (1996), Dresner et al. (2002)] that the effects of airport dominance are higher airfares, especially in the business

[15] Consider that air fares in business trips are usually paid by the user's firm rather than by the user.

[16] The generalized cost of a trip includes both the monetary cost and the time spent on it. In this way, the waiting time is the difference between the most preferred and the actual flight schedule and so, it is a component of the cost of the trip in terms of time.

segment of the market. In this way, Table 11.7 depicts the high proportion of total departures that hub carriers concentrate in the largest US airports (with the exception of airports from New York and Los Angeles) and in the largest EU airports.

11.3.2 Airport Competition

All airport services depend on the airlines offering flights at its site so that airport competition refers mainly to rivalry for attracting airline activities. In this way, airlines all over the world are developing two alternative strategies to compete in the markets. First, mainly major carriers follow the "network model". This strategy involves the establishment of international alliances in order to offer an extensive network of routes through an efficient exploitation of the connecting traffic. Second, the "low cost model" involves offering point-to-point services with low fares. Both competitive strategies require the development of a high scale of operations in one or several airports. Indeed, low cost airlines offer a high number of non-stop flights through secondary airports that are located near to big cities, while alliances feed their airport hubs through the connecting traffic that comes from short or medium-haul routes. This trend in the airline sector is likely to affect airport competition. In this way, we can outline two prominent forms of airport rivalry to attract airline services. First, airports can compete to attract low-cost carriers. Second, airports can compete to be some of the transfer hubs of international alliances[17].

(1) Regarding airport rivalry to attract low-cost airlines, it must be noticed that there has been a considerable increase in the share of air traffic carried by low-cost carriers. For congested airports, there are no incentives to attract low-cost airlines. However, airports with excess of capacity can obtain important benefits from being a base-operating site or (to lower extent) a destination of low cost airlines (Barret (2004)). Because low cost carriers do not follow the IATA interline system (enabling passengers to transfer between carriers using a single ticket) and because their average (single-class) fares are particularly low they tend to create their own market. As a result, they can offer new routes or expand services at existing routes. In this way, low-cost airlines have a strong record of generating new air traffic in small airports. In addition, low-cost airlines offer non-aeronautical revenue sources such as catering and shopping for services normally provided as in-flight services by full fare airlines.

Barret (2004) points out the following attraction factors for low cost airlines; low airport charges, quick turnaround time and check-in, single-storey airport terminals, no executive/business class lounges, good catering and shopping at airport

[17] ACI Europe (1999) has stated the following types of airport competition: Competition to attract new airline services - passengers and freight, Competition for a role as a hub airport and for transfer traffic between hubs, Competition between airports with overlapping hinterlands, Competition between airports within urban areas, Competition for the provision of services at airports and Competition between airport terminals. In this study, we focus particularly the attention in the first two forms of airport competition

and good facilities for ground transport. In terms of price competition, the large decline in airfares since the market entry of low-cost carriers has raised the share of airport charges in the price of an airline ticket. Thus, only a small fraction of the traditional airport charges is likely to be paid by the low-cost airline. Even in some cases, airports must offer subsidies to maintain low-cost services. In terms of non-price competition, passengers of low cost airlines require a simple airport product because they travel on point-to-point journeys.

(2) Regarding airport rivalry for attracting network airlines, airport managers must guarantee a significant amount of runway capacity to accommodate the banks of arriving and departing flights that operating a transfer hub requires. Airports also should assist airlines in the smooth operation of the hub by offering them sufficient gates in close proximity to each other and well-located business lounges. Baggage transfer also needs to be efficient and connecting times reduced to the minimum. In many instances, airport charges levied on transfer passengers are also lower than on the rest of passengers.

As Starkie (2002) suggests, there are significant economies/network externalities that tie the individual airline to the hub airport and make it more difficult for rival airports to attract airlines and passengers through price or non-price competition. Indeed, both airlines and passengers gain from a concentration of air transfer services. Airlines gain from concentrating services at a transfer point because it permits the use of larger and more efficient aircraft at a higher utilization rate (i.e; higher load factors). Passengers gain from increased frequency and network scope.

However, airline alliances do compete with each other over their respective hubs with the consequence that there is a degree of competition (although indirect) between the hub airports. In this way, transfer traffic can account for a sizeable proportion of the total traffics of a hub airport and this traffic is considered to be sensitive to different price/frequency combinations offered via different hubs. This is the case, for example, of the four leading European hubs (London, Amsterdam, Paris and Frankfurt) that compete vigorously for the transfer traffic addressed to intercontinental destinations (Lijesen et al 2001).

Additionally, airlines incur in some sunk costs when moving their operating base (or splitting their operations over more than one airport location). Nevertheless, the market power of a hub airport might be restricted if it is held by one airline (as in Europe) or few airlines (as in US) and if there is the possibility that such airline (s) could move all or part of its operations to an alternative site. In Europe, Lufthansa and British Airways have set Munich and Gatwick as a secondary hub and Alitalia is moving its operating base from Rome to Milan. In US, Delta has recently announced that it is going to withdraw all services in one of its main hubs, Dallas Fort Worth.

In any case, although there are important opportunities for hub competition many other factors away from the control of airport managers influence on the decisions of airlines to provide hubbing services. These factors are the availability of slots and traffic rights, the potential traffic and yield at the corresponding routes (which depend on the local traffic generated by the local population) or the existing competition offered by other airlines.

Finally, airports located in the same urban area are in the best position to compete with each other. This would be case for example for New York, Los Angeles, Tokyo, Sidney, London, Paris, Rome or Milan. In Europe, such competition is often restricted through the common ownership of the major airports within the same urban area[18]. We can also find vigorous competition between airports that share the same hinterland, which would depend on several economic and geographical features, such as distance or the quality of ground transport.

Table 11.7. Hub Carrier share of departures in selected world airports (2002)

Airport	Hub carrier (%)
US Airports	
Houston	82
Minneapolis	80
Detroit	79
Atlanta	76
Portland	69
Philadelphia	69
Dallas/Fort Worth	66
Washington Dulles	66
Denver	60
Newark	60
San Francisco	56
Seattle	55
Phoenix	47
Miami	45
Chicago O'Hare	44
Las Vegas	38
European airports	
Zurich	66
Vienna	65
Helsinki	61
Frankfurt	59
Paris CDG	57
London Gatwick	56
Munich	55
Copenhagen	54
Madrid	52
Rome Fiumicino	49

[18] In UK, there is a debate around the convenience of have privatized BAA plc (the firm that owns and manages the three main airports of London) in a competing basis (see Barret (2000) for details). In particular, the countervailing power of British Airways against the airport manager would have been stronger if Gatwick and Heathrow were controlled by different firms.

Milan Malpensa	49
Barcelona	49
Oslo	48
Manchester	44
Amsterdam	43
London Heathrow	40
Brussels	27
Other airports	
Toronto	73
Vancouver	56
Sidney	52

Source: ATRS Benchmarking Report (2004)

11.4 Concluding Remarks

In this chapter, we have analyzed airport management practices in OEDC countries and their effects on airport and airline competition.

There is a diversity of ownership models across OEDC countries. Indeed, airports are managed as a public-owned group network in most of the smaller countries of the EU, Spain, Paris system and the new accession countries and Korea. However, airports tend to be managed on a separate basis. In this framework, regional governments full or partially own the majority of airports in US, Canada, Japan and several airports in France, UK, Germany and Italy. In these cases (except for North America) the involvement of the private sector is increasing in the last years. Finally, private sector firms are major shareholders of several UK airports (most notably the London system), other large European airports such as Vienna, Copenhagen or Rome, Mexican airports and major Australian airports.

Airport financing mechanisms follow trends that are more common across EU countries. There is an important exception in US, where such mechanisms are very influenced by the particular arrangements between airport and airlines with regard to the aeronautical charges setting and the use and financing of the terminal building facilities (desks, check-in counters and so on). However, the general principle in all the airports refers to the self-sufficiency of the system though revenues that can come from aeronautical charges (fundamentally landing fees and passenger facilities charges) and non-aeronautical incomes (fundamentally concessions for developing commercial activities). In spite of this general principle, grants and loans from governments of different territorial levels can be used to support smaller airports. On the other hand, there is usually a non-transparent cross subsidization across airports in the case of airport groups. Price regulation schemes are applied in the majority of airports though a great variety of forms, although it is seen that regimes are usually more formal when airports are privately owned or managed.

Access of airlines to airports, particularly to runways, is determined by international slot allocation procedures. There are two general principles that are applied in most of airports: (1) "grandfather rights" (an operator who currently uses a slot can retain the slot each season); and (2) the "use it or lose it" rule (an incumbent carrier may loose its grandfather rights on a series of slots if it did not use more than 80 per cent of the series). In addition, there are often clauses in favor of new entrants when new slots are available. The influence of these general principles is relatively less important in the case of US airports, where domestic traffic predominates, because the arrangements between airlines and airports regarding the use of the terminal building facilities condition to great extent the access of airlines to airports.

The lack of market mechanisms in the slot allocation process means that new entrants have many difficulties to develop a scale of operations sufficiently high to be competitive in all major airports, which, in turn, tend to be congested. We can recall in this sense that the largest airlines can enjoy both of demand and cost side advantages derived from airport dominance. A documented consequence of such airport dominance is higher airfares in routes departing from major hub airports.

Finally, we want to remark that airline deregulation and airport commercialization have brought new opportunities for airport competition. Indeed, airports can compete to attract airline services. Price competition is especially relevant in the attraction of low cost carriers, whereas non-price competition (runway capacity, minimum-connecting times and so on) is particularly important to attract network carriers. In general terms, competition should be stronger when airports are managed on a separate basis and when airports share a same urban area or hinterland.

Acknowledgements

Our research on infrastructure and competition has received financial support from the Spanish Commission of Science and Technology (CICYT, BEC2003-01679).

References

ACI Europe (1999) European airports: a competitive industry. Submitted by the ACI Europe Policy Committee.

ATRS (2004) Airport benchmarking report. The Centre for Transportation Studies. University of British Columbia, Vancouver.

Barret S (2004) How the demand for airport services differ between full-service carriers and low cost carriers. Journal of Air Transport Management 10 (1): 33-39.

Barret S (2000) Airport competition in the deregulated European aviation market. Journal of Air Transport Management 6 (1): 13-27.

Berry S, Carnall M, Spiller P (1996) Airline hubs: costs, markups and the implications of customer heterogeneity. NBER Working Paper 5561: 1-38.

Borenstein S (1989) Hubs and high fares: dominance and market power in the U.S airline industry. Rand Journal of Economics 20 (3): 344-365.

Brander JA, Zhang A (1990) A market conduct in the airline industry: An empirical investigation. Rand Journal of Economics 21(4): 567-583.
Brueckner JK, Spiller P (1994) Economies of traffic density in the deregulated airline industry. Journal of Law and Economics 37 (2): 379-415.
Caves DW, Christensen LR, Tretheway MW (1984) Economies of density versus Economies of Scale: Why trunk and locals service airline costs differ. Rand Journal of Economics 15 (4): 471-489.
Commonwealth of Australia (2002) Price regulation of airport services, inquiry report by the Productivity Commission.
Dresner M, Tretheway MW (1992) Modelling and testing the effect of market structure on price. The case of International Air transport. Journal of Transport Economics and Policy 26 (2): 171-183.
Dresner M, Windle R, Yao Y (2002) Airport barriers to entry in the U.S. Journal of Transport Economics and Policy 36 (3): 389-405.
Doganis R (1992) The airport business. Routledge, London.
European Commission DG-TREN (2002a) Study on competition between airports and the application of state aid rules. Final report, Volumes I and II.
European Commission DG-TREN (2002b) White paper: European transport policy for 2010: time to decide. COM (2001) 0370.
Evans WN, Kessides I (1993) Localized market power in the U.S. airline industry. The Review of Economics and Statistics 75 (1): 66-75.
Federal Aviation Administration (1999) Airport business practices and their impact on airline competition. FAA/OST Task Force Study.
Lijesen MG, Rietveld P, Nijkamp P (2001) Hub premiums in European civil aviation. Transport Policy 8: 193-199.
Maldoom D (2003) Auction capacity at airports. Utilities Policy 11 (1), 47-51.
Marín PL (1995) Competition in European Aviation: Pricing policy and market structure. Journal of Industrial Economics 43 (2): 141-159.
Morrison S, Winston C (1989) Enhancing the performance of the deregulated air transportation system. Brooking Papers: Microeconomics 1: 61-112.
NERA (2004) Study to assess the effects of different slot allocation schemes. A final report for the European Commission. DG TREN.
OEDC (1998) Competition policy and international airport services. DAFFE/CLP98(3).
Oum TH, Zhang A, Zhang Y (2004) Alternative forms of economic regulation and their efficiency implications for airports. Journal of Transports Economic and Policy, 38 (2): 217-246.
Oum TH, Zhang A, Zhang Y (1993) Interfirm rivalry and firm-specific price elasticities in deregulated airline markets. Journal of Transports Economic and Policy 27 (2): 171-192.
Roller LH, Sickles RC (2000) Capacity and product market competition: measuring market power in a ·puppy-dog· industry. International Journal of Industrial Organization 18 (6), 845-865.
Starkie D (2002) Airport regulation and competition. Journal of Air Transport Management 8 (1): 63-72.
Tretheway M, Oum TH (1992) Airline economics: Foundations for Strategy and Policy. The Centre for Transportation Studies (University of British Columbia), Vancouver.

Williams, G (2003) Airline competition: Deregulation's mixed legacy. Ashgate, London.
Zhang, A. and Zhang, Y (1997) Concession revenue and optimal airport pricing. Transportation Research-E 33(4), 287-296.

12 Dynamising Economic Impact Studies: the Case of the Port of Seville

José I. Castillo
University of Seville (Spain)

Lourdes López-Valpuesta
University of Seville (Spain)

María-José Aracil
University of Seville (Spain)

12.1 Introduction

One of the structural weaknesses of Economic Impact studies that rely on the Leontief Input-Output methodology resides in its static character. This limitation prevents us from forecasting the results of these studies, and also obliges us to update them periodically if what we want is to analyse the evolution of the most representative variables.

Moreover, Input-Output methodology has been the resource most widely used to elaborate economic impact studies on port infrastructure in Spain during the last 10 years (Consultrans and Centro de Estudios Económicos Fundación Tomillo (1998) for Port of Barcelona and Port of Tarragona; Martínez et al (1999) for Ports of Santa Cruz de Tenerife; Castillo et al. (2000) for Port of Ceuta; Coto et al. (2001) for Port of Santander; Castillo (coord.) (2001) for Port Bahía de Algeciras).

This paper proposes a potential way to avoid this problem, by linking the Input-Output methodology to the System Dynamics Simulation supported on econometric estimations of certain of the model variables.

Both methodologies together allow us to simulate the evolution of the economic impact and the economic variables related to port activity in the province of Seville, in a 10-year time span.

System dynamics is one approach to modelling the dynamics of population, ecological and economic systems. Systems dynamics was founded in the early 1960s by Jay W. Forrester of The Massachusetts Institute of Technology (MIT). What makes system dynamics different from other approaches to studying complex systems is the use of feedback.

Dynamic simulation models are interesting auxiliary tools to analyse regional economic behaviour, as much for their merely descriptive approach as for their normative one. Studying regional economies requires a method of investigation that can not only interpret complex dynamic processes, but also supports an interdisciplinary vision of the reality in question. Of the techniques available for the construction of simulation models of regional economies, J. W. Forrester System Dynamics has a preferred place (Martínez and Requena 1986).

The first regional model elaborated with Systems Dynamics as a basic tool concerned the Susquehanna river basin (Hamilton et al 1969). It described interactions between the demographic, industrial and hydrologic sectors of the region surrounding the Susquehanna river. Taking their cue from this model, which together with Forrester's Urban Dynamics model (Forrester 1961, 1969a, 1969b) represented a new method of regional analysis, authors from many countries have applied System Dynamics to regional analysis. It is now accepted as a technique uniting the right features to build models on the regional reality.

In this paper we have tried to go a step further and link both methodologies, Economic Impact and System Dynamics, in the belief that the advantages of the latter can overcome the staticity problems of the former. The System Dynamics characteristics that convinced us of its usefulness as a tool, especially for local-regional analysis, can be summarized as follows (Aracil 1982, 1986):

1. Helps to adopt a systemic perspective. In contrast to the reductionist perspective, where the whole is just the sum of the parts, it offers a holistic vision.
2. Offers a simple graphical model structure.
3. The model structure, which is not predetermined, rests upon the modeller's skills and experience.
4. It leaves room for specialist opinions as well as scientific laws.
5. Allows for partial, incomplete states of knowledge regarding the facts to be modelled and takes close account of expert opinions on the same.
6. Helps to explain how the system reacts to changes.
7. Allows for long-run trend forecasting.

Despite the benefits of the System Dynamics approach, the resulting estimates have to be interpreted with care, since much of the information factored into the model, which is most often incomplete, comes from the expert view on the facts, which may be biased by value judgments.

In other words, models are to be taken with a grain of salt. Beside, models are not definitive but, on the contrary, can be continually upgraded as more and better information becomes available on the behaviour of the system.

The System Dynamics model we have elaborated simulates the decision-making process of vessels carrying merchandise whose final destination is the province of Seville and which can choose to berth at the Port of Seville or some other competing ports. In this way, a forecast is obtained of Port of Seville traffic, highlighting how public investment influences this decision via improvements in the Port of Seville's infrastructure and thereby a reduction in its relative costs. These improvements are necessary, since Seville's is an inland port with difficult access.

The main problem to bear in mind relates to this differential characteristic of the Port of Seville. Entrance to the port is conditioned by the estuary and by the size of the lock that regulates the water level in the port's commercial area – the depth of the estuary waters and the length and width of the lock impose significant size limitations on the vessels that can call at the Port of Seville. The sources for financing investments would basically be European Funds (external financing), the sale of obsolete Port of Seville land, and internal financing (profit). These resources would allow the Port of Seville to gain competitiveness and prevent traffic deviation to competing ports, mainly Huelva and the Bay of Cadiz[1].

For impact results, we have based ourselves on the two studies available on the impact of the Port of Seville on the economy of Seville province, (López-Valpuesta and Castillo 2001; Castillo et al 2003), written by the authors.

The paper is organised as follows: this introductory section is followed by Section 12.2 describing the System Dynamics model of the Port of Seville. Section 12.3 shows the main economic impact results. Section 12.4 links the main employment impact results to the simulation model. Section 12.5 is devoted to a sensitivity analysis of the model, and conclusions are set forth in Section 12.6. Finally, model equations and a graphic overview are included in the Appendix.

12.2 System Dynamics Model of the Port of Seville[2]

The model describes the whole process from the moment that the Port of Seville is chosen for the goods to be unloaded to the moment that the vessel leaves the port, with special consideration to the limitations of the Port of Seville infrastructure. The Port's lack of capacity means that a significant percentage of Andalusian port traffic, which might consider Seville as a discharge port, ends up in some other competing port[3].

The origin of the port's activity is its traffic, TR (in thousands tons), which we have calculated as a linear regression (with a correction error term to avoid autocorrelation problems and to obtain a long-run relation between the variables) with respect to province GDP[4] (constant prices):

$$\nabla TR_t = \underset{(0.044)}{0.282}\ \nabla GDP_t - \underset{(0.221)}{1.130}\ (TR_{t-1} + \underset{(165.202)}{409.739} - \underset{(0.010)}{0.211}\ GDP_{t-1})$$

[1] We have assumed that the infrastructure of competing ports remains constant during the period in question.

[2] The model has been elaborated into one System Dynamics computer simulation environment. Specifically, we have used VensimDSS.

[3] We have only considered the entrance traffic originated by the Port of Seville hinterland, which we take to be the province of Seville.

[4] We use provincial GDP as a demand indicator for the Seville hinterland. We base this relation on International Trade Theory in which imports are a function of the income of the importing region.

n = 14, $R^2 = .869$, $\overline{R}^2 = .830$

The System Dynamics model has been structured into three parts, which basically coincide with the functional phases of harbour activity:

A) Port of Seville entrance decision. The variables LUW (Length Units waiting to berth at the Port of Seville) and LUB (Length Units of ships berthing at the Port of Seville per year) are analysed in this initial phase.

B) Dockage at Port of Seville docks, in which the variable analysed is LUD (Length Units berthed at Port of Seville docks at any given time).

C) Unloading of goods in Port of Seville warehouses and merchandise flow to market. In this last phase the variable GW is analysed (volume of goods in warehouses).

As we said above, the model is completed with an analysis of how public investment could impact on port functioning. This investment involves the following two projects:

D) Building a new lock and deepening the draught, which would enable larger vessels to access the Port of Seville. The influence of these investments on Port of Seville activity is analysed through the variable GTMPS (mean size in GT of vessels berthing at the Port of Seville[5]).

E) Building new docks, so a greater number of vessels call at the Port of Seville. This investment is analysed by means of the variable MDC (Maximum dock capacity at the Port of Seville[6]).

We now go on to describe and define each of the aforementioned model phases, analysing the level variables implied and how they interrelate:

A) Port of Seville entrance decision.

LUW. This variable shows the number of vessels (in length units) waiting to berth at the Port of Seville per year. It is defined as the difference between the rate of vessels (in length units) choosing to unload in the Port of Seville in each period (CHPSR) and dock entry frequency (EF).

This variable is related to dock capacity because, the Port of Seville being an inland port with limited capacity, there tend to be delays between vessels getting to the lock and finally berthing at the docks. LUW includes vessels that are on their way to berth but haven't yet reached the dock. Dock saturation problems may cause delays and thus push up global transport costs, although in this first version of the model we have not introduced those costs.

$$LUW = \int_0^{10} \left(CHPSR(t) - EF(t) \right) dt$$

[5] The bulk vessel has been chosen as the standard because of its high relative weight in total Port of Seville traffic.

[6] We have considered neither dock specialization nor each dock's specific facilities for distributing merchandise.

CHPSR represents the rate of vessels that choose Port of Seville for discharging in each period. We have stripped out the captive traffic (PSCT) that would berth at Seville in any case from global Port of Seville traffic. The remainder, termed potential traffic (PSPT), is the only part affected by the Port of Seville entrance decision, because it may choose between berthing at Seville and berthing at some other port. The traffic is initially expressed in tons, so it has been necessary to change it into length units (LU) by means of the TONUL ratio[7].

PSCT is defined as a function of the captive traffic entrance rate (CTER) and the rate of traffic in tons (TRAUX). PSPT is defined as residual, subtracting the captive traffic (PSCT) from the flow of traffic in tons (TRAUX).

CTER is a constant that shows the Port of Seville captive traffic rate, and has been calculated with reference to previous analyses by the Port Authority of Seville (Autoridad Portuaria de Sevilla 1999).

ED represents the Port of Seville entrance decision. It is a key variable because it determines the higher or lower number of vessels - represented by higher or lower traffic - that choose the Port of Seville for introducing their merchandise into Seville province. We have assumed that this decision is based on a comparison of the tariffs and costs of the Port of Seville with those of the competing port; only Huelva in this version.

1) In the event that berthing costs at the Port of Seville (PSC) are lower than those at the Port of Huelva, (PHC), the Port of Seville is chosen.
2) In other cases, the decision depends on the entrance rate (ER), defined as an inverse relation between the difference in costs of the Port of Seville vs the Port of Huelva (PCD), and the proportion of vessels that choose Seville. The function determines the proportion of length units that might choose the Port of Seville, despite its costs being higher than those of the Port of Huelva.

PSC represents the costs to potential traffic of berthing at the Port of Seville and is defined as a function of TRIPS and PSCGTM. TRIPS stands for the mean number of vessels that would berth at the Port of Seville - apart from captive traffic - considering the mean size of vessels (in GT) allowed to berth there at any given moment. So TRIPS is defined as a function of the mean GT of the Port of Seville (GTMPS).

PHC is equivalent to PSC for the Port of Huelva - costs to potential traffic of berthing at the Port of Huelva – and is defined in a similar way, TRIPH being equivalent to TRIPS.

PSCGTM and PHCGTM represent the cost structure of an average-size vessel at the Port of Seville and the Port of Huelva respectively[8]. They include the following items:

---

[7] The definition of CHPSR is similar to that of LUER – length units entrance rate – as described later in the text. This is because the entrance flow of vessels per year is similar to those that choose the Port of Seville as their berthing port.

[8] The vessel cost structures of the Port of Seville and the Port of Huelva have been calculated according to the published tariffs of these institutions, supplemented by information available from the Autoridad Portuaria de Sevilla (1995).

1. Tariffs[9]: of all tariffs charged by Port Authorities (T-0 Maritime Navigation, T-1 Vessels, T-2 Passage, T-3 Cargo, T-4, Fresh Fishery, T-5 Sport and Leisure Craft, T-6 Gantry Cranes, T-7 Storage, T-8 Supplies and T-9 Various Services) we have factored T-0, T-1 and T-3, because they are the most directly linked to vessel and merchandise traffic. In the case of the Port of Seville, tariff T-9.2 (Vessels mooring at the lock) has also been considered.
2. Indirect Services: vessels pilotage and mooring.
3. Stowing and unstowing costs.
4. Freight.
5. Land transport from Huelva to Seville, in the case of the Port of Huelva alone.

PSCGTM is based on the vessel's size - in GT- since some of the costs are not fixed but vary according to this parameter. If bigger vessels could berth at the Port of Seville, the costs associated to merchandise transport would be smaller.

The determination of pilotage and moorage costs (PILSE, MOORSE for Port of Seville and PILHU and MOORHU for Huelva), as well as Seville freight costs (FREIGSE), is also related to the vessel's size – in GT. So we have had to define them by relating each of these costs to the GT of the vessels calling at each port. Stowing costs (STOWSE and STOWHU) are set at a fixed amount per ton.

An additional term is factored (TCHTOS) in the case of the Port of Huelva to reflect the merchandise transport costs from Huelva to Seville, because we confine ourselves here to merchandise whose final destination is the province of Seville. This cost has also been set at a fixed amount of €3.005 per ton transported (Autoridad Portuaria de Sevilla 1995).

The vessel freight for Huelva has been defined as a function of Seville's, with the tonnage data consulted (Autoridad Portuaria de Sevilla 1995) showing an approximately 4.41% difference in Huelva's favour.

Each port competes to attract the potential traffic. The cost of the potential traffic is determined by comparing the relative costs of the Port of Seville and the Port of Huelva, PSCGTM and PHCGTM. The utility of these variables resides in their comparability, so it is possible to determine the most competitive port and, consequently, the one that will likely be chosen for calling at and for merchandise unloading.

[9] Neither discounts nor special tariff reductions have been considered.

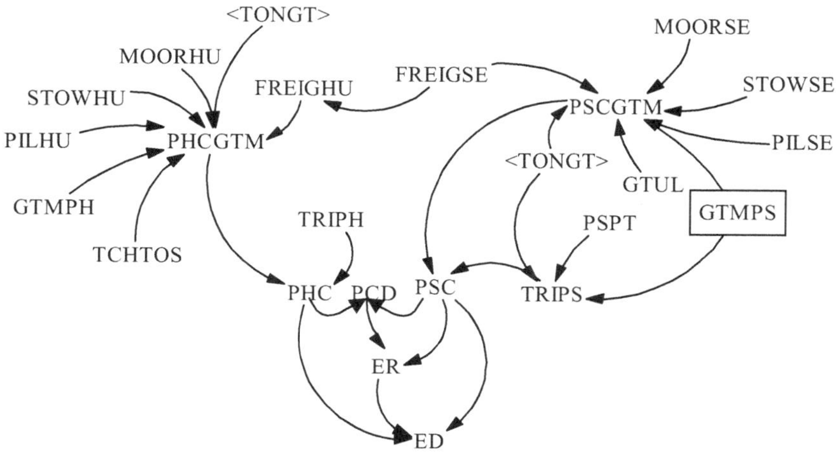

Fig. 12.1. ED and ER flow diagram

LUW is defined as the difference between CHPSR and EF. Having already defined CHPSR, we will now focus on EF. This variable, which represents dock entrance frequency, is based on dock capacity (MDC) relative to the vessels (in length units) berthed at each given moment. Hence:

1. If the dock is busy, that is to say, if the vessels berthed at the dock - in length unit (LUD) - occupy the whole dock capacity (MDC), the entrance frequency is necessarily 0.
2. Conversely, if there are metres of dock available, the entrance rate is determined by REF - real entrance frequency.

$$EF = \begin{cases} 0 & \text{if} \quad LUD = MDC \\ REF & \text{if no} \quad LUD = MDC \end{cases}$$

REF - real entrance frequency - is obtained by applying the rate of entrance (ERT) to the minimum between the vessels waiting (LUW) and the dock space available. The dock space available is calculated as the difference between maximum dock capacity (MDC) and the vessels berthed at dock (LUD).

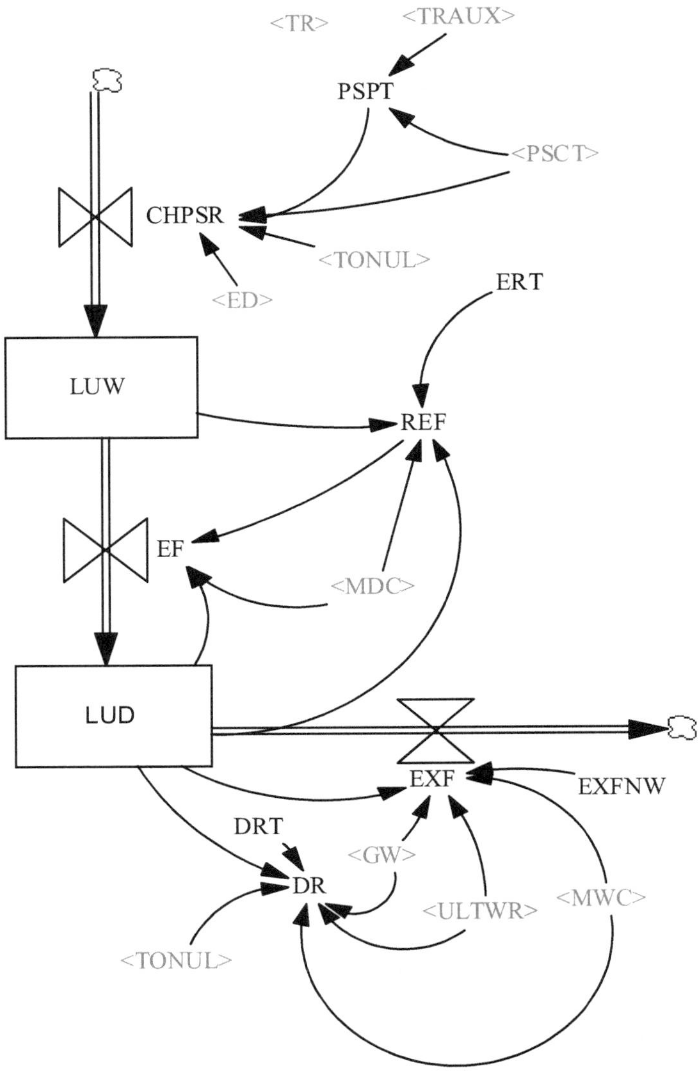

Fig. 12.2. LUW and LUD flow diagram

LUB is a variable defined with the aim of annualising the rate of vessels berthing at the Port of Seville each year, so we can calculate the tariff income obtained by the Port Authority of Seville and its corresponding profit. LUB is defined as the difference between the rate of vessels (length units) berthing in each period with respect to that of the former period (LUER and LUER1, respectively).

$$LUB = 57 + \int_{0}^{10} (LUER(t) - LUER(t-1)dt)$$

where LUER is the length units' entrance rate and it is similar to CHPSR defined above.

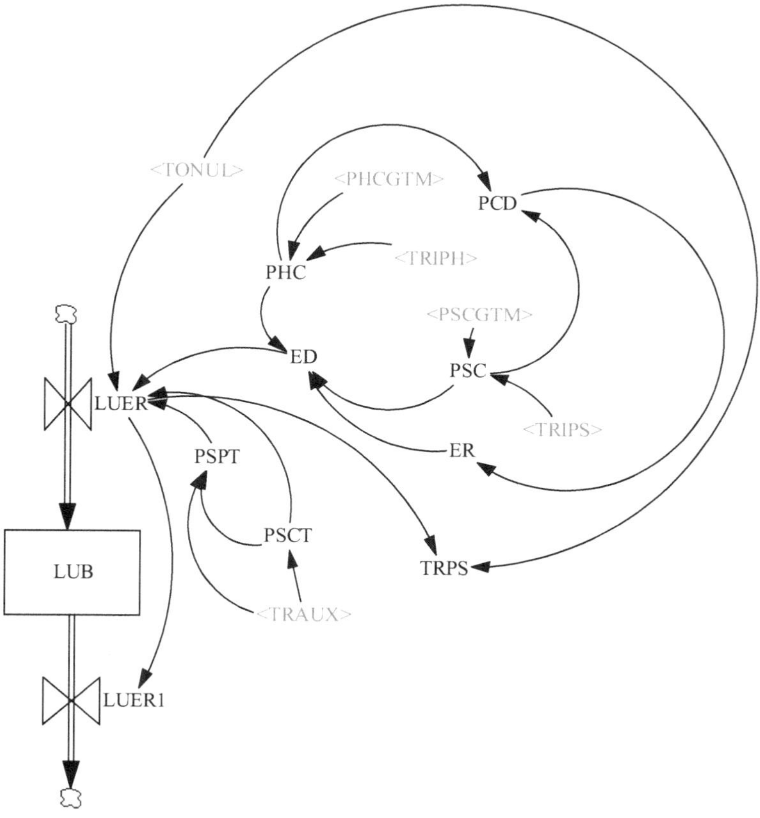

Fig. 12.3. LUB flow diagram

B) Dockage at Port of Seville docks

LUD represents the part of the Port of Seville dock which is busy at any given time. It is defined as the difference between entrance frequency (EF) and exit frequency (EXF), and depends mainly on dock capacity, MDC.

$$LUD = \int_{0}^{10} \left(EF(t) - EXF(t)\right)dt$$

Entrance frequency (EF) has already been defined in the previous section. Exit frequency (EXF) is defined as a function of maximum warehouse capacity, MWC[10]. Two alternative options may be used:

1) If the total warehouse capacity (GW) is occupied by discharged merchandise, those vessels wishing to unload their merchandise in the Port of Seville warehouses will not be able to, so will not leave the Port. However this is not the situation of those vessels whose merchandise is to be unloaded directly onto trucks or into external warehouses. The exit frequency of these vessels is determined by EXFNW (exit frequency of vessels not discharging at the Port of Seville's own warehouses) and their percentage share in total traffic by ULTWR.
2) Conversely, if there is warehouse room available, and assuming the merchandise discharging rate to be equivalent to the vessel exit rate from the Port of Seville, we also have to factor discharging flow (DR), which is defined as the minimum between the warehouse room available (MWC - GW) and the discharged merchandise from vessels whose cargo goes to Port of Seville warehouses, according to the discharging rate DRT.

$$\mathrm{EXF} = \begin{cases} \mathrm{EXFNW(1-ULTWR)LUD} & \text{if} \quad \mathrm{MWC = GW} \\ \mathrm{DR + EXFNW(1-ULTWR)LUD} & \text{if no} \quad \mathrm{MWC = GW} \end{cases}$$

C) Unloading of goods in Port of Seville warehouses and merchandise flow to market.

GW represents the level of occupancy of the Port of Seville warehouses devoted to storing merchandise from vessels. All the ships considered enter the Port of Seville to discharge merchandise into either Port of Seville or third-party warehouses, or else directly onto lorries for transport to the final destination. This variable indicates how warehouse capacities might influence Port of Seville traffic due to the impossibility of ships discharging if warehouses are busy. This being so, ships at the Port would be unable to leave, meaning no new ships could enter. In this version, however, we are not considering this to be the case.

GW is defined as the difference between the entrance rate and the exit to market rate, whose analytical expression would be:

[10] Representing the capacity of the Port of Seville warehouses in 2000. In the Port Authority of Seville Annual Report ("Memoria anual 2001"), this capacity is expressed in m2 so we have changed it into tons via the ratio 3 tons – 1 m2, provided by the Port Authority of Seville staff.

$$GW = \int_{0}^{10} (GEWR(t) - GME(t))dt$$

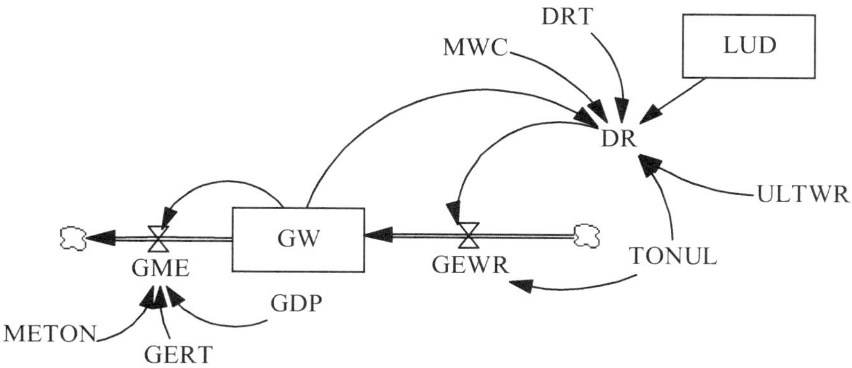

Fig. 12.4. GW flow diagram

GEWR is the rate of merchandise entrance to warehouses and can be taken as equivalent to DR, the discharge flow of vessels unloading at the Port of Seville warehouse. Length units must be converted to tons because of the different units of measurement involved.

GME represents the outflow of merchandise to the market. It has been defined such that merchandise leaves the warehouses at an exit rate (GERT) which depends on market demand at each given moment. In the present version of the model we have assumed this flow to be continuous.

D) Building a new lock and deepening the draught.

GTMPS represents the mean GT of vessels calling at the Port of Seville. GTMPS is a level variable that increases with investments via GTIPSI and does not decrease.

GTMPH stands for the mean size - in GT- of vessels calling at the Port of Huelva. In this port it has a fixed value.

GTMPS is defined as follows:

$$GTMPS = 4500 + \int_{0}^{10} GTIPSI(t)dt$$

We can calculate GTIPSI for two different scenarios:

1) If there is no Public Investment (PI), the size of the vessels that can call at the Port of Seville will not increase, so GTIPSI will be 0.

$$GTMPS = 4500 + \int_0^{10} GTIPSI(t)dt = 4500 \quad \text{if } PI = 0$$

2) Conversely, GTIPSI would be arrived at by multiplying public investment (PI) by the percentage devoted to draughting the lock, that is, the funds spent to increase the size of ship IGTR. It will also depend on the increase in GT admitted at the Port of Seville per monetary unit (million euro) invested (GTIUI). Finally, it also depends on the execution rate (ERI).

$$GTMPS = 4500 + \int_0^{10} GTIPSI(t)dt = 4500 +$$

$$+ \int_0^{10} \left(\left(PI(t) \times IGTR \times GTIUI \right) \times ERI \right) dt$$

$$\text{if no} \quad PI = 0$$

We calculate PI as an aggregate of 3 items: external investment (EXINV), the useful profit of the Port Authority of Seville (UP) weighted by the rate of invested profit (PIR), and Port Authority land sales (LS).

We calculate EXINV assuming an initial 0 (EXINVini = 0) with later contributions distributed as follows[11]:

- o 16 million euro in 2004
- o 17 million euro in 2005
- o 16 million euro in 2006
- o 14 million euro in 2007

In order to stop negative profits interfering in profit P calculation, we introduce the variable UP such that P having a negative value, UP is 0 and P being positive, UP equals P. P represents Port of Seville profit, so is calculated in terms of the difference between cost and income[12].

These are the three possible sources of income:

a) Tariff income (TEUL) which depends on the traffic calling at the Port of Seville. TEUL is calculated by aggregating income per length unit from T-0, T-1, T-9.2 and T-3 tariffs.
b) Income from storage tariff T-7 (TW) has been considered a constant.
c) PSAOI includes other Port Authority of Seville income.

[11] Data provided by Port Authority of Seville staff.

[12] For the sake of simplicity, profit has been calculated as the difference between income (port services - T-0, T-1, T-9.2, T-3 and T-7 tariffs - and concession fees and administrative authorizations) and operating expenses. Amounts received from/given to the Contribution Fund have not been considered.

PSAC represents the costs borne by the Port Authority of Seville, which include total operating expenses[13].

We have considered that non-tariff income and Port of Seville costs increase from their initial values, Iini and Cini, according to OIGR and CGR rates.
Expected land sales of the Port Authority of Seville have the following yearly distribution:

- 5 million euro in 2003
- 10 million euro in 2004
- 30 million euro in 2005
- 28 million euro in 2006
- 18 million euro in 2007

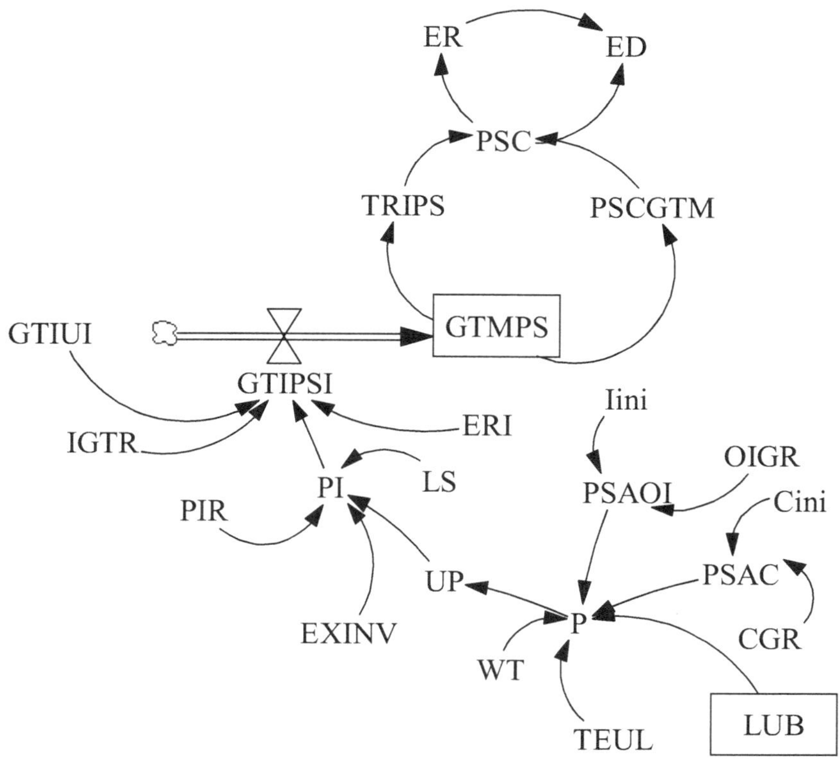

Fig. 12.5. GTMPS flow diagram

[13] Income and costs forecasts as provided by the Port Authority of Seville (2003).

E) Building new docks.

MDC is the maximum dock capacity, in length units. This variable shows how many length units are available for berthing. Its significance lies in that it can potentially limit the number of vessels that may berth, imposing a certain waiting time (**LUW**). This may even be one of the reasons why some vessels would not choose the Port of Seville as a berthing port. We have assumed that maximum dock capacity (MDC) increases from its initial level[14] along with the investment made (via DIPSI, dock capacity added) and does not decrease.

$$MDC = IDC + \int_{0}^{10} DIPSI(t)dt$$

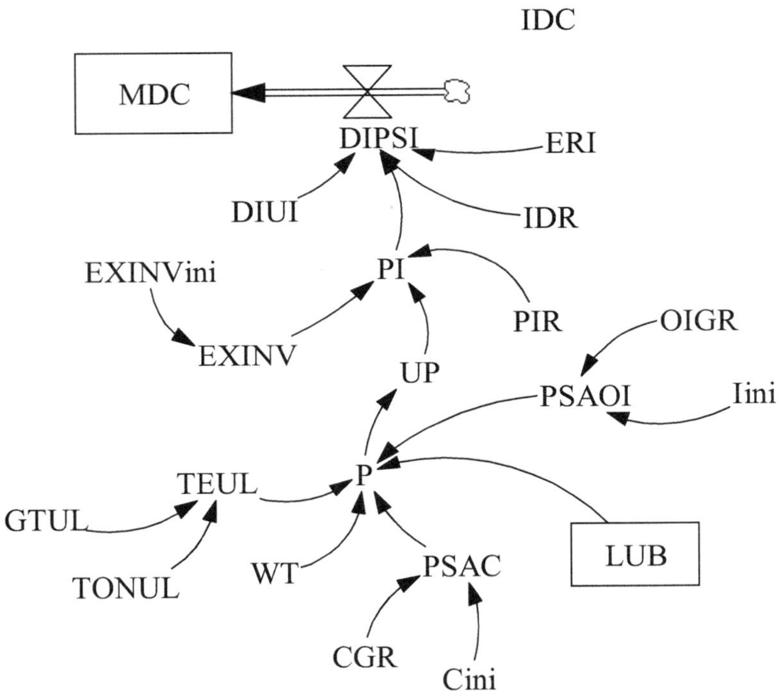

Fig. 12.6. MDC flow diagram

[14] Present dock capacity includes all the public docks in the commercial area.

DIPSI, that is, the dock capacity increase due to investments, has been defined as follows:

1) If there is no public investment (PI = 0), DIPSI will also be 0, that is, the dock will maintain its present capacity.

$$\mathrm{MDC} = \mathrm{IDC} + \int_0^{10} \mathrm{DIPSI}(t)dt = \mathrm{IDC} \quad \text{if } \mathrm{PI} = 0$$

2) Conversely (PI > 0), DIPSI will depend on the part of the global investment devoted to increasing dock capacity – depending on the dock investment ratio (IDR). We must also factor the growth of dock size per funds invested, DIUI. All of this will depend furthermore on the execution rate (ERI).

$$\mathrm{MDC} = \mathrm{IDC} + \int_0^{10} \mathrm{DIPSI}(t)dt = \mathrm{IDC} +$$

$$+ \int_0^{10} ((\mathrm{PI}(t) \times \mathrm{IDR} \times \mathrm{DIUI}) \times \mathrm{ERI})dt$$

$$\text{if no } \mathrm{PI} = 0$$

12.3 Economic Impact of the Port of Seville on the Province of Seville

The methodology for calculating the Port of Seville's economic impact is based on the Input-Output model. Our analysis is based on the adaptation of this model designed by "Puertos del Estado" for the Spanish Port System by the consulting firm TEMA (1994), applying different variations to this adaptation. The main change is due to the need to convert the last available input-output regional Table (TIOAN-95) into a provincial one, in order to model the indirect and induced effects of port activity.

The following Table shows the main global results of port activity in the province of Seville. There are three different ways to quantify the total impact of a port on its area of influence[15]. We have chosen the one that excludes from the induced effect both the indirect effect generated by the Port Industry and the consumption generated by the wages that the Port Industry generates indirectly. This approach

[15] The first way consists of adding direct, indirect and induced Port Industry and Dependent Industry effects; the second consists of adding direct and induced effects from both industries, but only taking into consideration the indirect effect caused by the Dependent Industry.

to quantifying the total impact appears to provide the best methodological solution to the problem of double accounting, since the Port Industry is only related to the rest of the economy through the Dependent Industry. It is therefore important to eliminate all the indirect impacts generated by the Port Industry (either in the indirect effect, or in part of the induced effect).

Table 12.1. Port of Seville Total Effect (1995 and 2000)

VARIABLE	TOTAL EFFECT 1995	Consumer Price Index 2000/1995	TOTAL EFFECT 1995 (capitalized)	TOTAL EFFECT 2000
STAFF EXPENSES (1)	179,922,350.87	1.13798	204,747,311.11	242,748,215.70
EBITDA (1)	111,823,157.69	1.13798	127,252,065.94	234,903,438.09
TAXES (1)	100,186,841.32	1.13798	114,010,217.57	133,824,838.92
SALES (1)	920,854,075.50	1.13798	1,047,909,806.50	1,619,972,059.86
EMPLOYMENT (2)	9,349.27		9,349.27	12,326.64

(1) Euro
(2) Employees

Taking the employment data for 1995 and 2000 shown in the previous Table, and using province of Seville employment in 1980-2000 as our reference, we have drawn up the Port of Seville employment generation series for the said period. From the total employment generated by port activity, we had to differentiate that attribuTable to Port of Seville entrance traffic. To do so, we calculated the weighting of Port of Seville entrance traffic in total traffic (1980-2000). Employment could then be linked to Port of Seville entrance traffic through a linear regression.

12.4 Dynamising Employment through the Simulation Model

The model described in section 12.2 simulates public investment effects on the functioning of the Port of Seville.

Once public investment effects had been determined, the variable EMP (employment) was introduced into the model with the aim of linking the results obtained from the economic impact study (Table 12.1) to the simulation model, so that we could obtain forecasts for job creation relative to infrastructure investments.

We constructed a linear regression with a correction error term from the employment EMP data obtained in section 12.3, and from entrance traffic to the Port of Seville (in thousands tons). We used the long-run relation between both variables from that linear regression:

$$\underset{}{\nabla EMP_t} = \underset{(0.469)}{2.542}\, \nabla TRPSAUX_t - \underset{(0.285)}{0.620}\, (EMP_{t-1} - \underset{(676.540)}{1775.903} - \underset{(0.354)}{2.288}\, TRPSAUX_{t-1})$$

n = 14, $R^2 = .759$, $\overline{R}^2 = .687$

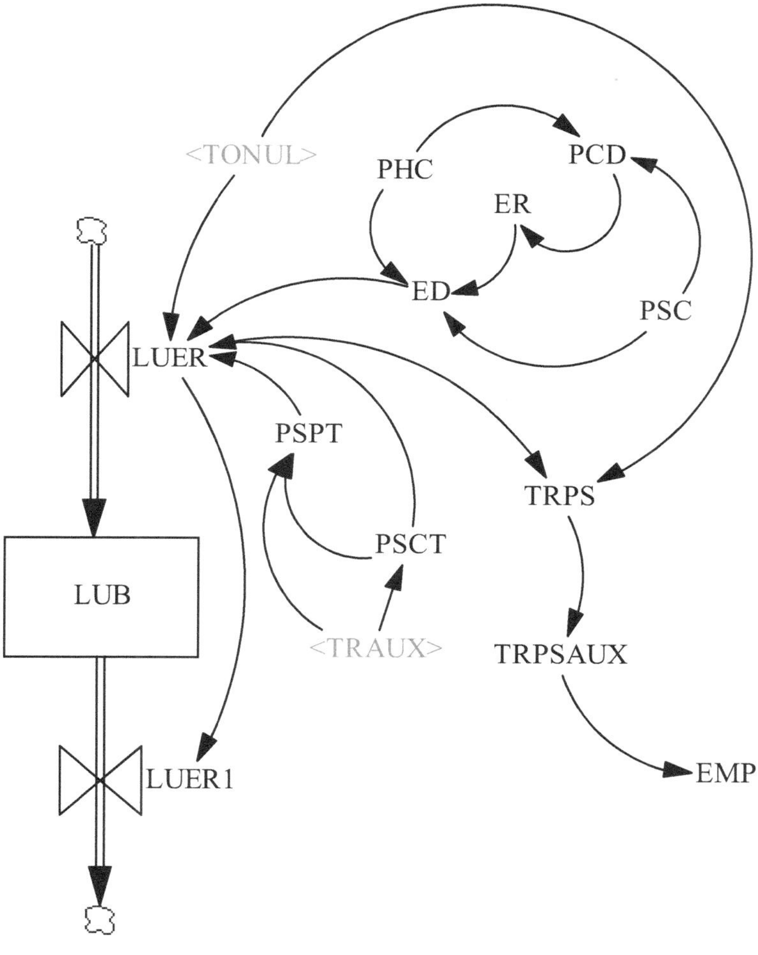

Fig. 12.7. Adding EMP to the LUB flow diagram

12.5 Sensitivity Analysis

System Dynamics has a real advantage over alternative procedures for mathematical modelling in situations where the nature of some of the variables involved makes it difficult to give them specific values. To address this difficulty, System Dynamics models are usually subjected to a sensitivity analysis, that is, running a series of simulations in which the model parameters are changed for each simulation. This can be of great help in testing the robustness of model-based policies.

Table 12.2. Sensitivity Analysis: Results for main parameters

Parameter nominal value	Range	Effect on LUB	Effect on EMP
DIUI = 0.07134	0.0535 to 0.089	None	None
IDC = 2.764	2.073 to 3.455	None	None
IDR= 0.08	0.06 to 0.1	None	None
MWC= 665733	499299 to 832166	None	None
WT= 1	0.75 to 1.25	None	None
METON= 246,76 / 10^6	0.00018507 to 0.00030845	None	None
ULTWR = 0.7	0.525 to 0.875	None	None
OIGR= 0.0812	0.0609 to 0.1015	None	Very weak
LS3= 5	3.75 to 6.25	None	Very weak
C_{ini} = 8.46	6.34 to 10.57	Very weak	Very weak
PIR= 0.8	0.6 to 1	Very weak	Very weak
LS4 = 10	7.5 to 12.5	Very weak	Weak
LS5 = 30	22.5 to 37.5	Weak	Weak
LS6 = 28	21 to 35	Weak	Weak
LS7 =18	13.5 to 22.5	Weak	Weak
LSG (above values)	Above values	Weak	Weak
CGR = 0.0799	0.0599 to 0.0998	Weak	Sensitive
EXINV4 = 16	12 to 20	Weak	Weak
EXINV5= 17	12.75 to 21.25	Weak	Weak
EXINV6= 16	12 to 20	Weak	Weak
EXINV7= 14	10.5 to 17.5	Weak	Weak
EXINVG (above values)	Above values	Weak	Weak
$EXINV_{ini}$= 0	0 to 10	Weak	Sensitive
I_{ini}= 5.51	4.13 to 6.88	Weak	Sensitive
IGTR= 0.92	0.69 to 1.15	Sensitive	Sensitive
GTIUI= 29.06	21.795 to 36.325	Sensitive	Sensitive
TONUL = 50000	37500 to 62500	Quite sensitive	Very weak
CTER = 0.6651	0.498825 to 0.831375	Quite sensitive	Quite sensitive
GTMPH = 15000	11250 to 18750	Quite sensitive	Quite sensitive
GDPGR = 0.03	0 to 0.08	Quite sensitive and Potential Behaviour Change	Quite sensitive and Potential Behaviour Change

Table 12.3. Sensitivity Analysis: Results for secondary parameters

Parameter nominal value	Range	Effect on LUB	Effect on EMP
DRT = 1	0.75 to 1.25	None	None
ERT = 1	0.75 to 1.25	None	None
EXFNW = 1	0.75 to 1.25	None	None
GERT= 1	0.75 to 1.25	None	None
ERI = 1	0.75 to 1.25	Sensitive	Sensitive
TONUL = 50000	37500 to 62500	Quite sensitive	Very weak

This section sets out the sensitivity analysis run on the model we constructed. The main variables we focused on to identify model sensitivity were LUB and EMP. Tables 12.2 and 12.3 show the results of this analysis for main parameters (Table 12.2) and secondary parameters (Table 12.3): the first column shows the parameters we considered, and the second, the fluctuation range set for each parameter[16]. The third and fourth columns show the effects of this parameter value change. We have performed univariate simulations, that is, changing only one parameter at a time, with the exception of external investments and land sales. In these two cases, we have performed both multivariate and univariate simulations. The reason is that we believed it could be more interesting to analyse the effect of changing all EXINV variables at once, and also all LS (Land Sale) variables. We present the results in the Table as EXINVG and LSG.

According to Table 12.2, parameters can be roughly classified into three main groups: parameters to which the model shows no sensitivity; parameters to which it shows some sensitivity; parameters to which it displays a high sensitivity.

The first group is formed by parameters whose changes of value are not relevant for the behaviour of the model, such as DRT, ERT or DIC. For example, the result of the sensitivity analysis for the parameter DIC is shown in Figure 12.8, where we can see that EMP follows the same trajectory for all DIC values within the range considered. Therefore, we conclude that variations in the value of DIC have no effect on model behaviour.

The second group is formed by parameters that have some effect on model behaviour, but whose effect is not that relevant. Examples would be CGR or GTIUI. In Figure 12.9 we can see a narrow range of variability.

The third group is formed by parameters to which the model displays a high sensitivity. There is a special case in this third group, which is parameter GDPGR. In this case, the sensitivity analysis detects qualitative changes in behaviour. Figure 12.10 shows the occurrence of a qualitative change, clearly evidenced in the two different long-term conducts; growth and stabilisation. In this Figure, EMP alters when we change the value of GDPGR and, as stated, we can observe two different behaviour modes.

---

[16] We have estimated that they vary 25% from their nominal value (up and down).

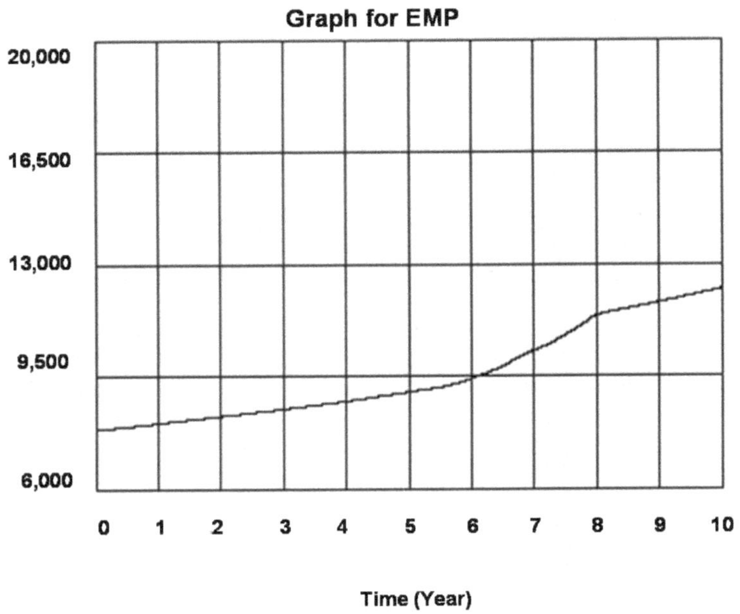

Fig. 12.8. Sensitivity analysis of variable EMP when parameter DIC is changed

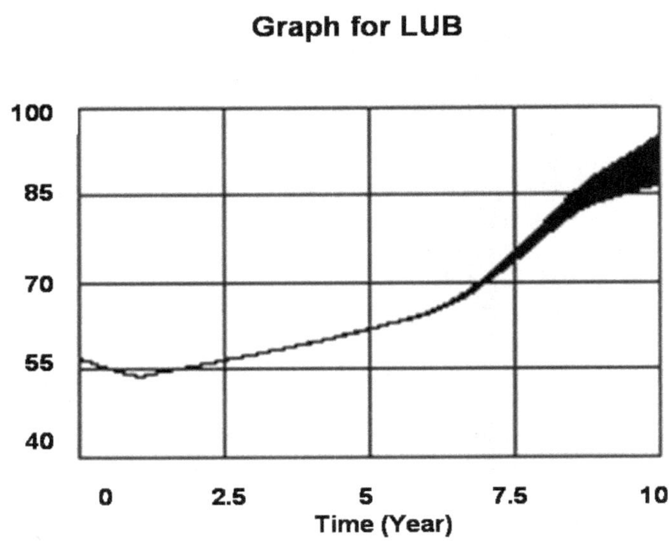

Fig. 12.9. Sensitivity analysis of variable LUB when parameter CGR is changed

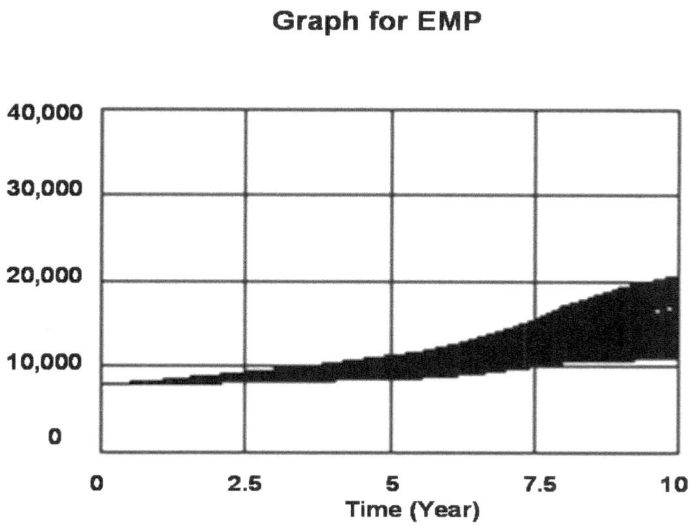

Fig. 12.10. Sensitivity analysis of variable EMP when parameter GDPGR is changed

12.6 Main Results and Conclusions

Simulating the model described in the previous sections allows us to obtain conclusions on some of the most relevant aspects related to the present and future of the Port of Seville. However, it should be noted that this is a first approach to a future global model of the Port of Seville - and for this reason simplifying assumptions have been adopted. Nevertheless, they do not weaken the result because our goal is to indicate the qualitative character of the model's behaviour, which shows a traffic increase.

Figures 12.11 to 12.15 show a foreseeable future of the port in which infrastructure reforms have been carried out in comparison to what would happen if no public investments were forthcoming.

Figure 12.11 a) shows the tendency of the traffic that would annually berth at the Port of Seville assuming no public investment occurs. As we can see, it does not reach 85 million length units (about 4250000 thousand tons of entrance traffic). In contrast, investments on the draught of the river go ahead as planned, the number of million length units that would berth at the port would reach 90 million (about 4500000 thousand tons of entrance traffic). In this last case, we can see that traffic growth is not so linear as it was with no investment, and intensifies as of the seventh year from the construction of improvement works on the Port of Seville entrance. This investment would give rise to the Port of Seville average vessel size increase shown in Figure 12.12.

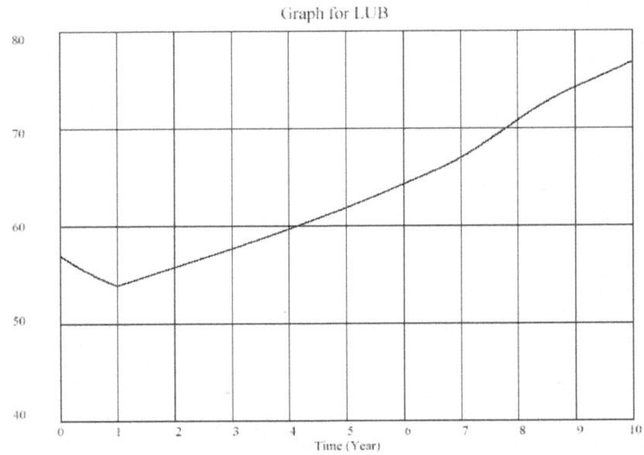

a) LUB evolution with no public investment

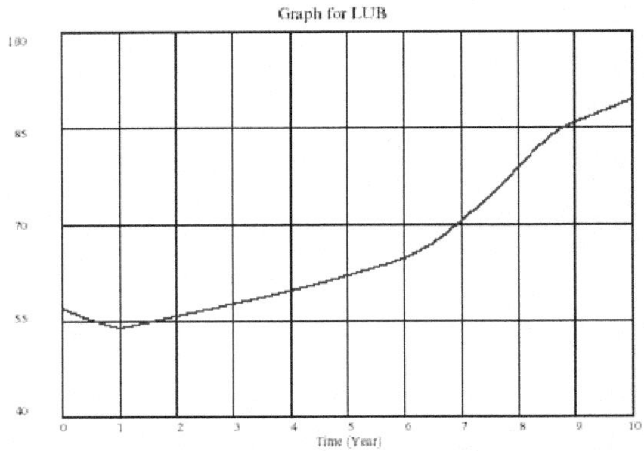

b) LUB evolution if planned public investment occurs.

Fig. 12.11. Port of Seville traffic (LU) evolution

We have also included the potential increase in the number of docks, which would allow more vessels to berth, therefore increasing the Port of Seville's profits. This increase is shown in Figure 12.13.

The possibility of admitting larger vessels would bring down relative costs, which would enhance the competitiveness of the Port of Seville. This competitiveness gain is even more important if we consider the Port of Seville's geographic location, surrounded by three ports of general interest, Huelva, Bay of Cadiz and Bay of Algeciras, within a radius of approximately 300 kilometres.

In this version of the model, this would lead to an increase in the percentage of traffic (in terms of potential Port of Seville traffic) that would choose the Port of Seville as a berthing port. The evolution of this percentage is shown in Figure 12.14.

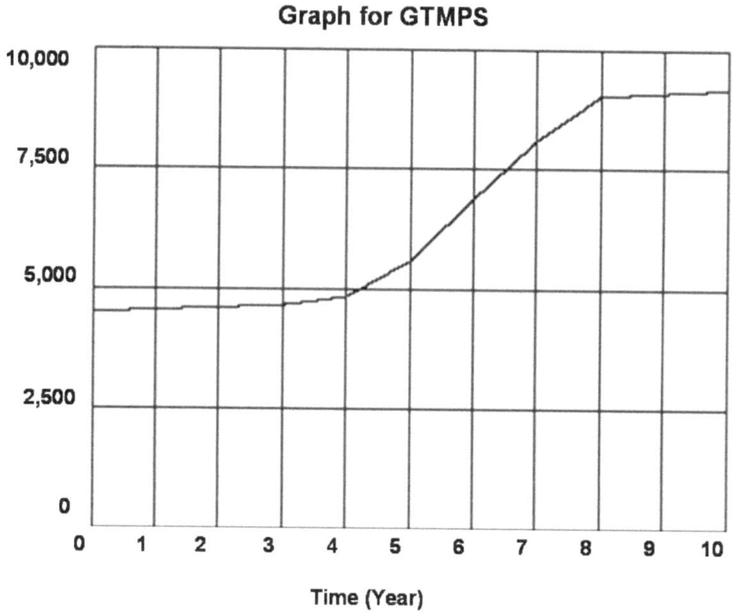

Fig. 12.12. Evolution of Port of Seville average GT

The positive impact on Port of Seville activity shown in previous Figures also has a marked influence on employment creation. Thus, according to Figure 12.15 b), in ten years time, the number of jobs created by Port of Seville activity - considering the increase in entrance traffic as a result of public harbour infrastructure investment - would sum about 12,500 in the province of Seville. If no investment occurred, the employment generated would be as shown in Figure 12.15 a).

Independently of the nominal values obtained, the most significant aspect of this analysis involves the introduction of methodological solutions to dynamise static Economic Impact studies based on the Leontief Input-Output model.

The proposed solution can be applied to any of the numerous Economic Impact studies on transport infrastructure conducted in Spain in the last fifteen years.

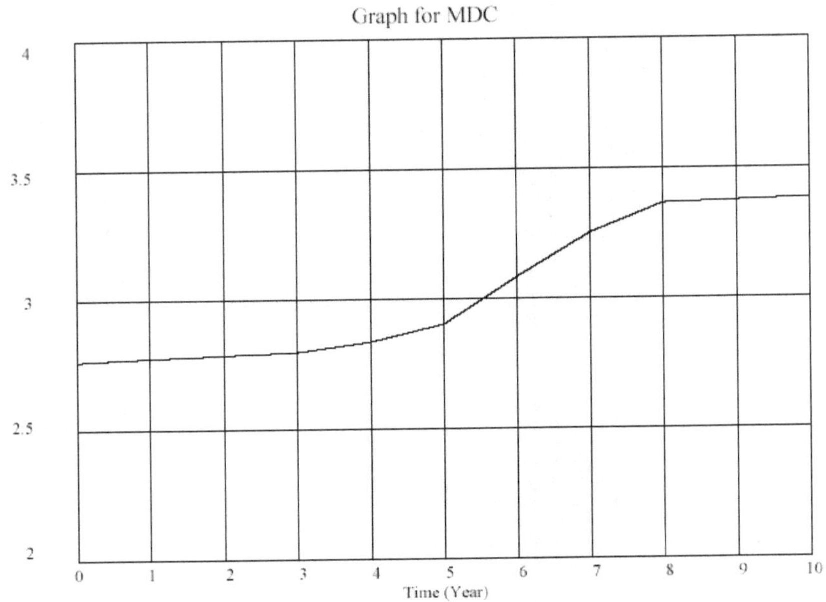

a) MDC evolution with no public investment

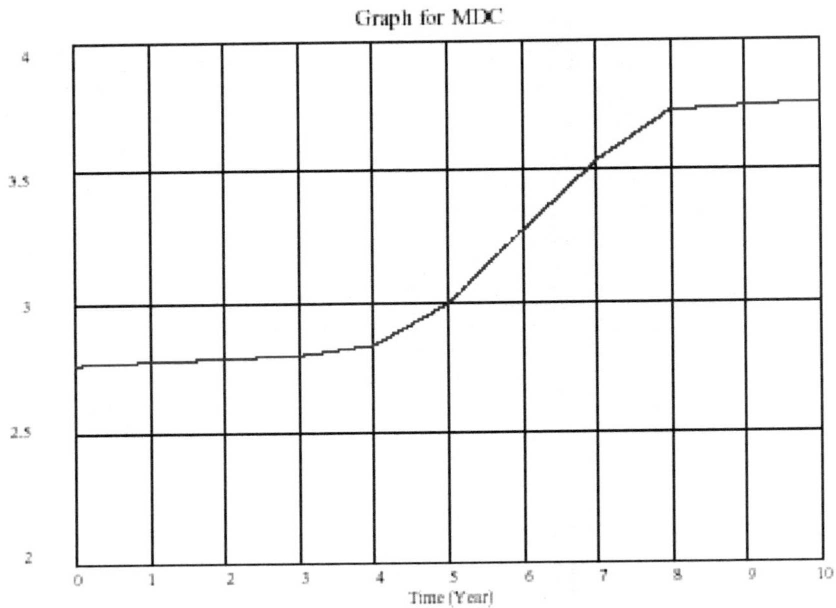

b) MDC evolution if planned public investment occurs

Fig. 12.13. Port of Seville dock capacity evolution (LU)

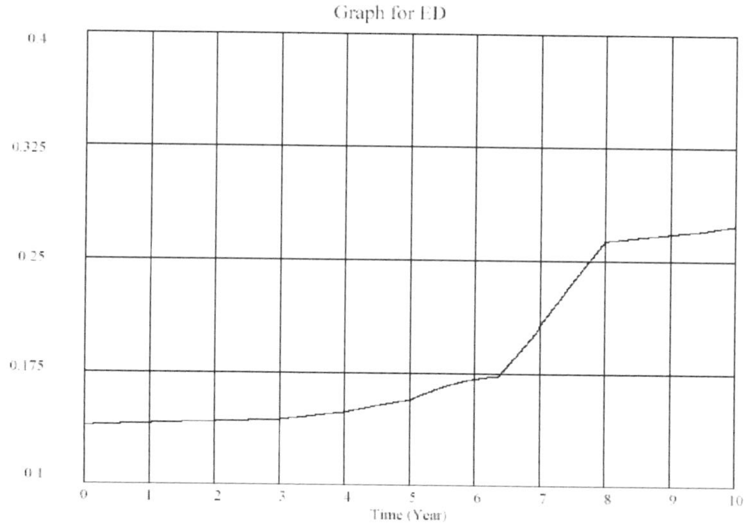

a) ED evolution with no public investment

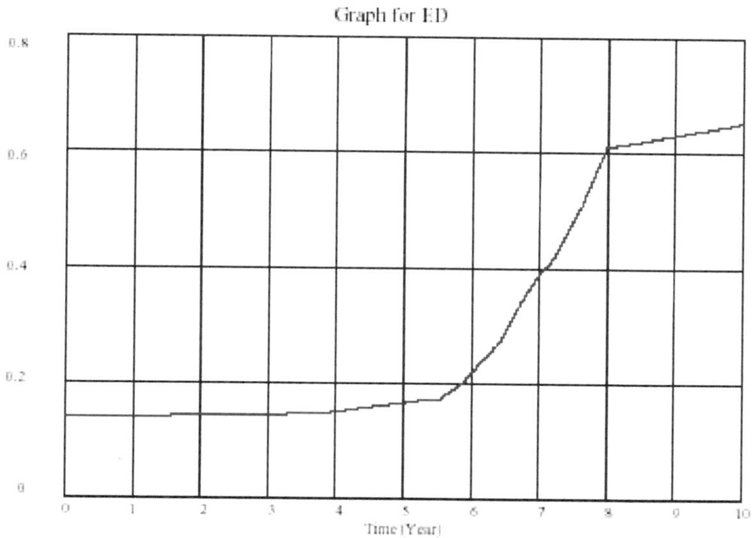

b) ED evolution if planned investment occurs

Fig. 12.14. Port of Seville entrance decision evolution

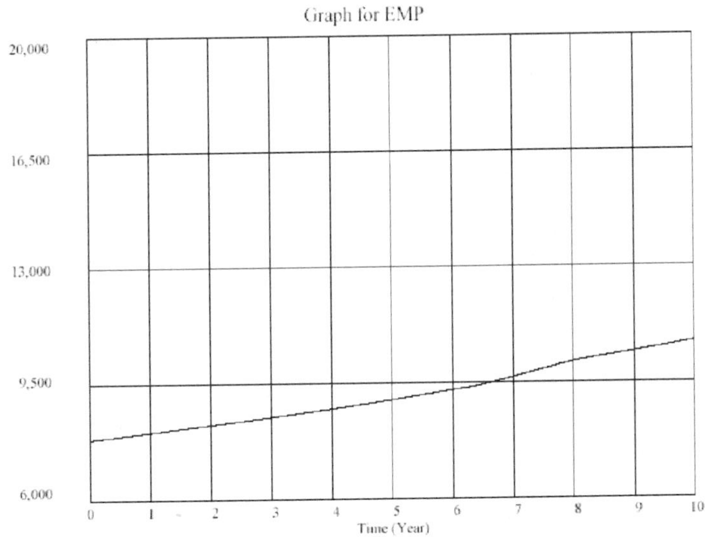

a) EMP evolution with no public investment

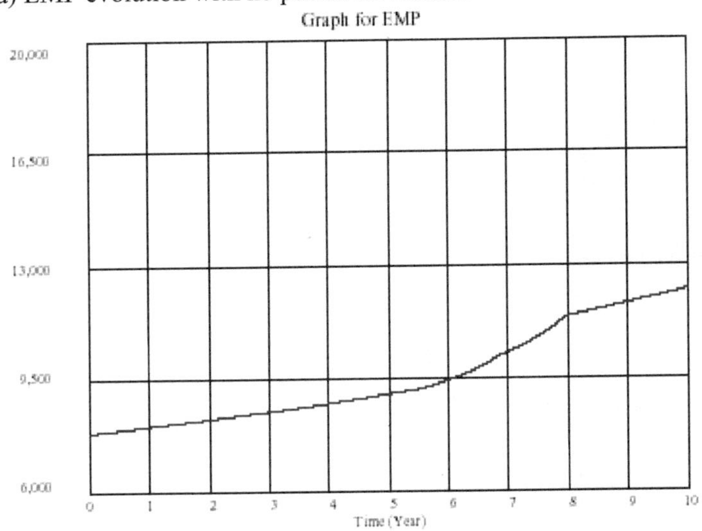

b) EMP evolution if planned investment occurs

Fig. 12.15. Evolut. of employment generated by entrance traffic to the Port of Seville

References

Alatec-Haskoning. Ingenieros y Arquitectos Consultores (1998) Asistencia Técnica para el Estudio de alternativas de las obras para la modificación del acceso al puerto e incidencias previstas de tales obras en el tráfico, la operación portuaria y zonas de servicio.

Aracil J (1982) Aspectos de la aplicación de la dinámica de sistemas a modelos urbanos y territoriales. Tablas Input-Output y cuentas regionales. Instituto de Desarrollo Regional 19.

Aracil, J (1986) Introducción a la dinámica de sistemas. Alianza Editorial, Madrid.

Aracil, J (1996) Realidad y representación en sistemas dinámicos. Arbor 606, June: 9-33.

Autoridad Portuaria de Sevilla (1990-2001) Memorias anuales.

Autoridad Portuaria de Sevilla (1995) Estudio de la Estructura de Costes para la captación de tráfico en el Puerto de Sevilla.

Autoridad Portuaria de Sevilla (1999a) Plan Estratégico.

Autoridad Portuaria de Sevilla (1999b) Plan de Desarrollo del Puerto de Sevilla.

Autoridad Portuaria de Sevilla (2003-2004) Plan de Empresa.

Castillo Manzano JI (2001) El Puerto Bahía de Algeciras, el motor económico del Sur. Ministerio de Fomento y Autoridad Portuaria Bahía de Algeciras.

Castillo Manzano JI, López-Valpuesta L, Aracil MJ (2003) Estudio integral de la actividad portuaria en la provincia de Sevilla. Editorial Pirámide.

Castillo Manzano JI, López-Valpuesta L, Castro Nuño M (2000) El Puerto de Ceuta. Una pieza clave en la economía de la Ciudad Autónoma. Editorial Civitas.

Consultrans, Centro de Estudios Económicos Fundación Tomillo (1998) Análisis de impacto económico de los Puertos de Barcelona y Tarragona. Puertos del Estado.

Coto Millán P, Gallego Gómez JL, Villaverde Castro J (2001) Crecimiento portuario y desarrollo regional. Una aplicación al Puerto de Santander. Autoridad Portuaria de Santander.

Forrester JW (1961) Industrial Dynamics. Productivity Press, Cambridge (MA).

Forrester JW (1969a) Urban Dynamics. The MIT Press.

Forrester JW (1969b) World Dynamics. Wright-Allen Press, Cambridge (MA).

Fundación BBV (2000) Renta Nacional de España y su distribución provincial, Año 1995 y avances 1996-1999.

Hamilton HR et al (1969) System Simulation for Regional Analysis: An Application to River-Basin Planning. The MIT Press.

Instituto de Estadística de Andalucía. Contabilidad Anual Regional de Andalucía, Base 1995, serie 1995-1999.

López-Valpuesta L, Castillo Manzano JI (2001) Análisis de la actividad económica del Puerto de Sevilla y su influencia provincial. Servicio de Publicaciones de la Universidad de Sevilla.

Martínez Budría E, Gutiérrez Hernández P, López Martín LJ, Martín Álvarez F (1999) El impacto económico de los puertos de Santa Cruz de Tenerife sobre la provincia. Hacienda Pública Española, nº 148, I, 175-185.

Martínez Vicente JS, Requena A (1986) Dinámica de Sistemas. 2 vols. Alianza Editorial.

Spim (1997) Estudio sobre el desarrollo de la ZAL en el puerto de Sevilla. Sevilla.

Sastry M, Anjali, Sterman JD (1992) Desert Island Dynamics: An Annotated Survey of the Essential System Dynamics Literature.

Mass NJ (1974) Readings in Urban Dynamics Vol. I. Cambridge MA, Productivity Press.
Schroeder WW, Sweeney RE, Alfeld LE (1975) Readings in Urban Dynamics Vol. II. Cambridge MA, Productivity Press.
Alfeld LE, Graham AK (1976) Introduction to Urban Dynamics. Cambridge MA: Productivity Press.
Forrester JW (1989) The System Dynamics National Model: Macrobehavior from Microstructure. Computer-Based Management of Complex Systems: International System Dynamics Conference, ed. P. M. Milling & E. O. K. Zahn. Berlin. Springer-Verlag.
Vensim. Ventana Systems, Harvard MA.
TEMA (1994) Elaboración de una metodología para la evaluación de los impactos de la actividad portuaria sobre la economía. Puertos del Estado.

Appendix

In this appendix we reproduce the equations of the model for the sake of completeness. Table 12.4 shows the model variables while Table 12.5 gives the nominal values of the parameters.

Table 12.4. Model variables

Variable	Meaning	Definition	Units
CHPSR	Choosing PS Rate	(PSCT + PSPT x ED) x (1/TONUL)	LU/year
DIPSI	Dock Increase in PS through Investment	IF THEN ELSE (PI = 0, 0, PI x IDR x DIUI) x ERI	LU/year
DR	Warehouse Discharge Rate	(1/TONUL) x [MIN (MWC - GW, TONUL x ULTWR x LUD) x DRT]	LU/year
ED	Entrance Decision to PS	IF THEN ELSE (PSC < PHC, 1, ER)	Dmnls[17]
EF	Entrance Frequency to Dock	IF THEN ELSE (LUD = MDC, 0, REF)	LU/year
EMP	Employment	1775.90+2.2881 x TRPSAUX	Employees
ER	PS Entrance Ratio	φ_6 (PCD)	Dmnls
EXF	Exit Frequency from Dock	IF THEN ELSE (MWC = GW, EXFNW x (1-ULTWR) x LUD, DR + EXFNW x (1-ULTWR) x LUD	LU/year
EXINV	External Investment	EXINVini + STEP (EXINV4, 4) - STEP (EXINV4, 5) + STEP (EXINV5, 5) - STEP (EXINV5, 6) + STEP (EXINV6, 6) - STEP (EXINV6, 7) + STEP (EXINV7, 7) – STEP (EXINV7, 8)	Mill. €
FREIGHU	PH Freight Costs	FREIGSE x (1 – 0.0441)	€
FREIGSE	PS Freight Costs	φ_5 (GTMPS)	€
GDP	GDP	GDP_{ini} x EXP(GDPGR x Time)	Mill. €

[17] Dimensionless.

Variable	Meaning	Definition	Units
GEWR	Goods-Entrance-to-Warehouses Rate	DR x TONUL	Ton/year
GME	Goods-to-Market Rate	(GERT x IF THEN ELSE (GW > (GDP/METON), (GDP/METON), GW)	Ton/year
GTIPSI	GT Increase in PS through Investment	IF THEN ELSE (PI = 0, 0, PI x IGTR x GTIUI) x ERI	GT/year
GTMPS	PS Medium GT	INTEG (GTIPSI, IGTMPS)	GT
GTLU	GT – LU Ratio	φ_3 (GTMPS)	Dmnls
GW	Goods in Warehouses	INTEG (GEWR - GME, IGW)	Ton
LS	Land Sales	STEP (LS3, 3) – STEP (LS3,4) + STEP (LS4, 4) – STEP (LS4, 5) + STEP (LS5, 5) - STEP (LS5, 6) + STEP (LS6, 6) - STEP (LS6, 7) + STEP (LS7, 7) - STEP (LS7, 8)	Mill. €
LUB	Length Units that Berth every year	INTEG (LUER - LUER1, ILUB)	LU
LUD	Length Units in Docks	INTEG (EF – EXF, ILUD)	LU
LUER	Length Units Entrance Rate	(PSCT + PSPT x ED) x (1/TONUL)	LU/year
LUER1	LUER delayed one period	DELAY FIXED (LUER, 1, 57)	LU/year
LUW	Length Units Waiting (from Lock to Dock)	INTEG (CHPSR – EF, ILUW)	LU
MDC	Maximum Dock Capacity	INTEG (DIPSI, DIC)	LU
MOORHU	PH Moorage Costs	φ_{2HU} (GTMPH)	€
MOORSE	PS Moorage Costs	φ_2 (GTMPS)	€
P	Profit	TEUL x LUB + WT + PSAOI – PSAC	Mill. €
PCD	Port Costs Differential	((PSC - PHC) / PSC) x 100	Dmnls
PHC	PH Costs (LU that Berth at PH)	PHCGTM x TRIPH	Mill. €
PHCGTM[18]	PH Costs (Medium Vessel)	(0.003065 x GTMPH + 0.042912 x 6 x GTMPH + 1.0295 x TONGT x GTMPH + PILHU + MOORHU + FREIGHU + STOWHU) / 10^6 + TCHTOS	Mill. €
PI	Public Investment	MAX (0, EXINV + UP x PIR + LS)	Mill. €
PILHU	PH Pilotage Costs	φ_{1HU} (GTMPH)	€
PILSE	PS Pilotage Costs	φ_1 (GTMPS)	€

[18] For the T1 tariff, second addend, 8 3-hour periods (2 days) have been considered for the Port of Seville and 6 periods (1.5 days) in the case of the Port of Huelva.

Variable	Meaning	Definition	Units
PSAC	Port Authority of Seville Costs	Cini x (1+ CGR)^Time	Mill. €
PSAOI	Port Authority of Seville Other Income	I_{ini} x (1+OIGR)^Time	Mill. €
PSC	PS Costs (LU that Berth at PS)	PSCGTM x TRIPS	Mill. €
PSCGTM	PS Costs (mean vessel size)	(0.003065 x GTMPS + 0.042912 x 8 x GTMPS + 730.632 x 2 x (1/GTUL) x GTMPS + 1.40401 x GTMPS x TONGT + PILSE + MOORSE + FREIGSE + STOWSE) /10^6	Mill. €
PSCT	PS Captive Traffic	CTER x TRAUX	Ton
PSPT	PS Potential Traffic	TRAUX – PSCT	Ton
REF	Dock Real Entrance Frequency	ERT x MIN (LUW, MDC - LUD)	LU/year
STOWHU	PH Stowage Costs	2.28 x TONGT x GTMPH	€
STOWSE	PS Stowage Costs	2.4 x TONGT x GTMPS	€
TCHTOS	Transport Costs from Huelva to Seville	0.000003005 x TONGT x GTMPH	Mill. €
TEUL	Tariff Earnings per LU	(0.003065 x GTUL + 0.042912 x 8 x GTUL + 730.632 x 2 + 1.40401x TONUL)/ 10^6	Mill.€
TONGT	Ton – GT Ratio	φ_4 (GTMPS)	Dmnls
TR	Traffic Rate to hinterland	-409.74 + 0.2106x GDP	Thousands Ton
TRAUX	Traffic Rate to hinterland (auxiliary)	TR x 1000	Ton
TRIPH	Traffic if PH is chosen	(PSPT x (1/TONGT))/GTMPH	Ships
TRIPS	Traffic if PS is chosen	(PSPT x (1/TONGT))/GTMPS	Ships
TRPS	Traffic Rate to PS	LUER x TONEL	Ton
TRPSAUX	Traffic Rate to PS (auxiliary)	TRPS/1000	Thousands Ton
UP	Useful Profit	MAX (0, P)	Mill. €

Table 12.5. Model parameters

Parameter	Definition	Value	Units
CGR	Costs Growth Rate	0.0799	Dmnls
Cini	Initial Costs	8.46	Mill. €
CTER	Captive Traffic Entrance Rate	0.6651	Dmnls
DIUI	Dock Increase in PS per Unit Invested	0.07134	LU
DRT	Warehouse Discharge Rate	1	Ton/year
ERI	Works Execution Rate	1	1/year
ERT	Dock Entrance Rate	1	1/year
EXFNW	Exit Frequency of Ships not unloading in Warehouses	1	1/year
EXINV4	External Investment in 2004	16	Mill. €
EXINV5	External Investment in 2005	17	Mill. €
EXINV6	External Investment in 2006	16	Mill. €
EXINV7	External Investment in 2007	14	Mill. €
EXINVini	Initial External Investment	0	Mill. €
GDPGR	GDP Growth Rate	0.03	Dmnls
GDPini	Initial GDP	19620.9	Mill. €
GERT	Goods Exit Rate	1	1/year
GTIUI	GT Increase in PS per Unit Invested	29.06	GT
GTMPH	Mean GT at PH	15000	GT
IDC	Initial Dock Capacity	2.764	LU
IDR	Investments in Dock Ratio	0.08	Dmnls
IGTMPS	Initial PS Mean GT	4500	GT
IGTR	Investments in GT Ratio	0.92	Dmnls
IGW	Initial Goods in Warehouses	0	Ton
Iini	Initial Other Income	5.51	Mill. €
ILUB	Initial Length Units that Berth every year	57	LU
ILUD	Initial Length Units in Docks	0	LU
ILUW	Initial Length Units Waiting (from Lock to Dock)	0	LU
LS3	Land Sales in 2003	5	Mill. €
LS4	Land Sales in 2004	10	Mill. €
LS5	Land Sales in 2005	30	Mill. €
LS6	Land Sales in 2006	28	Mill. €
LS7	Land Sales in 2007	18	Mill. €
METON	Mill. € per Ton	0.0002467	Mill. €
MWC	Max Warehouse Capacity	665733	Ton
OIGR	Other Income Growth Rate	0.0812	Dmnls
PIR	Profit Investment Ratio	0.8	Dmnls
TONUL	Ton – LU Ratio	50000	Ton
ULTWR	LU to Warehouses Ratio	0.7	Dmnls
WT	Warehouses Tariff	1	Mill. €

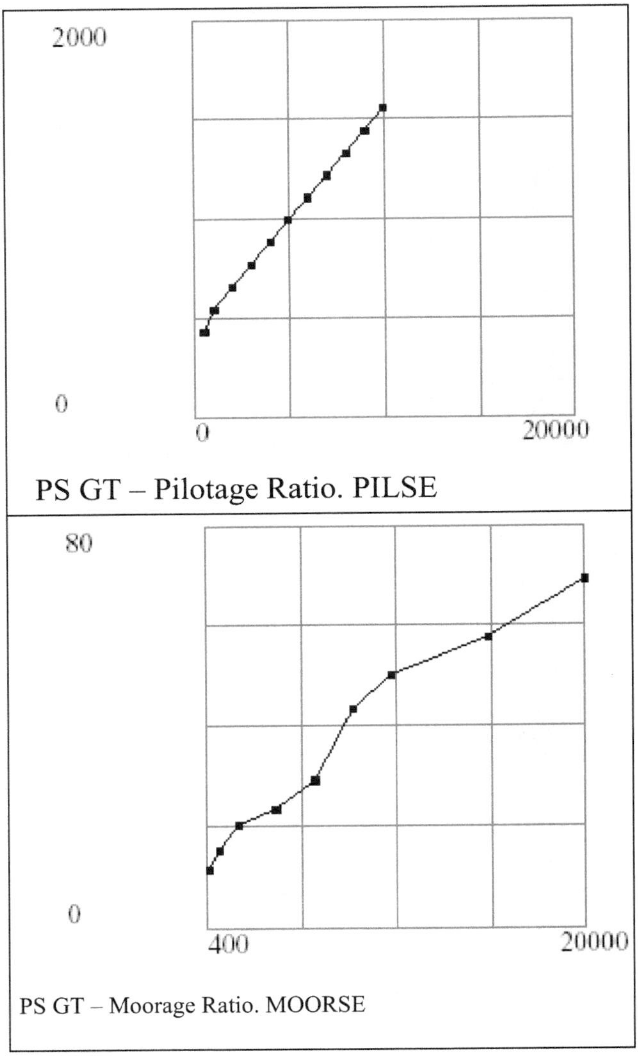

Fig. 12.16. PILSE, MOORSE, FREIGSE, PILHU, MOORHU and PCD-entrance ratio lookups

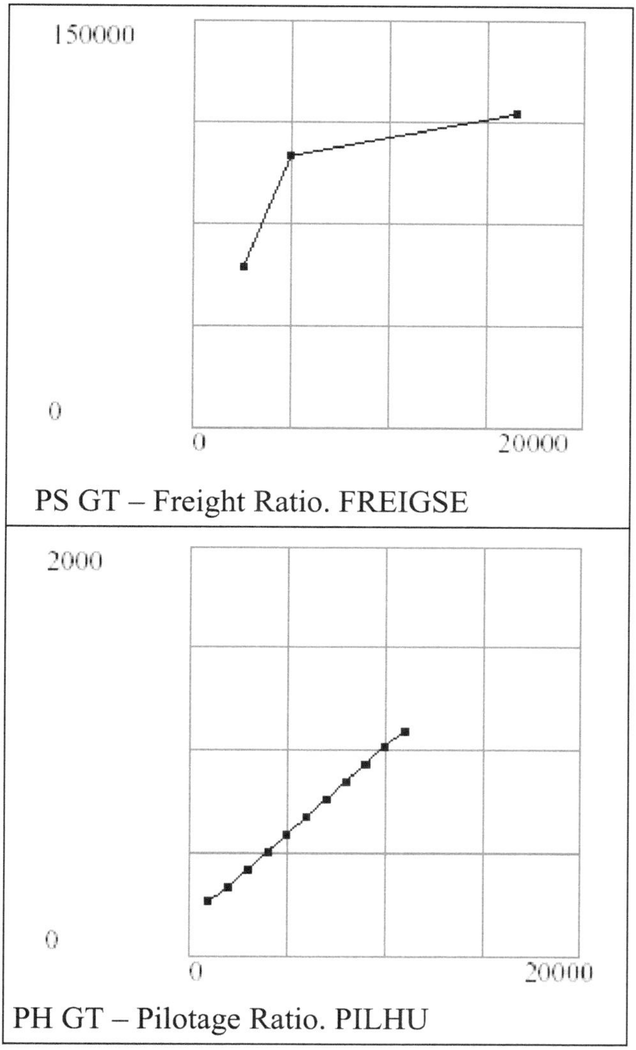

Fig. 12.16. Continued

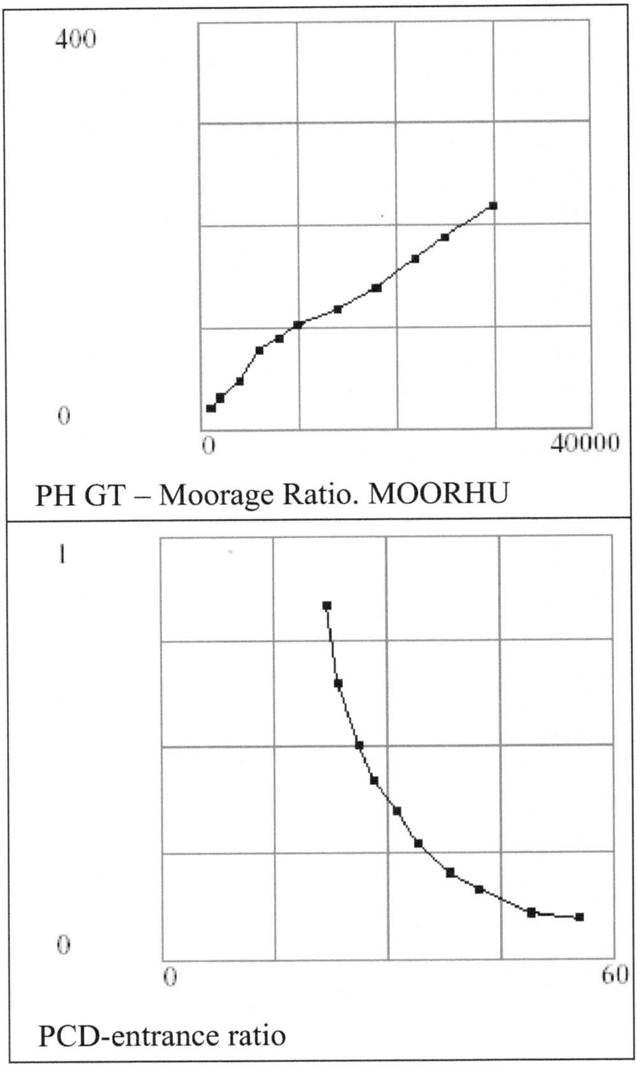

Fig. 12.16. Continued

PART IV VALUATION OF BENEFITS AND COSTS

13 Estimating the Economic Benefits of Bicycling and Bicycle Facilities: an Interpretive Review and Proposed Methods

Kevin J. Krizec
University of Minnesota (U.S.A.)

13.1 Introduction

Planning and policy efforts at all levels of transportation planning aim to increase levels of walking bicycling. In many cases, initiatives are motivated by a desire to reduce auto use and its attendant environmental consequences (e.g., pollution, natural resource consumption). Alternatively they are motivated by concerns of livability, public health, or physical activity. In response, urban planners, transportation specialists, elected officials, and health advocates are all looking to non-motorized travel to address myriad concerns, whether they are environmental, congestion, health or quality of life.

An initial step in doing so is to ensure that adequate facilities exist to encourage use of these modes. For walking, this includes sidewalks, public spaces or street crossings. For bicycling, this includes relatively wide curb lanes, on-street or off-street bike paths, and even parking or showers at the workplace. But bicycle facilities cost money, their merits are often called into question, and many consider spending on them a luxury. Planners and other transportation specialists often find themselves justifying that these facilities benefit the common good and that they induce increased use. Especially in austere economic times, they are often grasping for ways to "economize" such facilities.

Estimating the economic aspects of cycling remains a topic often discussed in policy circles but has yet to be tackled head on. Urban planners, policy officials, and decision-makers lack a consistent framework from which to understand the merits of such facilities. These officials are often bombarded with information and arguments about how much these facilities cost. Opponents of bicycle projects consistently use such information to argue how trimming particular projects would preserve funds. Cost data is readily obtained; it is relatively straightforward to account for the acquisition, development, maintenance and other costs for site-specific or aggregate cases. The benefits, however, are considerably more difficult to estimate.

To respond to such policy and planning needs, the purpose of this paper is twofold. The first is to review and interpret existing literature evaluating the economic benefits of bicycle facilities. The second is to suggest methods and strategies for doing so in future work. As such, the remaining sections of this paper are as follows. We first provide an overview of issues central to this pursuit and identify factors that confound the manner in which bicycle benefits are estimated in a consistent framework. We comment on 25 studies that speak to economic dimensions of bicycle facilities. The third section interprets the existing literature by describing six core benefits of municipal and regional bicycle facilities and suggests example strategies for how each could be estimated. The final section suggests issues to consider and recommendations for future work.

13.2 Overview of Issues Central to Estimating Bicycle Benefits

To set the stage for any effort estimating the economic benefits of bicycle facilities it is necessary to overview of the main issues involved, the matters that confound such endeavors, and a justification for more structured research.

Conventional evaluation techniques suggest that any bicycle facilities should be considered in the same manner as other transportation facilities (e.g., roadways, light rail, HOV lanes) or, for that matter, any major public capital investment (e.g., wastewater treatment plant, sports stadium). Doing so subjects bicycle facilities to the same methodologies or criteria used in these projects such as benefit-cost analysis, economic impact assessment (local, regional or state), cost-effectiveness evaluation, and financial or risk analysis. Of these approaches, benefit-cost analysis is the most well-known and most frequently relied on in transportation projects. It compares the effects of proposed policies or projects on social welfare. It requires identifying all project impacts (positive or negative) in the present and the future and then assigning an economic value to these impacts.

A handful of research studies attempt to calculate benefit cost ratios for bicycle-specific projects. The general approaches and data used in doing so are presented in Table 13.1, together with ratios. All show that benefits exceed costs. Such consensus is a reflection of a variety of factors, including the inexpensive nature of bicycle facilities (i.e., a low valued denominator) and optimistic adoption rates of such facilities. Most often, however, these studies are troubled by the relatively unreliable manner in which demand is estimated and benefit values are derived.

Table 13.1. Listing of Cost Benefit studies

Author/Date	Context	Ratio	Comments
Everett (1976)	University of So. Mississippi	1.7 : 1	Uses computer and hand-calculations to estimate benefits and costs on a university campus. Dated, difficult to replicate
Buis (2000)	Amsterdam, Netherlands	1.5 : 1	Each case attempts to answer: "What economic benefits can be attributed to an increase in bicycle use due to local bicycle policies?" Wealthier, currently bicycle-friendly countries benefit at a lesser significance than do poorer, less well-invested countries
	Bogotá, Columbia	7.3 : 1	
	Morogoro, Tanzania	5 : 1	
	Delhi, India	20 : 1	
Saelensminde (2002)	Hokksund, Norway	4.09 : 1	Ratio based on "best estimates" of future cycling/pedestrian traffic. Cities with the least amount of infrastructure in place see the most benefit from new infrastructure.
	Hamar, Norway	14.34 : 1	
	Trondheim, Norway	2.94 : 1	
Przybylski & Lindsey, (1998)	Central Indianapolis Waterfront Greenway	1.43 : 1	Estimates benefits by Unit Day Values and costs (based on construction costs) to establish cost-benefit ratio.
	Ohio River Greenway	1.9 : 1	

The overarching problem is reliably attaching and economic value to a facility for which there is no market value and little data for its use. Bicycle facilities, like wilderness, a clean environment, and access to open space, represent non-market goods not bought and sold. Markets for their price and use fail to exist. There are no prices for their use that can be manipulated and as a result, they represent a good for which it is extremely difficult to derive an economic value. Furthermore, given current levels of bicycling use, the majority for most facilities could be considered a good that is both non-rivalrous and non-excludable. They exhibit characteristics closely resembling "public good" (or at least a quasi-public good).

But if certain goods are thought to contribute positively to human well being, they are considered to have economic value (the reverse is also true). The Fields of economics and transportation have devised general methods for estimating economic values attached to non-market goods and services. These include strategies to measure both revealed and stated preferences for a good. The former aim to identify ways in which non-market goods influence the actual market for some other good are can be estimated using methods such as hedonic pricing, travel cost or unit day values. The latter attempts to construct markets, asking people to attach an economic value various goods and services and is estimated using methods such as contingent valuation or conjoint analysis.

Measuring any aspect of bicycling facilities is further complicated because transportation facilities are typically discussed in terms of auto, transit or non-motorized travel; this aggregates walking and cycling. For abstract or general purposes this may suffice and is often done in transportation research. In terms of daily use and facility planning, however, bicycling and walking differ significantly. Pedestrian travel and infrastructure have the following unique characteristics. First, all trips—whether by car, rail transit, or bus—require pedestrian travel because they start and end with a walk trip. Second, sidewalks and other pedestrian related amenities are now often required in zoning codes. Third, pedestrian concerns typically relate to relatively confined travel-sheds or geographic scales (e.g., city blocks). Bicycle travel and facilities, on the other hand, apply to longer corridors, fail to be used as frequently as walking facilities, and are considered more discretionary in nature. Where pedestrian planning applies to a clear majority of the population (nearly everyone can walk), bicycle planning applies to a considerably smaller market of travelers—those who choose to own and ride a bicycle. During the summer months in most of the U.S., this includes just over a quarter of the American population (U.S. Department of Transportation 2003).

The black cloud looming over all analysis of non-motorized transportation (bicycling or walking) is poor data. There exist a variety of sources from which bicycle behavior can be gleaned; for example, the census, metropolitan/nationwide travel surveys, facility specific surveys or counts, or national surveys such as that administered by the Bureau of Transportation Statistics (U.S. Department of Transportation 2003). Specific use and facility information may be available for select areas throughout the country. The strengths and weaknesses of these data sources are adequately documented (U.S. Department of Transportation 2000). A common theme is that existing behavioral bicycle data lacks the both the breadth and quality necessary for reliable analysis. Analysis of cycling use has been especially marginalized because of its relatively low levels of use.

Such data deficiencies are well recognized by the transportation planning community; procedures and protocol for collecting improved bicycle data are in place. In addition, matters of bicycle and pedestrian travel are increasingly on radars outside the transportation community. For example, transportation and urban planning researchers are joining forces with public health researchers to better understand both derived and non-derived forms of "active" transportation (i.e., bicycling and walking). Given that better data is a well recognized matter, it is best to direct attention to other issues important.

There remains considerable range in how to measure bicycle facilities. Confounding issues include: (a) at what geographic level, (b) for whom, (c) specific to which benefits, and (d) using what units. How does one compare the economic benefits gained from Colorado's mountain biking industry to the quality of life or neighborhood-scale benefits from building a neighborhood bike path for children? How do the air pollution benefits of increased cycling relate to quality of life benefits from the serenity of a nearby rail-trail? How reliable are the safety estimates for different types of bicycle facilities, especially given existing debate over on-road versus off-road facilities (Forester 2001; Pucher 2001)? The studies and approaches to date represent initial attempts to understand such benefits. They often do so, over inconsistent geographic scales and making a host of assumptions. Below, we describe in more detail each consideration.

At what geographic scale or type of facility?

The first consideration pertains to the geographic scale of the inquiry or facility in question. Past work has analyzed the benefits of a specific greenway or active recreation trail (Moore, Graefe et al. 1994; PKF Consulting 1994; Siderlis and Moore 1995; Sumathi and Berard 1997; Przybylski and Lindsey 1998; Schutt 1998; Betz, Bergstrom et al. 2003), a specific trunk roadway (Sharples 1995a), a region (Fix and Loomis 1997; Fix and Loomis 1998), an entire city (Buis 2000), or an entire state (Argys and Mocan 2000). Some studies focus on a system of bicycle trails across the state, while others focus the benefits of on-road versus off-road facilities. Different geographic scales demand different data, ranging from individual counts of a facility to aggregated or numbers for a specific area interpolated to an entire state.

For whom?

A second matter relates to the population for whom the benefits apply. Any question of benefits can been tackled in a number of ways depending on the audience of interest and the geographic scope. State legislators may be interested in understanding how bicycling, the bicycle industry or bicycle-oriented tourism impact a state's economy. Such analysis would resemble input/output models examining expenditures across an entire state. In contrast, a city council member may seek to learn how bicycle facilities enhance quality of life for a given municipality. Advocates want to document induced demand for facilities or relationships to decreased traffic congestion. Public health professionals are concerned about the use and safety benefits of such facilities.

Can a single review do justice to the myriad interests and beneficiaries involved? An answer depends on the level of specificity and need of the study. There are competing interests and multiple perspectives to capture. While actual users are likely to be similar for any given facility (i.e., people riding bicycles), the information likely to be of benefit to the state bureau of tourism differs from a municipality looking to justify different types of bicycle investments.

One report identifies three user groups impacted by cycling facilities: road-users, non road-users (e.g., occupants of adjacent properties) and planning/financing agencies (Sharples 1995a). The first group of 'road users' includes all users, cyclists, motorists, pedestrians and horse riders, and public transport. Alternatively, some studies divide the benefits of non-motorized travel into internal versus external benefits. The former include the financial savings, health benefits, increased mobility, and enjoyment for cyclists; the latter include the benefits to others, such as reduced congestion, road and parking facility expenses, accidents, pollution, and natural resource consumption.

Which benefits?

The range of benefits of cycling facilities include (but not limited to) reduced pollution, congestion, capital investments (at least compared to roads and auto use), and increased livability, health, well-being, and quality of life. But anecdotally describing such benefits has limited value. Politicians and lobbyists seek quantifiable estimates. Benefits range from the direct and easy-to-understand to the almost impossible to reliably calculate. Counting the number of cyclists using a new bicycle trail is relatively straightforward. The difficulty is translating such levels of ridership into monetary amounts.

Table 13.2. Comparing the values of different benefits from six studies

	Betz	Fix & Loomis	Lindsey	Litman	Nelson	Sharples
Benefit						
Air Pollution				$0.20 - $0.40	$0.24 - $0.40	184 kg of CO2
Congestion				$0.04 - $0.40	$0.03 - $0.32	varies
Earnings			$14,434,000			
Ecological/ Environmental				$0.23	$0.23	
Economic Benefits	$18.46 - $29.23 (surplus)	$197 - $205 (surplus)	$1.43-$6.13 UDV			
Energy Costs					$0.10 - $0.12	
Jobs			982 FTE			
Noise				$0.05 - $0.10	$0.02	1.5 dB
Parking				$0.25 - $1.50	$0.23 - $2.25	varies
Road Maintenance				$0.05 - $0.10	$0.02	varies
Road Safety						£450,000
Sales (from derived demand)			$21,000,000 est.			
User Savings/ Driver Costs				$0.55 - $0.85	$0.40 - $0.60	£7,472
Total				$1.37 - $3.20	$1.27 - $3.42	

One study suggests seven benefits to consider when estimating the economic value of walking: livability, accessibility and transportation costs, health, external costs, efficient land use, economic development, equity (Litman 2004). Focusing just on greenways, Lindsey (2003) articulates six valued benefits: recreation, health/fitness, transportation, ecological biodiversity and services, amenity visual/aesthetic, economic development. Which benefits are most important? Is it those that are accrued, those in which the sponsoring agency is primarily interested, or those for which there is available data? As an example, Table 13.2 depicts values calculated for different benefits from six different studies.

Using what units/method?

A final matter lies in the units and/or methods used to calculate different benefits. An ideal analysis considers benefits in a framework using a common unit. But how does an increase in riders compare to a reduced need for parking spaces? How does increased livability compare with decreased health concerns? Only one article focuses exclusively on methods, reviewing the Travel Cost Method (TCM) for imputing economic value and suggesting better alternatives for measurement (Randall 1994). Quite simply, most studies simply throw their best "guesstimates" at the problem. Methods and units are different, yielding varied output that precludes the desired aim of a common unit.

These include simple counts (e.g., reduced casualties), decibels, monetary amounts (e.g., vehicle operating costs), and descriptive measures (e.g., overall convenience). More specifically, hedonic pricing could measure livability or amenity visual/aesthetic values; economic input/output models could describe economic development; time could measure transportation savings; and surveys of different kinds (e.g., contingent valuation) could capture a host of values or benefits.

13.3 Review of Previous Research

Reviewing past research on this subject in a systematic manner is troublesome on two accounts. First, existing literature can be described "spotty" at best. While growing, the geographic scale, research depth, overall quality, and focus of past study varies considerably. Little is cumulative. Second, there is no clear strategy to delineate what constitutes such a paper. We cast a relatively wide net in what we consider a study of bicycle benefits. Our definition includes any research effort describing or attributing an economic value to bicycling or bicycle facilities.

By our tally this includes more than 25 studies; this comes close to representing the universe of all available and published research efforts. Each of these studies are presented in alphabetical order (authors name) in Table 13.3, showing the date, title, geographic level, and an indication of whether the report appears in a peer-reviewed outlet. The research ranges from general overview pieces anecdotal in nature to those examining ridership data within a traditional benefit-cost framework. Only ten or so are published in peer review outlets. Among other issues, this suggests that most studies have not been prepared to meet the levels of research quality required in peer reviewed publications. Furthermore, it suggests that many of the studies have a tone of advocacy to their analysis and findings. Such literature needs to be considered in that light. Below we provide a brief review of each of these studies. In lieu of a good strategy to organize the discussion, we use the level of geography to do so.

The largest geographic area includes a series of studies conducted for individual states to calculate the economic impact of cycling and related industries. In Colorado, more than 6,000 households and a sample of bicycle manufacturers, retail bicycle shops and ski resort operators were surveyed to glean a better understanding the impact bicycling has on Colorado's economy in the form of production, sales, jobs and income and tax revenue (Argys and Mocan 2000). A study from Maine conducted for the Department of Transportation surveyed bicycle tour operators to estimate the total economic impact of bicycle tourism in the state and to develop marketing recommendations (Maine Department of Transportation 2001). From this research, they estimated the size and characteristics of the bicycle tourism market in terms of socio-economic class, spending patterns, direct and indirect impacts. Finally, Michigan has also estimated spending by users of local rail-trails while participating in organized bike rides (Nelson, Vogt et al. 2001).

Table 13.3. Summary of all literature

Author (date)	Title	Geography	Summary	Peer Review
Argys, Mocan (2000)	Bicycling and Walking in Colorado	State	Provides statistical information regarding the economic impact of bicycling in Colorado, and documents bicycling behaviors and attitudes of residents of Colorado.	No
Buis (2000)	The Economic Significance of Cycling	City	The results of four cost-benefit calculations: Amsterdam, Bogotá, Delhi, Morogoro	No
Everett (1976)	Measuring the Economic Value of Exercise in Labor-Intensive Urban Transportation Systems	University campus	Analysis of how labor-intensive transportation modes provide needed exercise. Quantifies health benefits and the economic benefit of reducing coronary heart disease.	Yes
Everett, Dorman (1976)	New Approach to Economic Evaluation of Labor-Intensive Transportation Systems	University campus	Applies managerial economics tools to quantify the benefits of a proposed bicycle-pedestrian transportation system.	Yes
Fix, Loomis (1997)	The Economic Benefits of Mountain Biking at One of Its Meccas	Mountain bike trails, Moab, Utah	Compares non-market valuation techniques by applying a data travel cost method and contingent valuation method to mountain biking.	Yes

Author (date)	Title	Geography	Summary	Peer Review
Fix, Loomis (1998)	Comparing the Economic Value of Mountain Biking Estimated Using Revealed and Stated Preference	Mountain bike trails, Moab, Utah	Estimates the value of mountain biking using travel cost method.	Yes
Lindsey et. al (2002)	Use of Greenway Trails in Indiana	Greenway system	Informational report on trail use in Indiana.	No
Lindsey, Knaap (2003)	Sustainability and Urban Greenways (Indiana)	Greenway system	This case study examines whether the greenways system in Indianapolis, Indiana, is sustainable using a framework based on six principles of sustainability recently proposed in the planning literature.	Yes
Lindsey, et al (2003)	Amenity and Recreation Values of Urban Greenways (Indiana)	Greenway system	Presents a taxonomy of the values of greenways and demonstrates how different values can be measured using complementary techniques.	No
Litman (2002)	Economic Value of Walkability	General	Uses economic evaluation methods to investigate the value of walking. Analysis may be applied to other non-motorized travel modes.	No
Litman (1999)	Quantifying the Benefits of Non-Motorized Transport for Achieving TDM Objectives	General	Examines the degree to which non-motorized travel help achieve Transportation Demand Management objectives, including congestion reduction, road and parking facility cost savings, consumer cost savings etc.	No
Maine DOT (2001)	Bicycle Tourism in Maine	State (three trails)	Summarizes study to estimate the total economic impact of bicycle tourism by estimating the tourism market.	No

Author (date)	Title	Geography	Summary	Peer Review
Moore (1994)	The Economic Impact of Rail-Trails	Three trails	Examined economic impact generated by three diverse rail-trails in Iowa, Florida and California. Impacts were broken down into users' expenditures related to trail visits.	Yes
Moore, Barthlow (1998)	The Economic Impacts and Uses of Long-distance Trails	Trail	Investigates use patterns and economic impacts of long distance trails. Case study of Overmountain Victory National Historical Trail.	No
Nelson A. (1995)	Private Provision of Public Pedestrian and Bicycle Access Ways	National	Presents findings to support that implementing bicycle and pedestrian access ways will result in economic benefit.	Yes
Vogt, Nelson (2002)	A Case Study Measuring Economic and Community Benefits of Michigan's Pere Marquette Rail-Trail	Trail	Compiles executive summaries from research reports that have been completed as part of this case study. Includes economic benefit generated by trails use for organized rides, property owners' opinions.	No
PKF Consulting (1986)	Analysis of Economic Impacts of the North Central Rail Trail (Maryland)	State	Investigated seven categories including tourism, property values, local resident expenditures and public sector expenditures to determine an economic value.	No
Przybylski, Lindsey (1998)	Economic Evaluation of Major Urban Greenway Projects	State	Describes procedures used in economic evaluations of two major greenway projects in Indiana. Includes benefit-cost analyses and regional economic impact analyses.	No

Author (date)	Title	Geography	Summary	Peer Review
Saelensminde (2002)	Walking- and cycling-track networks in Norwegian Cities	City	CBAs of walking- and cycling-track networks based on use of the networks.	No
Schutt (1998)	Trails for Economic Development: A Case Study	Trail	Summarizes a user and economic impact study of the Bruce Trail in Ontario.	Yes
Sharples (1995)	A framework for the evaluation of facilities for cyclists – Part 1	General	Suggests framework for how to determine who will be affected by new cycling infrastructure and how.	Yes
Sharples (1995)	A framework for the evaluation of facilities for cyclists – Part 2	Roadway	Applies the above framework to Wilmslow Road Corridor in Manchester, England.	Yes
Siderlis, Moore (1995)	Outdoor Recreation Net Benefits of Rail-Trails	Trails in multiple states	Estimates net economic values with the individual travel cost method for three rail trails in different U.S. Regions.	Yes
Sumathi, Berard (1997)	Mountain Biking the Chequamegon Area of Northern Wisconsin	Trail system	Profiles mountain biking user characteristics from the Chequamegon Area Mountain Biking Association trail system	No
Wittink (2001)	On the Significance of Non-Motorized Transport	City	Presents the effectiveness of non-motorized transport in relation to economic growth, poverty reduction and quality of life urban areas and on the applicability of arrangements in the Netherlands.	No

A second level of analysis focuses on regional geographic areas or entire cities. Buis (2000) offers an international application describing calculations in Amsterdam, Bogotá, Delhi and Morogoro. Using existing data from each municipality about proposed or existing bicycle policy, such as investments in infrastructure and saved motorized journeys, this research captures cost . The benefits in the four different cities, while not calculated consistently for each setting due to the availability of data, employed infrastructure, user, and safety information which were translated into U.S. dollars. The calculations demonstrate that the benefits exceed the costs; the benefit-cost ratio was more pronounced in cities that have not yet invested in cycling facilities. A study prepared on behalf of the Institute of Transport Economics in Oslo is perhaps the most robust among available work (Saelensminde 2002). This research estimates the average bicycle ridership in three Norwegian cities (Hokksund, Hamar and Trondheim) to determine a project's calculated profitability or net benefit. This research claims to have used low benefit estimates and concludes that spending on future infrastructure serves to benefit society in those three cities. Saelensminde ascribes monetary values to all aspects from security and accident reduction to health benefits and parking.

Research by Fix and Loomis (1997) use a travel cost model to estimate the economic benefits to users of mountain bike trails in Moab, Utah. They did so measuring consumer surplus and individual per-trip values. The second of these studies, also focusing on the Moab area, compares non-market valuation techniques by applying the TCM and the dichotomous choice contingent valuation method (CVM) (Fix and Loomis 1998). Also included in this group of studies is an exercise, now over a quarter-century old, to create a computer model analyzing savings reaped from increased cycling on a college campus (Everett 1976). The computer simulation results generate a benefit-cost ratio by multiplying the benefits per mile for each commuter type by the miles per year traveled by that commuter type and sums it over commuter types and years. Subsequent research discusses the applicability of applying management economic techniques to bicycle and pedestrian transportation systems (Everett and Dorman 1976).

The Sharples work (1995a) is valuable because it lists a variety of applicable issues and demonstrates how to evaluate related costs and benefits (Sharples 1995b). She generates specific values around diverse costs as air pollution and accident reduction. However, her benefits rely almost exclusively on first-hand experience of one particular corridor using personally collected data. Lindsey and Knaap (1999) use contingent valuation to understand how much residents are willing to spend for a greenway facility. A different approach applied unit day values to estimate the benefits of proposed greenway projects (Lindsey and Przybylski 1998). Using a rating system established by the U.S. Army Corps of Engineers (USACE), scores based on the USACE project evaluation scheme are converted to dollar values, also established by the USACE. While useful for estimating value, this work is limited because it only estimates use value. The same study also estimates use and net benefits of the greenway projects and includes a regional economic impact analysis for the two trails.

Betz et al. (2003) combine contingent valuation and TCM methods to estimate demand for visiting a greenway in northern Georgia and measures of consumer surplus. More recently, Lindsey et al. (2003) demonstrated how different values of a specific greenway could be estimated using complimentary techniques. They measured the impacts of greenways on property values in Indianapolis using residential real estate sales data, GIS, and hedonic price modeling. Recreation values for the trail were estimated using the TCM method. A more general work absent of a geographical context (Litman 2004) focuses on walking aspects that can also serve as useful reference for cycling research. This piece suggests that benefit-cost analysis offers the broadest brush at identifying the full range of benefits but again, stops short of suggesting specific methods and strategies for doing so.

13.4 Proposed Benefits and Methods

Past research offers widely varying perspectives to show how audiences demand different information on bicycle facilities. Attempting to satisfy all often ends up satisfying few. The central challenge for urban planners, policy officials, and researchers focuses on the benefits of bicycle facilities that pointedly satisfy certain criteria. After reviewing existing literature, canvassing available data and/methods, and consulting a variety of policy officials, we suggest that to be most useful, bicycling benefits need to satisfy five criteria. They need to be (1) measured on a municipal or regional scale; (2) central to assisting decision makers about transportation/urban planning; (3) estimable via available existing data or other survey means; (4) converted to measures comparable to one another; (5) be measuring benefits for both users and non-users.

It is also important to describe the range of benefits, to whom they apply, and to suggest compelling methods in which they could be measured. Our itemized list of benefits are guided by previous research and include direct benefits to the user—in the form of mobility, health, and safety benefits—and indirect benefits to society—in the form of decreased externalities, increased livability, and fiscal savings).

Other benefits certain exist and the beneficiaries are not always that clear. Our aim is not to dismiss their significance but merely suggest that practical considerations related to data, methodologies, and measurement often preclude more detailed analysis. The six benefits mentioned usually have different beneficiaries. These range from society-at-large to individual users (potential and current) to agencies; there is crossover between beneficiaries for each benefit. Consider, for example, that the most common argument in favor of cycling suggests that an increase in facilities will result in increased levels of cycling. This assumed increase in cycling will be derived from: (1) existing cyclists whose current levels of riding will be heightened (because of more attractive facilities), and/or (2) potential cyclists whose probability for riding will be increased. Thus, we see potential benefits for two different populations of beneficiaries (current and potential cyclists). But if any of these heightened levels of cycling result in decreased auto use, then an third beneficiary results—society-at-large—in terms of reduced congestion and resource consumption.

Below we describe what each benefit refers to, the primary user group to whom it applies, and a thumbnail sketch for a method that could be used to estimate each benefit. The proposed method is not to imply there is a single strategy for estimating this benefit but to merely provide the reader and researcher with an example of how it could be measured. Figure 13.1 shows a simplified depiction of potential beneficiaries along with an indication of the primary benefit as alluded to above.

Beneficiary					
To the User (direct)			*To the Community (indirect)*		
Mobility	***Health***	***Safety***	***External***	***Livability***	***Fiscal***
-enhanced conditions -shorter travel distance	-increased physical activity -decreased health care costs	-decreased crashes -increased comfort	-decreased congestion -reduced pollution	-proximity to recreational amenities -increased open space	-increased economic activity -decreased taxes

Fig. 13.1. Beneficiaries of bicycle facilities

(Based on an analysis of several sources (e.g., travel diaries such as the National Household Travel Survey, direct questionnaires administered by the Bureau of Transportation Statistics), we project that approximately three percent of the U.S. population cycles one day per week and an estimated one percent of the population cycles three times per week. When people do ride a bike, it appears as if they do so for approximately 30 minutes at a time. Overall, however, current statistics suggest that less than one percent of the U.S. population receives their recommended weekly level of physical activity by cycling.)

(1) Mobility

The most directly cited benefits are often gleaned from users of the bicycle facilities. These come in the form of greater satisfaction of existing cycling (e.g., cyclists would be able to reach their destination faster, safer, via a more attractive means). A major problem, however, is that existing information by itself (e.g., ridership counts) cannot reliably shed light on this issue. For this reason, the different transportation benefits for the user are best uncovered through stated preference surveys or experiments. Since stated preference methods provide individuals with hypothetical situations, it becomes feasible to analyze situations that are qualitatively different from the actual ones seen in practice (Bradley and Kroes 1990).

Because individuals respond to several different hypothetical choice situations offered to them, the efficiency of data collection is improved; enough data is hence available to calculate functions describing their preferences or utility. Against this backdrop, the disadvantage in stated preference methods is that people may not always do what they say. Individuals' stated preferences might not be similar to the preferences they actually show (Wardman 1988). This arises because of the systematic bias in survey responses or because of the difficulty in actually carrying out the posed task.

Two techniques used in stated preference analyses are contingent valuation and conjoint analysis. The former is based on the premise that the best way to find out the value that an individual places on something is known by asking. Like other non-market goods, the concept has been applied to wilderness, open space, or even more specifically to greenways (Lindsey and Knaap 1999). The second stated preference technique, conjoint analysis, applies designed of experiments to obtain the preferences of the individual (customer). This market research technique can provide important information about new product development, forecasting market segmentation and pricing decisions. In this case it would help understand the type of cycling facilities that residents value. Conjoint analysis enables researchers to calculate the value that people place on the attributes or features of products and services; the aim is to assign specific values to the options that buyers look for when making a decision to use a good. It is a highly respected technique to explore trade-offs to determine the combinations of attributes that satisfies the consumer.

In these cases, an individual is provided a choice of alternatives; for example, the various travel routes by which a particular travel destination can be reached. The choice of a particular mode is assumed to depend on the relative attractiveness of the various travel options that the individual faces. These methods use experimental procedures to obtain individuals preferences based on the individual's evaluation of the various options given. Typically, these experiments generally provide hypothetical travel scenarios to obtain an individual's preferences (Fowkes and Wardman 1988).

An important point is that stated preference surveys need to be stratified by audience: current users versus potential users. For the former, current cyclists could be asked to respond to questions about factors that would provide for a more attractive cycling environment through different types of environments or facilities. It is necessary to have forced trade-offs so that a better environment might be coupled with higher costs for bicycle storage or a higher travel time. This will allow one to value each component of the user's preference. These preferences can then be translated to economic benefits using consumer's surplus measures (Ben-Akiva and Lerman 1989) to determine, for example, the value of an off-road bicycle facility for users of that facility.

For the latter category, potential users, it would be important to create scenarios based on constructed markets, asking people to attach a value to a goods or services. This technique is applicable to quantify the benefits that non-bicycling residents would accrue from a more desirable bicycling infrastructure. For example, questions could ask what mode they would choose for work and non-work trips based on the quality of the transportation environment, including auto, walk, transit, and bicycle travel. It would query residents about the degree to which they perceive different bicycling services or how facilities will improve the conditions of their commute, recreational activities, etc. By measuring how demand might change, one can ascertain the preferences for current non-users, some of whom would become users if a certain infrastructure package were constructed.

(2) Health

Researchers and practitioners from a variety of disciplines are building the scientific literature to better understand relationships between community design, transportation facilities, and levels of physical activity (Handy, Boarnet et al.

2002; Sallis, Frank et al. 2004). So-called "sprawling" land use practices and resulting auto-dependent travel are themes that now have moved front and center into the American consciousness; the link to public health and the declared obesity epidemic remains an important component of this discussion (Frank 2000; Wilkinson, Eddy et al. 2002; Pucher and Dijkstra 2003). One overarching goal of this active line of inquiry is to learn the extent to which rates of physical inactivity can be linked to features of the built environment (see for example, Krizek, Birnbaum et al. 2004). At a regional or neighborhood scale, most inquiries focus on land use patterns characterized by relatively scattered, single use and low-density development. At a street or facility level, such research focuses on access to sidewalks, trails, other non-motorized facilities, and destinations. While the past dozen or so years have seen a proliferation of research linking neighborhood design to travel behavior (Crane 2000; Ewing and Cervero 2001), surprisingly little of it has exclusively focused on relationships between specific facilities, bicycling and walking travel, and levels of physical activity.

To establish a health-care, cost-based reason for bicycle facilities, several types of specific empirical evidence must be gathered and broadly communicated to interested parties. Doing so is a tall order and one that some claim to be insurmountable. Borrowing reasoning from Goetzel et al. (1998), researchers must first demonstrate relationships between a given feature of the built environment (e.g., a bicycle facility) and levels of cycling. Doing so would be similar to methodologies previously described to measure the demand induced from various facilities. The active line of international research tackling this question is likely to have reliable results that can inform this line of inquiry in relatively short order time (i.e., a couple of years). Second, any amount of induced cycling that could be "teased" out from a facility would then need to be translated into an average percentage of one's weekly physical activity. For example, the daily recommended level of physical activity is defined as 30 minutes of moderate physical activity on five or more days per week (Pronk, Goodman et al. 1999; Blair, LaMonte et al. 2004). Cycling five miles in 30 minutes or four miles in 15 minutes would meet these current public health guidelines for physical activity for health (Pate, Pratt et al. 1995; U.S. Department of Health and Human Services 1999; U.S. Department of Health and Human Services 2003).

Third, researchers must then demonstrate that lack of physical activity—because it is indicative of certain risk factors—imposes a financial burden to the individual or to society. A fourth step would be to show that improved certain risk factors (i.e., increasing physical activity) does result in reduced cost. The final step is for researchers to demonstrate that health habits can be changed and that the resultant lower risk can be maintained over time. As can be seen, the challenges associated with documenting a "health" financial payback from a bicycle facility are significant. Looking at the problem optimistically and from the perspective of needing analytical justification, we see such exercise not completely out of the realm of possibility. For this reason, these later steps (three through five) comprise the focus of the below review.

The benefits of physical activity in enhancing overall health are well established. The task of attaching monetary amounts to levels of physical activity is a more challenging endeavor. One attempt is offered by Wang et al. (2004) who derive cost-effectiveness measures of bicycle/pedestrian trails by dividing the costs of trail development and maintenance by selected physical activity-related outcomes of the trails (e.g., number of trail users). The average annual cost for persons becoming more physically active was found to be $98; the cost was $142 for persons who are active for general health, and the $884 for persons who are active for weight loss.

Estimating the effect of physical inactivity on direct medical costs is a strategy more often employed, though considerably less straightforward. Part of the reason for ambiguity in this line research is that the amount of physical activity required to realize certain health benefits is relatively unknown (i.e., what is the elasticity?) (Hansen, Stevens et al. 2001; Rankinen and Bouchard 2002; Blair, LaMonte et al. 2004). In the field of public health, this matter is often approached from the perspective of dose-response relationships. The aim is to learn what change in amount, intensity, or duration of exposure (in this case, cycling) is associated with a change in risk of a specified outcome (in this case, cost of health care).

Existing literature examining relationships between levels of physical activity and health costs varies considerably in methodology and scope. The majority of existing studies pursue a dichotomized approach, separating respondents into two classes: those that satisfy the accepted "dose" of 30 minutes per day for five days and those who do not. In this first group of studies, there are at least five statewide reports whose methodology and assumptions are relatively general in nature. In most cases, estimates are derived from an aggregation of medical expenditures that can in some form be traced back to physical inactivity. For example, a study commissioned by the Michigan Fitness Foundation (Chenoweth, DeJong et al. 2003) concentrated on the economic costs to the residents of Michigan. The authors used estimates (acknowledged to be conservative) to derive direct costs (e.g., medical care, workers' compensation, lost productivity) and indirect costs (e.g., inefficiencies associated with replacement workers). The final amount totaled $8.9 billion in 2003 ($1,175 per resident). A 2002 report from the Minnesota Department of Health (Garrett, Brasure et al. 2001) estimates that in 2000, $495 million was spent treating diseases and conditions that would be avoided if all Minnesotans were physically active. This amount converts to over $100 per resident. Additional reports claim that too little physical inactivity was responsible for an estimated $84.5 million ($19 per capita) in hospital charges in Washington State (Claybrooke 2001), $104 million ($78 per capita) in South Carolina (Powell, Greaney et al. 1999), and $477 million in hospital charges in Georgia ($79 per capita) (Bricker, Powell et al. 2001).

These reports from various state agencies are complemented with more academically oriented research. For example, Colditz (1999) reviewed past literature on the economic costs of inactivity and concluded that the direct costs for those individuals reporting lack of physical activity was estimated to average approximately $128 per person. A separate analysis by Pratt et al. (2000) analyzed a stratified sample of 35,000 Americans from the 1987 national Medical Expenditures Survey. Examining the direct medical costs of men and women who reported physical activity versus those who did not reveals that the mean net annual benefit of physical activity was $330 per person in 1987 dollars. An alternative method used a cost-of-illness approach to attribute a proportion of medical and pharmacy costs for specific diseases to physical inactivity in 2001 (Garrett, Brasure et al. 2001). The authors first identified medical conditions associated with physical inactivity and then collected claims data related to those conditions from approximately 1.6 million patients 16 and older from a large, Midwest health plan. While the resulting conditions from lack of physical inactivity include depression, colon cancer, heart disease, osteoporosis, and stroke, the results from this study conclude that the costs of claims to the health plan attributable to physical inactivity translates to $57 per member. One challenge of these analyses is the decision whether to include diseases causally related to obesity.

A different approach than the dichotomized strategy estimates the impact of different modifiable health risk behaviors and measures their impact on health care expenditures. After gathering information from more than 61,500 employees of six employers gathered over a five-year study period, Goetzel et al. (1998) focused on a cohort of just over 46,000 employees. The analysis found that a "risk-free" individual incurred approximately $1,166 in average annual medical expenditures while those with poor health habits had average annual medical expenditures of more than $3,800. Thus they estimated the per-capita annual impact of poor exercise habits to be approximately $172. Pronk et al. (1999) also identify the relationship between modifiable health risks and short-term health care charges. This research surveyed a random sample of 5689 adults aged 40 years or older enrolled in a Minnesota health plan. Multivariate analysis on the modifiable health risks (diabetes, heart disease, body mass index, physical activity and smoking status) concluded that an additional day of physical activity (above zero) would yield a 4.7 percent reduction in charges (or a $27.99 reduction). The overarching result of the study is that obesity costs approximately $135 per member, per year and those with low fitness (inactivity) cost approximately $176 per member per year.

A couple of matters stand out to inform applicable methods. First, annual per capita cost savings vary between $19 and $1,175 with a median value of $128 (See Table 13.4). Second, some studies are disaggregate in nature and estimate costs by inpatient, outpatient, and pharmacy claims; others compare average healthcare expenditures of physically active versus inactive individuals. Third, some use a dichotomized approach to operationalize physically active individuals while others employ a modifiable health risks approach and do so in a relatively continuous scale. The studies are difficult to compare, however, because some include different conditions, outpatient and pharmacy costs, and actual paid amounts rather than charges. Nonetheless, existing literature provides adequate, though developing, methodologies for estimating the public health impact of bicycle facilities in terms of economic impacts.

Table 13.4. Different values of per capita cost savings

Study/Agency	Per Capita Cost Savings ($)
Washington State Department of Health	19
Garrett et al.	57
South Carolina Department of Health	78
Georgia Department of Human Resources	79
Colditz (1999)	92
Minnesota Department of Health	>100
Goetz et al.	172
Pronk et al.	176
Pratt	330
Michigan Fitness Foundation	1,175

(3) Safety

Increased cyclist safety is an often assumed, poorly understood, and highly controversial benefit of bicycle facilities. The task of establishing a safety derived, cost-based justification for bicycle facilities is similar to the process described in the previous section estimating public health benefits, albeit with different data. Researchers must first demonstrate relationships between a given cycling facility and safety outcomes. They then need to demonstrate that the measured outcomes of conditions with decreased safety imposes a financial burden to the individual or to society.

In general, the literature about the safety dimensions of bicycling manifests itself in three respects: (1) helmet use, (2) safety programs, and (3) levels of accidents or perceived level of safety that can be ascribed to facility design. The latter category is most germane to the construction of facilities and therefore comprises the heart of the below discussion. A key question seeks to marry data about safety (e.g., accidents or perceived comfort) with different attributes of cycling facilities. Our perspective on this literature aims to understand the degree to which different cycling facilities lead to an incremental safety benefit, measured in terms of decreased accidents or medical costs.

Existing literature in this respect measures safety in one of three ways: (1) number of fatalities, (2) number of accidents, and (3) perceived levels of comfort for the cyclist. Key explanatory variables behind these outcome measures are myriad and complex to identify. For example, the overwhelming majority of bicycle accidents resulting in fatalities are caused by collisions with motor vehicles (Osberg, Stiles et al. 1998). Less severe accidents tend to occur at intersections or at locations where motor vehicles and bicycles come in contact with each other (Hunter, Pein et al. 1995); it is further suggested that accidents are caused by differing expectations between auto drivers and bicyclists (Rasanen and Summala 1998). However, there is also evidence to suggest that some bicycle accidents do not involve any other party (Eilertpetersson and Schelp 1997); this is especially true for children (Powell and Tanz 2000).

The prevailing argument is that enhanced facilities—bike lanes, bikeways and special intersection modifications—improve cyclist safety (Pucher and Dijkstra 2003). This claim, however, is the source of a rich controversy within the literature as evidenced by the debate between Forester (2001) and Pucher (2001). Part of the controversy around this topic is fueled by differences between what cyclists state they prefer (i.e., their perception) and what studies with collision data actually reveal.

It is widely acknowledged that increased perception of safety is important to encourage cycling as a means of transportation and recreation (Noakes 1995); (Federal Highway Administration 1999). Subsequently, providing separated bicycle facilities along roadways is mentioned as a key ingredient in the burgeoning literature related to bicycle related stress factors (Sorton and Walsh 1994); bicycle interaction hazard scores (Landis 1994), relative danger index (Moritz 1998), compatibility indexes (Harkey, Reinfurt et al. 1998).

While a variety of labels appear in the literature, the overriding goal of these works is to determine and predict conditions for safe bicycling based on different cyclists perceptions of safety. The culmination of these works can best be described under the banner of Level of Service models, originally developed in 1987 in Davis, California and level of service (LOS) models (Epperson 1994; Landis, Vattikuti et al. 1997). The participants of this study were of diverse demographic and skill backgrounds and cycled 30 roadway segments. Including the variables of traffic volume per lane, posted speed limit weighted with the percentage of heavy vehicles, adjoining land use, width of outside through lane, and pavement conditions, the researchers were able to explain almost 75% of the variation. The model consists of four basic factors—pavement conditions, traffic speed, lane width, and traffic volume per lane which aim to serve as a tool for predicting accident along roadways between automobiles and bicycles.

The bulk of the existing literature on bicycle level of service and perceived safety focuses primarily on through mid-block roadway segments. It rarely separates bicycle lanes from other shared use conditions (wide curb lanes or paved shoulders) and rarely considers the role of intersections. While stretches of roadways are important, often the most significant and complex design and safety challenges occur at street intersections (Jackson 2002). In response to this void, two recent research papers have aimed to shed light on this matter (Landis 2003; Krizek and Roland 2004). Landis' recent work (2003) derived a model to evaluate the perceived hazard of bicyclists riding through intersections. Again, with a highly varied demographic and cyclist ability sample, this study produced a model with a high degree of explanatory power (R2=0.83) for bicycle intersection level of service. Significant variables included motor vehicle volume, width of the outside lane, and the crossing distance of the intersection. In this study there was no control for the presence or absence of a bicycle lane, but the width of the outside lane variable did include the bicycle lane were it present. The research by Krizek and Roland (2004) analyzed the severity of instances where existing bicycle lanes and the corresponding physical characteristics. Using multi-variate analysis, the findings suggest that bicycle lane discontinuities ending on the left side of the street, with increased distance of crossing intersections, having parking after the discontinuity, and wider width of the curb lane are statistically elements that contribute to higher levels of discomfort for the cyclist.

The degree to which perception of safety translates into actual increased safety, however, is still debated. It proves difficult to translate perceived measures of safety into quantifiable or economic estimates. We therefore turn to discussing research showing correlations between bicycle facilities and accidents which yields far from a clear picture.

There is evidence to support the notion that collision-type accidents are lower on off-road paths (Aultman-Hall and Kaltenecker 1999). Using before and after analysis, Garder's research (1998) found raised bicycle crossings to be more appealing and safer for cyclists than at-grade crossings. However, there exists an equal, if not greater body of research suggesting no relationships or relationships in the opposite direction. Research examining conflicts at approaching intersections on bike lane and wide curb lane segments determined that both facilities improve riding conditions for bicyclists, but that the two facilities themselves are not different in safety (Hunter, Stewart et al. 1999). Smith and Walsh analyzed before and after accident data for two bike lanes in Madison, Wisconsin finding no statistically significant difference (Smith and Walsh 1988). Also, Hunter's analyses of bike-boxes in Eugene, Oregon (Hunter 2000) and blue bike lanes in Portland, Oregon (Hunter, Harkey et al. 2000) demonstrate that no bike-car conflicts took place while the boxes were used as intended, but that the bike boxes did not seem to improve the number of conflicts in general (Hunter 2000).

There appears to be good reason for the existing debate over the safety benefits of bicycle facilities. While there is considerable literature suggesting cyclists perceive greater safety with facilities—and advocates certainly argue for such—the bottom line is that there little conclusive evidence to suggest such. For this reason, it is extremely difficult to prescribe guidelines, though, the research methodologies certainly exist as described above.

(4) Decreased Externalitites, Congestion

The most common assumption asserted is that cycling trips substitute for auto trips, yielding transportation benefits to society-at-large such as decreased congestion, improved air quality, and decreased of energy sources such as non-renewable natural resources. While the substitution element may hold true for some cyclists it is extremely difficult to reliably parse out such trips that would otherwise be made by car.

The nature and magnitude of any substitution is important to determine and could be estimated via a variety of means. In some instances, a bike trip may replace a car commute; in many cases, however, bicycle are likely made in addition to trips that would otherwise occur (Handy 1992) or for a different reason (e.g., recreation). Assuming a fixed demand of overall travel, a best-case scenario for bicycle substitution stems from an assumption well known in the field of travel behavior modeling referred to as Independence from Irrelevant Alternatives (IIA). That is, bicycles draw from other modes in proportion to their current mode shares. For instance, bicycles would draw 85 percent from current drive alone trips, five percent from auto passenger trips, five percent from transit trips, and five percent from walk trips. This of course is unlikely to be strictly true, so an important part of the benefit analysis would be to determine which of these groups is more likely to switch to bicycling and furthermore, and which socio-economic characteristics could be targeted to result in higher rates of cycling.

Assuming bicycling can help bicyclists travel faster, more safely, in a better environment or for shorter distances, its utility compared to other modes will increase. There may be an estimable effect in terms of substitution and there are different approaches for measuring this phenomenon. At a crude level, one could estimate the number of bicycle miles of travel and auto miles of travel. Assuming a fixed rate of substitution (i.e., 60 percent of all cycling trips are utilitarian in nature and are substituting for a car trip), one could estimate an upper bound of all mileage that is substituted and the overall social costs being saved. However, this does not account for the possibility that bicycle trips may be substituting for other modes than driving. Furthermore it says little about how many additional trips from potential cyclists that could be induced. Such information would be most reliably obtained by estimating a mode-choice model for different types of cycling trips and calculating the likelihood of substitution rates in that manner. The latter strategy is one subject to elaborate modeling schemes and survey data.

It is important to recognize, however, that any reduced congestion benefit to society needs to be tempered by "induced demand" phenomenon which may obviate congestion or pollution reductions due to diversion (Downs 1992). This implies that reduced traffic congestion that may result from the construction of an additional bike lane may largely (though not entirely) be consumed by other drivers making additional trips, drivers lengthening trips, and additional development. This suggests that any reduction in congestion (and subsequently pollution and energy benefits) will be small at best. (Nevertheless, the additional opportunities for drivers to pursue activities that previously had been too expensive prior to the capacity expansion (of roads or bike lanes) engender some benefits on part of those new drivers).

(5) Livability

A third benefit refers to social attributes accrued by individuals who receive benefits of such facilities, either directly or indirectly. One of the reasons people pay a premium to live in desirable areas is that they are paying for the option to use specific facilities, whether or not they actually do. For instance people may pay a premium to live near a bike path despite not cycling themselves because they might want to in the future. In this respect, such proximity would be valued by current and potential users. These benefits are revealed through preferences which represent an elusive phenomenon to which an economic value can be attached. A compelling strategy to measure these non-market goods analyzes the choices households reveal in their purchase of home locations in efforts to understand how they implicitly or explicitly evaluate the desirability of a certain good. A revealed preference approach would measure individuals' actual behavior and this can be done through hedonic modeling to learn if and how much residents value accessibility to bicycle facilities.

Discerning the relative value of non-market goods using hedonic modeling techniques is a method that has been employed for years ever since first applications by Lancaster (1966) and Rosen (1974). An extensive review of this literature (Sirmans and Macpherson 2003) documents nearly 200 applications that have examined home purchases to estimate values of several home attributes including structural features (e.g., lot size, a home's finished square feet, and number of bedrooms), internal and external features (e.g., fireplaces, air conditioning, garage spaces, and porches), the natural environment features (e.g., scenic views), attributes of the neighborhood and location (e.g., crime, golf courses, and trees), public services (e.g., school and infrastructure quality), marketing, and financing. The application germane to this inquiry focuses on the relative impact of bicycle lanes and trails. It is important, however, to understand the relative value of different types of facilities as they may have substantially different appeal. Some trails are on existing streets (demarcated by paint striping), some are next to existing (separated by curbs), while others are clearly separated from traffic and are often contained within open spaces. The latter category, being the most attractive for many bicyclists is likely to have the largest effect. To effectively estimate the value of such facilities it is important to be able to explain and control for the degree to which open space versus the bike trail contained within the open space contribute to a home's value. In many metropolitan areas bike trails and open space share a spatial location and at minimum exhibit similar recreational qualities. Any research failing to account and control for such correlation would be misguided in its attempt to estimate the independent value of bicycle trails. For this reason, not only is it important to control for structural attributes of the home, characteristics of the neighborhood, geographic location, but it is important to consider the value of adjacent open space. The value of open space has been estimated several applications of hedonic regressions (Quang Do and Grudnitski 1995; Benson, Hansen et al. 1998; Luttik 2000; Irwin and Bockstael 2001; Geoghegan 2002; Anderson and West 2004).

The hedonic pricing method is appealing because it is rooted firmly in market prices and provides a strategy to perform an economic valuation for non-market facilities. To our knowledge the only attempt to extend such methodology to bicycle facilities is offered by Lindsey et al. (2003) who analyze the property value using a half-mile buffer around a greenway. The outcome of this methodology would then be econometric models that can be used to reliably measure if residents value access to bicycle facilities and if so, to what degree. This value could be then be easily converted to monetary amounts.

(6) Fiscal

Right-of-way preservation is the process of preserving land needed for future infrastructure, most often in the form of transportation. It is a benefit reaped exclusively by the public agencies planning such facilities. Consider the situation where there may be a plan to build a rail transit corridor in ten years; it may be economically prudent to acquire the land sooner rather than later for several reasons (Dye Management Group 2002). First, the price of land may rise faster than inflation. Second, acquiring the land now may ensure it is not developed, while not acquiring it now may require the destruction of recently constructed buildings. There are, of course, risks associated with right-of-way preservation. Land may be acquired but the resources never found to complete the project. Right-of-way acquired prior to use for a future road or transit line may still be used for transportation. Placing a bicycle facility along the right-of-way is relatively inexpensive, ensures a transportation use for the corridor (ensuring it will not be viewed as a park land) and provides user benefits instead of allowing the land to lie fallow.

The economic value of right-of-way preservation can be estimated by multiplying the probability of use in the future by the difference of the net present value of future cost if not preserved and the present cost. Since acquiring right-of-way that is already developed is more expensive, this should output a positive value. The probability of future use is an important variable that is usually case specific, but it gets at the idea of preserving options. For example, a plan may suggest three alternative rights-of-way for a route. The probability of any route would then be less than one-third. Thus, the right-of-way preservation benefit would depend on the difference in costs multiplied by that probability. There are similar ways of estimating this value that might produce different results.

For example, the present cost of the right-of-way could be estimated in the cost category, and then consider "selling" the right-of-way in the future to the other transportation project as part of the salvage value of the bicycle facility. This salvage value is an estimate of the market value of the land. If the net present value of the salvage value exceeds the present cost, there may also be a right of preservation benefit. In such deliberations, it would be important to account for the discount value of completing the project—the present value of using available funds to complete a project and buying land for future projects later. For example, a benefit/cost ratio of 1.1 that would imply that one million dollars spent on a project will generate stream of benefits worth 1.1 million in present dollars. We could take this as the baseline and compare early ROW purchase to it. That is, the baseline is that some amount of money "x" greater than $1M will be spent to buy ROW in the future.

To estimate the present value of using the million dollars to buy ROW for future use, delaying a hypothetical project that would have been done with that money, consider how that benefit stream would change. First, a given project may eventually generate the same stream of benefits, but delayed by "n" years, giving a lower present value. However, the money that is saved (x minus $1M) by not paying a higher price later for the land, means that an additional project can be done at that time, yielding extra benefits, again starting "n" years in the future.

13.5 Summary and Conclusions

This essay interprets literature analyzing the benefits of bicycling or bicycle facilities. We do so by discussing the relatively sporadic nature of this body of knowledge (a primary shortcoming of this work is that it is not cumulative) and other confounding issues inherent to this endeavor. We articulate the population of interest in most studies, the benefits that are measured, the geographic scale at which they are measured, and discuss the difficulties involved with varying methodologies. We next review almost 25 studies that attach an assumed or economic benefit to such goods or areas. A main finding of the review is that studies in different locations use varied data and methodologies to arrive at widely varying conclusions.

For such information to be useful in policy circles, several actions need to be taken (in addition to improving data collection efforts). First, the majority of past work has a clear advocacy bent; it is not always known how and where much of the data is derived. It is unclear from most of the studies if the available data was analyzed in a completely objective manner. Second, it is important that continued discussion be most appropriate and useful scale for analysis. The content of this type of work is often called for in policy discussions. In its current condition, however, it lacks appeal because many of the studies are conducted at a relatively abstract scale rather than a project scale. For this reason, we suggest in this paper that benefits be estimated on a municipal (or regional) scale or for even more disaggregate unites. Finally, there exists considerable room for improving the manner in which these methodologies are approached. Our intent is to provide the foundation for urging a consistent framework in which different benefits could be estimated and subsequently compared. If the goal is to implement plans that systematically integrate or account for such consideration, then such methods and improvements will ultimately lead to more sound policy decisions and bicycle facility investment.

Acknowledgements

The author would like to thank several individuals who, through various conversations, have considerably contributed to and shaped the content of this manuscript. These colleagues include David Levinson, Gary Barnes, Rich Killingsworth, Bill Hunter, David Loutzenheiser, and Don Kidston. Katherine Reilly assisted in reviewing past literature and constructing figures and tables. Initial work on this topic is largely sponsored by support from the Minnesota Department of Transportation. This essay helped lay the foundation for guidelines that are available at: http://www.bicyclinginfo.org/bikecost/. All opinions and errors are those of the author.

References

Anderson ST, West SE (2004) The Value of Open Space Proximity and Size: City versus Suburbs. Macalester College, Department of Economics, working paper.

Argys L, Mocan, N (2000) Bicycling and Walking in Colorado: Economic Impact and Household Survey Results. Colorado Department of Transportation.

Aultman-Hall L, Kaltenecker MG (1999) Toronto bicycle commuter safety rates. Accident Analysis and Prevention 31: 675-686.

Ben-Akiva M, Lerman S (1989) Discrete Choice Analysis - Theory and Application to Travel Demand. Journal of Transport Economics and Policy.

Benson ED, Hansen JL, Schwartz AL Jr, Smersh GT (1998) Pricing Residential Amenities: The Value of A View. Journal of Real Estate Finance and Economics 16(1), 55-73.

Betz C, Bergstrom J, Bowker JM (2003) A Contingent Trip Model for Estimating Rail-trail Demand. Journal of Environmental Planning and Management 46(1): 79-96.

Blair SN, LaMonte MJ, Nichaman MZ (2004) The evolution of physical activity recommendations: how much is enough?. American Journal of Clinical Nutrition 79(5): 913-920.

Bradley M, Kroes PE (1990) Forecasting Issues in Stated Preference Survey Research. 3rd International Conference on Survey Methods in Transportation.

Bricker SK, Powell KE, Parashar U, Rowe AK, Troy KG, Seim KM, Eidson PL, Wilson P S, Pilgrim VC, Smith EM (2001) Physical Activity Report. Georgia, Georgia Department of Human Resources, Division of Public Health and the American Heart Association, Southeast Affiliate.

Buis J (2000) The Economic Significance of Cycling: A study to illustrate the costs and benefits of cycling policy. Den Haag, Interface for Cycling Expertise.

Chenoweth D, DeJong G, Sheppard L (2003) The Economic Cost of Inactivity in Michigan. Lansing, Michigan Fitness Foundation.

Claybrooke C (2001) Physical Activity in Washington State. Washington State Department of Health.

Colditz GA (1999) Economic costs of obesity and inactivity. Medicine and Science in Sports and Exercise 31(11 (Suppl)): S663-S667.

Crane R (2000) The Influence of Urban Form on Travel: An Interpretative Review. Journal of Planning Literature 15(1): 3-23.

Downs A (1992) Stuck in Traffic: Coping with Peak-Hour Congestion. Washington D.C., Cambridge, Brookings Institution, Lincoln Institute of Land Policy.

Dye Management Group (2002) Assessment of Techniques of Corridor Preservation in South Dakota, South Dakota Department of Transportation.

Eilertpetersson E, Schelp L (1997) An epidemiological study of bicycle-related injuries. Accident Analysis and Prevention 29(3): 363-372.

Epperson B (1994) Evaluating Suitability of Roadways for Bicycle Use: Toward a Cycling Level-of-Service Standard. Transportation Research Record 1438: 9-16.

Everett M (1976) Measuring the Economic Value of Exercise in Labor Intensive Urban Transportation Systems. Transportation Research Record 599.

Everett M, Dorman J (1976) New Approach to Economic Evaluation of Labor-Intensive Transportation Systems. Transportation Research Record 599.

Ewing R, Cervero R (2001) Travel and the Built Environment: A Synthesis. Transportation Research Record 1780: 87-112.

Federal Highway Administration (1999) National Bicycling and Walking Study Five Year Status Report by the U.S. Department of Transportation. Washington, D.C., U.S. Department of Transportation.

Fix P, Loomis J (1997) The economic benefits of mountain biking at one of its Meccas: an application of the travel cost method to mountain biking in Moab, Utah. Journal of Leisure Research 29(3): 342-352.

Fix P, Loomis J (1998) Comparing the economic value of mountain biking estimated using revealed and stated preference. Journal of Environmental Planning and Management 41(2): 227-236.

Forester J (2001) The Bicycle Transportation Controversy. Transportation Quarterly 55(2): 7-17.

Fowkes T Wardman M (1988) The design of stated preference travel choice experiments. Journal of Transport Economics and Policy 22: 27-44.

Frank LD (2000) Land Use and Transportation Interaction: Implications on Public Health and Quality of Life. Journal of Planning Education and Research(20): 6-22.

Garder P, Leden L, Pulkkinen U (1998) Measuring the Safety Effect of Raised Bicycle Crossings Using a New Research Methodology. Transportation Research Record 1636: 64-70.

Garrett N, Brasure M, Schmitz K, Schultz M (2001) The Direct Cost of Physical Inactivity to a Health Plan. St. Paul, Minnesota, Minnesota Department of Health.

Geoghegan J (2002) The Value of Open Spaces in Residential Land Use. Land Use Policy 19(1): 91-98.

Goetzel RZ, Anderson DR, Whitmer RW, Ozminkowski RJ, Dunn RL, Wasserman J (1998) The Relationship Between Modifiable Health Risks and Health Care Expenditures: An Analysis of the Multi-Employer HERO Health Risk and Cost Database. The Journal of Occupational and Environmental Management 40(10): 843-854.

Handy SL (1992) Regional Versus Local Accessibility: Neotraditional Development and its Implications for Non-work Travel. Built Environment 18(4): 253-267.

Handy SL, Boarnet MG, Ewing R, Killingsworth R (2002) How the Built Environment Affects Physical Activity: Views from Urban Planning. American Journal of Preventative Medicine 23: 64-73.

Hansen CJ, Stevens LC, Coast JR (2001) Exercise duration and mood state: How much is enough to feel better?. Health Psychology 20(4): 267-275.

Harkey DL, Reinfurt DW Mnuiman M (1998) Development of the Bicycle Compatibility Index. Transportation Research Record 1636: 13-20.

Hunter WW (2000) Evaluation of Innovative Bike-Box Application in Eugene, Oregon. Transportation Research Record 1705: 101-115.

Hunter WW, Harkey DL, Stewart JR, Birk ML (2000) Evaluation of Blue Bike Lane Treatment in Portland, Oregon. Transportation Research Record 1705: 107-115.

Hunter WW, Pein WE, Stutts JC (1995) Bicycle/Motor Vehicle Crash Types: The Early 1990's. Transportation Research Record 1502: 56-74 (1995).

Hunter WW, Stewart JR, Stutts JC (1999) Study of Bicycle Lanes Versus Wide Curb Lanes. Transportation Research Record 1674: 70-77.

Irwin EG, Bockstael NE (2001) The Problem of Identifying Land Use Spillovers: Measuring the Effects of Open Space on Residential Property Values. American Journal of Agricultural Economics 83(3): 698-704.

Jackson N (2002) Bike Lane Design Guide. Chicago, Pedestrian and Bicycle Information Center, City of Chicago Department of Transportation, Chicagoland Bicycle Federation.

Krizek KJ, Birnbaum AS, Levinson D (2004) A Schematic for Focusing on Youth in Investigations of Community Design and Physical Activity. American Journal of Health Promotion 19(1): 57-63.

Krizek KJ, Roland R (2004) What is at the End of the Road? Factors Affecting Discontinuities of On-Street Bicycle Lanes in Urban Settings. Active Communities Transportation (ACT) Research Group, University of Minnesota working paper.

Lancaster KJ (1966) A New Approach to Consumer Theory. The Journal of Political Economy 74(2): 132-157.

Landis BW (1994) Bicycle Interaction Hazard Score, A Theoretical Model. Transportation Research Record 1438: 3-8.

Landis BW, Vattikuti VR, Brannick MT (1997) Real-Time Human Perceptions: Toward a Bicycle Level of Service. Transportation Research Record 1578: 119-126.

Landis BW, Vattikuti VR, Ottenberg RM, Petritsch TA (2003) Intersection Level of Service for the Bicycle Through Movement. Journal of the Transportation Research Record. 1828: 101-106.

Lindsey G, Knaap G (1999) Willingness to pay for urban greenway projects. Journal of the American Planning Association 65(3): 297-301.

Lindsey G, Man J, Payton S, Dickson K (2003) Amenity and Recreation Values of Urban Greenways. The Association of European Schools of Planning Congress, Leuven, Belgium.

Lindsey G, Przybylski M (1998) Economic Considerations in Planning Urban Greenways: A Brief Review. Indianapolis, Center for Urban Policy and the Environment, School of Public and Environmental Affairs, University of Indiana 20.

Litman T (2004) Economic Value of Walkability. World Transport Policy & Practice 10(1): 5-14.

Luttik J (2000) The Value of Trees, Water and Open Space as Reflected by House Prices in the Netherlands. Landscape and Urban Planning 48: 161-167.

Maine Department of Transportation (2001) Bicycle Tourism in Maine: Economic Impacts and Marketing Recommendations. Augusta, Maine Department of Transportation.

Moore RL, Graefe AR, Gitelson RJ (1994) The economic impact of rail-trails. Journal of Park and Recreation Administration 12(2): 63-72.

Moritz WE (1998) Adult Bicyclists in the United States, Characteristics and Riding Experience in 1996. Transportation Research Record 1636: 1-7.

Nelson C, Vogt C, van der Woud A, Valentine B, Lynch J (2001) 2000 Midland County Recreation Needs Assessment: The Pere Marquette Rail – Trail. East Lansing, Department of Park, Recreation and Tourism Resources.

Noakes TD (1995) Fatal Cycling Injuries. Sports Medicine 20(5): 348-362.

Osberg JS, Stiles SC, Asare OK (1998) Bicycle safety behavior in Paris and Boston. Accident Analysis and Prevention 30(5): 679-687.

Pate R, Pratt M, Blair SN, Haskell W, Macera CA, Bouchard C, Buchner D, Ettinger W, Heath GW, King A, Kriska A, Leon A, Marcus BH, Morris JM, Paffenberger RSJ, Patrick K, Pollock ML, Rippe JM, Sallis J, Wilmore J (1995) Physical Activity and Public Health: A Recommendation from the Centers for Disease Control and Prevention and the American College of Sports Medicine. Journal of the American Medical Association 273(5): 402-407.

PKF Consulting (1994) Analysis of economic impacts of the Northern Central Rail Trail. Annapolis, Maryland Greenways Commission, Maryland Department of Natural Resources, 47.

Powell EC, Tanz RR (2000) Cycling injuries treated in emergency departments - Need for bicycle helmets among preschoolers. Archives of Pediatrics Adolescent Medicine 154(11): 1096-1100.

Powell KE, Greaney ML, Huang Y, Whitt M (1999) Physical Activity in South Carolina. Columbia, University of South Carolina School of Public Health.

Pratt M, Macera CA, Wang G (2000) Higher Direct Medical Costs Associated with Physical Inactivity. The Physician and Sports Medicine 28(10).

Pronk NP, Goodman MJ, O'Connor PJ, Martinson BC (1999) Relationship Between Modifiable Health Risks and Short-term Health Care Charges. Journal of the American Medical Association 292(23): 2235-2239.

Przybylski M, Lindsey G (1998) Economic Evaluation of Major Urban Greenway Projects. Indianapolis, Center for Urban Policy and the Environment.

Pucher J (2001) Cycling Safety on Bikeways vs. Roads. Transportation Quarterly 55(4), 9-11.

Pucher J, Dijkstra L (2003) Promoting Safe Walking and Cycling to Improve Public Health: Lessons From The Netherlands and Germany. American Journal of Public Health 93(9): 1509-1516.

Quang DoA, Grudnitski G (1995) Golf Courses and Residential House Prices: An Empririical Examination. Journal of Real Estate Finance and Economics 10: 261-270.

Randall A (1994) A difficulty with the travel cost method. Land Economics 70(1): 88-96.

Rankinen T, Bouchard C (2002) Dose-Response Issues Concerning the Relations Between Regular Physical Activity and Health. Washington, D.C., President's Council on Physical Fitness and Sports. Series 3.

Rasanen M, Summala H (1998) Attention and Expectation Problems in Bicycle-Car Collisions: An In-Depth Study. Accident Analysis and Prevention 30(5): 657-666.

Rosen S (1974) Hedonic Prices and Implicit Markets: Product Differentiation in Pure Competition. The Journal of Political Economy 82(1).

Saelensminde K (2002) Walking- and cycling-track networks in Norwegian cities: Cost-benefit analyses including health effects and external costs of road traffic. Oslo, Institute of Transport Economics, 50.

Sallis J, Frank LD, Saelens BE, Kraft MK (2004) Active Transportation and Physical Activity: Opportunities for Collaboration on Transportation and Public Health Research. Transportation Research Part A-Policy and Practice 38: 249-268.

Schutt AM (1998) Trails for Economic Development: A Case Study. Journal of Applied Recreation Research 23(2): 127 - 145.

Sharples R (1995a) A framework for the evaluation of facilities for cyclists - Part 1. Traffic Engineering and Control: 142-149.

Sharples R (1995b) A framework for the evaluation of facilities for cyclists - Part 2. Traffic Engineering and Control: 221-223.

Siderlis C, Moore RL (1995) Outdoor recreation net benefits of rail-trails. Journal of Leisure Research 27(4): 344-359.

Sirmans GS, Macpherson DA (2003) The Composition of Hedonic Pricing Models: A Review of the Literature. National Association of Realtors.

Smith RL Jr, Walsh T (1988) Safety Impacts of Bicycle Lanes. Transportation Research Record 1168: 49-56.

Sorton A, Walsh T (1994) Bicycle Stress Level as a Tool to Evaluate Urban and Suburban Bicycle Compatibility. Transportation Research Record 1438: 17-25.

Sumathi NR, Berard DA (1997) Mountain biking in the Chequamegon Area of Northern Wisconsin and Implications for Regional Development, University of Wisconsin-Extension.

U.S. Department of Health and Human Services PHS, Centers for Disease Control and Prevention, National Center for Chronic Disease Prevention and Health Promotion, Division of Nutrition and Physical Activity (2003, 1999) Promoting physical activity, a guide for community action, National Center for Chronic Disease Prevention and Health Promotion, Division of Nutrition and Physical Activity.

U.S. Department of Health and Human Services, P. H. S., Centers for Disease Control and Prevention, National Center for Chronic Disease Prevention and Health Promotion, Division of Nutrition and Physical Activity (2004, 2003) How active do adults need to be to gain some benefit?, National Center for Chronic Disease Prevention and Health Promotion, Division of Nutrition and Physical Activity.

U.S. Department of Transportation (2000) Bicycle and Pedestrian Data: Sources, Needs, & Gaps. Washington, D.C., Bureau of Transportation Statistics.

U.S. Department of Transportation (2003) National Survey of Pedestrian and Bicyclist Attitudes and Behaviors. Washington D.C., National Highway Traffic Safety Administration; Bureau of Transportation Statisitics.

Wang GJ, Macera CA, Scudder-Soucie B, Schmid T, Pratt M, Buchner D (2004) Cost effectiveness of a bicycle/pedestrian trail development in health promotion. Preventive Medicine 38(2): 237-242.

Wardman M (1988) A Comparison of Revealed Preference and Stated Preference Models of Travel Behavior. Journal of Transport Economics and Policy 22: 71-91.

Wilkinson WC, Eddy N, MacFadden G, Burgess B (2002) Increasing Physical Activity Through Community Design: A Guide for Public Health Practitioners. Washington, D.C., National Center for Bicycling and Walking.

14 Valuation of Transport Externalities by Stated Choice Methods

Juan de Dios Ortúzar
Department of Transport Engineering
Pontificia Universidad Católica of Chile

Luis Ignacio Rizzi
Department of Transport Engineering
Pontificia Universidad Católica of Chile

14.1 Introduction

An externality is defined as any action taken by an economic agent that has an impact on the utility or on the production function of one or more third agents without incorporating the economics effects of those impacts in his/her private accounting. As the provision of urban transport generates negative externalities, transport authorities willing to adopt a cost-benefit approach to project appraisal require to properly estimate the value people place on reducing such externalities. As there are no real markets to measure this, economists must resort to techniques that allow them to infer the corresponding prices. From a theoretical standpoint, it is straightforward to develop these techniques; however, applying them to obtain meaningful results is quite complex. Some techniques can accommodate the use of revealed preference (RP) data; i.e., data gathered by observing people behaviour in real markets. The drawback with this sort of data, however, is that economists need to make rather dubious assumptions. For example, it is customary to assume that people are fully aware of the environmental goods being modelled and that they consider these in the same way the modeller does.

As an alternative approach, stated preference (SP) data provides a different perspective. Here a pseudo-market is created in which respondents have to act as they would do in real life. For a pseudo-market to work people must be aware of the environmental good the modeller is trying to value. According to Nash (1997), methods designed to elicit people's preferences on environmental goods should be more successful when valuing local externalities. These constitute adverse effects of transport systems on which most people may have already defined their preferences. Road accidents, local atmospheric pollution and noise clearly fall within this category and are currently deemed to rank among the most negative impacts of road transport at a local scale. Hence, it is believed that appropriate valuation case studies could be designed in order to come up with willingness to pay (WTP) measures for reducing each of these externalities.

In this chapter, we will describe one of the most promising technique to estimate prices that are not revealed by simple market observation; this technique rests on the estimation of discrete choice models based on SP data and is most frequently referred to as Stated Choice (SC) in the transport literature, or Conjoint Analysis in the marketing literature (Louviere et al 2000); Daniels and Adamowicz (2000) provide a valuable overview on some important issues concerning environmental valuation. Here will discuss three applications of SC undertaken in Santiago, the capital city of Chile, to elicit WTP for improving urban road safety, better air quality and increasing levels of quietness. The rest of the chapter is organised as follows. In section 14.2, a brief description of discrete choice models and their application to stated choice data is provided in order to guide both experimental design and econometric analysis. Sections 14.3, 14.4 and 14.5 contain SC applications for the valuation of interurban road accidents, atmospheric pollution and quietness respectively. These applications were undertaken in a large urban area: Santiago, Chile. The chapter closes with a summary.

14.2 Discrete Choice Models and Stated Choice Data

Many daily economic decisions involve choosing one among a set of mutually exclusive alternatives. To mention a few examples, consider the choice of transport mode for a trip to work, choice of a TV set brand, choice of a physician and choice of residential location. In all these cases people have to evaluate the attractiveness of each alternative and then choose, if rational behaviour is assumed, the option that provides the highest level of utility. Following Lancaster (1966), the attractivenes, or utility of each alternative, can be decomposed into the utility of each of the attributes characterising the alternative. For instance, the attributes of a trip by bus to work may include the access time to the bus stop, the waiting time, travel time, access time to the place of work from the bus stop, fare, level of comfort, safety and so on. The traditional microeconomic framework is not well suited to analyse this type of decisions and it is preferable to apply discrete choice models. In this section, we provide guidance to perform an econometric analysis based on sound microeconomic principles.

Assume an individual has to choose one option out of a given choice set. Her utility maximisation problem will look like this (Jara Diaz and Videla 1989):

$$\max_m \langle \max_x \mathrm{U}(x, q_m) / m \in \mathrm{M} \rangle \tag{14.1}$$

subject to $p\,x + c_m = \mathrm{I}$

where x is a vector of goods, M the discrete choice set (its cardinal is N), m an element of that set, p the vector price of goods x, c_m the cost of alternative m, q_m the vector of attributes of alternative m, and I is income. This constitutes a discrete maximization problem, which can be decomposed into N differentiable sub problems:

$$\max_{x} U(x, q_m) / m \in M \tag{14.2}$$

subject to $p\,x = I - c_m$

The individual will choose the option that reports the highest level of U among the N differentiable problems. Thus, we obtain a conditional indirect utility function for each of the N alternatives:

$$V_m = V(p, I - c_m, q_m). \tag{14.3}$$

Assuming an additively conditional indirect utility function, Eq. (14.3) yields:

$$V_m(p, I - c_m, q_m) = v_m(p) + v_m(I - c_m) + v_m(q_m)$$

and as the first term is the same for each alternative m, it drops out. Next assume a linear-in-income utility function, so that the preceding Eq. looks like this:

$$V_m(p, I - c_m, q_m) = \alpha(I - c_m) + v_m(q_m)$$

and now income drops out. Observe that the marginal utility of income is given by minus the parameter of cost. Finally, if we also assume and additive $v_m(q_m)$ term, the following simple expression is obtained:

$$V_m(p, I - c_m, q_m) = \alpha^{\circ} c_m + \sum_{l} \beta_l q_{ml} \tag{14.4}$$

where α° and β_l are the parameters associated to cost and each of the l attributes of each option m (α° accounts for the sign change in α). This result can also be obtained by a first order Taylor expansion of Eq. 14.3. The reader should be fully aware of the restrictions that Eq. 14.4 imposes on preferences. Although this model is correct from the consumer's perspective, it is not from the modeller's standpoint. As he cannot observe all the relevant information used by the individual to choose her preferred alternative, he can just estimate choice probabilities. To that end, Eq. 14.4 should read like this:

$$U_m = U(p, I - c_m, q_m, \varepsilon_m) \tag{14.5}$$

where ε_m represents an error term. Note that these terms are not just statistical noise which deviate observations from their expected value, but components of preferences themselves from the modeller's perspective; hence, error terms will have an impact on both the underlying preferences and welfare measures that can be derived from the models (Hanemann and Kanninen, 1999). As an analogy to Eq. 14.4, we can write the most usual random utility expression:

$$U_m = \alpha^{\circ} c_m + \sum_{l} \beta_l q_{ml} + \varepsilon_m = V_m + \varepsilon_m \tag{14.6}$$

and note that errors are introduced in additive form. If they distribute identically and independently (iid) Gumbel between alternatives, the popular multinomial logit (MNL) model is obtained (see for example, Ortúzar and Willumsen 2001), where the probability of choosing alternative i from the set M, is given by:

$$Prob(i) = Prob\left(U_i > U_m,\ i \neq m,\ \forall m \in M\right) \left(= \frac{\exp\left(\lambda V_i\right)}{\sum_{m \in M} \exp\left(\lambda V_m\right)} \right) \tag{14.7}$$

where λ is a scale factor inversely related to the unknown standard deviation of the errors ε, and in normal applications has to be normalised (i.e. taken as one) as it is not identifiable.

If the modeller is interested in valuing a specific attribute l, he can consider the ratio β_l / α^0. This gives the maximum amount of money an individual would pay for a marginal improvement in attribute l, and is simply obtained by fixing the level of conditional indirect utility and allowing to vary the cost and the level of attribute l only in Eq. 14.6. By marginal, it is implied an improvement in the alternative currently being chosen and which will continue to be chosen. In the case studies presented below we will only compute this type of welfare measure. In particular, if the β_l refers to a non-market good such as environmental amenities, road safety or travel time, it is then immediate to derive WTP measures for these goods.

For non-marginal improvements and/or improvements in the attributes of non-chosen options affecting the probability of choice, the simple ratio above does not work because it fails to take into account that people can switch between alternatives in order to attain the highest level of utility. As we are dealing with probabilistic choice models, the expected change in welfare needs to be computed. For the MNL model with linear-in-income utility it can be shown that the appropriate expected welfare measure is given by the change in the inclusive value (composite utility) before (bc) and after (ac) the change (Small and Rosen 1981):

$$-\frac{1}{\alpha}\left\{ \log\left[\sum_{m \in M} \exp\left(V_m\right)\right]^{ac} - \log\left[\sum_{m \in M} \exp\left(V_m\right)\right]^{bc} \right\} \tag{14.8}$$

When the assumption of a linear-in-income utility function does not work the formula needed to compute the expected welfare measure is much more involved (Mc Fadden 1995; Karlstrom 2000), although the MNL model (and even its generalisation, the nested logit model) is still applicable. However if we relax the assumptions of fixed α^0 and β_l parameters for the whole population and/or that of identical and independent Gumbel errors, the MNL model is no longer valid. The first relaxation gives rise to random parameter (taste) models such as mixed logit (Train 2003) which are relevant in the context of this chapter as we explain below.

Analysts use two types of data for econometric analysis, revealed and stated preference data. RP data is based on real market behaviour but suffers two limitations. First, it does not allow us to study situations beyond the existence of real markets (i.e. how people would behave in new choice contexts). Second, the data itself is many times subject to problems of collinearity (Maddala 1992) and/or insufficient variability, thus, precluding the estimation of the effect of many relevant explicative variables. In addition, RP data may be quite expensive to collect.

On the other hand, SP data is more akin to the laboratory experiments. A hypothetical choice situation is set up and the respondent is requested to state what she would do; in our case, she would have to state which option she would choose. In these experiments, the analyst has total control of some of the explicative variables, basically, of those variables representing attributes of an alternative; thus avoiding problems of collinearity and insufficient variability. It also has the advantage of being relatively cheap to collect, since many answers can be sought from every respondent. The disadvantage, though, is rooted in its hypothetical nature: will people really behave as they say they would?

To address the issue that many responses may be provided by each individual in the SP case, our Eq. 14.7 for MNL models has to be modified. One simple way to do that is to consider that the parameters α^0 and β_l distribute according to a certain distribution in the population; in other words, random taste variation is present. This implies that all choices made by one person are treated the same and different to the choices made by any other person in the sample, a most sensible assumption within the context of SC experiments. The new formula for the probabilities of choice has a logit kernel that has to be integrated over the distributions of each taste parameter. Eq. 14.9 applies to the case where each parameter distributes in the population according to an independent Normal distribution (Train, 2003):

$$Prob(i) = \int \frac{\exp(V_i)}{\sum\limits_{m \in M} \exp(V_m)} f\left(\alpha^0 \middle| \alpha^0, \sigma_{\alpha^0}\right) \prod_l g\left(\beta_l \middle| \beta_l, \sigma_{\beta_l}\right) d\alpha^0 \prod_l d\beta_l \tag{14.9}$$

For a detailed discussion on the microeconomic foundations of random utility models, its applications to SP surveys and on how to develop welfare measures, the reader is referred to Adamowicz (2000), Hanemann and Kanimenn (1999), Louviere et al (2000), Ortúzar and Willumsen (2001) and Train (2003).

14.3 First Case Study: Urban Road Accidents

In Chile, as in most developing nations, the values used to assess safety related projects are based on the Human Capital approach (Landenfeld and Seskin 1982); the value of a life saved is given by the present value of the expected income flow the individual would have earned, had she not died. This approach is flawed from an economic standpoint as what actually counts are individual preferences. However, the idea is not to put a tag price on a given life, but on reductions in the probability of a fatality (Schelling 1993). This concept gave rise to the *value of risk reductions* (VRR) – also known as the value of a statistical life – and, since public safety is a non-rival good, it is equal to the summation of the marginal rate of substitution between income and fatal accidents over all the population affected by the safety problem. Jones Lee (1994) and Rizzi and Ortúzar (2005) provide a detailed microeconomic analysis on how to establish the VRR.

Rizzi and Ortúzar (2003) successfully estimated VRR in an interurban transport context in Chile based on SC data. Iraguen and Ortuzar (2004) built on the previous work to treat the more difficult urban case which will be described in this section. A route choice SC survey for car-trips using different types of streets in the Santiago metropolitan region was designed. The survey instrument had four parts; in the first, information about trip habits by individuals was collected and they were asked to mention a usual journey and its characteristics; this information was used to customise the second part. In part 2, respondents were presented with the choice context and the SP exercise (i.e. a series of binary route choices). In part 3, respondents were asked about their feelings on the SP experiment (i.e. did they consider the choices realistic?), and also about road accident experience and general attitudes towards risk. Finally, in part 4 respondents were asked some socio-economic data. The full survey form (albeit in Spanish) can be examined and/or played in the page: http://www.ing.puc.cl/~piraguen.

The characteristics of the contextual journey were chosen bearing in mind all factors affecting risk perceptions. The specific attributes for each respondent were allowed to vary as the survey was customised to each individual. An example of context is shown in Fig. 14.1 (in Spanish in the actual survey form); it was designed on the basis of the information (about travel habits) provided initially by the respondent. This data allowed the analysts to generate some items to which respondents should pay special attention (shown in italics in Fig. 14.1). These were journey purpose, type of day, arrival time and street predominantly used during the trip; among these, those that could vary were allowed to do so in realistic ranges. To make sure that each individual considered the same street features in all choice situations, a picture of the street indicated as predominantly used during the journey was shown at the SP exercise. Carson et al (1994) recommend the use of graphic representations as an aid for respondents, and cite the experience of Anderson et al (1993) who used video recordings of the various attributes defining their choice situations with good results.

Now we request you to put yourself in a hypothetical case, to be described below, where you will need to choose one route in each of a set of choice situations.

The context of the questions that follow was formed on the basis of the information that you provided in the previous page:

Assume that you must travel to *work*, from your house to your destination in Santiago. You make this trip regularly and it has the following characteristics:

»It takes place on a regular *working day*
»You must arrive at your destination approximately at *7:45 am*
»You drive your car and pay for all the travel costs involved.

You should also consider the following: A trip that takes between *30 to 35 minutes* at the time you travel, has an average travel cost of *US$ 1* (considering fuel and car maintenance). Finally, assume that during your trip you must choose between two routes by similar streets to the one shown in the figure:

We ask you to consider the following three characteristics when choosing your route:

- Travel time
- Travel cost
- Number of fatal car accidents per year.

In what follows you will be presented with nine (9) trip situations. We request that in *each one*, you select one of the two routes described; however, if neither option pleases you just move on to the next choice situation. Consider that the choice situations have no relation between them.

Figure 14.1. Choice context presented for the SP exercise

The following three variables were selected for the experiment: travel time, travel cost and some indication of the level of risk. A key design feature was to determine a clear way of presenting these variables in the survey; to aid this task focus groups were carried out in which the behaviour of several Santiago residents, of different age and sex, was examined in relation to various forms of presenting the variable accident risk. It was concluded that the word *fatality* was a key element in conveying the meaning of the risk variable that respondents should consider. So, the original variable definition proposed by Rizzi and Ortúzar (2003) was maintained as it had also been thoroughly tested in their interurban route choice experiment; i.e. *Number of car accidents with fatalities per year.*

The travel cost variable also required some thinking. A definition was needed that was both understood and assumed by the sample, and that at the same time was associated to the level of risk variable to measure. The problem was that in the Chilean urban case it is difficult to conceive of a payment instrument related to reductions in accidents. If a toll charge was postulated (which was acceptable in the interurban case), it would run the risk of *policy bias* (as tolls are not charged in cities) introducing *noise* in the experiment by diverting the respondents' attention to the cost variable. It was finally decided to use car operating costs, defined as the cost of fuel plus car maintenance, as payment instrument.

Statistical Design of the Stated Choice Experiment

A factorial design to estimate main effects and interactions for three attributes and three variation levels requires defining 27 choice situations (Winer 1971). However, submitting respondents to such burden runs the risk of loosing their attention and obtaining inconsistent answers (Caussade et al 2004). For this reasons, a fractional factorial design was implemented dividing the 27 original treatments into three different blocks (of nine situations each) at the very marginal cost of not being able to estimate the three-way interaction. A further manipulation was needed to avoid dominant alternatives, using the technique developed by Huber and Zwerina (1996). As an example, Table 14.1 shows the situations finally presented in the first block; for a reference on fractional factorial designs for SC surveys see Louviere et al 2000.

Table 14.1. Choice situations in block 1

Route 1			Route2		
Travel time (min.)	Travel cost (US$)	Accidents per year	Travel time (min.)	Travel cost (US$)	Accidents per year
24	0.74	5	14	1.29	2
24	0.92	4	14	1.11	9
24	0.92	6	14	1.29	4
30	0.92	5	15	1.11	2
15	1.29	4	30	0.92	9
30	0.74	6	15	1.29	4
24	0.92	5	19	1.29	2
24	0.74	4	19	1.29	9
24	0.92	6	19	1.11	4

Data Collection

The survey was administered via a web page. Advantages of an Internet survey are a) the elimination of response coding and digitising, b) the capacity to customise the survey to each respondent; c) reduction in costs as there is no need to pay interviewers for each completed form. The main disadvantage is the possibility of a biased sample. This could have been serious in our case, as access to the Internet in developing countries is fairly limited. In fact only individuals with medium to high income have access to the Internet in Chile (Subsecretaría de Telecomunicaciones 2002); so, there is no denying that our sample is not completely representative. However, in this study that problem should not be an important issue as the great majority of car owners in Chile are of also of medium to high income (Ortúzar et al 1993). Another possible bias is given by the fact that most Internet users tend to be distributed in certain ages, thus, people above 50 years old may be underrepresented.

To reach the sample, first senior management staff was contacted at a series of private and public institutions in Santiago (banks, universities, ministries and large companies). These contacts, previously recruited by phone, were informed in detail about the study objectives and were requested to send an e-mail containing a cover letter (including the Web page address) to a sample of car users at their organisations. In this form, the survey was considered as officially sanctioned by those who received it, decreasing the likelihood of point-blank refusals. A problem with this approach is that it was not known exactly how many people got knowledge of the survey, so it was impossible to estimate an accurate response rate.

After intense pre-testing and a pilot, the main survey was carried out during April and May 2002. 441 responses were received but only 320 were complete including eight cases where respondents did not answer all choice situations. The sample gender was predominantly masculine (63%) and their income distribution clearly showed them to be medium to high income people (only 15% of people belonged to the low income category). Other interesting data were that 59% of respondents did not have children younger than 18 years old, and that 77% of the sample always used safety belts (i.e. they do not appear to be risk takers in terms of accidents). On the other hand, as only 26% of respondents had been involved in a car accident previously (or had a friend or relative that died in a car accident), there were no grounds to expect an overestimation of the WTP for reducing accidents.

Table 14.2 summarises the age distribution of the final sample; as expected, the large majority corresponds to people under 50 years of age as older people still present a certain reticence to the use of computers and, with that, to the use of Internet.

Table 14.2. Age distribution of the sample

Age Category	Sample Distribution (%)
Less than 30	46.25
Between 30 and 49	34.60
Between 50 and 65	17.87
Over 65	0.95
No response	0.33

Discrete Choice Modelling

Both MNL and mixed logit (ML) models were estimated with linear indirect utility functions. The indirect utility for alternative *i* (in this case either of the two routes), V_i, is given by Eq. 14.1:

$$V_i = \alpha c_i + \beta t_i + \gamma a_i \qquad \text{i=1,2.} \tag{14.10}$$

where *c* stands for travel cost, *t* for travel time and *a* for number of accidents.

Based on the estimated parameters in Eq. 14.10, it is possible to obtain the subjective value of travel time (SVT) and the subjective value of accident reduction (SVAR). The first figure is given by Eq. 14.11 and the second by Eq. 14.12. To determine the VRR, we need to sum the SVAR across the affected population, as in Eq. 14.13:

$$SVT_j = \frac{\partial V_j / \partial time}{\partial V_j / \partial \cos t} = \frac{\beta}{\alpha} \tag{14.11}$$

$$SVAR_j = \frac{\partial V_j / \partial accident}{\partial V_j / \partial \cos t} = \frac{\gamma}{\alpha} \tag{14.12}$$

$$VRR = \sum_j SVAR_j \tag{14.13}$$

The standard binary logit model is not able to consider the fact that each respondent is answering to nine choice scenarios, whereas the binary ML model is. Table 14.3 shows estimation results for these two models. All parameters possess the correct sign and are all significative. The log-likelihood of the ML model is quite superior to the loglikelihood of the MNL, suggesting the presence of correlation among responses of each individual. In particular the value of α, γ and β sharply increase when passing from the MNL to the ML model; this implies an increase in the scale factor inversely related to variance (recall Eq. 14.7). In other words, the ML model has reduced unexplained variance. The SVT and the SVAR, however, are not very different between the models although the first decreases and the second increases when passing from the MNL to the ML (this is well explained by Sillano and Ortúzar 2005).

Table 14.3. Binary MNL and ML models

Coefficients (t-ratios)	MNL	ML
Cost (10^{-3} Ch$)	-3.04	-11.90
(α)	(-12.0)	(-7.79)
Std. dev.		0.0107
		(7.96)
Accidents	-0.1468	-0.5973
(γ)	(-12.5)	(-8.26)
Std. dev.		0.5755
		(8.64)
Time (min)	-0.1307	-0.4047
(β)	(-15.8)	(-9.09)
Std. dev.		0.2582
		(8.26)
β/α (US$/min.)	0.066	0.052
γ/α (US$/acc.)	0.074	0.077
$L(\theta)$	-1183.87	-890.39

*At the time of the survey 1 US$ = 650 Ch$

Variability around the mean is most significant for the cost and the accidents parameters; this variability should be interpreted this way: each individual j has a fixed value of α, γ and β, say, α_j, γ_j and β_j. For each individual, her particular set of values is taken from three independent Normal distributions with mean and standard deviation as indicated in Table 3. This would also produce a distribution for the SVT and the SVAR; in other words not every individual will display the same willingness to pay for a marginal reduction in travel time and/or fatal accidents as implied by the MNL model. The unfortunate feature of the above result is that for some individuals the ML model might predict a positive values of α and γ, a result which does not make sense.This issue has been discussed at great length by Hensher and Greene (2003) and Sillano and Ortúzar (2005) and will not be treated further here.

To estimate the VRR one modification is needed to apply Eq. 14.13. A fatal accident in the urban streets of Santiago produces on average 1.08 fatal victims. Thus, for an annual flow of 3.5 million cars per year, the VRR amounts to US$ 240.759 for the MNL model and US$ 250.251 for the ML. Besides, both the SVT and the SVAR are in line with previous results in other studies undertaken in Chile (Ortúzar and Rodríguez 2002; Perez et al 2002; Rizzi and Ortúzar 2003). Therefore, we have good grounds to believe that respondents answered the survey seriously in spite of the fact that it was implemented in a different (non traditional) format than previous cases.

We now interpret the VRR figures in the context of road safety management. The VRR is the economic worth to society of avoiding one death on urban streets. Thus, if the cost of a road safety scheme is below the VRR, the scheme yields an economic positive benefit to the society and it should be eligible for implementation. If the cost of the scheme exceds the VRR, the net economic return to society is negative, and the project should not qualify for public financing. This is the so called cost-benefit approach to project appraisal, determining the social worth of a project by its net economic benefits. This approach is quite different to a private financial evaluation. As there is no market for buying "road safety", a private investor will not receive any benefits and thus she should not be interested in the scheme at all.

14.4 Second Case Study: Valuation of Local Air Pollution

Ortúzar and Rodriguez (2002) designed a SP ranking experiment to estimate WTP for reduced atmospheric pollution in Santiago. The authors looked for a choice context where each option could be associated with different individual pollutant exposures. It was found that a realistic way of 'offering' distinct atmospheric conditions consisted in presenting different residential locations associated with different air quality levels. This context was supported by the notion that when families decide where to live, they consider not only the dwelling characteristics but also the features of its location (Hunt et al 1994), including air quality and accessibility conditions. As residential location represents a medium/long term decision and can be labelled a complex decision process, rank-order data was used. It has been found that this format is particularly appropriate in these cases. In addition, Hunt et al (1994) and Ortúzar et al (2000b) had used ranking data in a residential choice context with good results. The latter experience was especially meaningful because that survey was carried out in the same geographical area and using a similar survey format.

Definition of the Air Quality Attribute

The attributes characterising an option in a SP exercise should have a clearly defined and unique interpretation, so that individuals manifest their preference valuing objectively 'the same thing'. This was a complex task as it involved identifying an appropriate attribute to represent different air quality conditions (and the analytical measurement units of pollutant concentrations are unknown for a large share of the community). The authors looked for an air quality measure that was part of the daily references of a typical citizen and that had a direct relationship with the concentration of atmospheric pollutants.

After several pilots, the current air quality index (ICA) for Santiago was considered an adequate measure. The ICA index converts concentrations of five major air pollutants: Carbon monoxide (CO), Sulphur dioxide (SO_2), Nitrogen dioxide (NO_2), Ozone (O_3) and fine particulate matter (PM_{10}), into a single number and a matching description using a linear approximation. These pollutants are continuously monitored at several stations in the city where an index value is calculated daily. Then, the concentration of each pollutant is converted to its ICA equivalence and the highest number becomes the ICA level for that station. Finally, the station with the highest number yields the global ICA level for the whole city.

This information is disseminated daily through the media. Every television and newspaper meteorological report includes the ICA index, emphasising the area where the station recording that level is located. The environmental contingence day qualification (Alert, Pre-emergency, and Emergency days) receives special attention. This is directly determined on the basis of ICA levels measured during the year. According to this local profile, it was concluded that an adequate attribute to represent air quality conditions for a particular location was the number of days that the zone index would qualify for a city contingence day status.

Identification of Attributes and Selection of Measurement Units

Although there are many factors influencing housing choice behaviour (Hunt et al 1994) it was considered reasonable to include only a subset of these attributes (emphasising that any others would stay constant), as the main goal of the study was not to model housing market behaviour. So, two attributes belonging to the same category of air quality, accessibility to work and accessibility to study were chosen, both expressed in minutes of travel time for each individual in the household. The last factor considered was the rent paid, which was essential to obtain a monetary valuation for the other attributes and also gave an important dose of realism to the hypothetical exercise.

The task of choosing appropriate measurement units was straightforward for the accessibility attributes (minutes) and the rent (Ch$) but it was not the case for air quality. It was decided to use the number of days per year with a contingence level as a *second-best* measurement unit. After conducting a pilot study, the number of days per year with an *Alert* level associated to each residential location was selected, as there was more variations between areas than in the case of *Pre-Emergency* and *Emergency* days.

Data Collection Strategy

A 3^4 fractional factorial design leading to nine hypothetical situations (Louviere et al, 2000) was used, adding an option depicting the current situation of the household (in terms of the variables used). This was done in order to test for the existence of an aversion-to-change-location effect (i.e. reflecting an overvaluation of the current situation when compared to the alternatives offered), which had been observed in a previous study (Ortúzar et al 2000b). The survey was customised, ensuring that situations were well within a context familiar to each household. The levels were adjusted if the variations were smaller than thresholds based on absolute differences. A data collection strategy which had proved successful before

(Ortúzar et al 2000b) involved two stages and the participation of a small group of well-trained interviewers. They made two visits to each family contacted. In the first, the main characteristics of the dwelling and basic information about the family members were sought. Once this data was processed, the interviewer made a second visit, two days later, where the customised SC exercise was presented and a few complementary questions were asked.

After the ranking process was completed, the interviewer formulated 12 extra questions to detect how consistently the family had addressed the choice process, and to investigate if the attribute levels had been considered realistic. An important feature of this approach is that the ranking task was carried out by the whole family, trading-off good attributes of certain options for some members (say travel time) with worse features for others. To improve response quality the study focused on families that had occupied their present residence for less than two years. Also only tenants were considered under the assumption that they would have found a hypothetical move (and consequently the SC exercise proposed) more realistic than house-owners.

Modelling Results

One hundred and seven households were interviewed. The socio-economic information from the sample was representative of middle and high-income people in Santiago. The variables used at the modelling stage were TVW_{hi}: travel time to work by individual *h* from location *i* (min. per trip); TVS_{hi}: travel time to study by individual h from location i (min. per trip); and f_{Th}, f_{Eh}: frequency of trips to work and study by individual h (trips per week). Using these variables, household accessibility variables as shown in Eqs. 14.14 and 14.15 were defined:

$$TVW_i = \sum_{h \in H_t} f_{Th} TVW_{hi} \tag{14.14}$$

$$TVS_i = \sum_{h \in H_e} f_{Eh} TVS_{hi} \tag{14.15}$$

Other variables were DA_i, days of alert associated to residential location *i* (days per year); R_i, value of the house rental (thousands of Ch$ per month) and a dummy δ_{Actual}, which takes the value one if option i represents the household's current location, and zero otherwise. The indirect utility function specification used was linear-in-parameters and consistent with the proposed microeconomic framework:

$$\mathrm{V_i} = \theta_{Actual}\delta_{Actual} + \theta_{TVT} TVW_i + \theta_{TVE} TVS_i + \theta_{DA} DA_i + \theta_R R_i \tag{14.16}$$

Table 14.4 shows the results for binary MNL and ML models; the latter were estimated assuming Normal random taste parameters (Sillano and Ortúzar 2005); the second specification also allows to treat correctly the repeated observations from an individual through a distribution of tastes in the sample.

All parameters have the expected sign and the coefficients of the dummy variable δ_{Actual} turned out to be significantly positive, implying an inertia effect in the sense of adding a plus to the utility of the current residential location. The ML model presented again a better fit as expected, and as all parameters related to the standard deviation of the taste parameters were significant the null hypothesis of fixed taste parameters across the population was rejected.

Table 14.4. MNL and ML estimated models

Attributes		Parameters (t-test)	
		MNL	ML
TVW	Mean	-0.00417 (-10.6)	-0.00992 (-7.9)
	Std. dev.		0.00573 (4.5)
TVS	Mean	-0.00250 (-7.8)	-0.00577 (-8.2)
	Std. dev.		0.00266 (2.7)
DA	Mean	-0.27370 (-11.0)	-0.47863 (-6.8)
	Std. dev.		0.40567 (4.7)
R	Mean	-0.02641 (-12.5)	-0.0574 (-7.0)
	Std. dev.		0.04748 (6.2)
δ_{Actual}	Mean	0.89690 (5.9)	1.05325 (5.5)
Log-likelihood		-849.6	-747.0

Table 14.5 presents WTP estimates and their 95% confidence intervals following Armstrong et al (2000). The ratios of parameters tend to be quite stable. When compared, ratios of parameters from the MNL and ML specifications lie within each others' confidence intervals, except for the WTP value for Days-of-Alert reductions. It is interesting to mention that, as in the previous case, the values of time obtained were consistent with values obtained previously in the country using much simpler set-ups. This could be taken as an indication that respondents both understood the experiment and played the game seriously.

Table 14.5. WTP as ratios of population means

Attributes	Willingness-to-pay values (confidence interval)	
	MNL	ML
TVW (Ch$/min)	36 (29 – 45)	37 (25 – 54)
TVS (Ch$/min)	22 (16 – 28)	25 (14 – 40)
DA (Ch$/DA per year)	124,362 (100,818 – 152,301)	98,009 (70,127 – 135,793)

At the time of the survey, 1 US$ = 500 Ch$

Unfortunately it is not possible to say what people are actually valuing when stating a WTP for fewer days of alert. It could be related to health effects or to visibility, or to a combination of both. Research in progress on environmental risk perception should help to clarify this issue.

14.5 Third Case Study: Valuation of Quietness

Galilea and Ortúzar (2005) designed a SC experiment to value reductions in urban noise levels. For similar reasons to those mentioned above a residential location context was chosen to estimate WTP for quietness. Adapted to this case, one of the attributes affecting residential location was considered to be the level of noise. Based on focus groups results, the set of attributes chosen for the SP experiment were the rent or mortgage paid, noise level, travel time to work and sun orientation; it was assumed, as in the previous case, that the housing quality of the apartment was the same for all options.

Selection of Measurement Units

This task is again trivial for attributes related with time and money because they are familiar to all kind of people. Unfortunately, this is not the case for variables such as noise level or sun orientation. From focus groups, it was confirmed that although noise levels are measured using the decibel scale (dB), people do not know what it means and neither do they know that it is logarithmic. The authors tested presenting the noise variable in relation to recalled levels at different intersections in Santiago (e.g. some objectively louder than others). For this, participants were asked to rank them using a five-point scale; however, the results did not reflect a clear pattern and none of the respondents was close to the objective data in their assessments.

Laboratory experiences were discarded in spite of the fact that they would allow to simulate a wide range of situations because, as Arsenio et al (2000) explain, the experiments are costly and there is no way to know if respondents feel 'at home' in this simulation, or if they would be really annoyed by that noise level in practice. Finally, it was decided to use a rating 10-point scale. In the case of sun orientation, cardinal points were used; this is not only the natural way of presenting the attribute but was easily understood by focus group participants and this was confirmed at the subsequent pre-tests.

Experimental Design

Once the attributes and the way to represent them were chosen, the next step was to select the number of levels for each attribute. The factorial design chosen for this survey was a 2^4 experiment (Street et al 2001). A full factorial needs 16 choice situations but this had been observed to test respondent's patience in previous focus groups. For this reason, it was decided to use two blocks with eight treatments each, confounding the four-way interaction. Table 14.6 presents this result in terms of the attributes. If a respondent answers block 1 seriously, she should rank alternative 8 first and alternative 2 last. On the other hand, a respondent answering block 2 seriously should put alternative 3 before alternatives 1, 5, 6 and 8. This knowledge enabled us to check the data for inconsistencies.

Table 14.6. Attributes levels in each block

	Block 1				Block 2			
	Attribute levels				Attribute levels			
Alternative	Time	Noise	Sun	Rent	Time	Noise	Sun	Rent
1	High	High	Best	Low	High	High	Best	Low
2	High	High	Worst	High	High	Low	Best	Low
3	Low	High	Worst	Low	Low	High	Best	Low
4	High	Low	Best	High	Low	Low	Worst	Low
5	High	Low	Worst	Low	High	High	Worst	Low
6	Low	Low	Worst	High	High	High	Best	High
7	Low	High	Best	High	Low	Low	Best	High
8	Low	Low	Best	Low	Low	High	Worst	High

Sample Strategy

The same data collection strategy that had proved successful in the previous case study was used. It has two stages involving a small group of well-trained interviewers making personal visits to each family contacted. At the first stage, the main characteristics of the dwelling and basic information about the family members (i.e. identification and travel attributes) are sought. Each interviewer was provided with a survey form to register the household data and an interviewer manual containing the precise set of questions to be formulated and an exact definition of the data required. The manual specified that an adult family member should be the first to be contacted in order to ask him/her the general household information.

The socio-economic characteristics required from each person were: first name, relation to the household head, gender, age, educational level, possession of a driving license and occupation. The general household and dwelling data gathered were: borough where the dwelling was located, nearest street intersection, monthly rent/mortgage paid, origin of this money, number of household vehicles and family income. The interviewer also gathered trip data from every worker in the family: travel modes used, borough where the work place was located, nearest street intersection to the work-place, and current travel time and weekly number of trips to work. Finally, the interviewer asked the family which sun orientations were considered best and worst respectively by them, and requested the family to grade the current level of noise inside the dwelling according to the ten-point scale.

Once this data was processed, the interviewer made a second visit (two days later) where a customized SP exercise was presented to the household. Once a introductory description of the rank-order exercise context and the varying attributes was made, the interviewer delivered eight cards to the family (Fig. 14.2), each representing a different residential location. The family had to rank these cards and after completing the process the interviewer formulated some questions designed to detect how consistently the family had played the game, how important they considered the variable noise, and to investigate if the attribute levels had been considered realistic.

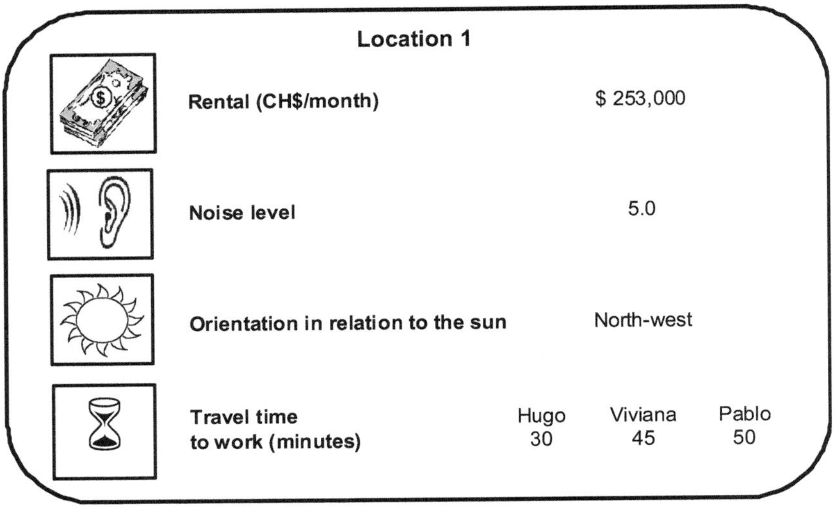

Fig. 14.2. Example of personalised ranking card

Because the main purpose of the exercise was to value reductions in noise levels, it was important to measure each household noise level objectively. Due to the high cost of this measurement (done by outside professional experts), it was decided to interview only families living in predetermined buildings. An important step was to get permission to do the survey in each of these buildings; a registry of noise levels was offered in return.

Flats in a total of nine buildings located in different areas of Santiago (four in the high income district, two in a medium-high income sector and three in the exact boundary between middle and low income sectors of the city) were surveyed; the buildings were selected on the basis of their socio-economic characteristics and noise levels. The number of households interviewed at each building varied from three and four (in high income buildings) to 27 and 33 (in low-medium income buildings). The sampling strategy was simply to get as many households as possible in each building because the interest was mainly exploratory and not policy oriented; for this same reason records of response rates were not kept.

Households in 150 flats were finally interviewed with a high level of supervision on the interviewing process. Socio-economic information was representative of middle and high-income people in Santiago: 63.5% of households answering the income question stated that their income was over 850 000 Ch$/month. This is easily over the highest 10% of income in the country, the minimum wage being little over 100 000 Ch$/month (at the time of the survey 1 US$ = Ch$ 650).

Discrete Choice Modelling

The definition of the variables used at the modelling stage was the following:

NL_i : noise level in location i (one to ten, where ten is an unbearable level of noise)
RM_i : value of the flat rent or mortgage (thousand of Ch$ per month)
SUN_i : dummy which takes the value one if option i has the best orientation in relation to the sun, as declared by household h, and zero if it has the worse.

A household accessibility variable, given by the travel time to work by all workers in the family, was also defined following Pérez et al (2003):

$$TTW_i = \sum_{h \in H_i} f_{ih} TTW_{hi} \tag{14.17}$$

where TTW_{hi} is the travel time to work by individual h from location i (minutes per trip) and f_{ih} is the frequency of trips to work by individual h, from location i (trips per week).

Once more we just present the results for binary MNL and ML models (Table 14.7), both of them based on the linear-in-parameters indirect utility function in Eq. 14.18:

$$V_i = \theta_{RM} RM_i + \theta_{NL} NL_i + \theta_{SUN} SUN_i + \theta_{TTW} TTW_i \tag{14.18}$$

As can be seen, the ML has again clearly superior fit and also the mean value estimates are higher suggesting a higher scale factor (See Sillano and Ortúzar 2005). Note also the high significance of each standard deviation, specially for the variables NL and, in particular, SUN. This is consistent with the subjective nature of these variables, and with the fact that there is no consensus about their importance within the sample.

The importance of a variable in the utility function can be gauged by looking at the product of its coefficient and its mean sample value. Doing this it can be shown that in both cases the most important variables are clearly the rent and the noise level, followed distantly by the sun orientation and finally travel time.

Table 14.8 compares the subjective values for the linear MNL and ML models. The two WTP point estimates increase in the ML due to the non-uniform increase in the mean estimates of its parameters with respect to MNL (note that we have found that as sample size increases the scale factor effect becomes more uniform). On the other hand, the WTP values for reducing noise have the same order of magnitude than the monetary values that should be invested to put double glazing in the dwellings, and recall that these are values based on people's perceptions of noise (i.e. based on a 10-point scale) and not based on objective (i.e. decibel scale) values.

Table 14.7. Binary MNL and ML models

Attributes	Parameters (t-test)		
	MNL	ML	
		Mean	Std. dev.
RM	-0.0432	-0.1398	0.0863
	(-16.3)	(-5.5)	(4.7)
NL	-0.6609	-2.2852	1.1504
	(-14.3)	(-10.3)	(8.0)
SUN	1.697	3.718	4.699
	(16.2)	(9.4)	(7.9)
TTW	-0.00628	-0.0241	0.0137
	(-7.3)	(-7.4)	(5.4)
$l(\theta)$	-967.03	-787.74	

Table 14.8. Estimation of willingness-to-pay values

	WTP Values	
	MNL	ML
Noise Level (US$/NL per month)	23.54	25.14
	(20.26 – 27.37)	(18.56 – 37.63)
Travel Time to Work (US$/hr)	3.14	3.69
	(2.31 – 3.97)	(2.58 – 5.63)

Subjective v/s Objective (dB) Perceptions of Noise Level

As the final objective of any exercise in valuation should be to estimate an objective monetary value, in this case for noise levels reductions, the authors attempted to relate their 10-point scale subjective values with decibel scale measurements taken at 96 dwellings where they succeeded in performing this task.

An important problem was that the dB(A) measures were in general fairly high whilst its range was not wide (i.e. from 37 to nearly 61 dB); this meant that many respondents with a "low" objective noise level reported a "high" grade as their subjective noise level. So a simple linear regression did not achieve a reasonable fit even when separate regressions were estimated for each building.

To improve estimation it was decided to incorporate the extra information provided by the households at the interview stage in order to achieve ceteris paribus conditions. In particular, the results of two questions were used: (i) whether they were aware that their dwelling had a significant noise level and, (ii) if they thought that noise level was an important attribute when searching for a place to live. Thus, a multiple regression was estimated using the ten-point scale subjective grades as the dependent variable, and the decibel scale plus two dummies representing Awareness (one, if the household was aware that the dwelling had a significant noise level) and Importance (one, if the household thought that noise level was an important attribute) as independent variables.

The results of this regression are shown in Table 14.9; as can be seen they appear quite reasonable. With these results the estimated parameter for the noise level was transformed by simply multiplying it by the coefficient for dB(A) in Table 14.9, as it is obviously not necessary to re-estimate the model with the transformed variable.

Table 14.9. Multiple regression results for the ten-point scale

Attribute	Parameter	(t-test)
dB(A)	0.0893	(6.1)
Awareness	2.1295	(3.6)
Importance	1.3184	(2.3)
Multiple correlation coefficient	0.5124	
Sample size	96	

The transformed noise level parameters allow to derive new subjective values of noise level (SVN) for each model (Table 14.10). These represent the WTP, in US$, associated to decreasing the noise level inside a dwelling in one dB(A) per month. Although the values seem reasonable, a caveat related to their use in social project evaluation is that there are other terms and elements that should form part of the total WTP for reducing noise level; for example, the health costs incurred as an effect on human health because of noise.

Table 14.10. Subjective values for noise level reduction in dB

Model	SVN (US$/dB(A) per month)		
	Lower bound	Mean	Upper bound
MNL	1.81	2.10	2.43
ML	1.66	2.25	3.36

As a caveat, we must recall that the relationship established above has to be considered tentative in so far as no external validity assessment was conducted for the results. Therefore, it is debatable whether it could be adopted immediately by the environmental authority. More work should follow in this direction.

14.6 Summary

A brief discussion on discrete choice models served to motivate the practice of valuing transport externalities by means of stated choice surveys. As in most applications, a sound microeconomic theory is required if the modeller pretends his research to be an adequate input for cost-benefit analysis.

Three case studies were described in this chapter. The aim of each was to elicit the values people place on three local environmental goods (urban accidents, air pollution and noise); although proper markets are not available for these, preferences are deemed to be well defined. These studies show that stated choice surveys provide a way forward to derive such monetary values. However, to obtain values that could be consistently used at governmental level in official cost-benefit analysis there is still a long way to go. More empirical evidence is needed and a great deal of external validation of the derived values is required.

The most important conclusion with respect to the three case studies is the realism that the stated choice technique needs to achieve if the experiment is to yield satisfactory and truthful results. Simulated markets should mimic real-life markets in order to provide a sensible input for cost–benefit analysis. Besides, these experiments should also help to understand how people could adjust their behaviour in the presence of externalities so that appropriate forecast can be made when the level of an externality changes.

The three studies considered show that stated choice survey techniques can be implemented in developing countries. Transferring values from developed countries to the developing world is not warranted and many caveats should be considered. Hence, it is apparent that there is a need for undertaking this kind of studies in countries at various levels of development.

Acknowledgements

The authors wish to thank Professor Huw Williams for many useful discussions related to the issues of interest in this paper. We also want to acknowledge the support of the Chilean Fund for Scientific and Technological Research (FONDECYT) through Project 1020981, and the post-doctoral MECESUP/PUC 9903 Project.

References

Adamowicz WL (2000) Environmental valuation case studies. In: JJ Louviere, DA Hensher, JD Swait (eds) Stated Choice Methods: Analysis and Application. Cambridge University Press, Cambridge.

Armstrong PM, Garrido RA, Ortúzar JdeD (2000) Confidence intervals to bound the value of time. Transportation Research 37E: 143-161.

Arsenio E, Bristol A, Wardman M (2002) Values of traffic noise from a stated preference-choice experiment in Lisbon. The 2002 International Congress and Exposition on Noise Control Engineering, Deaborn, MI, USA.

Carson R, Louviere JJ, Anderson DA, Arabie P, Bunch DS, Hensher DA, Johnson RM, Kuhfeld WF, Steinberg D, Swait J, Timmermans H, Wiley JB (1994) Experimental analysis of choice. Marketing Letters 5: 351-368.

Caussade S, Ortúzar JdeD, Rizzi LI, Hensher DA (2004): Assessing the influence of design dimensions on stated choice experiment estimates. Transportation Research B, (in press).

Daniels R, Adamowicz WL (2000) Environmental valuation. In D.A. Hensher and K.J. Button (eds.), Handbook of Transport Modelling. Pergamon, Amsterdam.

Gaudry MJI, Jara-Díaz SR, Ortúzar JdeD (1989) Value of time sensitivity to model specification. Transportation Research 23B: 151-158.

Hanemann WM, Kanninen B (1999) The statistical analysis of discrete response data. In: I. Bateman and K. Willis (eds), Valuing Environmental Preferences. Oxford University Press, Oxford.

Hensher DA, Greene WH (2003) The mixed logit model: the state of practice. Transportation 30: 133-176.

Huber J, Zwerina K (1996) The importance of utility balance in efficient choice designs. Journal of Marketing Research XXXIII, 307-317.

Hunt JD, McMillan JDP, Abraham JE (1994) Stated preference investigation of influences on attractiveness of residential locations. Transportation Research Record 1466: 17-35.

Iragüen P, Ortúzar, JdeD (2004) Willingness-to-pay for reducing fatal accident risk in urban areas: an Internet-based Web page stated preference survey. Journal of Accident Analysis and Prevention 36: 513-524.

Jara Díaz S, Videla, J (1989) Detection of income effect in mode choice: theory and application. Transportation Research 23B: 393 - 400.

Jones Lee M, Loomes G (2002) Valuation of safety. In: DA Hensher, KJ Button (eds), Handbook of Transport and the Environment, Pergamon, Amsterdam, 2002.

Karlström A (2000) Non-linear value functions in random utility econometrics. Pre-prints 9th International Association for Travel behaviour Research Conference, Gold Cost, Queensland, Australia.

Lancaster K (1966) A new approach to consumer theory, Journal of Political Economy 74: 136-156 .

Louviere JJ, Hensher DA, Swait JD (2000) Stated Choice Methods: Analysis and Application. Cambridge University Press, Cambridge.

Maddala G (1992) Introduction to Econometrics. Prentice Hall, Englewood Cliffs.

Mc Fadden D (1995) Computing willingness to pay in random utility models. Working Paper, Department of Economics, University of California at Berkeley.

Nash, C (1997) Transport externalities: does monetary valuation make sense? In: Gde Rus, C Nash (eds), Recent Developments in Transport Economics. Ashgate Press, London.

Ortuzar JdeD, Rodríguez G (2002) Valuing reductions in environmental pollution in a residential location context. Transportation Research 7D: 407-427.

Ortúzar JdeD, Willumsen LG (2001) Modelling Transport. 3rd Edition, John Wiley & Sons, Chichester.

Ortúzar JdeD, Ivelic AM, Malbran H, Thomas A (1993) The 1991 Great Santiago origin-destination survey: methodological design and main results. Traffic Engineering and Control 34: 362-368.

Ortúzar JdeD, Cifuentes LA, Williams HCWL (2000) Application of willingness-to-pay methods to value transport externalities in less developed countries. Environment and Planning 32A: 2007-2018.

Ortúzar JdeD, Martínez FJ, Varela FJ (2000) Stated preference in modelling accessibility. International Planning Studies 5: 65-85.

Pérez, P, Martínez F, Ortúzar JdeD (2003) Microeconomic formulation and estimation of a residential location choice model: implications for the value of time. Journal of Regional Science 43: 771-789.

Rizzi LI, Ortúzar JdeD (2003) Stated preference in the valuation of interurban road safety. Accident Analysis and Prevention 35: 9-22.

Rizzi LI, Ortúzar JdeD (2005) Road safety valuation under a stated choice framework. Journal of Transport Economics and Policy, (in press).

Subsecretaria de Telecomunicaciones (2002) Caracterización socioeconómica de los servicios de telefonía y tecnologías de información y comunicación. Informe Estadístico 4, SUBTEL, Gobierno de Chile (in Spanish).

Saelensminde K (2001) Inconsistent choices in stated choice data. Transportation 28, 269-296.

Schelling, T (1993) The life you save may be your own. In: R Dorfman, N Dorfman, (Eds), Economics of the Environment: Selected Readings. W. W. Norton and Company, New York.

Sillano M, Ortúzar JdeD (2005) Willingness-to-pay estimation with mixed logit models: some new evidence. Environment and Planning 37A (in press).

Small K, Rosen S (1981) Applied welfare economics with discrete choice models. Econometrica 49: 105-130.

Street DJ, Bunch DS, Moore B (2001) Optimal designs for 2^k paired comparison experiments. Communications in Statistics - Theory and Methods 30: 2149-2171.

Train: Discrete Choice Methods with Simulation (2003) Cambridge University Press, Cambridge.

Winer BJ (1971) Statistical Principles in Experimental Design. McGraw - Hill, New York.

15 Externalities Analysis of Investments in Infrastructure: a Practical Approach

Pablo Coto-Millán
Department of Economics
University of Cantabria (Spain)

Vicente Inglada
Department of Economics
University Carlos III of Madrid (Spain)

Juan Castanedo-Galán
Department of Transports
University of Cantabria (Spain)

Miguel A. Pesquera
Department of Transports
University of Cantabria (Spain)

Ramón Núñez-Sánchez
Department of Economics
University of Cantabria (Spain)

15.1 Introduction

Together with the economic benefits reaped from transport on business sectors and consumers as a direct consequence of time reduction in journeys, a broad set of negative effects is stated (noise, particles, vibration, accidents, emissions, natural- resource destruction, congestion and visual intrusion), which constitutes a high cost in terms of loss of social benefit to the economy and society. Most of these external effects do not carry a price due to their own nature, in other words, there is not a clear market system which provides users with sufficient evidence and is able to charge the social costs to the polluter. Therefore, there is a distortion in the market functioning and the social costs do not coincide with the private costs. Since the mechanism of prices does not act, there is an overuse of the service above the corresponding social equilibrium of transport market. To summarize, there are shortcomings of and barriers to the efficient development of markets and the current price is below the optimum.

In Spain, the volume of investments in railway infrastructure surprisingly exceeds those directed to road in the recent decades. An ambitious action plan which consists on having over 7,000 km of High-Speed Train network for 2010, is certainly stated. In the event that such an objective were fulfilled, Spain would occupy the leading position in total length of high performance railway network.

This study includes five sections and the final conclusions. The second section analyses the main guidelines observed in the evolution of Spanish passenger and goods transport demand, as well as the corresponding modal distribution. The third section studies transport externalities focusing on the analysis of the optimal price's theoretical framework, the internalization instruments and the evaluation in money terms of the considered external effects (congestion, environment, conservation and accidents). Sections fourth and fifth compare the effects on social benefit and modal distribution of the two transport policy approaches in the Madrid-Seville corridor: a) the levying of a tax on the price of fuel not only in road transport but also in the remaining means, that internalize the social costs of each transport mode; and, b) the primary investment in railway infrastructure implied in the introduction of the high-speed train.

Finally, the sixth, and last section, shows the most relevant conclusions derived from the obtained results.

15.2 Evolution of Transport Demand

The first significant feature inferred from the evolution of Spanish passenger and goods transport demand is its marked growth over the last fifty years. Likewise, this evolution has been parallel to that of the economic activity, although with a higher rhythm, both in the up and down periods of the economic cycle.

However, we cannot speak at all about generalized guidelines in this growing tendency of the demand for transport modes, since the increase in the volume of railway traffic has been slightly lower with respect to that of its competitors, specially that of the road. In fact, only during the few periods of weak economic activity, railway traffic has grown above the remaining transport means. All this process has led to a quick decrease in railway modal share, both for passenger transport and - even in a higher volume - for goods transport.

An evidence of the marked prevalence of road transport over rail is that, in the case of passenger transport, only in the Madrid-Seville corridor, road traffic volume is exceeded by rail due to the implementation of the high-speed train in 1992. In none of the other corridors, the railway modal share exceeds 20%. The increasingly dominant role of road transport is seen, even more widely, in the case of goods transport, as only in long distances, over 600 km, and for the transport of certain products - as for example minerals and containers - does railway have considerable importance. This tendency is almost generalized for all Spanish corridors.

Finally, the extension of this analysis to other countries, make us state that the process observed in the Spanish case are in general applicable to other countries, although the loss of modal share of railway transport is much less marked than in Spain.

Among the factors which have been implied in the evolution of transport demand, it is worth mentioning the significant improvements - specially in qualitative terms - of our road network with the incorporation of 7,200 km of high-capacity roads (motorways and highways) during the 1980-2001 period. On the contrary, Spanish railway infrastructure has remained almost unchanged, with the exception of the new Madrid-Seville high-speed train, only used for passenger transport. As regards the financial resources absorbed by each transport mode, the ratio between investment in roads and railway infrastructure - lower that 2 over the first years of the eighties - has increased by over 5 in the nineties.

Also in line with the factors that favor the development of road transport, it has been observed that, in the field of road passenger transport sector, according to the information about the Spanish families' expense structure, provided by the successive Family Budget Surveys, the income elasticity value of private transport widely exceeds that of public transport. All this implies that the share of cars on the modal distribution of passenger transport demand is increasingly higher.

As far as goods transport is concerned, there is no doubt that the transcendental changes undergone by the productive process as well as the distribution chain, have encouraged the role of road transport due to its higher reliability and flexibility to adapt to changes in demand. Deep transformations have taken place in the productive structure of the different industrial sectors. On the one hand, the goods which were traditionally transported mainly by train have widely lost percentage within the total of industrial production, and these products show the lowest growth rates over recent decades. On the other hand, the percentage of the total of industrial production of other productive sectors, characterized both by a higher unit value and lower volume, so that goods can be better transported by road, has widely increased.

In line with this, a detailed analysis of the main features of the present economic scenario, shows in favor of road transport, since, in particular for its high degree of flexibility, is able to meet the challenges offered by this new scenario successfully. Thus, as regards production, it is worth mentioning that, in the current economy, the development of the whole process is directed to each user's needs, and is guided in accordance with his/her specifications. In line with this, in the field of distribution, a generalized process of inventory reduction in line with the boom of logistics and "just in time" system, is taking place. All this demands the availability of efficient transport systems which are based on a high-quality infrastructure network, with a high degree of flexibility and capable of adjusting service to the changing needs of companies' operations. Definitely, as a consequence of the deep changes undergone by production and distribution processes, the elasticity shown by railway goods transport, with respect to the economic activity, is significantly lower than that of road transport, and there is consequently a regressive tendency in its modal share on the market of goods transport.

Finally, the evolution of modal prices does not seem to have constituted a particularly relevant explicative factor of the weakening tendency shown by railway transport, as, both in passenger and goods transport, railway fares have not increased at a higher rate than those of the alternative modes.

15.3 Transport Externalities

15.3.1 Concept

Only the externalities which Rothengatter (1994) denominate relevant are studied. These are, to summarize, activities outside the market but sufficiently relevant to alter their efficient functioning, forcing, therefore, state involvement to reduce their impact. In this sense, only technological externalities will be included as the effects of the so-called pecuniary externalities on other markets, are transferred through the mechanism of relative prices and thus, when aggregating on all of them, the final effect is nil.

In order to study transport externalities, a classification in four clearly differentiated groups constitutes a useful starting point: damage to the infrastructure due to the use and wear of pavement, congestion costs, accident costs and costs closely related to the environmental damage and noise.

15.3.2 Internalization

For the internalization of the external effects of transport according to ECMT (1998), there are four major types of instruments: economic incentives, regulatory instruments, actions on infrastructure and transport service supply and information and persuasion measures. From the point of view of the economic efficiency, the economic instruments based on acting on the prices are the adequate ones. The instrument chosen in this study for the internalization of the external effects on roads is the tax levied on fuel, as it has the advantage of being easily implemented and also shows an acceptable degree of efficiency for the internalization of all the externalities, with the exception of congestion, which, in the case of interurban transport, does not reach a significant value. For the remaining transport modes, the tax is included in the corresponding fares.

15.3.3 Theoretical Framework

We have used the theoretical framework employed by Jansson (1993), whose objective is to maximize the sum of consumer and producer surpluses, once the costs of the negative externalities borne by the rest of the society have been subtracted.

Thus, the Net Social benefit must be maximized as follows:

$$BSN = \int_0^Q U(Q)dQ - Q \cdot CM^{usuario} - CT^{prod} - CT^{ext} \quad (15.1)$$

Where:

BSN: Net Social benefit.

U (Q): Marginal utility function.

$CM^{usuario}$: User's average cost.

CT^{prod}: Producer's total cost.

CT^{ext}: Externality total cost.

An equilibrium condition which must be satisfied is that, the generalized cost, equivalent to the sum of price and the user's average cost, may be equal to the marginal unit:

$$P + g(Q) = U(Q) \quad (15.2)$$

Finally, if the first-order condition is imposed to a maximum, which requires that the derivative of the Net Social benefit with respect to quantity Q, be zero, the following price is obtained:

$$P = CMA^{prod} + Q\frac{\partial CM^{usuario}}{\partial Q} + CMA^{ext} \quad (15.3)$$

Therefore, we have achieved a known result, which implies that a necessary condition to maximize net social benefit is that the price should be equal to the sum of the marginal cost, in the short-term, of the producer of transport infrastructure services, the cost imposed on the rest of infrastructure's users and the cost imposed on the rest of society by an additional user of transport infrastructure. In this sense, with the objective of facilitating this price setting, we have chosen for this study the analysis of conservation, environmental, congestion and accident externalities separately.

By applying the described methodology, Figure 15.1 shows the value of the HB tax which must be levied on the cost borne by the user for the price to be optimal. In addition, it can be observed that the area of the HLE triangle is the gain of social benefit obtained when adopting a generalized price value for transport, equivalent to the marginal social cost.

15.3.4 Valuation

The need to evaluate monetarily the external effects has brought about the new valuation techniques which have been applied with special emphasis on the case of environmental goods. Environmental goods, even if they are non-market goods, may be linked to other goods which indeed are, being part with them, as substitutes, of a particular production function. A first possibility is that the environmental good may be part of a production function of a good or service as an additional productive input. Another possibility is that the environmental good is part, together with other private goods, of a specific person' or family's utility production function. In the first case it is possible to have a monetary value of the environmental good by means of the denominated drive-response function and the avoided or borne costs. The second technique is based on the fact that the environmental good is a substitute for other elements contained in the social benefit (Azqueta 1994).

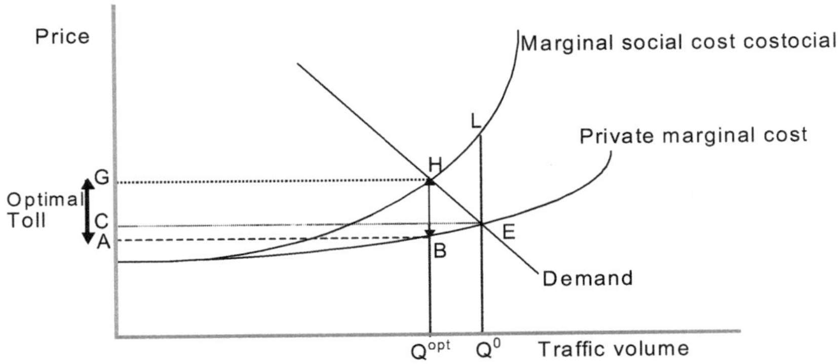

Fig. 15.1. Value of optimal toll

Parallel to this, a second type of methodological tool for the valuation of environmental goods has arisen, denominated of links or behavior relations. In these techniques, the evaluation depends not only on a physical relation but also on the behavior of the individuals who must face the change or the possibility that it may take place. This behavior may be observed either in a real or in a hypothetical market. Moreover, the evaluation may be direct or indirect via other interrelated goods. The hedonic price method values an environmental good by examining the effect that its presence causes on another good whose price is fixed at the market. The other valuation technique, which combines the observed markets by using the direct evaluation, is the travel cost method, which is an extension of the consumer demand theory keeping special focus on time value. As regards the contingent valuation method, the surveyed individuals are asked whether how much they are willing to pay in order to guarantee a social benefit gain, provided by a change in the provision of a non-market environmental good; or how much they are willing to accept as compensation for facing a loss of social benefit produced by a reduction in the level of provision of that good. Finally, by combining hypothetical market and indirect evaluation we have the definition of the method for valuing the declared preferences. This technique, which also uses individual surveys, differs from the contingent valuation method in that the individual is not directly asked how much he/she is willing to pay for the change in the provision of an environmental good, but each surveyed individual chooses from a set of choices with various characteristics.

We have employed in this work specific methodologies for each type of external effect, thus avoiding the mere transfer of values obtained in different studies made in other regions or in Europe. In particular, we have intended to reflect the specific characteristics of Spain, exclusively in relation with interurban transport.

Congestion

This externality has been specifically studied for road transport. In connection with this, the individual decision of traveling by road depends on the generalized cost of the journey, which includes either the variable operating costs of privately-owned vehicles or the fare in public transport, and the value of the time employed. An increase in traffic volume implies a reduction in the speed of vehicles, which leads to an increase in travel time and in the operating costs. When the user decides if he/she will travel or not, and which mode of transport to use, he/she only takes into account the additional cost which his/her decision represents for him/her, ignoring the effect on the level of congestion and the travel cost for the remaining users. There is therefore a difference between the average social cost and the marginal social cost. This difference is the external marginal cost which can be obtained as the product of the traffic volume by the derivative of the average operating cost (private) with respect to the number of vehicles.

In order to determine the external social cost given by congestion, we should firstly have a function which connects the traveling speed with the traffic volume. The opposite of this function enables us to know how the average travel time varies depending o the number of vehicles. Apart from the algebraic expression which may be adopted for this function, other important factors such as the capacity, the geometric features and the design of the road, the percentage of heavy vehicles and the equivalent number of cars allocated to each type of heavy vehicles in connection with their capacity consumption, are worthy of mention. There is a wide range of specialized literature on the topic. We have used in this study parabolic-type functions for highways or motorways and linear functions for conventional roads on each chosen stretch of the Roads Network. Given that the cost of congestion does not vary linearly with the level of traffic, the Madrid-Seville corridor has been divided into 8 stretches, using the homogenous traffic volume criterion on each stretch. This characteristic – that the cost of congestion does not depend linearly on the traffic volume – leads us to develop the marginal social cost of congestion after the evaluation of the remaining external effects, and use a value of price elasticity of demand, that shows the sensitivity of the demand to transport price, once the cost of congestion has been introduced.

In line with this, it is necessary to estimate the travel time value which enables us to convert time into monetary cost for the user. The values mentioned in MOPT (1991) have been used.

Conservation

The social cost of conservation of the infrastructure includes two clearly discernible components. Firstly, we must take into account the cost incurred by the Administration in the maintenance of the infrastructure. On the other hand, we must also consider the additional or marginal cost imposed by each specific type of vehicle. Once the hypothesis that the increase in the operating costs of the vehicles given by the deterioration of the road, is not considered due to its low magnitude, has been accepted, the social cost associated with the conservation of our transport infrastructures would only be the public investments that are not transferred to the user by fixing a price. The methodology employed is based on the analysis of the various cost sectors of the interurban road infrastructure and on the use of common criteria in the railway and road transport modes, for their application to that infrastructure's users. The various cost sectors of road transport have been distributed among the types of vehicles according to the different allocation criteria. For example, the sectors on leveling and factory works have been considered to be a function of the equivalent vehicles, while roadbed reinforcement is a function of the equivalent of the equivalent centerlines and accessory works and the administration costs are considered to be directly related to traffic units.

There are two technological facts essential to understand the process of conservation of a road. Firstly, the damage produced to the tarmac is not proportional to the burden it bears, but increases quickly with it. Secondly, the key parameter is not the total price of the vehicle but its weight per axle. In connection with this, it is worth mentioning that, when doubling the number of equally loaded axles, the damage produced is reduced by almost one eighth of the initial level. Therefore, a huge part of the damage caused to the road is due to the heavy vehicles' action, specially trucks. In order to determine the part of the cost applicable to the various vehicles, it is necessary to distribute the considered cost areas (in this case, conservation and use) among each type of vehicles. It is worth highlighting that, of the three allocation parameters that exist (equivalent-vehicle, equivalent-axles and vehicle); only the last two are taken into account for the estimation of the marginal cost. The obtained allocation parameters are the weighting factors applied to the kilometers traveled annually by the vehicles, to obtain the marginal costs (vehicle-kilometer) of each type of vehicle. In line with this, according to Muñoz-Alamillos (1996), for the railway infrastructure, the weighting factors of the kilometers traveled, which enable us to distribute the costs among the various types of movable material, are: equivalent axles, equivalent trains, train unit and electric-traction unit.

Once the corresponding costs per vehicle-kilometer have been determined for each selected type, and divided by the average number of units transported by each one of them, we finally have the marginal social unit costs of road and railway infrastructures for passenger and goods transport.

Accidents

This transport externality constitutes, from the economic, and specially from the social point of view, one of the topics which arouses greatest interest and concern in our society. The nature of the external effects associated with accidents in transport, lies in the fact that the user only takes into account his/her own risk (as he/she perceives it) rather than the risk generated to the rest of the society, including not only road users but also those who do not use this transport mode. The incorporation of a new vehicle implies a penalization and, definitively, an increase in the cost for the remaining users. However, there are other accident costs external to the transport system, such as the medical assistance costs, payable by public administration; or the losses in the production capacity, which are neither included in the private costs of each user nor taken into account in the process of deciding whether or not to travel. These external costs should be internalized by means of a type of tax, or by an adequate insurance system, if applicable.

Following this methodological line, the total cost of accidents may be obtained as the sum of two components. The first component would be the willingness to pay for avoiding such a risk, either by the vehicle owners or their close family. The second component would be intended to represent the purely economic costs borne by the rest of society.

According to this methodology, if the risk elasticity with respect to exposure to this risk were nil, we would only have to consider the third component of the cost, in other words, the costs which affect the rest of society. Therefore, the key point of this cost is the relationship between the risk and the number of users that will determine the extent of the external costs. The initial model has been extended by considering the existence of two types of vehicles: light and heavy vehicles. In this case, if the sum of the corresponding elasticities of the number of accidents with respect to the number of vehicles, is equal to one, the first external effect does not exist; and if each user's risk were completely internalized, it would only be necessary to consider the component associated with the rest of the society.

The estimations made for the Spanish case enable us to observe that the sum of the mentioned externalities is not significantly different than one.

The process carried out to obtain the social cost of the accidents on each mode of transport includes the following steps (Inglada, 1998): firstly, the total hospital and administrative costs are determined with a view to working out the non-internalized part. Secondly, the cost component called "net production losses", has been obtained. Then, the immaterial component of the social cost of accidents is valued by subtracting from the value that citizens are willing to pay for the loss of a human life and for an injured person, the already internalized part through the corresponding legal indemnities. Finally, in order to determine these unit values from the methodology based on users' willingness to pay, the value provided by the European Commission in the ECMT (2000) has been considered, adapting it to the Spanish case. Finally, the total of the social costs relative to road accidents, has been distributed among the different users – car, bus and truck – in accordance with the respective probabilities of accidents of these means of transport.

Environmental

This externality includes noise, local pollution and the denominated, climatic change. For noise we have used the INFRAS/IWW (1994 and 2000) methodology based on that employed for the cost-benefit analysis of road investment in Sweden. This methodological approach has two main advantages: on the one hand, it provides data for the values of the social cost of noise below 60 db(A); on the other hand, the values represent an average value of numerous works. From the above-mentioned study, we have taken the basic costs of noise per exposed person and year. By applying the distribution of people exposed to noise in Spain, we can ascertain the magnitudes of the noise costs corresponding to passenger and goods transport. Finally, it is worthy of mention that, a review of the studies made on the social cost of noise shows that no differences are appreciated - within the usual range of values - between marginal and average costs, being possible to consider the values obtained as unit marginal social costs of noise for interurban transport in our country. For the valuation of the external effects associated with pollution, based on the CONRINAIR inventory - specifically made for Spain by the European Environmental Agency - the emission factors for each type of vehicle have been transferred to the corresponding ratios per passenger-kilometer and ton-kilometer through the average occupation coefficients in interurban transport. This inventory has been used for air transport, and the values provided by INFRAS/IWW (1994 and 2000). In passenger and goods railway transport, there are two different types of traction energy: electric and diesel, so that different methodologies must be used in order to determine their emission factors. For pure electric traction, we should analyze the original sources of electric energy production, shown in the table below. The emissions per passenger-kilometer in the electric-traction railway (long distance, AVE and goods) have been determined from the distribution for each type of primary energy of the electric energy production, by applying the energetic consumption to the corresponding occupation factors. In line with this, diesel-traction railway and the remaining modes of transport have been operated by applying the amounts of units emitted to energetic consumption.

Once the factors of the units emitted for each mode of transport, both for passengers and goods, have been determined, it is necessary to have unit costs available. These values have been obtained from the ECMT (1998) as average value of numerous studies and besides this, have the advantage of considering interurban transport separately for each polluting factor. By applying these unit costs to the amounts of each polluting factor emitted by each mode of transport, we have the final values of the social unit cost given by the pollution on each mode of passenger and goods transport.

15.4 Policy of Prices: the Case of Madrid-Seville

15.4.1 Elasticities

Once the chosen methodology has been defined, it is necessary to modelize transport demand with the aim of simulating the effects on modal distribution of the price variations of each mode as a consequence of introducing the optimal price. For this reason, we have used the values of the price elasticities of the demand for each mode of transport, as well as those values relative to the alternative modes obtained in Coto-Millán, Baños-Pino and Inglada (1997) by using cointegration techniques. For the case of petrol and gas-oil consumption, considered as proxy variables of car and coach transport respectively, additional estimations have been made by using the Box-Jenkins methodology for the time series analysis. Data on the traffic of each mode of transport as well as on the consumption of petrol and gas-oil, have been obtained from the reports of the different situations by the Ministry of Development and the Ministry of Economy respectively. In connection with the values of these elasticities, shown in Table 15.1, it is worth pointing out major rigidness of the prices of petrol and gas-oil consumption and the few substitution relationships between the various modes of transport.

Table 15.1. Price elasticities considered in passenger transport

	Estimated values			
	Car (petrol)	Coach (gas-oil)	Train	Plane
Car (petrol)	– 0.25			
Bus (gas-oil)		– 0.16		
Train		0.42	– 1.24	
Plane				– 1.26

Source: Coto-Millán, Baños-Pino and Inglada (1997) and own work

15.4.2 Results

Table 15.2 records the values of each one of the external social cost areas per passenger-kilometer in the Madrid-Seville corridor for each mode of passenger transport obtained in section 4. These values have been ascertained taking as base year 1991 in order to have a similar horizon to that of the implementation of the high-speed train and being thus able to efficiently compare both policies. Moreover, as the AVE only transports passengers, we have only estimated the external social costs of passenger transport market. It is worth pointing out that the highest value of the external social cost corresponds to the car (5.18) and the coach is the transport mode with the lowest external cost (1.39). From these values we would have to discount the specific taxes applicable to fuel.

Table 15.2. External social costs of passenger transport modes in the Madrid-Seville corridor including taxes (Centimes of 2001/passenger-kilometer)

	-Car-	-Train-	-Plane-	-Coach-
Congestion	0.46	--	--	0.08
Conservation	0.69	2.14	--	0.13
Accidents	2.49	0.15	--	0.64
Environmental	1.54	0.49	2.01	0.54
Total	5.18	2.78	2.01	1.39

Source: Own work from the methodology mentioned in the text

Once the social costs relative to each externality, have been valued, we have proceeded - by using price elasticities of demand - to jointly determine the optimal price and the associated traffic volume for each mode of transport. The obtained results, shown in table 15.3, lead us to state that the introduction of a price equivalent to the marginal social cost in the Madrid-Seville corridor, within the internalization process of the multiple externalities on each mode of transport, would probably give rise to a sharp change in modal distribution within the field of interurban passenger and goods transport. For example, if we take into account the base scenario (a value of human life of 0.8 million euros, special taxes discounted), only the car would lose nearly four percentage points of modal share, passing from 52% to 48.15% mainly to the benefit of the train.

Table 15.3. Modal distribution of passenger transport in the Madrid-Seville corridor after application of the optimal price. (Modal percentages)

	Value of human life: 0.812 Million euros of 2001		Value of human life: 1.219 Million euros of 2001	
	Taxes included	After discount of special fuel taxes	Taxes included	After discount of special fuel taxes
Car	41.16%	48.15%	36.53%	44.19%
Train	20.14%	14.93%	23.50%	17.80%
Plane	29.76%	27.71%	31.21%	28.96%
Coach	8.94%	9.21%	8.75%	9.05%

Source: Own work

One cause of this process is that competition between the different modes of transport, of passengers and goods, takes place mainly (García et al., 1998) by using the different components of the generalized cost (time, reliability, comfort, safety, etc.), and to a lesser extent, through the fare price, as inferred from the low values of the price elasticities of the competing models. However, from the point of view of social benefit, the application of a policy of optimal prices, based on the marginal social cost in said corridor and year, would have generated a profit of 4.5 million euros in 2001 in the Madrid-Seville corridor for the adopted base scenario.

15.5 Investment Policy: the Case of the Madrid-Seville AVE

15.5.1 Impact on Modal Distribution

The High-Speed Train (AVE), which uses the standard European gauge, started being in operation in the Madrid-Seville corridor in April 1992. This new mode of transport is characterized by its high speed, higher than double that of conventional trains, and its high infrastructure cost, with a fixed character, almost independent of the number of transported passengers and which, therefore, needs to attract high levels of demand in order to achieve an acceptable level of profitability. The implementation of High-Speed rail brings about a significant reduction in the generalized cost of the railway mode. This reduction does not take place in the monetary component of said cost, but it does in the rest of components (time, comfort, etc.).

The AVE's implementation produces on transport demand – through the subsequent heavy reduction in the value of the non-monetary components of the generalized cost – two clearly visible effects, called "induction" and "substitution" respectively, and which are relative to the journeys which would not have taken place if this service did not exist, and those which would have taken place in another mode of transport, respectively. Given the large extent of the substitution effect, the implementation of the high-speed train produces very significant effects on the demand for the remaining modes of transport which compete with it in the Madrid-Seville corridor. Apart from the almost complete disappearance of conventional trains in this corridor, the implementation of the AVE has triggered an important fall of nearly 50% in air traffic on the Madrid-Seville corridor. As far a the car is concerned, losses are lower than in the above cases, being nearly 30% in the above-mentioned corridor. Finally, as regards the coach, it does not seem to have suffered a strong impact in long distance corridors (11% of losses), as both products are little substitutive.

Thus, it can be concluded that the implementation of the high-speed train produces a drastic change in the modal distribution of the demand, and it is possible to speak in terms of the transport market before and after the AVE. In this sense, as shown in Table 15.4, it is worth pointing out that rail becomes the dominating mode in the Madrid-Seville corridor, exceeding the car's market share - a rare case in Spanish transport market.

Table 15.4. Variation in the modal distribution of the Madrid-Seville corridor (Thousand of passengers)

Mode of Transport	Without the Ave (1991)	(%)	With the Ave (1996)	(%)
Car	1436.4	52.0	1407.4	40.5
Plane	694.4	25.1	352.2	10.1
Bus	239.2	8.7	182.9	5.3
Conventional Train	392.3	14.2	96.4	2.8
Ave	------	------	1438.2	41.3

Source: Own work

15.5.2 Cost-Benefit Analysis

We have used here a generalized methodology of the one used in Dogdson (1984), widely described by De Rus and Inglada (1994, 1997). The considered cost-benefit areas are shown in table 15.4. The costs include fixed costs - those relative to construction of infrastructure (in the broad sense) and its maintenance (although in the long-run these costs have a parallel development to demand) – and semi-fixed costs, which are those relative to the acquisition of movable material; and finally, variable costs, which are those commonly denominated of use, characterized by having a high sensitivity to demand evolution.

The following benefit issues have been considered:

- Cost reduction in the remaining transport operators.
- Time savings for AVE users.
- Time savings for road users given by a reduction in congestion.
- Reduction in the environmental impact (local and global pollution, and noise).
- Reduction in other generalized cost components of travel (comfort, security, etc...)
- Reduction in accident indexes (road and rail).
- Income derived from project performance.
- Reduction of the costs of conservation of road and conventional rail infrastructure.

15.5.3 Results

Table 15.5. Social benefit of high-speed in the Madrid–Seville corridor (Million euros of 2001)

	AVE's basic benefit	Most favorable scenario[1]
Costs		
Infrastructure	2356.3	1987.6
Residual value	179.9	62.1
Movable material	593.6	691.7
Maintenance	398.1	433.0
Performance	1401.6	1713.9
Time savings for the users provided by:		
Conventional rail	415.2	543.5
Coach	48.1	63.0
Bus	20.7	26.4
Plane	21.7	28.0
Generated journeys	1072.8	1406.6
Reduction in the costs of:		
Conventional rail	203.1	265.5
Plane	209.0	288.8
Buses	19.5	25.5
Cars' operating costs	239.7	314.1
Congestion	11.3	15.9

[1] It is the maximum value of accidents, GDP growth of 3%, 40 years of project duration and the consideration of the shadow price of the work factor.

Accidents	116.1	218.9
Environmental	62.5	88.9
Conservation	139.8	183.0
Net Current Value of the AVE	-1990.1	-1295.7

Source: Own work from the methodology specified in the text

However, the economic evaluation made through the cost-benefit analysis of the project, make us state that, as seen in table 15.5, the cost of this project exceed the benefits provided, with a total social cost of 1295 million euros of 2001 in the most favorable scenario (40 years of project duration, maximum value of human life, economic growth tendency of 3%, etc.). The basic reason for this negative result lies in the existence of a very low level of demand, which means that the willingness to pay for the capacity may be lower than the costs of said capacity. In this sense, in comparison with other modes of transport, the high-speed rail's profitability depends much more than the rest on the density of traffic on the corridor, as the supply of additional rail service units includes a much lower additional cost due to a strong effect of the economies of scale. Therefore, this type of policy intended to improve railway infrastructure, in connection with supply, with the subsequent high reduction of the time component of the generalized cost of the railway mode, seems to be very efficient in order to alter modal distribution, although in turn of a high social cost.

15.6 Conclusions

In this study, we have compared the results obtained from the application of the different transport policies – price and investment – which pursue the objective of reducing negative external effects in the Madrid-Seville corridor since 1992 until present. An initial, very interesting conclusion inferred from the results obtained, is that, with the alternative based on the internalization of the externalities through an increase in the prices of transport modes, modal distribution suffers changes of little relevance, the introduction of the new and modern high-speed train in the railway transport mode has a major impact on passenger transport market, which makes high-speed rail a predominant means of transport for that corridor, a very uncommon case in Spanish transport market. This effect only takes place on the passenger transport market as the AVE does not transport goods. The conventional rail remains almost exclusive for goods transport and has a broad margin of capacity given the release produced in passenger transport with the implementation of the AVE.

However, to strictly compare both alternatives, it is necessary to use an approach based on the social benefit variations. In line with this, the cost-benefit analysis carried out for the high-speed train shows that the social cost implied by the implementation of the High-Speed Train exceeds 1295 million euros of 2001 for all the considered hypotheses, as the improvements and benefits derived from time saving, the reduction of accidents and from other costs, cannot compensate the high cost of the infrastructure used by this mode of transport. Without any doubt, on corridors with higher traffic volumes, as for example Paris-Lyon, this alternative would generate an increase in the social benefit. However, an increase on the modal prices equivalent to the external marginal social cost, would have implied a social benefit of 4.5 million euros of 2001 in the base scenario studied. Definitely, from the analysis made, we can conclude that, from the point of view of economic efficiency and social benefit optimization, the high-speed train should not have been implemented that year (1992) in the Madrid-Seville corridor. Moreover, the above conclusion is strengthened by the fact that that year, and on the same corridor, important actions for the improvement of road and airport infrastructure were carried out. In this study, we also want to state that there were other transport policy approaches, as the introduction of an optimal modal price based on the respective marginal social costs, which would have increased social benefit.

Therefore, from the results obtained in this investigation, we infer the necessity to introduce higher economic efficiency in transport market through the application to each mode of transport of a price based on the marginal social cost. This is how the numerous negative external effects relative to passenger and goods transport are internalized. In the case of road transport, this internalization – until there exist more efficient systems, as in the case of the electronic toll – could be carried out by the imposition of a specific tax on fuel: petrol and gas-oil. Through this method, we would have achieved an increase in the social welfare or surplus.

In the field of the infrastructure policies, the investments that may involve a greater balance in terms of social welfare should be covered for the sake of higher economic efficiency, as properly shown by the economic theory.

Therefore, the future transport policy should be based on the internalization through the prices of negative externalities, and on the investment in those infrastructure projects that present better balance in terms of social welfare. In this sense, probably other corridors with different characteristics to those of the one studied (for example Madrid-Barcelona), should have constituted in 1992 more adequate scenarios for investments in the improvement of the railway offer, which would have made it possible for this means of transport to strengthen its weak present role without bringing about a significant reduction in social welfare.

References

Azqueta Oyarzun D (1994) Valoración Económica de la Calidad Ambiental. Editorial Mac Graw Hill.

Coto-Millán P, Baños-Pino J, Inglada V (1997) Marshallian demands of intercity passenger transport in Spain: 1980-1992: An economic analysis. Transportation Research E 33: 79-96.

Coto-Millán P, Carrera-Gómez G, Inglada V, Pesquera MA (2005a) Promoting competition in regulated markets: Application to a study of transport services in Spain. The Annals of Regional Science 39-1: 73-84.

Coto-Millán P, Inglada V, Rey B (2005b) Effects of Network Economies in High Speed Rail: The Spanish Case. The Annals of Regional Science. (forthcoming).

De Rus G, Inglada V (1993) Análisis coste-beneficio del tren de alta velocidad en España. Revista de Economía Aplicada 3: 27-48.

De Rus G, Inglada V (1997) Cost-Benefit analysis of the high-speed train in Spain. The Annals of Regional Science 31: 175-188.

Dogdson J (1984) Railways costs and closures. Journal of Transports Economics and Policy 18: 219-235.

ECMT (1998) Efficient transport for Europe: Policies for internalisation of external costs. OECD, París.

ECMT (2000) Economic Evaluations of Road Traffic Safety Measures. Round Table 117, OECD, París.

García A, Cillero A, Rodríguez P (1998) Operación de trenes de viajeros. Fundación de los Ferrocarriles Españoles.

INFRAS /IWW (1994) External effects of transport. UIC, París.

INFRAS/IWW (2000) External costs of transport, UIC, Paris.

Inglada V (1998) El coste social de los accidentes de carretera. Valoración e internalización. III Congreso de Ingeniería de Transporte: 169-176, Barcelona.

Inglada V, Coto-Millán P (2003) Introduction of an innovative product: the High Speed Train. In: Coto-Millán (ed) Essays on Microeconomics and Industrial Organization. Springer-Verlag-Heidelberg, Germany: 29-41.

Inglada V, Coto-Millán P (2003) Social benefit of Investment Projects: the Case for High-Speed Rail. In: Coto-Millán (ed) Essays on Microeconomics and Industrial Organization. Physica-Verlag 2nd edition: 361-385.

Jansson JO (1993) Government and transport infrastructure investment. In: Polak,J and Heertje, A (eds) European Transport Economics. CEMT/Blackwell: 221-243.

MOPT (1991) Manual de Evaluación de Inversiones en Ferrocarriles. Ministerio de Obras Publicas y Transportes, Madrid.

Muñoz-Alamillos A (1996) Tarificación por el uso de la red ferroviaria. II Symposium Ingeniería de los Transportes, Madrid.

Layard R, Glaister S (1994) Cost-benefit Analysis. Cambridge University Press.

MOPT (1991) Manual de Evaluación de Inversiones en Ferrocarril de Vía Ancha. Ministerio de Obras Públicas y Transportes, Madrid.

Nash CA (1991) The Case for High Speed Rail. Investigaciones Económicas, XV: 337-354.

Owen AD, Phillips GDA (1987) The Characteristics of Railway Passenger Demand. Journal of Transport Economics and Policy 21: 231-253.

Plassard F (1992) El impacto espacial de los trenes de Alta Velocidad en Europa. Transporte y Medio Ambiente, MOPT.

RENFE (1993) Encuestas realizadas a los viajeros del AVE. RENFE.

Rothengatter W (1994) Do external benefits compensate for external costs of transport?. Transportation Research, A 28: 321-328.

UNITE (2000) Unification of Accounts and Marginal Costs for Transport Efficiency. V Programa Marco de la UE.

PART V TRANSPORTATION NETWORK AND INFORMATION AND COMMUNICATIONS TECHNOLOGY

16 ITS-Based Transport Concepts and Location Preference: Will ITS Change 'Business as Usual'?

Raffael Argiolu
Nijmegen School of Management
Radboud University Nijmegen (The Netherlands)

Rob van der Heijden
Nijmegen School of Management
Radboud University Nijmegen (The Netherlands)
Delft University of Technology (The Netherlands)

Vincent Marchau
Delft University of Technology (The Netherlands)

16.1 Introduction

The development of Intelligent Transport Systems (ITS) has taken a leap in the past decade. Under strong influence of improved Information and Communication Technology (ICT) industries, automotive suppliers and scientific institutes have put much effort on developing a range of ICT based applications for vehicles to drive safer, more comforTable, to make more efficient use of current and future infrastructure and to manage fleets more accurately. Policymakers show increasing interest in ITS as a tool for solving traffic and transport problems facing society (e.g. congestion, environmental damage and traffic safety). This interest of policymakers is backed by findings of preliminary scientific research which show that promising perspectives seem within reach (Marchau and Van der Heijden 2003). '*ITS is different from transportation advancements that it promises to increase the system's throughput substantially* [...] (Tayyaran and Kahn 2003). However, with respect to ITS policymaking many uncertainties exist regarding for instance real traffic impacts of ITS (drivers might adapt their behaviour) and conditions for implementation (e.g. acceptance among users, liability in case of malfunctioning devices), legal issues (Van der Heijden and Van Wees 2001) and safety potentials (see e.g. Hegeman *forthcoming*). Hence, on the short term, the way in which ITS will affect traffic and transport system performance is still everything but sure. Although throughout the past years more and more knowledge is gained on the validity of intended ITS impacts and conditions for implementation, there is still a lot of work to be done in this area.

In addition, the long-term effect of ITS on spatial dynamics is even more uncertain. Despite this uncertainty, the expectation that ITS concepts will, in the long term, have significant spatial effects on the location pattern of, in particular firms, is plausible. We can conclude from history that innovations in transportation systems have had significant influence on spatial patterns of activities (see e.g. Filarski 1999). In general, distances between activities like for example residing and working have increased. Although some patterns of development are clear and can be explained easily, the nature of the relation between new transportation services and infrastructure and spatial patterns of locational development remains difficult to make explicit (see e.g. Banister 1995). Therefore, we have to develop hypotheses on these relationships with regard to the introduction of ITS. First, we assume that the implementation of ITS will change the preferences of actors regarding office locations of companies. Secondly, we assume that if preferences will change, they follow the pattern of ITS implementation. The theoretical background and the methodological exploration to research these hypotheses are described in this paper.

In doing so we need more insight in the possible role of ITS in location theory. Why do offices emerge at a certain spot and not elsewhere? Is there any difference in preferences between companies[1]? How important are preferences of companies? How influential is supply of office locations? What role do municipalities play? Which ITS are considered to be so attractive? Have researchers already gathered some empirical evidence? How can we study the role of ITS in location development of firms? Can we learn from practice? Or do we need more explorative research methods? These questions, and others, are part of our puzzle and will be discussed in this paper. The contribution of this paper is threefold.

First, section 16.2 briefly discusses the link between transportation and location development. During the 20th century the importance of transportation development as an explaining variable, within location theory has changed. Its importance has decreased while other factors have become more important. Still, it is assumed that the *attractiveness* (nearness and quality) of the transportation system has an important influence on location preferences. The *attractiveness* of a transportation system is dependent on the perception on the travel time, comfort, reliability and other elements of service. In most studies conducted on stated preferences of companies regarding locational alternatives, companies refer to the importance of accessibility, proximity and image. In contrast to research that focuses on current location preferences of companies; our future exploration also takes into account the preferences of suppliers of locations. Municipalities and real estate developers play an important role in developing new locations.

---

[1] Although we do not make this explicit we are aware of the fact that it is not 'companies' as such that make judgments and corresponding decisions on (re)locations but locations preferences actually depend on the decision making process within the company. For more on decision making processes within relocating companies see e.g. Pen (2002).

So if we want to know how whether ITS contributes to the attractiveness of a transportation system and as a consequence influences location preferences, we have to study its perceived gains as compared to other variables influencing *attractiveness*.

Section 16.3 subsequently explores the nature of future ITS, which is plausible in being so attractive. ITS systems cover, among others, systems that support the driver in controlling his/her vehicle in a better way (Advanced Driver Assistance Systems (ADAS), systems that support the traveller in finding an optimal mode and route, (Advance Traveller Information Systems (ATIS) and systems that are concerned with a more efficient organisation of traffic flows throughout the existing road infrastructure network (Advanced Traffic Management Systems = ATMS). We argue that most potential to reach a higher service level in transportation is expected from integration between ADAS and ATMS and ATIS. Further, integration seems very appealing in terms of safety benefits, throughput in networks and environmental issues (Van der Heijden and Marchau 2002). However, in practice integration of ADAS, ATIS and ATMS systems hardly occurs and therefore has not resulted in many new ITS modes.

Section 16.4 proposes a combination of methods to explore the influence of ITS on the development of firm location. An attractive way of studying these future impacts of ITS is by means of scenarios. ITS scenarios are first constructed based on existing cases and relevant knowledge, as described in literature. These scenarios are next assessed on their feasibility and likeliness in order to come up with set of so called plausible scenarios. These plausible scenarios will be used in our future research in a survey among actors that are involved in the location development of firms.

16.2 Theorizing Preferences Regarding Business Locations

The motives that firms have for (re)locating have been a scientific issue since 200 years approximately and can be summarized by so-called (re)location theories. Pellenbarg et al (2002) distinguish three approaches of (re)location theories: the neo-classical, the behavioural, and the institutional approach. These could be extended with a fourth, namely: the 'classic' theories.

These older 'classic' theories, as described by Von Thünen (1826)[2] and Weber (1906), presumed landlords (in the case of Von Thünen) and industrial companies (in the case of Weber) behaving as a 'homo economicus', which characteristic was totally formed by maximising profit. Transportation costs were considered as very

---

[2] Von Thünen, presented a theory, in which a agricultural business man, who strives for maximization of profits (W), must realise an optimal difference between the given market price (VM) and the sum of production (P) and transport costs (T). In formula: $W=VM-(P+T)$.

important variables in this maximization[3]. Later, these classic theories were elaborated by neo-classic location theories, with several changes in the assumptions, for instance from perfect to imperfect competition (see e.g. Hoteling 1929). Despite the differences, both classic and neo-classic theories considered transportation costs as an important settlement factor for firms. The emphasis on costs and profit shifted away when so-called 'behaviourists' introduced the notion of the 'homo psychologicus' (see e.g. Simon 1957, 1960). People were now assumed to behave as 'satisficers', instead of 'optimisers'. The notion of 'bounded rationality' was introduced. The behaviour of firms was regarded similarly. This meant that they would accept certain limitations in their choice. This also accounted for choices regarding locations. In the decision making process, firms had to cope with uncertainties and incomplete knowledge. These 'behavioural' theories where further elaborated with notions as the construction of mental maps, spatial cognition and regional image. The notion of spatial cognition can best be explained as: '*knowledge of spatial entities and consequently of possible locations*' (Lambooy et al 1997, *translation ours*). Spatial cognition is regarded as the bases on which locations are valued. This leads to the other two notions mentioned: mental map and regional image. The former is the image of certain locations or regions. Regional image has a somewhat broader definition, which also contains an element of prejudgement, personal correct or incorrect information and stereotypes. An example is that people regard Paris as the 'city of romance' and perceive the Ruhr area in Germany as 'dirty'.

Other than the former three approaches, institutional approaches do not only look at the firm, but also consider the social and cultural context in which this behaviour is embedded. This view is based on the idea that firms have to negotiate with deliverers and suppliers, local, regional or national governments, labour unions and other institutions, about prices, wages, taxes, subsidies, infrastructure, and other key factors in the production process of the firm. Locational behaviour is the result of the outcome of these negotiations (Pellenbarg et al 2002). Because of a risen complexity and less belief in deductive approaches, more research has focussed on empirical data. Characteristic about these data is the aim to explain location development according to preferences or so-called settlement factors.

To predict or explain movement of companies, various stated preference surveys have been conducted. Although some results differ, little change seems to have occurred in the last decades regarding the nature of these location- or so-called settlement factors in the Netherlands. Lukkes et al (1987) described four factors of increasing importance: accessibility, representation, proximity of clients and the quality of the building in comparison with the price.

[3] Webers' theory (1909) focussed on the location of industrial businesses. Therefore, he addressed other location factors than Von Thünen did (see Von Thünen, 1826). He called those factors 'standortfaktoren'. Webers' theory argued that minimization of transportation costs of raw materials ('Lokalisiertes Material') was the impetus for businesse to locate. He also addressed the importance of labour costs (1909).

Later, Atzema and Wever (1994) note that lack of accessibility plays an important role as a *push*-motive[4] for companies. Further, accessibility was the most important *pull*-factor[5], which included proximity to clients, suppliers, local unlocking and parking lots. More recently, Pellenbarg et al (2002) emphasise the work of Louw (1996); he found that the most important motive to leave a location is the fact that a firm has not enough space to expand.

Table 16.1. Location preference of different companies

	General location preferences
'Stationeries'	Organisations with a strong preference for locations near pubic transport facilities. Other important factors are: working conditions, such as a nice atmosphere, flexibility within the interior design and organization of the building and accessibility of the entrée. Representation is of less importance. This group consists of governmental and non-profit organisations.
'Modals'	'Modals' need common buildings with standard facilities. Accessibility by car and the presence of parking lots are important. There is no need for a representative building, and the proximity of public transport is even less important, whereas the rent price should be as low as possible. Core activities of this group are mainly non-office companies like industries, trade companies and transport organisations.
'Visuals'	'Visuals' consider representation and aesthetics very important. Further, the company name or logo needs a prominent position on the outer wall. The image of the building has to be congruent with its own product. 'Visuals' are willing to pay relatively high rents. Commercial organisations, service businesses, banks and insurance companies are considered as visuals.
'Ambulatories'	Most important location factor for ambulatories is accessibility by car. This group provides its services predominantly outside the building, with the building as base. Representation is of less importance as most of the clients are spread throughout the country. Ambulatories are mostly smaller businesses (less than 20 employees) in the services sector: banks and insurance businesses.
'Classicists'	These users prefer settlements characterised by historical and dignified milieus. They opt for traditional buildings. They settle in city centres and accept less accessibility by car. This group consists of law firms, accountant offices, notaries, brokerages and some governmental institutes, like embassies, for whom representation is of less importance

Source: Louw 1996

[4] Push-motives are reasons to move from a location. An example is the lack of space to expand.

[5] Pull-factors are reasons that relate to a new location. An example is an ideal accessibility in the new situation.

In latter stages of the decision making process to relocate, location specific features, like for example accessibility and representation, become increasingly important. The last stages are characterised by negotiations about prices of location and parking space. As described, companies prefer multiple settlement factors. Furthermore, the emphasis on the specific factors is influenced by the differences in the nature of companies. Table 16.1, which is based on an overview described by Louw[6] (1996), is a typology based on this distinction. According to this Table 'stationeries' are considered to be more interested in public transport facilities than for instance 'modals' are. Companies that are mainly attracted by representation and aesthetics are regarded as 'visuals'. Embassies, account offices and universities can be seen as 'classicists'. They prefer settlements characterised by historical and dignified milieus.

Louw (1996) criticizes this typology for three reasons: a decrease in importance of the settlement factors does not mean that the explanatory function also decreases. Spatial differences can be described to settlements factors that are considered to be less important. The second criticism of Louw (1996) is that preferences of companies do not account for the supply side which influences spatial outcomes too. The third critique is that such a distinction does not include the combinations in decision-making or the internal relations. We would like to add another point of critique, which is based on the topic of this paper. If we want to study location development and spatial differences, we are mainly focussed at spatial impact. And spatial impact is also based on the size of the companies and the 'spatial' life cycle[7] of companies.

It is clear that most of the location theory has changed in three major steps and has become more sophisticated than the oldest classic theories. At first current research uses an institutional approach and also considers the social and cultural context; the idea that firms have to negotiate with a multitude of actors, about prices, wages, taxes, subsidies, infrastructure, and other key factors in the production process of the firm. This approach is miles away from the first classic theories that explained location by a simple formula. Another improvement concerns the distinction between the nature of the company and the differences in location preferences. A third theoretical elaboration is aimed at the removal process of companies. The importance and relevance of settlement preferences seem to correlate with different stages in the process of moving from location a to location b. In accordance to this removal process is a fourth aspect which is described in the next paragraph: location development as a result of matching between demand *and* supply.

---

[6] The table is based on research performed by the Dutch real estate company DTZ Zadelhoff.

[7] Similar to products also companies have a life cycle. The motive to move from one location to another is strongly related to the stage of the company in the cycle.

16.2.1 Location Development, Matching Supply and Demand

According to Louw (1996) there are three theoretical gaps in location theory: the neglect of market processes, the neglect of the relation between location factors and business removal, and the overemphasis in literature on economic processes and its influence on spatial structures. This has resulted in an '*overemphasis on the demand side of the urban system: the location preferences of firms and households are held responsible for urban development*' (Van der Krabben and Lambooy 1993). Locational development cannot merely be explained by demands of companies. A description of locational development should also account of the spatial development policy, especially in the Netherlands with its active land policies. These policies involve the land market. Although the nature of the Dutch spatial development policy is changing (see e.g. Louw et al 2003), a focus on the explanation of the why's and who's of firm location development should include more preferences than only those of firms. Pen (2002) already shows that 'external actors' like for example architects and accountants play an important role in the relocation process of companies. Irrespective of this involvement, we think that some of these 'external actors', for example real estate developers and municipalities are also involved in the development of new location sites, without knowledge of the specific companies it will accommodate.

An exploration on the influence of ITS on the development of office locations should aim at more actors than companies solely. It should also focus on actors as for example municipalities that both influence land usage and infrastructure development. Their statement on the importance of an ITS scenario on location preferences is therefore very important.

Louw concludes that '*considering the fact that suppliers of office space make location choices in their new estate plans, they are full actors in the field of force of actors that influence the spatial dispersion of office companies*' (1996, translation ours). Moreover it is very likely that actors involved in the development of an ITS concept would use any tool, in this case for example an urban development project, to make a technological advanced ITS project, successful.

Suppliers of business locations (e.g. municipalities and real estate developers) create themselves images on the level of accessibility required by the potential companies locating in these zones. For example, Bok et al (2003) show that especially firms in the public sector tend to follow the Dutch ABC-location-policy and move towards α-locations. α-Locations are typified by Bok et al (2003) as locations with a distance to an intercity station less then 800 meters. Further, it seems for instance that 'location policies' of municipalities in the Netherlands, although not anymore explicitly driven by the national government[8], focus implicitly on the proximity of transportation systems. This could be explained as a result of a process policy-making (see e.g. Parsons 1999). We assume that the development or re-

[8] The Fourth Report on Physical Planning Extra (VINEX 1991) formulated an ABC-location policy. A-locations were situated next to road infrastructure, B-locations next to road infrastructure and public transportation and C-locations only next to public transportation. Later in the nineties, the policy was stopped, due to poor results.

newal of an important (in other words: expensive) public transportation systems, such as ITS, is likely to become an issue for policy making (e.g. Marchau and Van der Heijden 1998). If so, other policies like spatial development could become seriously influenced by that.

The assumption that actors such as municipalities could combine the interest in for example public transport ITS and the development of nearby firms locations is supported by research (see e.g. Edwards and Mackett 1996). After studying 11 new public transport systems in the UK they distinguished two objectives of constructing the transport system. The reasons were generally either transport issues or economic and development issues. A major reason for many systems was to stimulate economic and thus spatial development. Although there is little evidence that building new public transport systems does stimulate such a development, '*it is more likely to do so if a comprehensive plan is being followed or if complementary means of encouraging development are used*' (Edwards and Mackett 1996). What should be noted is that governmental bodies perceive only those public transport systems, which have fixed infrastructure, to attract developers and users of areas near the public transport systems (Edwards and Mackett 1996).

If we look at new public transport systems and spatial development plans in the Netherlands similarities are not difficult to find. Since technology seems to have a special role in decision making processes and dedicated transport systems and spatial development plans are often linked, this research should study on preferences of actors both at the demand and the supply side of office area developments.

16.3 Unfolding '*Attractiveness*' of ITS

In the previous sections we have explained the main part of the theoretical framework. What is not explained yet is what it is in ITS that would influence location development. Considering the theoretical part of section 16.2 it is expected that ITS influences locational development if it changes the nature of one of the settlement factors of a location. It speaks for itself that if ITS influences any settlement factor it would be *accessibility* and/or the image of a location. We define the extent to what ITS can increase the accessibility and/or image of a location as the *attractiveness* of a transportation system. Related to accessibility is the proximity of relevant services to a location.

Before discussing the nature of ITS, we have to explore the meaning of attractiveness of a transportation system. According to our preliminary definition attractiveness has to do with the extent to which the transportation system is capable of increasing the service level in travel. At its turn, this is strongly related to what is often called 'accessibility'. Accessibility is '*the number of persons/households per transportation system per class of movement resistance to the business location in relation to other, similar, locations, as perceived by an actor involved in the development of business locations*'[9]. This definition needs some explanation.

[9] Partly based on the definition of Hakkesteegt (1991: 4.7:)

First, a *business location* is a zone where, according to the land use plan, businesses are settled or allowed to settle. Secondly, a *transportation system* is a means to accommodate a geographical transport of information, freight or passengers. At least infrastructure and vehicles are important elements of the transportation system (in case of physical transportation). Thirdly, the notion of '*movement resistance*' refers to the effort to move information, goods or persons from one geographical position to another. This effort can for example be measured by time, costs, distance and comfort. The importance of the applied indicator is dependent on what is transported. For instance, the travel distance does not matter for the transportation of information. In that case, speed and costs matter. For freight transport costs and time have become dominant for measuring movement resistance (Muilerman 2001; Runhaar 2002). In passenger transport comfort, trip duration and travel time reliability have become increasingly important. Hence, distance as such has become less important as compared to the past. The fourth element to be explained is the phrase: '*in relation to other, similar, locations..*'. Measuring accessibility of a zone in absolute terms has limited informative value, since the valuation (and influence on decision making of firms and households) is always related to and dependent on the accessibility of other locations within the search area. The fifth element is that a valuation of accessibility is always dependent upon the perception of accessibility because '[...] *there is no such thing as unmediated data or facts: these are always the results of interpretation*' (Alvesson and Sköldberg 2000). Hence, there is no such thing as 'absolute' accessibility.

The perception of accessibility could be seen as a construction of two important elements: by 'tangible' and 'less-tangible' elements of accessibility. To explain 'tangible' accessibility we use another definition of accessibility. Hakkesteegt (1986) defines accessibility as '*the possibility that activity spaces can be used by individuals within stated budgets of time, costs and discomfort*' (Hakkesteegt, 1986). This implies that for instance ITS can contribute to accessibility if it supports faster, cheaper and more comforTable transport. Such a measurement would describe effects in hard numbers, which leave little room for interpretation. Such an interpretation would only differ from the approach which was used to describe accessibility. Geurs and Ritsema van Eck (2001) distinguish different measurements to describe accessibility. One difference for example is between activity based accessibility and infrastructure based accessibility. Infrastructure based accessibility measures do not incorporate a land-use component, in contrast to activity based. This can lead to different conclusions and consequently different perceptions. For example, in the Netherlands, employment is concentrated in the highly urbanised western part of the Netherlands (The Randstad). In this area, the main road network is heavily congested during peak hours. '*From an infrastructure-based accessibility measure as 'average speed on the main road network', one may conclude that the level of accessibility in the Netherlands is lowest in the Randstad, whereas from an activity- based accessibility measure (e.g. the number of jobs within 45 minutes travel time by car) one may conclude that the Randstad area shows the highest level of job accessibility of the Netherlands, despite the higher average travel times as a result of congestion*' (Geurs and Ritsema van Eck

2001). So even if tangible data is at forehand it could easily be misinterpreted by for example companies.

The second important element of *attractiveness* is the perception on less-tangible data. Less-tangible features of a transportation system are less easy to measure. Examples of 'less-tangible' factors are, trust, reliability or flexibility of transport facilities. The valuation of accessibility impacts of for example ITS should reckon with both aspects.

We distinguish a second possible element that could increase the *attractiveness* of a transportation system in relationship to locations: *image*. Image is related to those features of a transportation system that does not involve the travel based services. For instance the design of the transportation system could be of a high standard. Further it is possible that innovations in transportation help creating a more positive image of the system. For example, firms could regard a technologically advanced transportation system as a signal that the location is settled within an innovative region.

Although we suggest to study the influence on the *attractiveness* of ITS regarding a location, it remains difficult to separate the influence of one variable, namely attractiveness of a transportation system, from the influence of other factors on the decision to (re)locate. Over time, several surveys have been conducted in the Netherlands to gain understanding about the role of the different settlement factors. However, they do not show a clear pattern. In their first empirical exploration on the importance of accessibility in migration patterns of firms, Bok et al for instance find that '*accessibility appears to express itself in the migration pattern of firms significantly at different scale levels but further research is necessary to determine the exact relationship*' (2003). So, it seems that accessibility is indeed very important, but it is not clear to what extent changes in accessibility can be decisive in case of a (re)location of a company. Some companies might focus more on for instance the quality of the building and its immediate environment, whereas others see '*good access*' as a '*status determinant*'. For instance: '*Some firms want to be located near an international airport or a high quality public transport terminal, whether or not the employees, costumers or clients regularly us these travel modes*' (Geurs and Ritsema van Eck 2003). Bok et al (2003) conclude that firms in business services and finance display concentration patterns: it is observed that these firms move to locations with a larger number of jobs nearby. These are often peripheral locations that are accessible by car and closer to on-ramps but in general with worse public transport and with a less good accessibility for residents or employees. In contrast, government departments show a location pattern which is much more oriented to the city centre: closer to intercity stations and more jobs and inhabitants within reach of 15 minutes from new locations (Bok et al 2003).

In short, the theoretical framework contains two main difficulties. The first difficulty lies in the theoretical assumptions on location theory. In most studies location development is totally explained by stated and revealed preferences of companies. However, this seems to be inadequate since location development is also dependent upon the supply of locations (Louw 1996). For example, in scenario-building it is argued that active land policies, seen as a '*supply-oriented*' approach, result in different locational development than approaches that are more influenced by demanders preferences, which are so-called '*demand oriented*' approaches (Geurs and Ritsema van Eck 2001). Our study aims to reckon with this complexity. Secondly, it is still rather unclear how important the attractiveness of the transport system is relative to other settlement factors. The importance seems to vary with the type of company. Thus considering both difficulties, in the methodological exploration we will also focus on the relative importance of ITS attractiveness on parties involved in the supply side. And what is the nature of the ITS that is considered to be so important?

16.4 Location Development, the Link with ITS

In the previous section, we discussed a hypothetical relation between ITS and the (re)location of firms. We also mentioned that there is no large scale implementation of infrastructure based ITS within our reach at present to test our hypotheses in practice. Therefore, we have to follow another research strategy.

First, in this section, ITS systems are specified that are assumed to contribute to attractiveness and influence different actors involved in the location development process. We will discuss plausible images of large scale implementation of ITS in an urban region. One could say why at the level of the region? One important reason for looking at the urban region is that this seems the appropriate environment for which ITS will be implemented initially as new modes. A second reason is that we have taken into account that most of the (re)locations of firms occur within the region of origin.

Secondly, what would this large scale implementation of ITS look like? And what can be said about the possible impact on attractiveness? How important are differences in penetration level? There fore we will briefly look at the theoretical differences in impact of these ITS concepts on (re)location of firms. Can we, for instance, explore differences in spatial dynamics between ITS in public transport and in car driving?

ITS as a Settlement Factor

Before discussing possible implementations and advantages of ITS systems, it is important to elaborate on a more systematic view of ITS. The notion of Intelligent Transportation Systems has been mentioned multiple times in this paper.

Generally, ITS can be described as '*systems consisting of electronics, communications or information processing used singly or integrated to improve the efficiency or safety of surface transportation*' (Tindemans *et al*, 2003: 2). This notion encompasses a large variety of applications[10]. Marchau and Van der Heijden (2000, 2002, 2003) use a structured view of ITS services. They conceptualise the

[10] For a more specific and complete overview on the nature of different ITS applications see for example publications by Ertico (e.g. 2002) and publications of Bishop (e.g. 2000).

transport system by seven subsystems: four subsystems comprising the transport system's physical features (infrastructure, vehicles, goods or passengers and spatial and economic organisation) and three markets representing the interactions between the transport system's physical features. The three markets are the transport need market, the transport market and the traffic market.

Table 16.2. Indicative relationship between transportation subsystems, ITS functionality and the variety of ITS applications (based on Van der Heijden and Marchau 2003)

Subsystem	ITS functionality	Examples ITS application
Transport need market	Systems for facilitating virtual mobility	Electronic commerce; tele-working; tele-education
Freight and passengers	ATIS	
	Information supply on transport services; booking services	Park and ride information; public transport services information; traffic information on radio, teletext; internet booking services
Transport service market	ATIS/ATMS	
	Pre-trip planning support systems	Trip reservation and route planning systems
	Systems for logistic optimisation	Telecommunications for fleet management; trip matching systems
Vehicles	ADAS	
	Smart Motor Technology	Self-diagnostic engine control systems, crash recorders;
	Driver support systems	Reverse parking aid; tutoring systems; navigation systems; adaptive cruise/speed control; lateral and longitudinal control; cooperative driving; intersection collisions warning; forward collision warning; intelligent speed adaptation; passenger warning systems
Traffic flow market	ATMS/ATIS	
	Dynamic traffic management systems	Dynamic route information screens; traffic information on radio; differentiated electronic payment; dynamic (directional) lane assignment; ramp metering; speed control (radar detection, cameras); VMS; incident detection; aid coordination systems
Physical transport infrastructure	ATMS/ADAS	
	Lane optimisation technology; infrastructure status control systems	Dynamic lane configuration adaptation; surface measurement and deterioration detection

Most gains in terms of safety, comfort and throughput in transportation networks is expected from technological developments within the field of driver support systems. These systems are called ADAS. However, these expectations are to a large extent dependent on future combinations of different ADAS applications and the integration of ADAS, ATIS and ATMS. An example of integration between ADAS is vehicles equipped with more than one ADAS application. Integration between subsystems occurs for example when ADAS systems use infrastructure to operate. Such integration could provide large gains in terms of safety, comfort and throughput in networks.

Examples of ADAS are Intelligent Speed Adaptation (ISA) and Adaptive Cruise Control (ACC). ISA is an in-car system that assists or controls a vehicles speed limit. If a car is equipped with ISA and enters an 80 km/u road, the car, slows down and adjusts its speed to what is permitted, either by getting a signal from infrastructural devices or by using the digital map in the vehicle on which maximum posted speed have been pre-programmed. One can think of large safety potentials when ISA would be used at large scale. ACC is an intelligent cruise control system. It detects vehicles in front and back of the car and anticipates their speed. Instant breaking of a front car could warn the driver or intervene by slowing down the speed. Like ISA, ACC has large safety potentials. Further, ACC could increase driving comfort and road usage efficiency. ISA and ACC are two examples of ADAS systems. A final stage of ADAS development could result in for example fully automated driving. Although such a concept is not plausible to become reality on a large scale in the near future, its potentials are sufficient great to conduct much research on automated driving.

Similar to integration of different ADAS we expect large gains from new ITS concepts that combine applications from other user service bundles with ADAS. As Table 16.2. shows these other services are mainly ATMS and ATIS. Contrary to the development of ADAS, ATMS and ATIS systems in transportation have largely matured (Bishop 2000). These are for example systems that inform drivers or passengers about the trip. Examples of such systems are Variable Message Signs (VMS) and Personal Intelligent Travel Assistant (PITA). VMS systems inform drivers on motorways about congestion or incidents. Alternative routes are suggested. Although the benefits of such a system are not considered to be impressive, they do stimulate traffic in usage of variable roads. PITA is a GSM system that gives real-time route information to passengers on arrival and departure of different public transport. In case of delay, alternative route information is provided.

Thus, our image of the future is probably coloured by new ITS concepts that are constructed from ADAS and further surrounded by several other ATMS and ATIS user services. Those ITS concepts would influence several parts of the transportation network. There are two possible scenario's as to how ITS will affect land-use decisions.

Thus, future ITS concepts that have great potential and have reasonable chance of being developed would focus on ADAS plus ICT- based travel information and traffic management. Such a concept is our focus of research. We will name it ADAS+ from now on.

The development process of *ADAS+* is difficult mainly because of large uncertainties within the technological development of ADAS and the market potential for ICT-services. With regard to ADAS for instance, the economic benefit of an automatic public bus system is potentially large. About three quarters of a bus companies' costs is spent on personnel. However, the automation of a bus system requires new technical and legal systems to insure passenger safety. More specific, the ITS applications that provide precise navigation need additional driver assistance systems. This requires extra political and financial investments. Given the fact that the implementation of such technological developments is expensive and municipalities face limited budgets a fixed strategy is needed. Therefore, municipalities are forced to choose to be selective in terms of the ITS strategy they prefer to accommodate. It is hardly possible to invest on ITS for the whole variety of transport activities. Consequently, these public actors can either support services regarding car driving, freight transportation, public transport or perhaps a low level of mixed services. ITS (in particular traffic flow control) has proven to be able to improve throughput in transportation networks (see e.g. Juan et al 2003) and consequently to improve access to nearby locations.

'Attractiveness' of ITS

How can a possible influence of ITS be made more specific? In other words: how can ITS contribute to the *attractiveness* of a transportation system? To start on an extensive answer to this question we must focus on the core: infrastructural applications, in-vehicle applications and their combination. A distinction should be made to the level of technological support the system provides to the driver. This refers to the degree of driving automation by the system: *Informative* (auditive or visual signals to the driver, who has to decide what to do with the information), *Assisting* (system takes over some driving tasks, but intervention by the driver) and *Autonomous* (system takes over certain driving tasks, without intervention options for the driver). The tendency is to intensify R&D on assisting and autonomous systems. For example, in the Netherlands pilots with automated people movers and freight trucks have been initiated in recent years.

The more attention for autonomous driving is intensifying, the more the link with the infrastructure system becomes important and the more the discussion on the transport services level and organisation is triggered.

The in-vehicle applications are linked to the basic driving tasks of the driver. These systems are ADAS. There are various ADAS under development. For instance, Intelligent Speed Adaptation, Lane keeping Assistance or Adaptive Cruise Control. Often a distinction is made in this respect between the drivers' controlling task (task associated with keeping the vehicle on the road), manoeuvring task (lateral and longitudinal vehicle positioning in relation to other vehicles) and the navigation task (route choices).

Until recently, hardly any links between ADAS and infrastructure management were made. Increasingly however, thoughts and experiments focusing on the combination of in-car and infrastructure-based ITS applications are debated. These have for instance been described by Van der Heijden and Marchau (2002) in terms of different transport service levels.

These developments, that are hardly to be expected to become reality on a large scale in the next years, are important for the discussion on the long term relationship between transport and spatial development triggered in this paper. In more specific terms of attractiveness we refer for example to the first deliverable of project STARDUST, a European research programme. STARDUST aims to explore the field of ADAS and Automated Guided Vehicles (AGV).

In this, it distinguishes Adaptive Cruise Control (ACC), Lane Departure Warning, Side-Obstacle warning Systems, Forward Vehicle Collision Warning Systems, Intersection Collision Warning Systems, Parking Assistance, Night Vision enhancement Systems, Intelligent Speed Adaptation (ISA) and Full-automated Driving. These systems are under development in the USA, Europe (including Israel) and Japan. The former mentioned ADAS systems and Full-automated driving are dependent upon a large variety of smaller technological developments, in particular sensors (laser and wave radar), navigation and detection systems.

Table 16.3. (Note: V Impact; VVStrong Impact; VVV Very Strong Impact)

System	Impacts			
	Safety	Comfort	Congestion	Environment
Adaptive Cruise Control		VV	V	V
Lane Departure Waning	VV			
Lane Keeping Assistance	V	VV	V	V
Side-obstacle warning	VV			
Intersection Collision Warning	VV			
Parking Assistance	VV	V		
Forward Collision Warning	VV		V	
Night Vision Enhancement	VV	V		
Intelligent Speed Adaptation	V	VV		V
Fully Automated Driving	V	VV	VVV	V

Source: STARDUST (2001: 24)

Table 16.3. shows the expected impact of different ADAS and AGV applications on safety, comfort, congestion and environment. The impact rates are expert expectations based on an extensive international literature study. Note that, as we mentioned previously, only Fully Automated Driving has a real strong impact on congestion. Next, Fully Automated Driving scores well on safety, comfort and environment. If we interpret attractiveness of ITS in terms of '*the number of persons/households per transportation system*' as was described earlier in this paper Fully Automated Driving has high potential. And if we interpret attractiveness in terms of '*movement resistance*' Fully Automated Driving has a strong impact on comfort and less impact on safety. Fully Automated Driving has the highest potential to increase what we called *attractiveness* of a transportation system. Looking at influences of ITS, this research will further solely aim at the influence of Fully Automated Driving. However, plausibility of implementation remains an important criterion. Hence, it is possible that some features of automation will not maintain our focus in research. Fully Automated Driving can be applied to freight transport, public transport and road traffic. Key technologies used are: dedicated lanes (e.g. CombiRoad and ULS projects in Netherlands), vehicle position technology (e.g. Parkshuttle projects in EC), obstacle detection, vehicle-vehicle and vehicle-roadway communication and sensor technology for vehicle ranging (STARDUST 2001).

Currently, Fully Automated Driving is only applied successfully in small public transport concepts. Expected is that within 5 to 10 years, Fully Automated Driving will be possible for freight transport and larger public transport systems. Implementing Automated Fully Driving in road traffic requires much more technological development regarding safety and new legislation by governments. Fully Automated Driving is an interesting concept to test whether location preferences will be influenced, at least theoretically.

Although Table 16.3. shows some promising impacts of AVG, we should remain cautious. Van Arem and Smits (1998) show for example that impact of AVG on levels of mobility and travel time is much less attractive. Moreover, the impact is dependent upon multiple aspects. Differences result for instance from the role of government, the level of regulation regarding AVG, implementation of dynamic traffic management (DTM), transportation mode and period of time.

Thus, it is expected that advanced levels of transport automation, based on the integration of ITS systems in infrastructure and in-car, such as Fully Automated Driving, require quite some investments in technological facilities and a dedicated organisation for operational management. Van Arem and Smits (1998) discuss that '*although the study shows that AVG can help solving mobility problems, it appears that AVG needs to be embedded in an integral transport policy* [...]' (1998). For example, sensor technology is required in each road network for real-time data-collection on traffic flows and incident management. Real-time, tailor-made information should be available on various modalities for travellers; guiding autonomous driving vehicles might require Global Positioning System (GPS) and sensor facilities on dedicated roads. Particularly when investments in supporting technology and traffic flow management are infrastructure-based, it seems rather plausible that these investments will be selective initially (that is: initially not everywhere but related to certain pieces of the transport system). The first reason for that is that (mainly public) budgets, usually needed for infrastructure adaptations, are limited. Of course extra budgets might be realised by charging transport users for improved transport service quality but there willingness to pay is uncertain. Secondly, not all infrastructures will be candidate for these applications, but selected parts of road networks will be, because traffic problems (e.g. congestion level, safety level) are not the same in all parts of the network and the contribution to the total performance improvement will be a serious criterion for investment. Thirdly, it is plausible that such an infrastructure transition program will be phased in time: new investments will be based on the evaluation on the impacts of former investments (effectiveness, the need for changing the concept): the evolutionary innovation process[11]. And as we argued before municipalities play an important role in location supply and the development of new transportation systems.

To indicate a plausible development of these ITS concepts, one can think of selective promotion by public policies of certain target groups, for instance public transport, business cars or urban freight transport. This might lead to investments in for example all the facilities accommodating high quality public transport, including dedicated lanes, automated vehicles, and full information supply for travellers. Argiolu (2002) has described experiments with such ITS-based approaches in the Dutch cities of Eindhoven and Rotterdam/Capelle aan den IJssel. For freight transport a full automated concept was already seriously studied (CTT, 1995-1997). Serious thoughts for applying such a freight transport technology in the Dutch urban agglomeration of Enschede-Hengelo are currently under study. A final possibility to be mentioned is to invest in the facilities required for multimodal chain mobility, linking the car system systematically with public transport facilities. A strong focus may be laid in that context on the performance of the transfer points. Both options will lead to the investments in smart and partly dedicated, pieces of infrastructure within the urban agglomeration.

Considering these plausible future ITS developments, we can assume that the implementation of ITS will follow a pattern of selective adaptation (based on geographical and functional considerations) of the transportation system. Given the pursued goals of ITS (improving safety, throughput in networks and travel comfort) it is assumed to generate competitive advantages for these parts of the transportation network from the perspective of transport performance and attractiveness for travellers.

For example, a dedicated lane for full automated driving inbound a metropolitan area with guaranteed travel time and parking place at the destination might turn out to be more attractive, irrespective the need for reservation of an individual access slot and the need for extra payment for the service, than to accept the present daily peak congestion and uncertainty of finding a parking place.

16.5 Methodological Framework

Hypothetically, ITS can contribute to the *attractiveness* of a location. As a consequence, it gains influence on future settlement-considerations. This influences actors that are involved in the development of firm location, whilst making spatial choices. Since ITS are state of the art in transportation and only few data is available, the methodological approach to test the hypothesis is explorative from nature (see figure 16.1. on the next page). A method that is commonly used to explore future situations is scenario-building.

Scenarios can be used for several reasons[12]. A general motive to use scenarios is to support decision-making by reducing uncertainties. In this project they serve

[11] For an in-depth discussion on technological development as a process, see e.g. Giovanni Dosi (1982) on 'Technological paradigms and technological trajectories'.

as a tool to gain more insight in possibilities of future ITS concepts. To use scenarios effectively[13] in this research we need to restrict the number of scenarios. Both the number and emphasis of scenarios can be determined by a procedure that uses morphological analysis[14]. The first step in this procedure involves the construction and initial exploration of alternative ITS concepts for the future. These ITS concepts are constructed by adding traffic and travel management services to ADAS. The main purpose of this step is to structure and limit the set of alternative ADAS+ concepts. The morphology of the scenario space is constructed by the appropriate value ranges of the dimensions. This morphology defines the maximum number of possible scenarios (Porter et al 1991). At first we identify basic dimensions constituting the variety of concepts. Secondly, we specify the values of these dimensions and finally we evaluate all possible combinations of these values. The unique combinations of possible values along the different features produce a variety of alternative concepts. Next, these concepts are evaluated to prune highly unlikely or unfeasible concepts. This involves, for instance, concepts that are unlikely to contribute to general transportation goals and/or concepts that are unfeasible from technical and/or societal point of view. The elimination of these concepts will lead towards the scenario narratives.

[12] For an updated scenario typology see e.g. Van Notten et al. (2003)

[13] For more information on how to develop and use scenarios in research, see for example Schnaars (1987)

[14] For a more detailed description on the nature of the morphological analysis see Van Doorn and Van Vught (1978). For an example of the use of the morphological analysis see Marchau (2000).

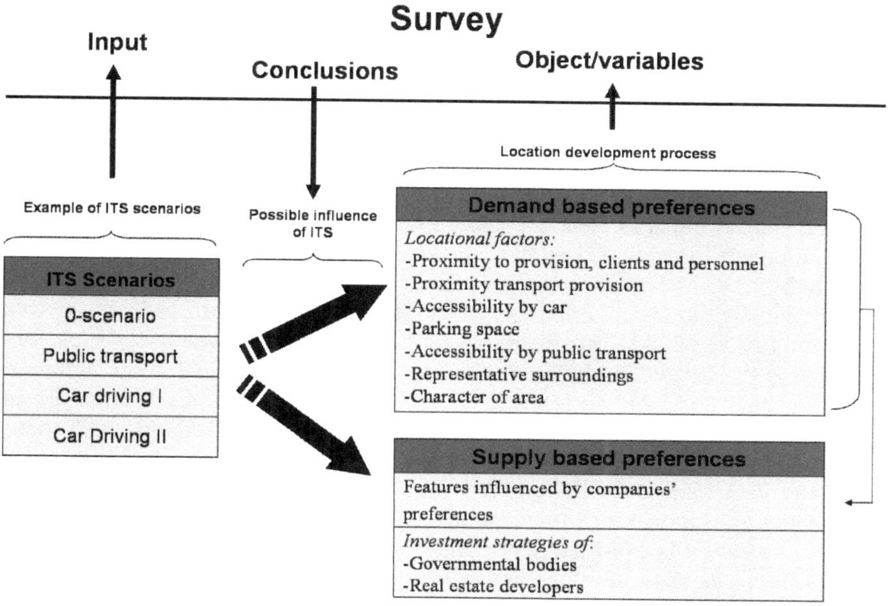

Fig. 16.1. Theoretical and methodological concept

The problem then is to identify those ITS scenarios that will be relevant in meeting the goals of the foresight. That is, which ITS can contribute to the *attractiveness* of a location? These final steps in limiting the scenarios will be based on features of ITS concepts that have been implemented already combined with the results of research, which have been described in literature.

The outline for the *validation* of the scenarios is based on expert opinion. Policymakers, scientists and companies involved in the development of ITS criticise and re-shape the scenarios. This expert data collection could for example be performed using a Delphi technique[15], in which consensus about for example feasibility of the different scenarios, is gained by repeating several rounds of judgement. Other ways to collect the date are for instance workshops or by using group model building tools.

The construction and validation of the scenarios result in narratives and/or images of different ITS implementations in an urban region. An important step from construction to narrative is to translate the scenarios from the sophisticated approach that safeguards plausibility to narratives or images that are useful in survey research. Thus, they should be appealing enough to make sense to actors involved in development process of companies. This conversion could for instance be conducted by using a Geographical Information System (GIS).

[15] For an example on the usage of the Delphi method to define the future of AVG see Marchau 2000.

Dependent variable in the survey research would be the preferences of relevant actors regarding firm locations. The specific contents of the questions are not defined yet. The aim of the survey is to unfold the possible influence of ITS on the preferences of firm location in an urban region[16], for which the scenarios[17] form the basis. The sampling of respondents should take relevant sub-populations into account.

At least, this means that samples are taken from both actors involved in the *demand* side, companies, and the actors involved in the *supply* side of the location development process. Possibly further differentiation between subgroups is needed.

Eventually, we need to reckon for the fact that the differences between scenarios might also trigger different subgroups. An important issue in research for example is the connection between plausible ADAS+ conceptualisation and its specific impact on location preferences. As we argued earlier, the type of transport which this ADAS integration would apply to differentiates strongly with the type of preference actors have. What if we regard Table 16.1. and link this with a concept such as Fully Automated Driving? Applied to public transport it would probably only appeal to firms regarded as '*stationeries*' and '*classicists*'. Besides, in such a case it is expected that municipalities will play a more important role in pinpointing location development than in case of regional roadway development. Finally, if we want to draw conclusions on possible impact on spatial development in the future we also need to take into account the penetration level. Fully Automated Driving within a public transport system probably has a smaller penetration level than in case of Fully Automated Driving on highways.

16.6 Conclusion

Geographical differences in ITS-based accessibility might result in changes in location patterns. It has been argued that location choices of businesses and actors in the supply side are to a significant degree sensible for perceived differences in accessibility, either in terms of the travel costs (time, money) or in terms of distance. A next step in reasoning is that these differences in accessibility at a certain moment might lead to gradually changing location choice behaviour of businesses

16 The spatial scale of the region as an entity seems well suited for such a scenario since it covers most of the urban areas on which transport problems occur and thus municipalities or regions will invest in. Pellenbarg (1996) found that 57% of the companies movements stay within the municipality and 97% within the province in 1992. Bok et al. (2003) found that the share of firms in the dataset who migrate within the boundaries of their municipality is 75% and original COROP-region (COROP=Dutch statistical spatial entities) is 97%. The Netherlands consist of 43 COROP regions. Example: Dutch cities of Arnhem and Nijmegen are one COROP.

17 For an elaboration on the specific contents of the ITS scenarios as they are constructed in this research project see Argiolu et al. (2004, *forthcoming*)

and commuters. These choices will be characterised by a preference for locations that are better accessible by ITS-based transport services as compared to locations that are not. Measured in terms of a long periods (decades), we expect a geographical pattern of (at least certain) business activities that increasingly will match with the geographical pattern of high level ITS applications.

To test the research hypothesis two main studies will be done. The first is a scenario study to specify the combinations of ITS applications that would increase location *attractiveness*. The second will be a survey among actors that influence spatial development. These are 'so-called' demanders and suppliers of locations. Comparable studies (see e.g. Tayyaran et al 2003; Tayyaran and Khan 2003) show that the proposed methodology can be fruitful in answering questions on impact of IT and ITS on location choice. Their results show that for residing '[...] *telecommunicating and ITS measures are highly significant factors in the residential choice model*' (Tayyaran et al 2003).

Clearly many operational decisions have to be taken for performing these substudies. A variety of issues has been mentioned already. Important is that by exploring the issue in this paper, and the first attempts to translate them into researchable questions, we made an important step for more systematically studying a challenging issue to link technological innovation and spatial development. Evidently, we will report on the progress in future.

Acknowledgements

The research project that is described in this paper is carried out as part of the NWO-CONNEKT Research program "Behavioural Analysis and Modelling for the Design and Implementation of Advanced Driver Assistance Systems" (BAMADAS). Our project is sponsored by the Cornelis Lely Foundation.

Helpful comments on earlier drafts of this paper by Edwin Buitelaar, Erik Louw and Egbert Wever are gratefully acknowledged. However, only the authors are accounTable for any remaining errors and omissions.

References

Alvesson M, Sköldberg K (2000) Reflexive Methodology, New Vistas for Qualitative Research. SAGE, London.

Argiolu R (2002) Innovatief openbaar vervoer. Anders of Beter?, master thesis spatial planning, Nijmegen School of Management, University of Nijmegen (In Dutch).

Argiolu R, van der Heijden R, Marhcau V (2006) Looking at ITS in the future: four scenarios, paper to be presented at the WCTR Istanbul, 4-8 July, Turkey, (Forthcoming)

Atzema O, Wever E (1994) De Nederlandse Industrie, Ontwikkeling, spreiding en uitdaging, Van Gorcum Assen (In Dutch).

Banister D (1995) Transport and urban development, E and FN SPON, London.

Bishop R (2000) A survey of Intelligent Vehicle Applications Worldwide. Richard Bishop Consulting USA.

Bok M, Blije B, Sanders F (2003) The influence of the transportation system on land use: A disaggregated analysis of the migration patterns of firms on the office market and the accessibility of locations, paper for Colloquium Vervoerplanologisch Speurwerk, Netherlands.

CTT (1994-1996) Combiroads reports, Center for transport Technology, Rotterdam.

Dosi G (1982) Technological paradigms and technological trajectories. Research Policy, 11, pp. 147-162.

Edwards M, Mackett R (1996) Mapping new urban public transport systems. Transport Policy, Vol. 3, No. 4: 225-239.

ERTICO (2002) Intelligent Transport Systems and Services, ITS – Part of Everyone's Daily Life. ERTICO – ITS Europe and Navigation Technologies, Brussels.

Fourth Report on Physical Planning Extra (1991) Ministry for Housing, Physical Planning and Environment, Sdu. The Hague (In Dutch).

Filarski R (1999) The rise and fall of transport systems: technology, human behaviour, mobility and spatial factors. Paper presented at the NECTAR conference, 20-23 October 1999 in Delft.

Geurs K, van Eck R (2001) Accessibility measures Review and applications. Research for men and environment (RIVM), Bilthoven, The Netherlands.

Hakkesteegt P (1986) Vervoerssytemen- en modellen. Deel A: Vervoerkunde. Delft: Vakgroep Verkeer, Faculteit der Civiele Techniek, TU-Delft. (In Dutch).

Hakkesteegt P (1991) Vervoersystemen en –modellen. Deel A: Algemene Vervoer- en Verkeerskunde. Delft: Vakgroep Verkeer, Faculteit der Civiele Techniek. TU-Delft (In Dutch).

Hegeman G (2004) Effect advanced driver assistance systems on overtaking on two-lane roads. Paper to be presented at IEEE conference Den Haag, The Netherlands.

Hotelling H (1929) Stability in competition. The economic journal 39: 41-57.

Juan Z, Wu J, McDonald M (2003) The socio-economic impacts assessment of advanced convoy driving on motorway. Transportation Research Part A 37: 731-747.

Krabben E, van der and Lambooy J (1993) A theoretical framework for the functioning of the Dutch property market. Urban Studies 30, 8: 1381-1397.

Lambooy J, Wever E, Atzema O (1997) Ruimtelijke economische dynamiek, Uitgeverij In: Coutinho BV, Bussum, The Netherlands (In Dutch).

Lukkes P, Krist A, van Steen P (1987) Kantorenmarkt Investeren en Ruimte, Vonk Uitgevers, Zeist (In Dutch).

Louw E (1996) Kantoorgebouw en Vestigingplaats, een geografisch onderzoek naar de rol van huisvesting bij locatiebeslissingen van kantoorhoudende organisaties. Stedelijke en Regionale Verkenningen 12, Delftse Universitaire Pers (In Dutch).

Louw E, Krabben E, van der and Priemus H (2003) Spatial development policy: changing roles for local and regional authorities in the Netherlands. Land use policy 20: 357-366.

Marchau V, Heijden R van der (1998) Policy aspects of driver support systems implementation: results of an international Delphi study. Transport Policy, 5, 4: 249-258.

Marhcau V (2000) Technology Assessment of Automated Vehicle Guidance: Prospects for automated driving implementation. Delft University Press: Delft.

Marchau V, Heijden R van der (2003) Innovative Methodologies for Exploring the Future of Automated Vehicle Guidance. Journal of Forecasting, 22: 257-276.

Marchau V, Heijden R van der, Vree W (2000) Strategische Ontwikkelingen rond Verkeersbeheersing, De rol van ITS. Faculty of Technology, Policy and Management, Delft University of Technology (In Dutch).

Muilerman GJ (2001) Time-based logistics. Delft University Press, Delft, The Netherlands.

Parsons W (1999) An Introduction to the Theory and Practice of Policy Analysis. Edward Elger, Cheltenham, United Kingdom.

Pellenbarg (1996) Struktuur en ontwikkeling van bedrijfsmigratie in Nederland. Planning, Vol. 48., INRO-TNO, Delft: 22-32 (In Dutch).

Pellenbarg P, Wissen L van, J van Dijk J (2002) Firm relocation: state of the art and research prospects: SOM Research Report 02D31, University of Groningen.

Pen CJ (2002) Wat beweegt bedrijven? Besluitvormingsprocessen bij verplaatste bedrijven. Netherlands Geographical Studies 297, Groningen (In Dutch).

Porter A, Roper A, Mason T, Rossini F, Banks J (1991) Forecasting and Management of Technology. John Wiley and Sons Inc., New York.

Runhaar H (2002) Freight transport at any price?. Delft University Press, Delft, The Netherlands.

Simon HA (1957) Models of a man: social and rational. John Wiley New York.

Simon HA (1960) The new science of management decision. New York: Harper and Row.

STARDUST (2001) Deliverable 1, Critical Analysis of ADAS/AVG options to 2010, selection of options to be investigated. European Commission Fifth Framework Programme, Energy Environment ad Sustainable Development Programme.

Tayyaran M, Khan A (2003) The effects of Telecommuting and Intelligent Transportation Systems on Urban Development. Journal of Urban Technology, 10, 2: 87-100.

Tayyaran, M., Khan, A. and Anderson, D (2003) Impact of telecommuting and intelligent transportation systems on residential location choice. Transportation Planning and Technology, 26, 2: 171-193.

Thünen J von (1842) Der isolierte Staat in Beziehung auf Landwirtschaft und Nationalökonomie, Zweite auflage (1842) (Reproduction in 1921, Jena: Gustav Fischer Verlag).

Schnaars S (1987) How to Develop and Use Scenarios. Long Range Planning, 20, 1: 105-114.

Van Arem B, Smits C (1998) An exploration of the development of Automated Vehicle Guidance Systems. TNO-report Inro/VVG 1997-3, TNO Inro, Delft.

Van Doorn, van Vught (1978) Forecasting: Methoden en technieken voor toekomstonderzoek. Van Gorcum, Assen. (in Dutch).

Van der Heijden R, Marchau V (2002) Innovating road traffic management by ITS: a future perspective. Int. J. Technology, Policy and Management, 2, 1: 20-39.

Van der Heijden R, van Wees K (2001) Introducing advanced driver assistance systems: some legal issues. European Journal of Transport and Infrastructure Research 1: 309-326.

Van Notten P, Rotmans J, van Asselt M, Rothman D (2003) An updated scenario typology. Futures 35: 423-443.

Weber A (1909) Ueber den Standort der Industrien, Ersten Teil: Reine Theorie des Standorts (Zweite auflage (1922)), Tübingen: J.C.B. Mohr Verlag.

17 The Economics of Transportation Network Growth

Lei Zhang
Department of Civil Engineering
University of Minnesota (U.S.A.)

David Levinson
Department of Civil Engineering
University of Minnesota (U.S.A.)

17.1 Introduction

A number of factors influence the efficiency, productivity, and welfare of transportation networks. Travel demand, user costs, and facility supply costs equilibrate on various time scales under a set of pricing (taxes and tolls), investment and ownership policies. Two types of equilibria exist in a transportation network, short-run traffic equilibrium and long-run supply-demand equilibrium. The phenomenon of traffic equilibrium is explored with a fixed transportation network where the capacity of links is given. Even though investment- and ownership-related policies are not of major concern for studies of traffic equilibrium, it is still a complex problem due to network congestion effects, variations of pricing rules, and multidimensionality of user choices. In order to understand the long-run supply-demand equilibrium in a transportation network, one has to consider all of the above-mentioned factors in a coherent analytical framework. We refer to this research problem as the transportation *network growth problem*, because the network evolves and link capacity is not fixed in the long run.

The growth (and decline) of transportation networks obviously affects the social and economic activities that a region can support, yet the dynamics of how such growth occurs is one of the least understood areas in transportation, geography, urban economics, and regional science. The growth of the transportation network is determined by the total amount of investment and the investment rule, both of which could change over time. What has become known as the *network design problem* in the transportation literature simplifies the *network growth problem* in three aspects: (1) investment decisions are considered independent of pricing rules and ownership structures; (2) only the optimal investment rule is considered; (3) inter-dependencies of sequential investment decisions are ignored. In reality, the budget is typically determined by the revenue generated from the pricing policy and inter-agency negotiations. Various practical investment rules have been adopted by public or private decision-makers with different goals in mind, that are not necessarily socially optimal. Historical dependency is also an important property of network growth. Economic studies on transportation network growth should recognize these facts. A salient feature of the network growth problem, defined in this chapter, is that it considers the growth of transportation networks as endogenous, in contrast with current transportation planning practice that strives to exogenously direct that growth. In other words, transportation network growth is not entirely an artifact of design, but driven by various market forces present in the network.

Today's decisions both depend on expectations of tomorrow, and constrain tomorrow's choices. Understanding how markets and policies translate into facilities on the ground is essential for both scientific understanding and improving forecasting, planning, policy-making, and evaluation. An improved understanding of long-term network dynamics should lead to better planning and design of transportation networks to exploit network economies and externalities. The challenge for solving the network growth problem is that travel demand, cost structures, and all relevant policies must be modeled with accuracy and sensitivity. This chapter is therefore exploratory in nature, investigating these modeling needs and possible solutions. Another purpose of this chapter is to demonstrate how a network growth model can improve transportation planning in ways short-run network models cannot achieve.

Most previous studies have considered network pricing, investment, and ownership structures separately, which are reviewed in the following section. The next section considers choices of prices, capacity, and ownership simultaneously on small parallel, serial, and parallel-serial networks, and develops an analytical network model. Section 17.4 of this chapter discusses properties of long-run network equilibria with different network layouts and ownership regimes, and the implications on network efficiency. Section 17.5 concludes the chapter with some critiques on the analytical model and suggestions for future research.

17.2 Literature Review

Transportation economists have long been investigating various road pricing policies for optimal allocation of scarce road resources, primarily from a theoretical framework (Dupuit 1844, Pigou 1920, Knight 1924, Mohring and Harwitz 1962, Vickery 1963, Walters 1968, Small 1992, Arnott *et al.* 1993, Button and Verhoef 1998, Gomez-Ibanez 1999, de Palma and Lindsey 2002, Verhoef 2002). The economic theory also suggests that the optimal level of road investment is to expand a road to the point that the cost of one additional unit of capacity just equals the benefits it brings. An important finding, due to Mohring and Harwitz (1962), states that the revenue generated from the optimal pricing scheme is just sufficient to finance the optimal level of capacity under certain conditions. A series of studies have examined the validity of this "self-financing rule", which are summarized by Verhoef and Rouwendal (2004). However, the theoretical analyses are typical performed under a strict set of economic conditions which, in some cases, hardly correspond with reality. Some have concerns that the revenue collected from short-run marginal cost pricing schemes may either significantly exceed or fall short of long-run cost of facility supply for reasons with regard to economies of scale and non-optimality of existing road capacity (Walters 1968, Gwilliam 1997). While the majority of road pricing literature considers a network of parallel roads, several studies examine revenue choices on a serial network managed by multiple jurisdictions (Levinson 1999, Levinson 2000).

While pricing policies are typically proposed with the goal of improving short-run network efficiency, studies on investment principles are generally concerned with long-run efficiency assuming *a priori* the pricing policy (Wohl and Hendrickson 1984). Previous research on the network design problem (NDP) seeks to find the optimal network that serves a certain travel demand, or the optimal network enhancement given a budget constraint (Boyce *et al.* 1974, LeBlanc 1975, Poorzahedy and Turnquist 1982, Yang and Bell 1998, Meng *et al.* 2001). However, these studies, focusing on investment only, do not address the conflict between long-run economic efficiency and financial feasibility in reality. Benefit-cost analysis has been extensively used in practice for strategic planning. Decision-makers have also developed practical investment rules dealing with problems of concern, most notably congestion, such as bottleneck removal and bottleneck bypassing (Zhang and Levinson 2005).

Another related issue is transportation commercialization and privatization. Gomez-Ibanez and Meyer (1993) have reviewed transportation privatization at an empirical level, though the cases of roadway privatization are few and not entirely successful. It is unlikely that even if roadways were privatized, that their price structure would be left entirely to the private sector. Roth (1996) reviewed positive aspects of road commercialization and privatization, and proposed a framework for creating a market economy of roads. In many ways, roadways are natural monopolies, as their provision and use has a declining average cost (aside from congestion effects). The relative advantages and disadvantages of various ownership regimes may also depend on the type of regulation (Kahn 1988, Train 1991).

Most previous economic studies consider the aforementioned three policy aspects (pricing, investment and ownership) of transportation network growth separately with a few exceptions. Keeler and Small (1977) developed a theoretical model to examine optimal peak-load pricing and investment on urban expressways. Verhoef and Rouwendal (2004) recently revisited this topic with additional considerations of second-best pricing policies. Several studies consider alternative ownership regimes and toll choices on a small network with one OD pair and two or more alternative routes (DeVany and Saving 1980, de Palma 1992, Viton 1995, Verhoef *et al.* 1996, de Palma and Lindsey 2000). No previous study has consider pricing, investment and ownership issues jointly on hypothetical or real-world networks.

There are also different methodological tools which could be used to model transportation network growth. Following the seminal work by Pigou (1920) and

Knight (1924), most economic studies on road pricing and financing adopt a theoretical framework and base the analysis on small hypothetical networks, which may be labeled as small network (equilibrium) models. Models of the transportation network as a physical system have been well developed in the transportation literature (Sheffi 1985). When there are multiple agents making pricing and investment decisions (e.g. private roads competing with public roads), an economic network arises which considers coordination and competition between decision-makers. Johansson *et al.* (1994) describe various economic networks from an empirical viewpoint, while Nagurney (1993) provides a computational framework, which links analysis of economic networks (supplier-customer relationships) with algorithms developed for the analysis of physical networks. Economides (1996) compares the economic structure of networks with vertically related industries. Economic systems with multiple decision-making agents may not contain a neat equilibrium solution. Game theory (Von Neumann and Morgenstern 1944, de Palma 1992) provides an alternative means for capturing the interactions between agents in deciding prices and investments. However, game theory assumes a certain amount of knowledge and information available to the players. A modeling approach using cellular automata (Langton 1989) suggests specifying simple rules and allowing the system to evolve. The transportation system is, in Sussman's (2000) word, a complex, large, integrated, and open system. Modeling tools developed for analyzing complex systems, such as agent-based techniques (von Neumann 1966, Zhang and Levinson 2004a), may also be used to model transportation network growth.

17.3 An Analytical Model of Pricing, Capacity Choice and Ownership Structure

17.3.1 Demand Side: Models of Road Users

Users in the transportation systems make a number of spatial and temporal choices that affect travel demand: residential and job locations, vehicle ownership, activity location, activity participation, timing, duration, trip chaining, travel mode, and routes. Traditionally, these choices are modeled in a sequential manner with trips as the basic analysis units, while integrated models have also received significant research interest (Boyce 2002). New activity-based approaches have also emerged since major breakthrough in behavioral geography in the 1970s (Hagerstrand 1970) and have also been applied to aid transportation planning (Pas 1985, Kitamura 1988, Jones 1990, Axhausen and Gärling 1992). In transportation economics studies, the problem of road pricing has been traditionally set up for simplicity with route choice and origin-destination travel frequency choice being the only two demand dimensions. Recently, several studies also consider departure time choice, employing Vichrey's (1969) bottleneck model (Bernstein and Muller 1993, Braid 1996, Liu and McDonald 1999, de Palma and Lindsey 2000). Verhoef and Rouwendal (2004) developed an analytical model with vehicle ownership as one of the endogenous variables. The analysis in this chapter considers departure time, route, and trip frequency choices with a flat toll, optimal capacity choices, and alternative ownership regimes. Although the assumption of flat toll corresponds to the current practice, it underestimates the effectiveness of road pricing with dynamic tolls varying with traffic conditions (de Palma and Lindsey 2000). The following sections in this chapter will discuss limitations of the analytical models.

Departure Time Choice

Vickrey (1969) derives the departure time equilibrium with flat tolls and the duration of the departure period (i^0, i^e) is determined by the total number of users or total flow (f) and road capacity (F):

$$i^e - i^0 = f / F \tag{17.1}$$

Total travel cost (U) excluding toll (τ) for each user is comprised of three parts: free-flow travel cost ($\gamma \cdot T^*$), queuing delay (D^q), and schedule delay (D^s). A summary of notation is given in the appendix. Throughout this chapter, superscripts are indexes and subscripts denote first-order (partial) derivatives.

$$U = \gamma \cdot T^* + D^q + D^s \tag{17.2}$$

Let i^* and i denote the desired and actual arrival times respectively, where i^* is further assumed to be the same for all users. A piece-wise linear schedule delay cost function is then specified where α and β are coefficients.

$$D^s(i - i^*) = \alpha \cdot Max(0, i^* - i) + \beta \cdot Max(0, i - i^*) \tag{17.3}$$

At the departure time equilibrium, all drivers using the same route should experience the same total travel cost (U*) whenever they depart. It is convenient to consider the earliest driver and the latest drivers as their queuing delays are both zero.

$$U = \gamma \cdot T^* + D^s(i^0 + T^* - i^*) = \gamma \cdot T^* + D^s(i^e + T^* - i^*) \tag{17.4}$$

Solve Eq. system 17.1, 17.3 and 17.4 and the following expression of travel cost under departure time equilibrium is derived:

$$U = \gamma \cdot T^* + \frac{\alpha \cdot \beta}{\alpha + \beta} \cdot \frac{f}{F} \tag{17.5}$$

The second term of Eq. 17.5 is the sum of queuing cost and schedule delay cost under departure time equilibrium, which is proportional to total number of users and inversely proportional to road capacity. In contrast, the classic BPR function raises the ratio of f/F to the power of four (BPR 1964). It is possible to use empirically derived schedule delay functions, such as the one developed in Small (1982), to specify the coefficients in Eq. 17.5. There is also a more fundamental difference between Eq. 17.5 and the BPR function. The BPR flow-travel-time function is often regarded as a supply side equation in transportation economics, while Eq. 17.5 is derived from user departure time choices and a given road capacity.

Route Choice and Trip Frequency Choice

Three small networks are considered in this study so that the equilibrium network properties can be examined for parallel, serial, and parallel-serial networks (see Figure 17.1). Different analytical route choice models exist with various assumptions about route choice behavior and are summarized in Sheffi (1985). Wardrop's (1952) first equilibrium principle states that all used routes between each OD pair have the same travel cost which is lower than costs of all unused routes connecting the OD pair. This route assignment criterion assumes that users have perfect knowledge about the network and can always identify the best route however defined. Although it is behaviorally questionable, the Wardrop principle, or the deterministic user equilibrium condition, is still the most widely used route choice protocol for its simplicity. Let C denote the total travel cost including toll, and q^{12} the total number of users between origin-destination pair 1-2. For the parallel network (Figure 17.1a), the Wardrop route choice equilibrium conditions are:

$$U^A + \tau^A = U^B + \tau^B = C^{12} \tag{17.6-1}$$

$$f^A + f^B = q^{12} \tag{17.66-2}$$

By assuming a demand curve to describe trip frequency choices, we also have the following equilibrium demand expression, where *P(.)* is the inverse demand function:

$$P(q^{12}) = C^{12} \tag{17.6-3}$$

Similar route choice equilibrium conditions and equilibrium demand expressions can be derived for the serial network (Figure 17.1b):

$$q^{12} + q^{13} = f^A \tag{17.7-1}$$

$$q^{23} + q^{13} = f^B \tag{17.7-2}$$

$$P^{12}(q^{12}) = C^{12} = U^A + \tau^A \tag{17.7-3}$$

$$P^{23}(q^{23}) = C^{23} = U^B + \tau^B \tag{17.7-4}$$

$$P^{13}(q^{13}) = C^{12} + C^{23} \tag{17.7-5}$$

and for the parallel-serial network (Figure 17.1c):

$$q^{12} + q^{13} = f^A + f^B \tag{17.8-1}$$

$$q^{23} + q^{13} = f^C \tag{17.8-2}$$

$$P^{12}(q^{12}) = C^{12} = U^A + \tau^A = U^B + \tau^B \tag{17.8-3}$$

$$P^{23}(q^{23}) = C^{23} = U^C + \tau^C \tag{17.8-4}$$

$$P^{13}(q^{13}) = C^{12} + C^{23} \tag{17.8-5}$$

It is assumed that there is no OD substitutional effects, i.e. demand functions for different OD pairs are independent of each other.

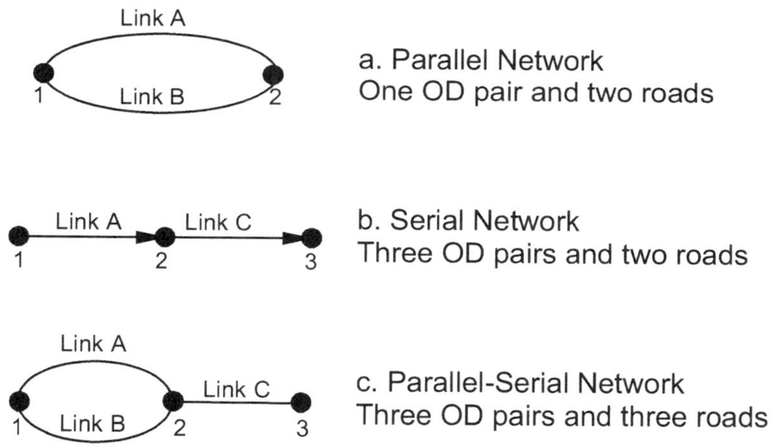

Fig. 17.1. Three stylized networks

17.3.2 Supply Side: Road Provision Cost

The cost of supplying road capacity usually involves land acquisition, construction, and maintenance cost (Keeler and Small 1977, Zhang and Levinson 2005). Several empirical studies have tested if constant returns to scale characterize the road supply cost function for its theoretical importance (Keeler and Small 1977, Krause 1981, Small *et al.* 1989, Levinson and Gillen 1998, Small 1999, Levinson and Yerra 2002, Levinson and Karamalaputi 2003). It is fair to conclude from these studies that the overall empirical evidence does not strongly disagree with the proposition that road supply cost exhibits approximately constant returns to scale. However, it should be kept in mind that a small deviation from constant returns to scale in either direction may have significant practical importance in terms of financial feasibility. The approach herein is that a cost function with constant returns to scale is taken as a base case and then sensitivity analysis with increasing and decreasing returns to scale is conducted. With constant returns to scale, the average amortized cost of providing a unit of capacity (*S*) is simply a constant:

$$S \equiv S^{*} \tag{17.9}$$

This simple average cost function does not differentiate between various components of road supply costs. It also implies that capacity expansion can be considered continuous.

17.3.3 Ownership and Policies: Models of Road Providers

Two types of road owners are considered, public and private. Each road owner sets prices and chooses capacity to build based on a pre-determined goal. It is assumed that private road authorities maximize profit, and public road authorities maximize social welfare without budget constraint or discounting. But it should be pointed out that how well these assumed objectives correspond the real objectives pursued by road owners in a real world fraught with principal-agent problems is still an open question.

The general welfare function for a network growth process over a period of time is:

$$W = \sum_{t} \left\{ \sum_{b} \left(\int_{0}^{q} P(q)dq \right) - \sum_{a} C(f^{a,t}, F^{a,t}) \cdot f^{a,t} + \sum_{a} \tau^{a,t} f^{a,t} - \sum_{a} S \cdot \Delta F^{a,t} \right\} \tag{17.10}$$

Where *t, b, q, a* are indices of years, OD pairs, users of an OD pair, and roads respectively, and delta indicates capacity changes. For the analytical models developed in this section, the time index is not meaningful and dropped because only the equilibrium network is considered and the equilibrating process is ignored in all equilibrium analyses. An evolutionary approach is necessary to take into account the growth process in addition to the final network. The first term is users' willingness to pay, and the second term is user cost including toll, and their difference is consumers' surplus. The third term is total revenue for the facility provider, and the last term is facility provision cost, and their difference is suppliers' surplus or profit. A private road company simply maximizes total profits that are produced from all roads it owns:

$$\pi = \sum_{a} \tau^{a} f^{a} - \sum_{a} S^{a} F^{a} \tag{17.11}$$

Since there are two roads for the parallel and the serial network, we have seven possible ownership regimes:

Free-Free: Welfare maximization with no-toll constraints on both routes and only capacity is optimized;

Public: Unconstrained welfare maximization in which capacity and toll are optimized simultaneously;

Private: Profit-maximization in which a monopoly apply profit-maximizing tolls and capacities on both routes;

Private-Private: A duopoly situation where each of the two companies builds, owns, and operates one road to maximize its profit;

Public-Free: Welfare maximization with no-toll constraint on one route – the public agency optimizes capacity on both roads and toll on only one road;

Private-Free: A monopoly builds and operates one of the two roads to maximize profit by setting appropriate toll and capacity while a public agency builds optimal capacity on the other non-toll road.

Public-Private: Same as the Private-Free case except that the public agency optimizes both capacity and toll on the public road.

The scenario with the parallel-serial network has somewhat more complicated possible ownership regimes. In fact, several ownership regimes on this network are special cases of the serial network when roads A and B are owned by the same agency and have the same travel cost function. We considerer two interesting ownership regimes on the parallel-serial network in order to explore market properties with private roads, which will be discussed in the next section.

If we define W_1 as the welfare of the *Free-Free* scenario, and W_2 the *Public* scenario. A measure of efficiency (e) for the each ownership regimes (R), with larger e indicating superior efficiency, can be calculated based on its welfare (W_R):

$$e_R = \left(W_R - W_1\right)/\left(W_2 - W_1\right) \tag{17.12}$$

17.3.4 A Numerical Example

Although the expression of the optimal prices can be derived in closed form as functions of road capacity, a closed-form expression of the optimal road capacity is not always available as shown in the next section. Therefore, a numerical model is constructed for the three stylized networks so that more useful insight can be obtained from the analysis. However, we do not intend to replicate any real-world decision scenarios with this example.

Inverse demand function for the parallel network

$$P = 20 - f/1000$$

Inverse demand function for the serial network

$$P^{12} = 20 - f/1000$$

$$P^{23} = 20 - f/1000$$

$$P^{13} = 40 - f/1000$$

Average construction cost function (same for all links)

$$S = 5 \qquad \text{(constant return to scale)}$$

$$S = 5F^{0.1} \qquad \text{(increasing return to scale)}$$

$$S = 5F^{-0.1} \qquad \text{(decreasing return to scale)}$$

Travel cost function excluding toll (same for all links):

$$U = 5 + 4\frac{f}{F}$$

Homogenous user group

Free-flow travel time is valued at $10 per hour for all users. Assuming away user heterogeneity and the possibility of product differentiation could cause underestimation of the benefit of road pricing, as shown by several previous studies (Arnott *et al.* 1992, Schmanske 1993, Small and Yan 2001).

The task of finding an equilibrium toll and capacity is a nonlinear programming problem for ownership regimes with only one authority managing all roads (cases Free-Free, Private, Public, and Public-Free for all networks), or for regimes with two road authorities on a symmetric network (case Private-Private on the parallel or the serial network) and a game theoretical problem for regimes with two road authorities having different objectives (e.g. cases Public-Private, Private-Free on all networks, and case Private-Private on the Parallel-Serial network). Various studies have developed algorithms to solve one or more of those cases, or to solve equilibrium toll only with fixed capacity (de Palma 1992, de Palma and Lindsey 2000, Verhoef 2002, among many others). The solution algorithm adopted for this study is as follows. For the nonlinear programming problem with the objective function defined by either Eq. 17.10 or 17.11, and with toll and capacity as decision variables, we take advantage of the equality constraints defined by Eq. 17.5 to 17.9 depending on the network in question, and solve for the Lagrangian stationary point. Non-negativity constraints are then checked at those stationary points. For the game-theoretical problem, we derive the pure strategy Nash equilibrium necessary conditions (i.e. first-order necessary conditions) based on the objective functions of players (Eq. 17.10 or 17.11 or both), and form a system of linear and non-linear equations by combining the first order conditions with user equilibrium conditions (Eqs. 17.5 to 17.9). The solution to this equations system is also a stationary point for the problem. If there are multiple stationary points (this only occurs for the parallel-serial network), a brute-force method is applied evaluating objective functions at all stationary points and identifying the true solution. The exhaustive search is acceptable with at most six decision variables on the three small networks being examined in this study. Applications to larger networks should pursue more efficient search algorithms. Provided in de Palma and Lindsey (2000) is the detailed solution procedures for a simpler case with only toll as the decision variable on a parallel network. Interested readers can refer to their paper for some mathematical details. When capacity choices are also considered, the equation systems will also include first order derivatives with respect to capacity, which are nonlinear in nature. Extending de Palma and Lindsey's (2000) solution method to include capacity choices on the three small networks requires solving a non-linear system of as many as twenty-four equations.

17.4 Equilibrium Toll and Capacity under Various Ownership Regimes

Although in most cases equilibrium tolls can be expressed as simple functions of equilibrium capacity, the closed-form solutions for tolls and capacity are either too complicated for one to draw meaningful policy insights or not available at all. Therefore, we will only analyze the expressions of equilibrium tolls as functions of capacity (called *toll equations* for the remainder of this chapter), and refer to the numerical solutions for equilibrium capacity to discuss policy implications.

17.4.1 Parallel Network

The toll equations for the parallel network have been previously derived in several previous studies (Verhoef et al. 1996, de Palma and Lindsey 2000) for most aforementioned ownership regimes, and some of them are presented in our notation for discussion below and for comparison with the equilibrium tolls on the serial network. Table 17.1 summarizes toll equations for both networks.

A private monopoly controlling both alternatives between the origin-destination pair always levies tolls higher than the marginal cost ($f \cdot U_f$). In the duopoly (Private-Private) case, the toll is always lower than that in the monopoly case for both roads. The duopoly toll on a road is higher if the demand elasticity is lower (i.e. larger c^1), and if the alternative road is more prone to congestion (i.e. larger U_f). The properties of the duopoly toll also hold for the Private-Free and Public-Private case. A public agency will set the toll on one road higher (lower) than the marginal cost if the toll on the alternative road is higher (lower) than the marginal cost (Public-Free, and Public-Private). In other words, in a second best situation with an untolled alternative (Public-Free), the optimal toll on the toll road should be somewhat lower than the true marginal cost. Also, the optimal toll should be even lower in order to avoid over-usage on the untolled alternative if the untolled alternative is more susceptible to congestion (i.e. larger U_f).

The solutions of optimal toll, optimal capacity, volume-capacity ratio, profit, and welfare are summarized in Table 17.2a for the parallel network. It should be noted that the volume-capacity ratio here is an indicator of the extent of bottleneck queuing congestion. This ratio should always be larger than one because a bottleneck model is used. Otherwise, the bottleneck is underutilized. The base case (Free-Free with capacity optimization only) assumes that the construction expenditure comes from other revenue resources and is not paid by the road users. This is why changes in consumers' surplus in all other scenarios are negative. In the numerical example, users must at least contribute 68% of total construction cost in the base case scenario so that they would support welfare-maximization pricing and investment policies. They would always oppose any form of privatization unless a sufficient portion of the toll profit is appropriately redistributed. Thanks to the assumption of constant returns to scale in the road supply cost function, the public agency can operate at a balanced budget when the levels of toll and capacity are both at the optimum. This will not be the case when there are increasing or decreasing returns to scale, as we shall see in the sensitivity analysis later in this chapter.

Since the public agency and the private sector have different objectives, they also adopted quite different levels of tolls and capacity. In all cases, the private sector significantly under-built capacity while charging much higher tolls than optimal, even though the extent of queuing is the same for the social optimal Public case and the private Monopoly case. This result, based on the numerical example, demonstrates that, although severe congestion on untolled roads may be an indicator of inefficiency (Free-Free, and Private-Free), the level of congestion is in general not a very good measure of system performance. One can find other examples by comparing the volume-capacity ratio between some other cases. Of the last five columns in Table 17.2, the Public-Private ownership regime is the most efficient, followed by private Duopoly, private Monopoly, and Public-Free. The Private-Free case is even worse than the base case (Free-Free). One conclusion from these results is that if road pricing is pursued on several alternative roads, it is better for efficiency purposes to levy tolls on all alternatives no matter what ownership structure is present. However, untolled alternatives maybe justified for equity purposes. If one compares capacity and VC ratios between scenarios Public and Public-Free, it is evident that a much larger number of users are priced off the roads when both roads are toll roads. Future studies should consider multiple user classes and possible product differentiation, and more seriously examine the equity issue, with toll and capacity choices under various ownership regimes. Finally, according to the computed rate of investment return (profit/construction cost), the private sector would most likely seek monopoly or duopoly status. The rate of return is abnormally high in this numerical example, but future studies applying similar analysis on real-world scenarios should be of interests to many parties.

17.4.2 Serial Network

While small parallel networks have been extensively studies by transportation economists for issues related to road pricing and ownership regimes, the serial network has received significantly less research interest. One reason is probably attributed to the fact that the parallel network is somewhat more relevant to the road pricing policy debates. However, any real-world network consists of both parallel roads and upstream/downstream roads.

Table 17.1 Toll Equations

Ownership	Parallel Network	Serial Network
Private $\tau_A = f^A U^A_{f_A} + ..$	$c^1\left(f^A + f^B\right)$	$\dfrac{(c^2 + c^3) f^A - c^3 f^B}{c^4}$
Private-Private $\tau_A = f^A U^A_{f_A} + ..$	$\dfrac{U^B_{f^B} c^1}{U^B_{f^B} + c^1} f^A$	$\dfrac{(c^2 + c^3) f^A U^B_{f^B} + c^6 f^A}{(c^3 + c^4) + c^5 U^B_{f^B}}$
Public-Free $\tau_A = f^A U^A_{f_A} + ..$	$-\dfrac{c^1}{U^B_{f^B} + c^1}\left(f^B U^B_{f^B}\right)$	$\left[\dfrac{c^3}{(c^3 + c^4) + c^5 U^B_{f^B}}\right]\left(f^B U^B_{f^B}\right)$
$\tau_B = 0$		
Private-Free $\tau_A = f^A U^A_{f_A} + ..$	$\dfrac{U^B_{f^B} c^1}{U^B_{f^B} + c^1} f^A$	$\dfrac{(c^2 + c^3) f^A U^B_{f^B} + c^6 f^A}{(c^3 + c^4) + c^5 U^B_{f^B}}$
$\tau_B = 0$		
Public-Private A-B $\tau_A = f^A U^A_{f_A} + ..$	$\dfrac{c^1}{U^B_{f^B} + c^1}\left(\tau^B - f^B U^B_{f^L}\right.$	$\left[\dfrac{c^3}{(c^3 + c^4) + c^5 U^B_{f^B}}\right]\left(f^B U^B_{f^B} - \tau\right.$
$\tau_B = f^B U^B_{f^B} + ..$	$\dfrac{U^B_{f^B} c^1}{U^B_{f^B} + c^1} f^B$	$\dfrac{(c^3 + c^4) f^B U^A_{f^A} + c^6 f^B}{(c^2 + c^3) + c^5 U^A_{f^A}}$

Note:
(1) Tolls for the Free-Free case are always zero, and for the Public case, always equal to the marginal cost $f \cdot U_f$.
(2) c^1, …, c^6 are constants defined below:

$$c^1 \equiv \left|P_f\right|; \quad c^2 \equiv \left|P^{12}_q P^{13}_q\right|; \quad c^3 \equiv \left|P^{12}_q P^{23}_q\right|; \quad c^4 \equiv \left|P^{13}_q P^{23}_q\right|;$$

$$c^5 \equiv \left|\sum_b P^b_q\right|; c^6 \equiv \left|\prod_b P^b_q\right|$$

The toll Eq.s for the small serial network are slightly more complex than those for the parallel network (see Table 17.1), but some useful insights can still be drawn. Let us first examine the private monopoly scenario (Private). In this case, if road A has much lower flow than road B ($f^A < c^3 \cdot f^B/(c^2+c^3)$), the profit-maximizing toll on road A would be lower than the marginal cost toll ($f^A \cdot U^A_f$), while the toll on road B would be higher than the marginal cost toll (the toll Eq. for road B can be obtained by exchanging superscripts of toll Eq. for road A due to network symmetry). The monopoly can gain more profits on the high-flow overcharged road than the lost profits on the low-volume undercharged road. This result implies that a private road monopoly may attract more users to the high-volume trunk roads by charging low tolls on local connector roads. Similarly, in the airline industry, a carrier maybe willing to provide cheap service on the secondary routes as long as they can charge high markups on the routes connecting hubs with much more passenger flow. However, if the amount of traffic on both upstream and downstream links is comparable, the profit-maximizing tolls on both roads will be higher than the marginal cost tolls. In the duopoly case (Private-Private), the toll is always higher than the welfare-maximizing toll. Furthermore, the duopoly toll is higher on one road if the upstream or downstream road is more congestible (i.e. larger U_f). It is interesting to compare second-best tolls in the parallel and serial networks (first row of the Public-Private case, or the Public-Free case). Whether the second-best toll is higher or lower than the first-best toll on one road depends on the relationship between the actual and first-best tolls on the other road in both networks, but in quite different ways. In the parallel network, the second-best toll and the actual toll on the other road should both be either higher or lower than the first-best toll. Whereas on the serial network, the second-best toll is higher (lower) than the first-best toll if the actual toll on the other road is lower (higher) than the first-best toll. One can easily see why it is a complex problem to determine the relationship between the second-best and the first-best tolls on a more complicated network. Verhoef (2002) offers a heuristic algorithm for finding second-best toll levels and toll points on a general network.

Table 17.2b provides numerical equilibrium solutions for the serial network. Again, the network under private ownership regimes would be significantly underbuilt compared to public ownership with or without optimal tolls. The toll levels are also consistently higher under private ownership regimes. Users would support marginal cost pricing only if they currently pay more than 76% of road construction cost. Even if all construction cost is currently borne by users, some redistribution would still be required to make them indifferent toward road privatization. To be exact, 66% of monopoly profit or 85% of duopoly profit needs to be redistributed.

Private roads compete with public roads by offering faster (small VC ratios) but more expensive services. Had the distribution of value of time among road users been considered, this phenomenon would be more apparent. One interesting finding is that the monopoly chooses a price ($7.50) lower than the two duopoly roads ($8.41), and is more efficient. This is reminiscent of the important result in vertical competition and integration due to Cournot (1738). In the serial network with vertically complimentary roads, a vertically-integrated monopoly actually faces a more elastic demand than two vertically-disintegrated duopolies. However, the incentive for the two firms to agglomerate almost does not exist according to the level of profits and rate of return. The most efficient ownership regime next to the social optimal benchmark is the Public-Free case, followed by Public-Private, Private Monopoly, Private-Free, and Private Duopoly. The private sector would prefer operating with a public complimentary road to operating with another private road upstream or downstream as the rates of return suggest, which is different from the parallel network.

Table 17.2. Equilibrium solutions for the numerical example

17.2a: Parallel network

Ownership Route A-Route B	Free-Free	Public	Private	Private-Private	Public-Free	Free-Private	Public-Private
Toll A ($/veh)	0	4.47	7.50	6.98	2.43	0	5.40
Toll B ($/veh)	0	4.47	7.50	6.98	0	5.475	5.62
Capacity A (veh/hr)	2624	2708	1354	1316	3194	1480	2320
Capacity B (veh/hr)	2624	2708	1354	1316	2406	1228	2175
VC Ratio A (no unit)	1.62	1.12	1.12	1.21	1.16	2.49	1.14
VC Ratio B (no unit)	1.62	1.12	1.12	1.21	1.77	1.12	1.09
Profit A ($)	-13120	0	4584	4528	-6983	-7399	2733
Profit B	-13120	0	4584	4528	-12030	1377	2437
Total Profit	-26240	0	9168	9056	-19013	-6022	5170
Rate of return A	–	–	68%	69%	–	–	–
Rate of return B	–	–	68%	69%	–	22%	22%
ΔCS	0	-17889	-31647	-31165	-4706	-23462	-23609
ΔWelfare ($)	0	8351	3761	4131	2521	-3244	7801
Total Welfare ($)	9989	18340	13750	14120	12510	6745	17790
Efficiency	0	1	0.45	0.49	0.30	-0.39	0.93

17.2b: Serial network

Ownership Route A-Route B	Free-Free	Public	Private	Private-Private	Public-Free	Free-Private	Public-Private
Toll A ($/veh)	0	4.47	7.50	8.41	6.42	0	2.67
Toll B ($/veh)	0	4.47	7.50	8.41	0	11.42	10.34
Capacity A (veh/hr)	19740	16250	8125	7405	16170	16220	14490
Capacity B (veh/hr)	19740	16250	8125	7405	18520	9349	8450
VC Ratio A (no unit)	1.42	1.12	1.12	1.02	1.12	1.22	1.12
VC Ratio B (no unit)	1.42	1.12	1.12	1.02	1.29	1.00	1.04
Profit A ($)	-98700	0	27505	26420	35130	-81100	-29180
Profit B	-98700	0	27505	26420	-92580	59550	48990
Total Profit	-197400	0	55010	52840	-57450	-21550	19810
Rate of return A	–	–	68%	71%	–	–	–

Rate of return B	–	–	68%	71%	–	127%	116%
ΔCS	0	-151090	-233590	-242110	-106550	-162740	-195320
ΔWelfare ($)	0	46310	18820	8130	33400	13110	21890
Total Welfare ($)	63690	110000	82510	71820	97090	76800	85580
Efficiency	0	1	0.41	0.18	0.72	0.28	0.47

It would be premature to make any recommendations on road commercialization and privatization based on the above results derived from a simple numerical example. But some insights are worth mentioning. First, the task of quantitatively evaluating the consequences of various forms of road privatization is an important yet difficult problem. Studies using different network layouts could draw different conclusions. The results in Table 17.2 exemplify this issue. A case-by-case examination maybe necessary. Since the analytical model does not scale very well in large networks, alternative modeling methods need to be pursued. Another issue has to do with deployment. Even though it is apparent that a new private toll road is socially desirable and profitable, the most socially desirable ownership arrangement could be different from the most profitable arrangement. Some sorts of constraints in terms of regulation policies or contracts need to be carefully forged.

17.4.3 Returns to Scale

The results presented above are all based on the assumption of constant returns to scale (CRS) in the road supply cost function. Cost functions with increasing (IRS) and decreasing returns to scale (DRS) are also specified and used to recalculate equilibrium tolls and capacity for the socially optimal case (Public) on both parallel and serial networks. Economic theory suggests that an IRS cost function causes a budget deficit and a DRS cost function leads to excessive revenue, as confirmed in Table 17.3. The main point of this sensitivity analysis is to demonstrate that a small deviation from CRS could cause significant budget-related problems, deficit or surplus, and large variations of the equilibrium network properties. It is anticipated that conclusive empirical evidence supporting any one of the three return-to-scale scenarios will not be available in the near future. Therefore, sensitivity analysis of this type should always be pursued in similar economic studies on road financing and ownership.

Table 17.3. Sensitivity analysis: Returns to scale of the construction cost function

	Parallel Network			Serial Network		
Ownership: Public	CRS	IRS	DRS	CRS	IRS	DRS
Ave. cons. cost fn. →	S=5	$S=5F^{-0.1}$	$S=5F^{0.1}$	S=5	$S=5F^{-0.1}$	$S=5F^{0.1}$
Toll ($/veh)	4.47	2.73	6.48	4.47	2.47	6.88
Capacity (veh/hr)	2708	7010	633	16250	48790	2149
VC Ratio (no unit)	1.12	0.68	1.62	1.12	0.62	1.72
Profit ($)	0	-50560	1206	0	-16580	4628
Welfare ($)	18340	42710	3305	110000	286700	9186

17.4.4 Parallel-Serial Network

For the three-road parallel-serial network, we only consider two scenarios, Private-Private, and Private-Private without capacity reduction (called Competition 1, and Competition 2 in the last two columns of Table 17.4). In scenario competition 1, company 1 operates road A and C, and company 2 wants to build a new alternative road B connecting OD pair 1-2. Scenario Competition 2 is similar to Competition 1 except that company 1 cannot reduce the capacity of roads A and C when company 2 decides to enter the market. The purpose of this analysis is to examine whether a new private company would have incentives to enter a market economy of roads where a monopoly dominates. In other words, we want to know what the degree of spatial monopoly is in a privatized road market.

Table 17.4. Numerical results: Parallel-serial network

Ownership	Welfare Max NoToll	Welfare Max.	Private Monopoly	Competition Scenario 1	Competition Scenario 2
Toll A ($/veh/link)	0	4.47	7.50	5.70	5.79
Toll B ($/veh/link)	0	4.47	7.50	5.70	5.47
Toll C ($/veh/link)	0	4.47	7.50	8.40	8.36
Capacity A (veh/hr)	9870	8125	8125	6753	(Fix.)8125
Capacity B (veh/hr)	9870	8125	0	3784	3372
Capacity C (veh/hr)	19740	16250	8125	8125	(Fix.)8125
Flow on A (veh/hr)	13995	9085	8125	7550	8441
Flow on B (veh/hr)	13995	9085	0	4231	3770
Flow on C (veh/hr)	27990	18170	9084	9084	9243
Total Revenue ($)	0	162500	136260	143472	146767
Comp. 1: A & C			136260	119347	126145
Comp. 2: B			0	24125	20622
Const. Cost ($)	197400	162500	81250	93310	98110
Comp. 1: A & C			82150	74390	81250
Comp. 2: B			0	18920	16860
Total Profit ($)	-197400	0	55010	50162	48587
Comp. 1: A & C			55010	44957	44830
Comp. 2: B			0	5205	3757
Rate of return 1	–	–	67%	60%	55%
Rate of return 2	–	–	–	28%	22%
ΔCS	0	-151090	-233590	-223002	-219907
ΔWelfare ($)	0	46310	18820	24560	26080
Total Welfare ($)	63690	110000	82510	88250	89770
Efficiency	0	1	0.41	0.53	0.56

Results suggest that new competition caused by the entry of company B significantly improves social welfare. After road B is built, the previous monopolist loses about 19% of profits and confronts a lowered rate of investment return. There is clearly a profit incentive for company 2 to enter the market with a rate of return higher than 20%. However, company 1 still has larger market share between OD pair 1-2 than company 2. These findings suggest that a privatized road market maybe able to attract enough companies to sustain a socially desirable level of competition. However, further confirmation on real-world networks is necessary for policy recommendations.

Finally, in the numerical example, company 1 has no incentive to apply discriminative intersection control at node 2 that prevents traffic on link B from using link C to reach node 3. Such discrimination would only cause redistribution of local and through traffic on links A and B, but not affect the profit of company 1. This conclusion holds as long as the amount of the through traffic (demand from node 1 to 3) is less than the current equilibrium flow on link A. Of course, this would not be an issue at all if a regulator prohibits any types of discriminating traffic control plans.

17.5 Conclusions

The dynamics of transportation network growth previously have not attracted significant research attention and have not yet been very well understood by planners and economists. This lack of understanding is revealed time and again in the long-range planning efforts of metropolitan planning organizations (MPOs), where transportation network change is treated exclusively as the result of top-down decision-making. Changes to the transportation network are rather the result of numerous small decisions (and some large ones) by property owners, firms, developers, towns, cities, counties, state department of transportation districts, MPOs, and states in response to market conditions and policy initiatives. In the 1960s, several studies examined possible forces shaping transportation networks (Boyce 1963, Garrison and Marble 1965). Only recently has their been a revived small but growing interest in studying the growth of transportation networks (Levinson and Yerra 2002, Levinson and Karamalaputi 2003, Yamins *et al.* 2003, Zhang and Levinson 2003, Verhoef and Rouwendal 2004). An important intellectual merit of studies of the network growth problem is that they could improve and extend the understanding of how transportation networks grow and decline, and help theorize the intertwined process of the growth in travel demand and the growth of the transportation network. In practice, this improved understanding could illustrate how decisions made in one point of time affect future choice, and help guide planners and decision-makers desiring to shape the future.

Traditionally, transportation economists have approached network financing problems by first constructing tractable and transparent analytical models on small networks like the one described in section 17.3 of this chapter and then with some insights gained from the analytical models developing models and algorithms applicable to large-scale realistic networks. Such a method is also suitable for studies of transportation network growth, as the analytical model has several inherent limitations. Models involving analytical equilibrium analysis evaluate the desirability of alternative policies based on the performance of the final equilibrium network only, ignoring the equilibrating process. It is now well known that in complex systems, historical dependency or path dependency is a major property. A small change of the system state at a time may profoundly impact the future network growth path. Another drawback of the analytical model described in section 17.3 lies in its inapplicability to large networks. Even for network economics problems with a static network for which pure mathematical programming models could be formulated for real-world scenarios, there is often the lack of efficient and reliable solution algorithms. As a result, various simplifying assumptions are required to make the problem tractable, while necessary validation of the assumptions is not seriously pursued. This problem will also be evident if analytical models of network growth are formulated for large dynamic networks.

Two approaches seem to be appropriate for exploring regularities in transportation network growth processes, with the observation that network growth stems from the behaviors of and interactions between a large number of heterogeneous agents (users, various levels of government, private roads etc.) having different goals and limited information. The expansion and contraction of a network could be modeled as the outcome of an evolutionary game played by those agents. The complexity in a transportation network also suggests an agent-based simulation approach, which has been pursued in several exploratory studies (Zhang and Levinson 2003, Zhang and Levinson 2004b). Future research may apply these methods to study the network growth problem and its planning implications.

References

Arnott R, de Palma A, and Lindsey R (1992) Route choice with heterogeneous drivers and group-specific congestion cost. Regional Science and Urban Economics 22: 71-102.

Arnott R, de Palma A, Lindsey R (1993) A structural model of peak-period congestion: A traffic bottleneck with elastic demand. American Economic Review 83: 161-179.

Axhausen KW, Gärling T (1992) Activity based approaches to travel analysis: Conceptual frameworks, models and research problems. Transport Reviews 12(4): 323-341.

Bernstein D, Muller J (1993) Understanding the competing short-run objectives of peak period road pricing. Transportation Research Record 1395: 122-128.

Braid RM (1996) Peak-load pricing of a transport facility with an unpriced substitute. Journal of Urban Economics 40: 179-197.

Boyce DE (1963) The generation of synthetic transportation networks. Report submitted US Army Transportation Research Command, Contract DA 44-177-TC-685, Fort Eustis, VA.

Boyce DE (2002) Is the sequential travel forecasting paradigm counterproductive. ASCE Journal of Urban Planning and Development 128(4): 169-183.

Boyce DE, Farhi R, Weischedel R (1974) Optimal subset selection: Multiple regression, interdependence and optimal network algorithms. Springer-Verlag: New York, LLC.

Bureau of Public Roads (BPR) (1964) Traffic assignment manual. Urban Planning Division, U.S. Department of Commerce, Washington, D.C.

Button KJ, Verhoef ET (1998) Road pricing, traffic congestion and the environment: Issues of efficiency and social feasibility. Cheltenham: Edward Elgar.

Cournot A (1838) Researches into the Mathematical Principles of Wealth. Paris: Hachette.

de Palma A (1992) A game-theoretic approach to the analysis of simple congested networks. American Economic Review 82(2): 494-500.

de Palma A, Lindsey R (2000) Private toll roads: Competition under various ownership regimes. Annals of Regional Science 34: 13-35 (2000).

de Palma A, Lindsey R (2002) Private roads, competition and incentives to adopt time-based congestion tolling. Journal of Urban Economics 52: 217–241.

de Vany A Saving T (1980) Competition and highway pricing for stochastic traffic. Journal of Business 53: 45-60.

Dupuit J (1844) On the measurement of the utility of public works. Reprinted in Munby D. (ed), Transportation: Selected Readings 1968.

Economides N (1996) The economics of networks. International Journal of Industrial Organization 16 (4): 673-699.

Garrison WL, Marble DF (1965) A prolegomenon to the forecasting of transportation development. Office of Technical Services, United States Department of Commerce, United States Army Aviation Material Labs Technical Report.

Gomez-Ibanez J, Meyer J (1993) Going private: The international experience with transport privatization. Brookings Institute: Washington, DC, 1993.

Gomez-Ibanez J (1999) Pricing. In: Gomez-Ibanez J, Tye WB, Winston C (Eds) Essays in Transportation Economics and Policy: A Handbook in Honor of John R Meyer. Brookings Institution Press: Washington DC.

Gwilliam KM (1997) Sustainable transport and economic development. Journal of Transport Economics and Policy 31: 325-330.

Hagerstrand T (1970) What about people in regional science? Papers and Proceedings of the Regional Science Association 24: 7-21.

Johansson B, Karlsson C, Westin L (1993) Patterns of a Network Economy. Springer-Verlag: Berlin.

Jones P (1990) Developments in dynamic and activity-based approaches to travel analysis. Brookfield, Vt.: Avebury.

Kitamura R (1988) An evaluation of activity-based travel analysis. Transportation 15: 9-34.

Kahn A E (1988) The economics of regulation: Principles and institutions. MIT Press: Cambridge, MA.

Keeler TE, Small KA (1977) Optimal peak-load pricing, investment and service levels on urban expressways. Journal of Political Economy 85(1): 1-25.

Knight FH (1924) Some fallacies in the interpretation of social cost. Quarterly Journal of Economics 38: 582-606.

Kraus M (1981) Scale economies analysis for urban highway networks. Journal of Urban Economics 9: 1–22.

Langton C (1989) Artificial life. Addison-Wesley Publishing Company: Redwood City, CA, 1989.

LeBlanc LJ (1975) An algorithm for the discrete network design problem. Transportation Science 9: 183-199.

Levinson D (1999) Tolling at a frontier: A game theoretic analysis. Proceedings of the 14th International Symposium on Transportation and Traffic Theory: 173-187.

Levinson D (2000) Revenue choice on a serial network. Journal of Transport Economics and Policy 34(1): 69-98.

Levinson D, Gillen D (1998) The full cost of intercity highway transportation. Transportation Research 3D: 207-223.

Levinson D, Yerra B (2002) Highway costs and the efficient mix of state and local funds. Journal of the Transportation Research Board 1812: 27-36.

Levinson D, Karamalaputi R (2003) Induced supply: A model of highway network expansion at the microscopic level. Journal of Transport Economics and Policy 37(3): 297–318.

Liu LN, McDonald JF (1999) Economic efficiency of second-best congestion pricing schemes in urban highway systems. Transportation Research 33B: 157-188.

Meng Q, Yang H, Bell MGH (2001) An equivalent continuously differentiable model and a locally convergent algorithm for the continuous network design problem. Transportation Research Part 35B: 83-105.

Mohring H Harwitz M (1962) Highway Benefits: An Analytical Framework. Nothwestern University Press.

Nagurney A (1993) Network economics: A variational inequality approach. Kluwer Academic Publishers: Norwell, MA.

Pas EI (1985) State of the art and research opportunities in travel demand: another perspective. Transportation Research 21A: 431-438.

Pigou AC (1920) The Economics of Welfare. Macmillan.

Poorzahedy P, Turnquist MA (1982) Approximate algorithms for the discrete network design problem. Transportation Research B 16: 45-56.

Roth G (1996) Roads in a Market Economy. Avebury Technical: England.

Schmanske A (1993) A simulation of price discriminating tolls. Journal of Transport Economics and Policy 27: 225-235.

Small KA (1982) The scheduling of consumer activities: Work trips. American Economic Review 72: 467-479.

Small KA (1992) Using the revenues from congestion pricing. Transportation 19, 359-381.

Small KA (1999) Economies of scale and self-financing rules with non-competitive factor markets. Journal of Public Economics 74: 431–450.

Small KA (1989) Winston, C. M. and Evans, C. A.: Road work. Washington, DC: Brookings Institution.

Small KA, Yan J (2001) The value of "value pricing" of roads: Second-best pricing and product differentiation. Journal of Urban Economics 49: 310-336.

Sheffi Y (1985) Urban transportation networks: Equilibrium analysis with mathematical programming methods. Prentice Hall: Englewood Cliffs, NJ.

Sussman, J (2000) Introduction to transportation systems. Boston, MA: Artech House.

Train KE (1991) Optimal regulation: The economic theory of monopoly. MIT Press: Cambridge, MA.

Verhoef ET (2002) Second-best congestion pricing in general networks: Heuristic algorithms for finding second-best optimal toll levels and toll points. Transportation Research 36B: 707-729.

Verhoef ET, Nijkamp P, Rietveld P (1996) Second-best congestion pricing: The case of an untolled alternative. Journal of Urban Economics 40: 279-302.

Verhoef ET, Rouwendal J (2004) Pricing, capacity choice and financing in transportation networks. Journal of Regional Sceince 44(3): 405-435.
Vickery W (1963) Pricing in urban and suburban transport. American Economic Review 53, 452-465.
Vickrey W (1969) Congestion theory and transport investment. American Economic Review 59: 251-261.
Viton PA (1995) Private roads. Journal of Urban Economics 37: 260-289.
Von Neumann J (1966) Theory of self-reproducing automata. Edited by A.W. Burk. University of Illinois Press.
Von Neumann J Morgenstern O (1944) Theory of Games and Economic Behavior. Princetion University Press: Princetion, NJ.
Walters A (1968) The Economics of Road User Charges. Baltimore: Johns Hopkins Press.
Wardrop JG (1952) Some theoretical aspects of road traffic research. Proceedings of the Institute of Civil Engineers Part II 1: 325-378.
Wohl M, Hendrickson C (1984) Transportation Investment and Pricing Principles. John Wiley&Sons, Inc.
Yamins D, Rasmussen S, Fogel D (2003) Growing urban roads. Networks and Spatial Economics 3: 69-85.
Yang H, Bell MGH (1998) Models and algorithms for road network design: a review and some new developments. Transport Review 18: 257-278.
Zhang L, Levinson D (2003) A model of the rise and fall of roads. Presented at the 50th North America Regional Science Council Annual Meeting, Philadelphia, Nov 20-22.
Zhang L, Levinson D (2004a) An agent-based approach to travel demand forecasting: An exploratory analysis. Journal of the Transportation Research Board (in press).
Zhang L, Levinson D (2004b) Road pricing with autonomous links. Presented at the 51st North America Regional Science Council Annual Meeting, Seattle, Nov 10-13.
Zhang L, Levinson D (2005) Investing for reliability and robustness in transportation networks. Presented at the 84th Transportation Research Board Annual Meeting, Washington, DC, January 9-13.

Appendix: Notation

a	index of link
b	index of OD pairs
C	generalized travel cost on a link
E	revenue
f	number of users on a link
F	capacity
$K(.)$	expansion cost function (for dynamic analysis only)
$M(.)$	maintenance cost function (for dynamic analysis only)
$P(.)$	inverse OD demand function that is continuously differentiable and $p_x(x) > 0$
q	number of users between an OD pair
$S(.)$	average amortized cost of supplying a unit capacity (for static analysis only)
r	interest rate

t	index of pricing cycles
T	travel time: $T(f/F)$
T^*	free-flow travel time
U	average user operating cost $U = \gamma T = U(f/F)$
α	schedule early cost
β	schedule delay cost
γ	value of travel time savings
τ	toll
π	profit

18 Transport Network Development and the Location of Economic Activity

Adelheid Holl
Department of Town and Regional Planning
University of Sheffield (U.K.)

18.1 Introduction

The relationship between transport infrastructure and economic development has been studied in wide range of academic disciplines, including economics, geography, and planning. Given the funds involved, it is also an important policy question. Although there exists now a wide literature, there is still little consensus on the exact impacts of transport infrastructure investment. The debate remains contentious with some analysts claiming important impacts, while others argue that with decreasing transport costs and the increasing importance of non-material flows, transport infrastructure investment has little effect on national or regional economic growth.

A large body of recent empirical research has been based on macro level analysis (for reviews, see, for example, Gramlich 1994; Boarnet 1997; Mikelbank and Jackson 2000). Most of these studies report a positive relationship between the level of infrastructure investment and the level of economic growth, but the results vary to a great extent from study to study and are far from conclusive. Since macro-level analyses identify average effects of infrastructure investment and are often carried out at a limited level of disaggregation due to problems of data availability, the results are prone to mask important sectoral and spatial variations. In particular, conclusions from macro-level analysis can not be easily applied to particular transport infrastructure projects. Impacts from a particular project will depend on the type of infrastructure but also on the characteristics of firms in the impact regions, their price and output changes, and importantly on location changes of these firms. The role of transport investment in influencing the location of economic activity is, however, an important subject that has received much less attention in recent empirical research (Haughwout 1999). In contrast, the role of transport has a long tradition in classical location theory. More recent new economic geography models again emphasise the importance of transport costs along with imperfect competition, market size and economies of scale in explaining the location of industry (Krugman 1991).

This paper is organised as follows. The next section reviews the literature on transport and the location of economic activity and presents some stylised facts. Section 18.3 presents an empirical contribution regarding dynamic location effects of transport infrastructure investment based on data for the Spanish road building programme over the period from 1980 to 2000. Section 18.4 provides concluding remarks and some recommendations for further research.

18.2 Literature Review: Transport Infrastructure Investment and the Location of Economic Activity

Location theory gives transport a central role in the location choice of firms. The first approaches originated from the work of Von Thünen (1826) and Weber (1928). Von Thünen focused on agricultural location and the transport of agricultural produce to the central market. Differences in land rents and transport costs determine what is produced. Falling transport costs allow production of a particular produce further away from the market centre. Weber, on the other hand, developed a location model with transport costs determining the location of manufacturing. Weber suggested that the optimal location of firms depends on the relation of input and output transport costs compared to relative costs of productions. Firms search for the least-cost location that allows for the lowest delivered cost to the market centre. Depending on the transport costs involved in the delivery of the inputs and outputs respectively, the least-cost location is either near the raw material source or at the market centre. Opponents of the least-cost framework centred their interest on the demand side and the locational interdependencies between competitors. Buyers are distributed over a market area as opposed to the least-cost approach where all buyers are concentrated at the market centre. In contrast, factor costs are assumed equal at all locations. Firms seek locations where they can serve the largest markets, taking into account the choice of location of their competitors, and where transport costs are minimised. The fact that the location decision is separate from decisions on technology or output levels exaggerates the importance of transport costs in this type of models. Reductions in transport costs will always reduce a firm's input prices and/or increase its market area (Vickerman 1996). A significant contribution in this regard is the seminal paper of Moses (1958) who linked location theory with production theory. Here transport is treated as an input cost factor. Location depends on the relative source prices of the inputs. A change in input prices leads to a change in the proportions of each input consumed which consequently changes the optimum location of the firm towards one input point. With regard to transport cost this means that larger variations than in the other input prices produce a centralising effect. Moreover, as McCann (1995) argues, once the relative proportions of the inputs are changed, the characteristics of the good produced will be different and the firm's potential suppliers and customers will have changed too, which makes the determination of location inherently complex.

Most of the recent literature in the field of firm location draws on agglomeration economies first identified by Marshall (1920) to explain industry agglomeration. Agglomeration economies are another form of interdependence among firms in their location decision. Agglomeration economies stem from a large number of economic activities located close to each other. Such clustering facilitates a pooled labour market with specialised skills, a greater variety of non-traded inputs at lower cost and information spillovers between firms. There is a transportation element to benefits of clustering, since by being close, economic agents save on transport costs involved in the exchange of goods and information, as well as travel to work for labour which can affect wage levels and the size of the labour market catchment area.

Important theoretical contributions have recently been developed within the field of new economic geography (Krugman 1991; Fujita et al 1999). Such models point to a complex mechanism by which transport infrastructure affects the spatial distribution of firms. Puga (2002) provides a recent review of the main mechanisms at work. The approaches concentrate on the role of market-size effects and linkage effects among firms (centripetal forces) that foster geographical concentration and the opposing force of factor cost differences and competition (centrifugal forces) working against such concentration. Reductions in transport costs change the balance between these forces and can therefore have opposing effects on firm location in different regions. The models predict a reorganisation of industrial location that follows an inverted U-shaped relationship between transport costs and agglomeration. If transport costs are high, firms have to supply markets locally. Hence, firm location will be dispersed. With reductions in transport costs firms can serve markets from a greater distance. This allows firms to spatially concentrate and take advantage of agglomeration economies. However, as transport costs continue to fall, proximity becomes less important, and peripheral regions with their lower prices for local factors and lower competition may gain in attractiveness for firm location.

18.2.1 Empirical Evidence

Among empirical location studies, several have adopted a survey approach (McQuaid et al 1996; Bruinsma et al 1997; Bryan et al 1997; Leitham et al 2000). Such studies generally involve a series of questions relating to firm characteristics and various location factors including issues of transport. Among the various types of transport infrastructure, roads are frequently reported as the most important type. Although firms perceive the availability of good transport infrastructure as very important, it is also seldom the decisive factor in a location decision. The findings of such survey research show that new transport infrastructure seems to relax location constraints, allowing firms to examine a wider range of locations. Nevertheless, most location decisions and relocations are made over very short distances, and firms are often found to relocate within the same region (Bruinsma et al 1997). The range of potential benefits to firms due to transport improvements, has been highlighted by Bryan et al. (1997) in their survey of local firms following the construction of the A55 motorway in North Wales. Their findings suggest important logistical impacts. Most firms are reported to have benefited in terms of reduced input ordering times, improved output delivery and customer service.

Whilst the findings reported above are useful, the main drawback of the survey approach is that the results are restricted to the particular research context and cannot easily be generalised, nor do they provide explanations of why a particular behaviour of a firm has been observed, i.e. a particular ranking of location factors. Still, the emphasis on entrepreneurs' perceptions can constitute a valuable complement to more formalised approaches especially for studies on specific infrastructure improvements (Rietveld 1989).

The availability of different types of transport infrastructure features in most survey studies on firm location, but firm location studies based on econometric models have paid less attention to transport infrastructure. A wide range of factors influencing the location decision of firms (Keeble and Walker 1994) is considered, involving variables on the demand side, the supply side and policy variables (Holmes 1998), such as for example, differences in taxes (Papke 1991; Devereux and Griffith 1998) or environmental regulations (Levinson 1996; McConnell and Schwab 1990), but transport infrastructure improvements have been largely overlooked in this literature.

Exceptions are Guimarães et al (1998) in an analysis of industrial location in Puerto Rico. They include a measure of distance to a major highway and the main economic centre as a proxy for transport costs and accessibility in a nested logit model. Guimarães et al (2000) use a multinomial logit model in studying foreign direct investment location in Portugal. Here road travel time to the main urban centres is included as an explanatory variable. In both studies a significant effect of road infrastructure is found on plant location. Holl (2004a) studies the impact of road infrastructure investment on the location of new manufacturing establishments in Spanish municipalities from 1980 to 1994 using Poisson regression. These results show that new motorways affect the spatial distribution of manufacturing establishments by increasing the attractiveness of municipalities close to the new infrastructure. Holl (2004b) reports similar results for manufacturing plant location in Portugal. Fotopoulos and Spence (1999) proxy the availability of infrastructure by the amount of public investment per capita as an explanatory variable in a regression model accounting for new plant openings in Greece. They find a significant and positive effect of public infrastructure on new plant openings. These findings are supported by Holtz-Eakin and Lovely (1996) who test the impact of public infrastructure in a general equilibrium context and find that impacts of public infrastructure primarily work through increases in the number of manufacturing establishments.

Locational studies highlight that impacts of projects depend not only on the nature of the projects themselves but also on the economic environment characterised by a wide range of factors, as well as the characteristics of the firms.

Sectors: Firms vary in their input-, output-, and consequently transport requirements and are therefore likely to be influenced differently in their location decision. Among econometric location studies, few have analysed industry-specific effects of different location factors. Notable exceptions are Papke (1991), Becker and Henderson (2000), but they do not take into account the specific role of transport. Holl (2004) analyses the role of road investment as a location factor among manufacturing sectors in Spain, and Holl (2004b) for manufacturing and service sectors in Portugal. There are sectoral differences in both countries and some similarities and differences between the two countries can be mentioned. In both countries, in the 'metal products, machinery and equipment' sector, the 'food and beverage', 'textile and clothing', the 'paper and printing sectors', and the 'plastics and other manufacturing' sector firms have clearly preferred locations closer to new motorways at the cost of more distant municipalities. For the 'transport equipment' sector locations outside transport corridors, i.e. beyond 50 kilometres to a nearest motorway appear particularly unattractive in Spain. In the case of the 'chemical products' sector, no clear conclusions with regard to the importance of closeness to the new infrastructure are observed for Spain, but in Portugal the sector shows a clear preference for closeness to the new motorway network. The opposite is the case for the 'wood and furniture sector', which only shows a significant preference in the case of Spain. Results reported in Holl (2004b) also support the idea that industries characterised by high transport costs are more likely to locate close to local demand. Overall, this is the case in the service sector.

Diamond and Spence (1989), in a survey study on infrastructure and industrial cost in the UK, found that expenditure on transport-related activities is about 5.7% of the total operating costs of industry. The cost share found for the distribution industry and for business services is, however, considerably higher with 12% and 9% respectively. Effects of road infrastructure improvements are likely to be concentrated in sectors where transport costs are relatively high or where the quality of delivery service plays an important role. Fernald (1999), for example, argues that road infrastructure investment is associated with larger productivity growth in industries that use roads more intensively. His selection of road-intensive industries is based on data on the average stock of cars and trucks in industries.

While interesting, such results have to be also viewed with caution since, in general, there is a lack of comprehensive measures of industries' transportation costs. A complete picture would have to include 'own account' as well as 'for-hire' transport for business travel and freight. What is often neglected is the increasing importance of bought-in trucking services in many industries. Furthermore, cost and stock measures do not take into account transport attributes like speed, regularity and reliability. This overlooks benefits derived from transport improvements in the form of improved delivery times and greater predictability. Such effects can be crucial for the reorganisation of a firm's activities and for logistical restructuring (McKinnon 1998). Shirley and Winston (2004), for example, show for the U.S. that firms have reduced their inventories in response to highway investment.

There is a need for more sector-specific studies, but in particular, the service sector deserves much more consideration than it has received so far. A substantial proportion of new firms are created in service sectors. In fact, services have replaced manufacturing as the predominant source of economic growth in most developed countries. The service sector is also to a greater degree reliant on direct face-to-face contacts, which makes the transport cost for service delivery high (Kolko 1999).

Location versus relocation: There are also differences in the location behaviour of completely new start-ups and firms that relocate to a new location. Holl (2004c) shows for manufacturing in Portugal that for both, road infrastructure is important, but relocations show an even stronger preference for being close to the new motorways built. This highlights that in addition to sectoral differences, the sensitivity of a firm depends on its particular transport requirements that are likely to be related to a firm's development. The fact that firms that relocate are on average larger in terms of the number of employees than new start-ups, suggests that firms are likely to relocate after an initial business growth. Following the argumentation of Taylor (1975), firms, as they grow, expand their 'knowledge space', 'action space', and 'decision space'. This means that at the time of a relocation, firms on the one hand may have transport requirements to cover larger market areas, given their growth and, on the other hand, may have better information on a larger area, which allows them to get closer to their optimal location.

Spillovers and redistribution effects: Aggregate studies are likely to capture a mix of two different relationships. Infrastructure investment is place-specific and consequently there might be output increases in some regions, whereas output decreases in other regions. Hence, aggregate results are difficult to interpret. Boarnet (1998) examines the locational impacts of street-and-highway capital in Californian counties from 1969 to 1988 and tests for spillover effects resulting from firm migration of mobile factors of production towards better endowed regions. Boarnet includes street-and-highway capital of other Californian counties which can be regarded as competitors for mobile factors into the production function along with labour inputs, private capital inputs and a county's own street-and highway capital. Depending on the definition of neighbouring regions, evidence for negative spillovers from transport infrastructure capital is found across similarly urbanised counties in terms of population density, per capita income and share of employment in finance, insurance and real estate. The results suggests that similarly urbanised counties are close competitors for mobile factors of production and that road infrastructure is associated with higher output within the same county and with lower output in competing counties. On the other hand, positive spillover effects are found across contiguous counties when the degree of connectivity provided by the highway network is taken into account. Chandra and Thompson (2000) in a study on earnings impacts of interstate highways in US non-metropolitan counties find that new interstate highways raise earnings in counties receiving a new interstate highway and reduce earnings in adjacent counties. Holl (2004a, 2004b) shows for Spain and Portugal that an important effect of the new transport infrastructure constructed over the period from 1980 to 1994 has been a densification of firms in the vicinity of the projects, with evidence that suggests negative spillovers at the intra-regional level. The new infrastructure has made locations in its vicinity more attractive for firm location, but reduced the attractiveness of more distant locations. At the urban level, Voith (1993) and Haughwout (1997) provide evidence that indicates that transport investments to and in central cities have positive effects on suburban house values.

While there is evidence of important redistribution effects of transport infrastructure investment at the local and regional level, at the state level Holtz-Eakin and Schwartz (1995) do not find any significant productivity effects on neighbouring states in the U.S. This suggests that important road infrastructure impacts operate within rather than across regions. A geographically detailed analysis of locational effects of transport infrastructure improvements that can take into account different impacts occurring at different distances from the new infrastructure is therefore important.

Relocations are shifts from one location to another and the general view adopted in transport project appraisal is that they don't yield additional benefits as economic activity just takes place at a different location. However, such transport induced relocations can bring economic benefits if they allow firms to operate more efficiently in the new locations or where they facilitate the emergence of agglomeration economies and thus raise the productivity of firms. Similarily, where shifts take place from congested to less congested areas they can potentially constitute positive impacts.

Concentration versus dispersion: The geographical concentration of economic activity is one of the most striking features of the economic landscape (e.g. Krugman 1991). A key question is whether transport infrastructure improvements can help dispersion of economic activity or will, as feared by some analysts, lead to greater concentration.

Where transport infrastructure improvements cause relocation of firms due to changes in accessibility, a central issue in this context is how it affects the patterns of employment change. Linneker and Spence (1992 and 1996) study the relationship between regional employment and accessibility changes due to the construction of the M25 London orbital motorway. The research follows an earlier UK study on the effects of the M62 (Dodgson 1974). The methodology used develops accessibility indices and relates them to employment levels and employment changes. Several potential accessibility measures are calculated for the 'with M25' and 'without M25' to estimate the impact of the M25 London orbital motorway on employment change. Their findings show that accessibility improvements can have varying impacts. In estimations using the level of accessibility, employment growth was found to be highest in areas with low accessibility. Areas of high accessibility have shown losses in employment, suggesting, as the authors argue, that the most accessible places also are the most costly places and therefore maybe not be the best places for business expansions. However, in addition to this negative relationship, changes in the level of accessibility have been positively related to employment growth. The M25 construction has allowed a decentralisation of employment, especially to those areas that have experienced high gains in accessibility. Very likely those are the areas along transport corridors. Linneker and Spence's (1996) results differ form the earlier UK studies of Dodgson (1974) and Botham (1980) that suggested that road building during the 1960's and 1970's has had a centralising effect by favouring employment in the most accessible areas. Haughwout (1999) studied employment growth in US counties and found that state infrastructure investment affected the distribution of employment within states leading to a more dispersed pattern of economic activity away from areas of dense employment. This is in line with the new economic geography literature, which predicts a weakening of agglomeration forces with decreases in transport costs beyond a certain threshold level.

The result in Holl (2004a) for Spain shows that different types of accessibility have different effects. Negative signs of inter-regional demand accessibility indicate that the new road infrastructure constructed has facilitated geographical dispersion by allowing firms to locate at greater distance from the main population and industrial centres. In contrast, improving a municipality's supplier accessibility as measured by proximity to the main centres of production in the same sector as the new plant, shows a generally positive effect on the probability of manufacturing plant location. This suggests a process of geographical specialisation.

To date there has been very little empirical work directly based on new economic geography models. A notable exception is Combes and Lafourcade (2004) who estimate the effect of transport cost reductions in France from 1978 to 1993 on changes in employment. Their findings indicate that transport cost reductions have decreased the concentration of employment at the national scale but have also widened intra-regional disparities.

Transport improvements that disperse growth may diminish agglomeration economies (Haughwout 1999). As Rosenthal and Strange (2003) show, agglomeration economies attenuate rapidly with distance. However, transport improvements that bring economic agents closer reduce the cost and increase the potential for interaction and can therefore enhance the benefits of agglomeration economies over larger geographical areas (Eberts and McMillen 1999). The empirical literature on agglomeration economies and transport infrastructure has largely developed separately. Integrating these two strands of literature could help to enhance our understanding of the spatial organisation of economic activity (Eberts and McMillen 1999). The interdependencies highlighted in new economic geography models make a spatial analysis necessary that takes into account where the infrastructure is located, its network character, and how the impacts change through space and time.

Dynamic effects: The new economic geography literature suggest that the relationship between transport investment and the effect on the location of economic activity is not constant over time. Thus, an important academic and policy question is how the relationship between transport investment and the spatial distribution of economic activity changes with better infrastructure endowment and reductions in transport costs.

A related question is whether transport infrastructure are becoming more or less important in the location of industry. The public capital literature argues that there are diminishing returns on the aggregate investment in transport infrastructure networks. Thus growth effects of transport infrastructure investment tend to become smaller as networks near completion (Fernald 1999) The existence of decreasing returns is also argued in Moreno et al. (1997) who study the link between infrastructure and regional growth in Spain over the period from 1964 to 1991 within the aggregate production function approach. If effects on productivity are becoming smaller, then the role of transport in firm location should also be decreasing in importance. Giuliano (1989) concluded for the U.S. that highway access is indeed becoming less important as the networks in most metropolitan areas become well developed. This is in line with some location studies that argue that where road networks are completed, transport is becoming less important as a location factor and industry is increasingly becoming 'footloose' (Forkenbrock and Foster 1996). The reasons for this declining importance are seen in the relative ubiquity of major highways. It is argued that most cities offer comparable access and consequently, firms' location decisions are influenced to greater degree by other factors than transport, notably labour quality and labour cost. This literature argues that where the network is already very dense, new investment would have little impact on firms' location choice among regions. In this context, the role of transport becomes more an issue of attracting firms to specific sites with good access to higher order transport infrastructure. There is, thus, an important issue of scale in the discussion of the importance of transport infrastructure which has to be taken into account in empirical research.

From a network perspective, an important criteria is the number of locations that are linked (Boarnet 1997). The network literature suggests that effects would be larger once a sufficient network size is achieved. For example, the first elements of a new motorway network would still make little difference and provide limited opportunities to firms located close to such infrastructure until individual motorway parts are linked up to a functioning network. Additional locations that get linked to such a network will increase the size and usefulness of the entire network (Boarnet 1997). However, once a network is completed, most investment is usually geared towards maintenance rather than extension of the network and this will bring smaller and more localised benefits, rather than effects throughout the entire network, unless important bottlenecks are overcome. Thus, from a network perspective one would expect increasing effects in the first place, but a levelling-off after completion of the primary network.

There are, however, also reasons to think that such a levelling-off might not happen. As transport networks become better developed, transport costs decline and this can facilitate changes in industrial organisation towards more transport intensive production and distribution processes such as for example, 'just-in-time', and outsourcing. Economic activities are also enabled to take place over wider geographical areas, as reflected in processes such as the increasing internationalisation of production. This is likely to make transport increasingly crucial for industrial strategies and, hence, in location decisions. Preston (2001, p.17) argues: "Paradoxically, transport may have become more important because its costs have become less important permitting new modes of production which are reliant on a high transport input …."

This is in contrast to arguments that the rise of telecommunication and information technology has lead to an important fall in communication and transportation costs for firms and hence lead to a diminishing role of distance and the location of economic activity in general (Cairncross 1997). If, however, communication and transport are complementary, rather than substitutes, as shown in Plaut (1997) for industrial uses, then technological improvements in telecommunications can cause additional travel as these too enable more intensive economic relations that take place over wider geographical areas.

18.3 Dynamic Effects – the Spanish Motorway Building Programme

The vast improvements in the Spanish road network that have been carried out over the last two decades have led to significant transport cost reductions and are an interesting development that offers a great opportunity to explore the role of major transport improvements on the spatial distribution of economic activity. The motorway network in Spain has been extended from just 1,933 kilometres at the beginning of the 1980's to over 10,000 kilometres by 2000. This covered two major planning periods that were to provide the basic motorway network and primary connections in Spain linking the major cities of the country.

a) The "Plan General de Carreteras": Planning of the first major road building programme started in 1983 and covered the period up to 1994. The basic strategy of the plan was to upgrade the principal road connection to free motorways and to provide the basic radial network linking the major cities to the capital Madrid. The plan was finished and made public in 1984. The same year as implementation of the plan started. However, it was not until the late 1980´s that the first important motorway links opened to traffic.
b) In 1994, the government introduced the "Plan Director de Infraestructuras", that were to complete the primary motorway network.

The current planning period 2000-2010 continues the extension of the motorway network through the provision of a complementary finer mesh network.

The aim of this section is to contribute to the understanding of the factors underlying firm location with regard to a) how the importance of transport changes with the development of a higher-order transport network that significantly reduces transport costs, and b) how far and in which direction the traditional spatial patterns of location change by virtue of decreasing transport costs.

For this purpose, an analysis is carried out using panel data for Spain covering a 20 year period over which important changes in road infrastructure have taken place. Furthermore, the spatial level of analysis adopted is the municipality (NUTS V) level. This is a very detailed geographical level of analysis. Most studies on transport infrastructure investments have used large geographic units due to lack of more disaggregated data which limited their results to inter-regional variations in transport infrastructure impacts but intra-regional differences have been neglected. Yet transport infrastructure is place-specific and impacts will depend on distances to the new infrastructure and on its network characteristics. To address this, the approach adopted combines GIS techniques with advanced location econometrics to analyse large scale micro-level data that result from such a spatially detailed analysis. Certainly, a comprehensive understanding of the relationship between transport and the location of economic activity must include the analysis of impacts taking place at the intra-regional and local level.

18.3.1 Data and Variables

The dependent variable used are the number of manufacturing plants that opened in each of the 7939 Spanish mainland municipalities (NUTS-5 level). This data has been obtained from the Register of Industrial Establishments (Registro de Establecimientos Industriales) compiled by the Spanish Ministry of Industry[1]. The data consists of new establishments that were set up between 1980 and 2000 covering the entire manufacturing sector. For the period from 1980 to 1994 the Ministry has a complete data set covering all Spanish municipalities. Unfortunately, for the more recent years the available data is not complete and for the period since 1994, the relevant information could only be collected for 40 out of the total of 47 mainland provinces in Spain[2]. The data for the 40 provinces covers, however, over 90 percent of the Spanish mainland population, as well as over 90 percent of production and new plant registrations in manufacturing.

The theoretical and empirical literature on industrial location shows that firm location is not a random process. Firms choose a plant site after having considered a set of locational characteristics that affect expected profits. These are characteristics specific to the individual municipality (NUTS5) and characteristics of the wider geographical area which relates here to the province where the municipality is located. The latter are factors that work over wider areas such as labour markets (NUTS3). The independent variables used in the firm location analysis are summarised in Table 18.1. Three groups of location determinants are distinguished: (1) measures of market demand (locally proxied by municipality population, and regionally with GDP per capita) and market access (motorway access, and market potential accessibility), (2) measures of agglomeration economies (diversity, specialisation, and size of the industrial basis), and (3) wage costs and labour force qualification. Given the focus of this paper, only the road transport infrastructure variables are discussed in more detail below. Transport is introduced in the analysis via accessibility indicators. This brings the advantage over simple infrastructure stock measures such as the ones used in most production function approaches, of taking into account the network character of transport infrastructure. Furthermore, the concept of accessibility more closely relates to the services provided by transport infrastructure of reducing the friction of distance and bringing economic agents together.

---

[1] All new physical plants belonging to the industrial sector are required to enter in the Industrial Establishments Register. Information on each establishment includes year of registration, industry code at 5 CNAE-93 digits (Clasificación Nacional de Actividades Económicas 1993), location (province and municipality), number of employees, initial capital investment and electricity power subscription.

[2] The missing data refers to the provinces of La Rioja, Navarra, Guadalajara, and the 4 provinces in Galicia.

Table 18.1. Independent variables: definition, expected effects and data sources

Variables	Definition	Geo. Scale[a]	Data Source
GDP/capita	Annual GDP/capita (in millions of 1986 constant pesetas)	NUTS III	BBV
Population	Absolute size of population (in hundred thousands)	NUTS V	INE
Population accessibility	Index of potential population accessibility	NUTS V	GIS own calculations
Motorway access	Distance to nearest motorway (in 10 kilometres)	NUTS V	GIS own calculations
Lack of diversity	Herfindahl index of sectoral employment concentration	NUTS III	BBV
Sectoral specialisation	Share of manufacturing employment in total regional employment	NUTS III	BBV
Industry base	Regional share in total national industry employment	NUTS III	BBV
Manufacturing wage	Index of manufacturing sector wage (base = national average)	NUTS III	BBV
Labour force qualification	% of labour force with higher education	NUTS III	EPA/INE

a NUTS III regions are provinces in Spain; NUTS V corresponds to municipalities

The accessibility measures used in this analysis are based on the evolution of the road network from 1980 to 2000 as reflected in Fig. 18.1. Part (a) shows the network as of 1980. The motorway network was basically non-existent. Motorways were limited in and around the major urban agglomerations and there were some motorway connections in the north-eastern part of the country. However, Madrid, the capital, was not linked by motorways to any of the other economic centres of the country. Part (b) of Fig. 18.1 shows the network as of the year 2000. The principal radial motorway network has been basically completed linking all autonomous communities and the major province capitals.

As in Holl (2004a), detailed accessibility measures have been calculated using Geographic information systems (GIS) to provide a way to quantify the effect of transport infrastructure improvements on firm location. First, a measure of motorway access is calculated. This is computed as the straight air-line distance from each municipality to the nearest inter-regional motorway. Table 18.2 gives some summary statistics. The statistics highlight that there have been very large differences in terms of access to the higher-order road transport networks in Spain. Before the road construction programmes were launched, the average straight airline distance to an inter-regional motorway was over 60 kilometres with a maximum value of 262 kilometres. After the massive road building, the average distance was reduced to slightly over 20 kilometres and the maximum distance was reduced to just over a 110 kilometres.

(a)

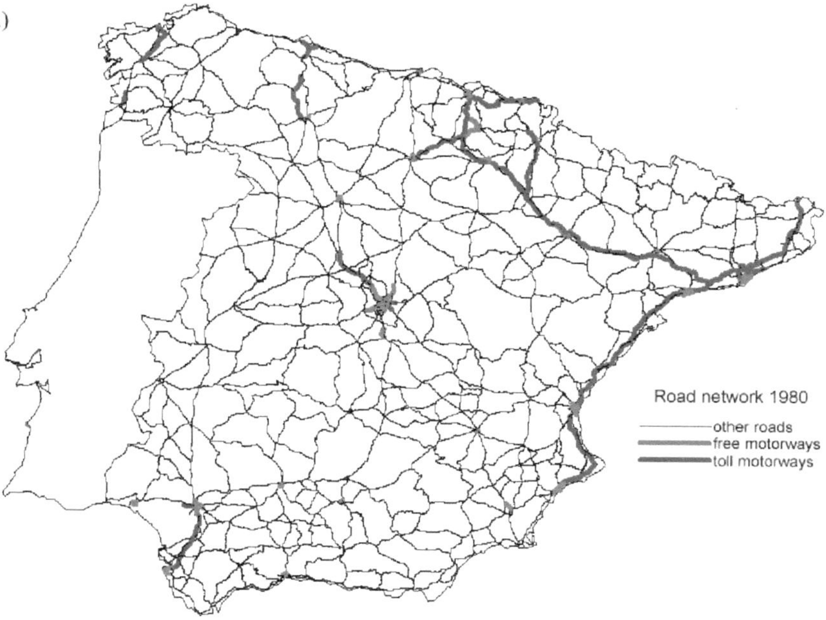

(b)

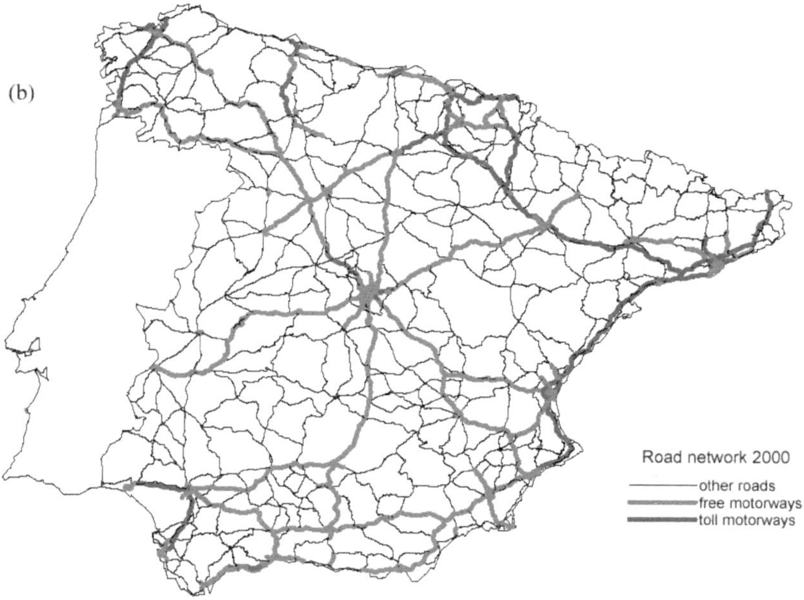

Fig. 18.1. The Spanish road network in: (a) 1980; (b) 2000

Second, an accessibility measure of market potential is constructed. Harris (1954) shows that market potential is determined by the distance to and the size of market demand in alternative locations. In his market potential function, the potential demand for goods produced in location j is the sum of the market size in all other locations M_k divided by their distance d_{jk} to j.

$$ACC_j = \sum \frac{M_k}{d_{jk}} \tag{18.1}$$

Here, market size is proxied by the population of municipalities of the 438 largest Spanish cities with more than 10,000 inhabitants. This covers over 75 percent of the total Spanish peninsular population. Distance between municipality j and k is measured in travel time where $d_{jk} = 1$ for all municipalities that are less than half an hour travel time apart[3].

Table 18.2. Distance to the nearest interregional motorway (in km)

Distance	1980	1985	1990	1995	2000
Mean	64.5	64.2	36.6	28.1	22.5
Std. Dev	54.7	54.6	33.5	26.4	21.4
Min (in meter)	0.2	0.2	0.2	0.2	0.2
Max	261.8	261.8	165.6	147.3	111.6

18.3.2 Estimation and Empirical Results

Estimations are carried out for 1980 to 1999. To add to the understanding of dynamic impacts of transport infrastructure investment, and in particular on where economic activity locates with changes in transport costs, these 20 years are divided into three subperiods:

- 1980 to 1987: covers the start of the network construction with no major links yet opened to traffic.
- 1988-1994: is the period when the most important links of the network were opened.

[3] Travel times between locations have been calculated using a minimum pathfinder programme written in Fortran. This programme has been kindly made available and adapted to the network used in this research by Peter Bibby, Department of Town and Regional Planning, University of Sheffield.

- 1995-1999: is the period when the primary motorway network neared completion.

Regarding the functional form of estimation, a conditional fixed effects Poisson model is used since the dependent variable is a count variable (Cameron and Trivedi 1998; Guimarães et al 2003). Results are reported in Table 18.3. In addition to standard errors from the expected Hessian in parentheses, robust standard errors are reported in brackets (see, Papke 1991; Wooldridge 1991, 1999). Annual year dummies are included to control for any cyclical effects stemming from the business cycle. Columns 1 to 3 show the results for the 40 provinces for which complete data has been obtained. Column 4 and 5 show the results for all 47 mainland provinces for the first two periods for which data is complete on all those provinces. The results are remarkably similar. This highlights the robustness of the results and also suggests that the results obtained for the second half of the nineties should not be too sensitive to the omission of the 7 provinces.

In the first period, a significant preference of manufacturing firms for locating in larger market areas can be observed. This is reflected by the positive and significant signs of the regional GDP per capita variable and the potential market accessibility. In contrast, with the motorway network hardly developed, distance to the nearest motorway is not significant. Turning to the agglomeration variables, area specialisation, that is lack of diversity, does not show a significant effect in the first period. However, areas that have been more strongly specialised in manufacturing and with a larger industrial base have attracted fewer new plants. Factor costs as reflected by wage costs did not significantly influence the location choice, nor did labour force qualification.

In the second period, potential market accessibility, indicating proximity to the main urban agglomerations, looses significance. Interestingly, however, distance to a nearest inter-regional motorway exerts a much stronger and significant effect in the second period. Relative manufacturing specialisation turns to exert a significant positive effect and higher wage costs significantly deterred manufacturing plant location in the second period.

In the third period, potential market accessibility shows a significant negative effect on manufacturing plant location indicating dispersion from the larger urban agglomeration. The coefficient for distance to the nearest inter-regional motorway is again negative and significant and larger than in the previous period. This suggests that as the motorway network near completion it is becoming increasingly important for firms to be close to the network. As in the first period, new manufacturing plants preferred more diversified areas but it also seems that the dispersion from the larger urban agglomeration has increased the importance for being closer to other manufacturing firms. Both the manufacturing specialisation and the industry share are positive and significant in the third period.

18.4 Conclusions

The relationship between transport infrastructure investment and the location of economic activity is complex. The literature indicate that impacts depend on infrastructure, location as well as firm characteristics. Such differences are often disguised in aggregate studies.

Table 18.3. Results of the fixed effects Poisson estimations: pooled sample

	40 mainland provinces for which data is complete from 1980-1999[a]			All 47 mainland provinces: complete data for 1980-1994	
Variables	1980-1987	1988-1994	1995-1999[b]	1980-1987	1988-1994
Regional GDP per capita	1.787*	1.792***	0.904	1.601*	0.516
	(0.319)	(0.315)	(0.417)	(0.294)	(0.292)
	[0.718]	[1.018]	[0.842]	[0.619]	[0.923]
Municipality population	0.075	0.337*	0.487	0.053	0.329*
	(0.041)	(0.047)	(0.204)	(0.041)	(0.047)
	[0.081]	[0.098]	[0.399]	[0.074]	[0.095]
Potential market accessibility	0.053*	-0.008	-0.047***	0.048*	-0.013
	(0.008)	(0.003)	(0.018)	(0.008)	(0.003)
	[0.021]	[0.007]	[0.029]	[0.020]	[0.006]
Distance to nearest motorway	-0.014	-0.036*	-0.052**	-0.009	-0.032*
	(0.016)	(0.003)	(0.021)	(0.016)	(0.003)
	[0.029]	[0.011]	[0.024]	[0.029]	[0.010]
Lack of diversity	-3.943	-1.812	-9.539**	-5.262**	-0.791
	(1.405)	(0.811)	(2.501)	(1.344)	(0.811)
	[2.753]	[1.256]	[3.812]	[2.545]	[1.321]
Sectoral specialisation	-0.109*	0.038**	0.112*	-0.094*	0.028
	(0.009)	(0.009)	(0.017)	(0.008)	(0.009)
	[0.025]	[0.020]	[0.025]	[0.020]	[0.020]
Industry share	-0.851*	-0.352*	0.523**	-0.818*	-0.237*
	(0.067)	(0.046)	(0.093)	(0.065)	(0.046)
	[0.166]	[0.084]	[0.258]	[0.156]	[0.083]
Wage	-0.026	-0.019***	-0.008	-0.010	-0.023**
	(0.006)	(0.006)	(0.008)	(0.005)	(0.006)
	[0.018]	[0.011]	[0.016]	[0.012]	[0.011]
Labour force qualification	0.0004	0.013	-0.008	-0.008	0.009
	(0.006)	(0.006)	(0.007)	(0.005)	(0.006)
	[0.013]	[0.008]	[0.008]	[0.012]	[0.008]
Observations	33024	26229	12412	36144	29743
Log-likelihood	-27307.54	-23527.15	-10346.01	-30769.53	-26716.37
Wald test	3600.69*	1825.10*	505.42*	3718.86*	1739.04*

Notes: Standard errors from the expected Hessian are provided in parentheses, robust standard errors are reported in brackets. Significant coefficients are indicated by *, **, ***, for significance at the 1%, 5% and 10% level respectively based on robust standard errors. Estimations include unreported year dummies. a) except for 1998 when no data for Andalucia is available. b) excludes 1998.

Using municipality-level manufacturing data for Spain from 1980 to 2000, this article empirically tested for dynamic impacts. The results suggest that the effect of transport improvements is not stable over time. Consistent with predictions of new economic geography models for transport costs falling below some critical level, the new road infrastructure constructed in Spain appears to have facilitated geographical dispersion. It has allowed firms to locate at greater distance from the main market centres, however, along the motorway corridors where they can still benefit from good accessibility, and close to firms in the same sector to take advantage of localisation economies. While the estimation results reported here are interesting and suggestive, they have to be viewed with care given the lack of a complete data set for all Spanish provinces.

The literature review as well as the empirical results of this paper do not support the hypothesis of a declining importance of transport infrastructure for industrial location. They do, however, indicate a changing role of scale. With good regional accessibility, the role motorways play will be more related to the location decision of firms regarding the intra-regional level or even to the local level regarding specific areas or parcels. As Vickerman (1995) points out, with the development of a higher order transport network, intra-regional distribution effects are becoming increasingly pronounced depending on differences in access to the new networks. This is also consistent with empirical evidence reported that such investment draws economic activity into the new transport corridors at the cost of more distant locations. This implies important redistritribution effects of transport infrastructure investment, which bring along policy implications in terms of the geographic incidence of transport improvements benefits and who has to bear the costs not only in terms of funding but also in terms of negative externalities. This re-enforces the need for a careful consideration of the spatial dimension in transport infrastructure studies. Results will depend on the spatial scale of analysis adopted and since redistribution effects, too an important degree, occur at the fine-grained geographical level, there is a clear need for more micro-level research in this area.

Another area, which is in need of more research, is the relation between transport improvements and agglomeration economies. An interesting subject for further research is how the geographical scale over that different types of agglomeration forces operate changes with transport and communication improvements.

Further research should also investigate the effects of transport improvements on industrial re-organisation such as the implementation of just-in-time production and the increased outsourcing of activities that have been traditionally carried out in-house. An important dimension in this context is the issue of reliability and how it affects modern logistical organisation.

Finally, empirical research to date has mostly relied on physical stock measures of infrastructure. This implicitly assumes that transport flows are the same across the network. Interesting insights could be gained by taking into account actual transport flows. Unfortunately, such data is rarely available at a sufficiently disaggregate level to be combined with a detailed sectoral and spatial location analysis.

Acknowledgements

This research has been carried out with financial support from the ESRC, grant RES-000-22-0056. The support is gratefully acknowledged.

References

Becker R, Henderson V (2000) Effects of Air Quality Regulations on Polluting Industries. Journal of Political Economy 108 (2): 379-421.

Boarnet MG (1997) Highways and Economic Productivity: Interpreting recent evidence, Journal of Planning Literature 11 (4): 476-486.

Boarnet MG (1998) Spillovers and the Locational Effects of Public Infrastructure, Journal of Regional Science 38: 381–400.

Botham RW (1980) The regional development effects of road investment, Transportation Planning and Technology 6: 97-108.

Bruinsma FR, Rienstra SA, Rietveld P (1997) Economic Impacts of the Construction of a Transport Corridor: A Multi-level and Multi-approach Case Study for the Construction of the A1 Highway in the Netherlands, Regional Studies 31 (4): 391-402.

Bryan J, Hill S, Munday M, Roberts A (1997) Road infrastructure and economic development in the periphery: the case of A55 improvements in North Wales, Journal of Transport Geography 5 (4): 227-237.

Cairncross F (1997) The Death of Distance. Boston: Harvard Business School Press.

Cameron AC, Trivedi PK (1998) Regression Analysis of Count Data. Cambridge University Press, Cambridge, UK.

Chandra A, Thompson E (2000) Does public infrastructure affect economic activity? Evidence from the rural interstate highway system, Regional Science and Urban Economics 30: 457-490.

Combes PP, Lafourcade M (2004) Trade Costs and Regional Disparities in a model of Economic Geography: Structural Estimation and Predictions for France. C.E.R.A.S working paper. Paris.

Devereux MP, Griffith R (1998) Taxes and the location of production: evidence from a panel of US multinationals. Journal of Public Economics 68: 335-367.

Diamond D, Spence N (1989) Infrastructure and Industrial Costs in British Industry. HMSO, London.

Dodgson JS (1974) Motorway investment, industrial cost and sub-regional growth: a case study of the M62. Regional Studies 8: 169-185.

Eberts RW, McMillan DP (1999) Agglomeration economies and urban public infrastructure. In: P. Cheshire and E.S. Mills (eds), Handbook of Urban and Regional Economics, Volume 3. New York: North Holland: 1455-1495.

Ellison G, Glaeser EL (1997) Geographic Concentration in U.S. Manufacturing Industries: A Dartboard Approach. Journal of Political Economy 105 (5), 889-927.

Fernald JG (1999) "Roads to Prosperity" Assessing the Link between Public Capital and Productivity. American Economic Review 89: 619–638.
Forkenbrock DJ, Foster NSJ (1996) Highways and Business location Decisions. Economic Development Quarterly 10 (3): 239-248.
Fotopoulos G, Spence N (1999) Spatial Variations in New Manufacturing Plant Openings: Some Empirical Evidence from Greece. Regional Studies 33 (3): 219-229.
Fujita M, Krugman P, Venables AJ (1999) The Spatial Economy. Cities, Regions and International Trade. MIT Press, Cambridge. MA.
Giuliano G (1989) Research policy review 27: New directions for understanding transportation and land use. Environment and Planning A 21 (2): 145-159.
Gramlich EM (1994) Infrastructure investment: A review essay. Journal of Economic Literature 32: 1147-75.
Guimarães P, Figueiredo O, Woodward DP (2000) Agglomeration and the Location of Foreign Direct Investment in Portugal Journal of Urban Economics 47 (1): 115-135.
Guimarães P, Figueiredo O, Woodward DP (2003) A Tractable Approach to the Firm Location Decision Problem. Review of Economics and Statistics 85 (1): 201-204.
Guimarães P, Rolfe RJ, Woodward DP (1998) Regional Incentives and Industrial Location in Puerto Rico. International Regional Science Review 21 (2): 119-138.
Harris CD (1954) The Market as a Factor in the Localization of Industry in the United States. Annals of the Association of American Geographers 44: 315-348.
Haughwout A (1997) Central city infrastructure investment and suburban house values. Regional Science and Urban Economics 27: 199-215.
Haughwout A (1999) State Infrastructure and the Geography of Employment. Growth and Change 30: 549-566.
Hausman JA, Hall BH, Griliches Z (1984) Econometric models for count data with an application to the patents-R&D relationship. Econometrica 52: 909-938.
Holl A (2004a) Manufacturing location and impacts of road transport infrastructure: Empirical evidence from Spain. Regional Science and Urban Economics, 34 (3): 341-363.
Holl A (2004b) Transport infrastructure, agglomeration economies, and firm birth. Empirical evidence from Portugal. Journal of Regional Science, 44 (4): 693-712.
Holl A (2004c) Start-ups and relocations: Manufacturing plant location in Portugal. Papers in Regional Science 83: 649-668.
Holmes TJ (1998) The effect of state policies on the location of manufacturing: evidence from state borders. Journal of Political Economy 106 (4): 667-705.
Holtz-Eakin D, Lovely ME (1996) Scale economies, returns to variety, and the productivity of public infrastructure. Regional Science and Urban Economics 26: 105-120.
Holtz-Eakin D, Schwartz AM (1995) Spatial Productivity Spillovers from Public Infrastructure: Evidence from State Highways. International Tax and Public Finance 2: 459-468.
Keeble D, Walker S (1994) New Firms, Small Firms and Dead Firms: Spatial Patterns and Determinants in the United Kingdom. Regional Studies, 28 (4): 411-427.
Kolko J (1999) Can I Get Some Service Here? Information Technology, Service Industries, and the Future of Cities. mimeo, Harvard University.
Krugman P (1991) Increasing Returns and Economic Geography. Journal of Political Economy 99 (3): 483-499.

Leitham S, McQuaid R W, Nelson JD (2000) The influence of transport on industrial location choice: a stated preference experiment. Transportation Research A 34: 515-535.

Levinson A (1996) Environmental regulations and manufacturers' location choice: Evidence from the Census of Manufactures. Journal of Public Economics 62: 5-29.

Linneker B, Spence N (1992) Accessibility measures compared in an analysis of the impact of the M25 London Orbital Motorway on Britain. Environment and Planning A 24: 1137-1154.

Linneker B, Spence N (1996) Road transport infrastructure and regional economic development: The regional development effects of the M25 London orbital motorway. Journal of Transport Geography 4 (2): 77-92.

Marshall A (1920) Principles of Economics, 8th edition. Macmillan, London.

McCann P (1995) Rethinking the Economics of Location and Agglomeration. Urban Studies 32 (3): 563-577.

McConnell VD, Schwab RM (1990) The impact of environmental regulation on industry location decisions: The motor vehicle industry. Land Economics 66: 67-81.

McKinnon AC (1998) Logistical Restructuring, Freight Traffic Growth and the Environment. In: Banister, D. (ed) Transport Policy and the Environment, 97-109, Routledge, London.

McQuaid RW, Leitham S, Nelson JD (1996) Accessibility and Location Decisions in a Peripheral Region of Europe: A Logit Analysis. Regional Studies 30 (6): 579-588.

Mikelbank BA, Jackson RW (2000) The Role of Space in Public Capital Research. International Regional Science Review 23: 235–258.

Moreno R, Artís M, López-Bazo E, Suriñach J (1997) Evidence on the Complex Link between Infrastructure and Regional Growth. International Journal of Development Planning Literature 12 (1&2): 81-108.

Moses, L (1958) Location and the theory of production. Quarterly Journal of Economics 72: 259-272.

Papke LE (1991) Interstate business tax differentials and new firm location: Evidence from panel data. Journal of Public Economics 45: 47-68.

Plaut PO (1997) Transportation-Communications Relationships in Industry. Transportation Research A 31 (6): 419-429.

Preston J (2001) Integrating transport with socio-economic activity – a research agenda for the new millennium. Journal of Transport Geography 9: 13-24.

Puga D (2002) European regional policies in the light of recent location theories. Journal of Economic Geography 2: 373-406.

Rietveld P (1989) Infrastructure and regional development: A survey of multiregional economic models. Annals of Regional Science 23: 255-274.

Rosenthal SS, Strange WC (2003) Geography, Industrial Organization, and Agglomeration. Review of Economics and Statistics 85: 377–393.

Shirely C, Winston C (2004) Firm inventory behavior and the returns from highway infrastructure investments. Journal of Urban Economics 55: 398-415.

Taylor MJ (1975) Organisational Growth, Spatial Interaction and Location Decision-Making. Regional Studies 9, 313-323.

Vickerman R (1995) The regional impacts of Trans-European networks. Annals of Regional Science 29 (2): 237-254.

Vickerman RW (1996) Location, Accessibility and Regional Development: the appraisal of Trans-European networks. Transport Policy 2 (4): 225-234.

Voith R (1993) Changing Capitalization of CBD-Oriented Transportation Systems: Evidence from Philadelphia, 1970-1988. Journal of Urban Economics 33: 361-376.

Von Thünen JH (1826) Der Isolierte Staat in Beziehung auf Landwirtschaftslehre und Nationalökonomie, Hamburg, English translation, Oxford: Pergamon Press, 1966.

Weber A (1929) Theory of the Location of Industry. Chicago University Press, Chicago.

Wooldridge JM (1991) Specification testing and quasi-maximum-likelihood estimation. Journal of Econometrics 48: 29-55.

Wooldridge JM (1999) Distribution-free estimation of some nonlinear panel data models. Journal of Econometrics 90: 77-97.

19 Mapping the Terrain of Information and Communications Technology (ICT) and Household Travel

Kevin J. Krizec
Active Communities Transportation (ACT) Research Group
University of Minnesota (U.S.A.)

Andrew Johnson
Oregon Department of Transportation (U.S.A.)

19.1 Introduction

New forms of information and communications technology (ICT) continue to emerge as primary forces influencing people's activities and travel. More than a century ago the telephone was instrumental in establishing new patterns of both communication and shopping. Rural residents, in particular, were not able to purchase products through catalogues (e.g., Sears) and have them delivered to their outlying locations. Later in the century the energy crisis of the late 1970's prompted increased attention on reducing travel and the potential role of emerging forms of computer assisted communication. Employers have always been attracted to telecommuting as a strategy to provide employee flexibility while still maintaining the array of services offered. Similar themes, albeit somewhat modified for current settings, persist as researchers and futurists examine the influence of rapidly changing forms of information technology on society. The nascent popularity of the internet has now placed e-commerce front and center on the minds of many. Burgeoning forms of computing communication (e.g., personal data assistants, cell phones) permeate even the simplest of transactions.

But what is the impact of these new forms of information and communication on household activity? What is their potential in eliminating, reducing or modifying travel? The effect of technology, and more specifically ICT, has been studied on a number of levels in previous work. For example, Edwin Parker (1976) estimated that the introduction of computers and telecommunications will change modern economics as "information" cannot be treated as a commodity. Alvin Toffler (1980) later surmised that ICT improvements will in fact make cities obsolete, while Lehman-Wilzig (1981) projected that telecommunications might eliminate all travel. More recently, others have offered exposes relating technology to contemporary urban life or policy agendas (e.g., Smart Growth) (Mitchell 2002; Moss and Townsend 2000). Interests in ICT remain varied. These include (a) geographical perspectives aiming to examine loosening the relationships between spatial patterns and development, (b) psychological perspectives aiming to uncover ways in which ICT changes communication patterns, or (c) economic analysis of increasing the efficiency of freight delivery.

A perspective receiving considerable attention, and one that is at the heart of this paper, relates to the influence of ICT on household travel. Motivation for interest in this specific topic remains varied. For example, employers are interested in enhancing employee flexibility, reducing overhead costs, improving operational efficiency and minimizing time spent in travel for their employees. Commercial businesses want to provide options for customers to not travel. The most publicized interests (environmental groups, government entities) are those who look to ICT to save energy, reduce congestion, and improve air quality. A premise of such interest rests on the likelihood that ICT will reduce the need for automobile travel (either in terms of vehicle miles traveled (VMT) or number of vehicle trips). The principle reason for such in economic terms–it is suggested–is because ICT eliminates the "geographic costs" of each trip (or activity)–travel will therefore less likely be pursued physically but rather virtually. Particular attention focuses on the potential of ICT to eliminate, reduce, or temporally shift peak-period commute travel. But interestingly enough, while deployment of ICT has skyrocketed in recent years, overall household travel in terms of distance and/or trips has increased as well. This suggests that our knowledge of relationships between ICT and travel, while growing, is still tentative at best.

The work that has been pursued to date relating ICT and household travel is varied. One only needs to refer to previous reviews (see, for example, Mokhtarian and Salomon 1997; Golob 2001; Salomon 1986) to gain a better understanding of the central questions and range of issues associated with this general line of inquiry. But these reviews are limited in at least two contexts. First, the bulk of previous literature focuses on one aspect of ICT: affecting the work commute (hereafter telecommuting). This aspect has been the focus of most activity and development. But everyday use of ICT has migrated well beyond the bounds of the work commute. As Golob claims, "we must do better than that [focusing on telecommuting] in order to keep our field relevant to planning and policy making" (Golob 2001). Secondly, technology, and the way in which people use it, is rapidly changing. It is necessary to keep abreast of recent developments, grapple with the emerging ranges of issues, and understand current work about these developments.

In response to at least these two calls, this paper uses a literature search as the primary means of inquiry to update our knowledge of relationships between ICT and travel. It uses existing studies to help frame and update a task that has been the target of a previous "research needs assessment" (Mokhtarian 2000). In doing so, this work first maps the terrain of existing work to date related to ICT and household travel. It identifies the predominant nature of existing study–conceptual or empirical–and identifies voids in the existing knowledge base. Second, the paper sheds light on emerging phenomena to help conceptualize future research. This review therefore serves to update our knowledge about a body of knowledge undergoing quick changes. The aim is that it will also serve as both a springboard and a blueprint for more detailed lines of inquiry related to ICT and household travel.

Before we begin it is important to frame the issues covered in this review. The present discussion is limited to understanding the behavior of households and individuals relative to different dimensions of ICT, broadly referred to telecommunications or information technology in some circles, and ICT in others. We use the term ICT because it encompasses a variety of terms describing a wide array of communication/technological enhancements. The most commonly cited examples include Internet improvements (i.e., broadband, e-mail, increased electronic accessibility to information and opportunities, more powerful personal computers), cell phones, ATMs, and teleconferencing. ICT is about using computers to work at home and cell phones to arrange a meeting place remotely. It is about ordering gifts on line and using internet availability to enhance home-schooling. It is about ordering an on-demand movie and using video-conferencing. This paper, however, is not about reviewing some of ICT's other impacts. It is less about the use of Global Positioning System (GPS), Advanced Vehicle Transportation Systems (AVTS), the general nature of Intelligent Transportation Systems (ITS), and the impact of ICT on commercial vehicle operations or business to business commerce. The focus in many of these categories is more on modifying or managing travel than replacing it. Our focus here lies in how ICT may affect the travel patterns of households and/or individuals.

19.2 Part I) Previous Research

Defining a Framework for Discussion

Our review uses three dimensions to map recent literature of relationships between ICT and travel. The first dimension specifies whether the study is conceptual or empirical in nature, a relatively self-explanatory pursuit. The former describes theoretical arguments or key relationships, while the latter measures changes in travel as a result of ICT. The second and third dimensions are based on, respectively: (a) the purpose of the specific activity being studied and (b) the effect that ICT has on travel. These two dimensions are described below and the literature is then mapped and discussed using this framework.

Purpose of the ICT Activity

A critical aspect relates to nature of activities that are being pursued using ICT. For example, previous study has classified eight activities in which telecommunications can be substituted for travel (telecommuting, teleconferencing, teleshopping, telebanking, tele-entertainment, tele-education, tele-medicine, and tele-justice) (Mokhtarian 1990). This list presents a healthy list of ICT applications; but being more than a decade also, it is one that has undergone much change in recent times. Rather than attempt to identify each of the ever growing list of ICT applications, we find value in using a relatively broader classification scheme–one that is also useful in helping us better understand how ICT relates to a household's overall travel. The typology we adopt is based on work first introduced by Reichman (1976) who defined three major classes of travel-related activities. These three classes represent:

- subsistence activities, consisting of activities that generate income, including work, business services, and sometimes schooling (travel associated with this activity is most commonly commuting),
- maintenance activities, consisting of the purchase and consumption of convenience goods or personal services needed by the individual or household, and
- leisure or discretionary activities, comprising multiple voluntary activities performed on free time, not allocated to work or maintenance activities.

This typology of activities has been employed by Pas (Pas 1982, 1984) and Bhat and Koppelman (Bhat and Koppelman 1993) to classify daily travel activity behavior. Such a framework also represents the cornerstone of current activity-based transportation modeling efforts (e.g., TRANSIMS) currently underway (Bowman et al 1998; Ben-Akiva and Bowman 1998; Bhat et al 1999; Misra and Bhat 2000; Jonnalagadda et al 2001; Kitamura 1988; Bradley Research and Consulting et al 1998; Gould and Golob 1997; Ma and Goulias 1997; Bhat and Misra 1999). This classification is directly applicable to this line of inquiry as it provides a parsimonious strategy to map the demand for central purposes of ICT activity (e.g., working versus banking versus shopping) and the degree to which existing study has tended to focus on one or more of these aspects.

The Effect of ICT on Travel

Almost 20 years ago, seminal work on ICT and travel by Salomon provided a foundation that helped outlined basic types of interaction (Salomon, 1986 and 1985). These types of interaction–substitution, modification, enhancement, and neutrality–have been employed in subsequent discussion and analysis (Mokhtarian 1990; Marker and Goulias 1999; Hjorthol 2002). We employ them here as a means to better understand the theories and evidence of past research.

- Substitution of travel refers to the elimination of trips -- trips that are no longer required as a result of ICT improvements. This interaction has been the focus of most of the ICT attention, and the substitution of subsistence trips, by definition, is a phenomenon inherent in the term telecommuting (Golob 2001). While the substitution hypothesis is one that holds great hope by many, the scale to which this is happening is estimated to be quite smaller than originally anticipated (Mokhtarian 1990).
- Modification refers to travel that is likely to be altered, primarily by a shift in the timing and routing of trips (spatial and/or temporal transformations). It may

also refer to the manner in which trips are linked together (i.e., trip chaining) or even the mode of travel. The benefits of shifting even a small amount of peak hour travel to different times (through telecommuting) are mentioned as a key strategy for reducing levels of congestion. The bulk of the literature agrees that ICT will modify travel behavior (Viswanathan and Goulias 2001; Pendyala et al 1991; Wells et al 2001); the outstanding issue is understanding how such modification will play out (e.g., more travel or less).

- Generation refers to any generation of travel that would not have occurred but for the existence of ICT. Little is known about how ICT may generate additional traffic, primarily due to the difficulty in determining causality and a lack of time-series data before and after ICT enhancement and deployment.
- Neutrality refers those instances in which ICT has no foreseeable effect on household travel behavior.

Mapping the ICT Literature

Our mapping of recent work (Table 19.1) reviews over 50 studies to understand the nature and orientation of existing work. We classify each study first as being primarily conceptual or empirical in nature. The second mapping dimension considers the primary nature of the specific study–its relation to subsistence, maintenance or discretionary travel. The purpose of this table and subsequent discussion is to help identify where existing research is concentrated and where future research would most usefully be targeted.

Subsistence

Subsistence activities, when viewed relative to ICT, refer to individuals working at home or other remote locations, most often with telecommunications links to a central office. Interest in telecommuting stems from the often heralded potential of relieving peak hour traffic congestion by reducing or modifying people's work trip (on average, considered to comprise one-third of all household travel). The widespread availability of telecommunications services, combined with the use of such services, has been the principle reason this aspect of ICT has been the target for the overwhelming majority of all study of ICT use (Mokhtarian 1990; Wells et al 2001; Mokhtarian and Salomon 1994, 1996a, 1996b; Mokhtarian 1998; Nilles, 1976, 1994; Yen, 1994; Kitamura et al 1990; Mokhtarian 1991; Kraut 1989). Additional reasons for the focus on this line of work are two-fold. First, transportation planners and modelers have long been preoccupied with the work commute (often considered the lion's share of household travel). Secondly, work related activities are typically "cleaner" to analyze than maintenance and discretionary activities because they tend to be more stable and predictable.

Table 19.1. Mapping the literature of travel and ICT relating to three purposes of activity

	Primarily Conceptual	Primarily Empirical
Subsistence	-Handy and Mokhtarian 1995 -Mokhtarian 1990 -Mokhtarian 1991 -Mokhtarian and Salomon 1994 -Mokhtarian and Salomon 1996a -Mokhtarian and Salomon 1996b -Mokhtarian 1998 -Handy and Mokhtarian 1996 -Lund and Mokhtarian 1994 -Nilles 1976 -Niles 1994 -Golob and Regan 2001 -Golob 2001 -Yen et al 1994 -Salomon 1986 -Bernardino and Ben-Akiva 1996	-Kitamura et al. 1990 -Pendyala et al. 1991 -Wells et al 2001 -Mokhtarian 1991 -Mokhtarian et al 1995 - Mokhtarian and Salomon 1996a - Mokhtarian and Salomon 1996b -Kraut 1989 -Shen 1999 * -Guiliano 1998 -Hamer et al 1992 -Hamer et al 1991 -Salomon et al 1991 -Nilles 1988 -Nilles 1993 -Yen et al 1994 -Mokhtarian and Meenakshisundaram 1999
Maintenance	-Salomon and Koppelman 1988 -Salomon and Koppelman 1992 -Gould 1998 -Gould and Golob 1997 -Marker and Goulias 1999 -Couclelis 2002 -Mokhtarian et al 2001 -Golob and Regan 2001 -Golob 2001 -Underhill 1999 -Batty 1997	-Handy and Yantis 1997 -Kraut 1989 -Cairns 1996 -Kilpala et al 2000 -Koppelman et al 1991
Discretionary	-Salomon and Koppelman 1988 -Salomon 1985 -Salomon and Koppelman 1992 -Underhill 1999	-Handy and Yantis 1997 -Hjorthol 2002 -Kraut 1989 -Preece 2001 -Koppelman et al 1991

Notes:
-Some papers describe both theoretical and empirical aspects and are listed in each column.
-Some papers relate to more than one category and may be listed in multiple rows.
* This research focuses less on the impact of direct work travel and more on the impact that telecommuting has on accessibility indices. It is grouped under subsistence because of the primary focus on employment opportunities.

Despite the telecommuting piece of the ICT puzzle being subject to the most mature models and conceptual frameworks, its orientation varies considerably. For example, previous work has focused on different dimensions of the issue, such as defining telecommuting (Mokhtarian 1991), forecasting telecommuting, (Mokhtarian 1998; Handy and Mokhtarian 1996) understanding individual and employer attitudes toward telecommuting (e.g., flexible working arrangements, increased proliferation of self-employment) (Mokhtarian 1994; Mokhtarian and Salomon 1996a, 1996b), and land use implications (Shen 1999; Giuliano 1998; Nilles 1991). Mokhtarian (1998) has attempted to assemble the substantive findings to date under a unified framework by examining current knowledge in forecasting the demand for telecommuting and the resulting transportation impacts.

The culmination of this line of work has, however, yielded somewhat conflicting findings. Some have found that telecommuters reduce their number of trips and distance traveled on telecommute days (Pendyala et al 1991; Wells et al 2001; Nilles, 1993), on non-telecommute days (Pendyala et al 1991; Nilles 1993), or on net travel (see Mokhtarian 1998 for other reviews, Mokhtarian et al 1995). Other work has uncovered anecdotal and empirical evidence suggesting travel stimulation or generation (Mokhtarian and Salomon 1997; Salomon 1986; Mokhtarian 1990; Niles 1994), sometimes only on non-telecommute days. Some go so far as to hint that levels of traffic jams and congestion may heighten because it provides an opportunity to catch up with telephone messages and email (Moss and Townsend 2000).

Maintenance

The effect of ICT on maintenance travel has enjoyed perhaps the longest history of study. Researchers examined the impact of early telephone order (and delivery) businesses on the ease of rural living and the vitality of town commercial centers. Central tenets of this line of inquiry continue today with the advent of the internet and e-commerce permeating the simplest of maintenance transactions. These types of activities account for over half of all household trips (and 40 percent of personal miles travel), but there is a lack of knowledge about how they are affected by ICT. Some of the existing work is oriented towards the freight and delivery aspects of e-commerce (Golob and Regan 2001; Cairns 1996). The bulk of the maintenance travel-related literature, however, focuses on shopping (as opposed to maintenance-type activities such as banking or paying bills).

More than a decade ago Salomon and Koppelman provided a theoretical framework to understand home shopping (Salomon and Koppelman 1988) which was later supported with an empirical investigation (Koppelman et al 1991). While its preoccupation with telephone shopping limits the applicability of such work to a contemporary setting, this work continues to enlighten current study. An initial contribution they made was to distinguish between the act of shopping (the acquisition of information) and purchasing–a distinction of growing importance related to ICT activity. A second contribution is that they articulated five primary steps in selecting a piece of merchandise: (1) entry into the market, (2) choice among alternative shopping modes, (3) information gathering, (4) evaluation of information obtained, and (5) choice between purchase, continuing to shop or exiting the market. In a contemporary expose, Couclelis (forthcoming) provided a more detailed breakdown of similar tasks (see itemized list in later section) more t to ICT purchases.

Gould and Golob (1997) and Golob (1998) offer an overview of the transportation implications emerging from home shopping and on-line commerce. Her review focused on possible changes and demands placed on delivery services, the possibility of goods with no physical delivery, and the possible growth of new retail venues. She touched on a number of the difficulties in estimating the use of home shopping, including the need for understanding the different stages of shopping, attitudinal issues and opinions of consumers, as well as how ICT travel is related to other physical travel. Marker and Goulias (1999) describe a framework for understanding and estimating the use of ICT and grocery shopping. In so doing, they outline salient issues as they relate to the likely effects on traffic (e.g., substitution, consolidating loads, trip chaining), forms of delivery, and methods in modeling such activities.

To our knowledge the most applicable empirical work on maintenance travel is provided by Handy and Yantis (1997). They examined in detail the potential substitutability of three different types of activities: movie watching, shopping (non-grocery), and banking. These activities were chosen to represent the spectrum of non-work activities from entertainment to personal business with movie watching at one end (discretionary), banking at the other (maintenance), and shopping somewhere in the middle. They conducted a household survey in three different cities to explore individual use of and choices about the each of the activities. Not surprisingly, their results suggest complicated relationships between in-home activities and those requiring physical travel. For the most part, they found that out-of-home versions of movie-watching, shopping, and banking offer qualities that are not currently duplicated by the in-home versions.

Previous research on maintenance travel, while limited, has served to successfully identify salient dimensions for consideration. One issue that keeps emerging is that different goods have different potential for successful e-commerce. Gould and Golob (1997) highlighted that consumers will make decisions based on the four primary costs related to shopping: the cost of the item, the cost of the time to search for the item, the time to travel, and the expense of travel. There also appears to be wide variation in how different products are perceived to be more or less convenient to purchase on-line. According to one survey, home electronics, computer hardware and software are the most convenient items to shop for online; clothing and apparel are the least (Bhatnagar et al 2000). Our responsibility as transportation behaviorists is to understand how these subtle nuances relate to household travel. Furthermore, consumers prefer using their senses for many types of shopping, for example trying on a shirt, smelling perfume, sitting in a chair. In-store shopping offers immediate gratification and social interaction (Underhill 1999). Though, there seems to be consensus that significant potential remains for many other goods, most notably books, music and movies (both downloaded and delivered), travel and theatre tickets, and computer software and hardware (Underhill 1999; Bhatnagar et al 2000).

Discretionary

As evident in Table 19.1 the linkage between the use of ICT and discretionary activity is a topic that has received the least amount study. While the boundaries between maintenance and discretionary activity blur (thus the cross listing of some of the studies in Table 19.1), at least two related thoughts come forward with respect to discretionary activity. The first refers to the inherently social and psychological needs of humans (Salomon 1985). Much of the social interaction and human contact we require is invaluable and cannot be adequately provided for via electronic means. This need has important implications in how we spend our free time. The second consideration is that few discretionary activities (e.g., theaters, sporting events, pleasure shopping) can be replicated electronically. For example, renting a movie is not a substitute for going to the theatre because the two are usually not considered to be equivalent experiences. The latter usually provides a greater degree of social interaction and a higher quality product. This notion is reinforced in the Handy and Yantis study (1997) which looked at home movie rental, television and theatre visits. Primary reasons for going to the theatre include the size of the screen, newer movies, better sound, getting out of the house and going out with friends that for many reasons cannot be duplicated without leaving home. Both of these considerations suggest that in-home and electronic versions of goods and services are not likely viable substitutes for out-of-home and physical versions. For this reason, one should expect minimal travel savings (at best) with respect to reducing the roughly one-fourth of all discretionary trips currently completed.

A final issue considers the elasticity that may be embedded within discretionary activities. Salomon suggests that the increased leisure time resulting from increased efficiency from telecommuting results in increased leisure travel (Salomon 1985). (In this respect, reducing the time allotted to subsistence and maintenance activity may free up time for discretionary activity.). Although discretionary activity itself may not be becoming electronic, as ICT makes subsistence and maintenance activity more efficient, people will have more discretionary time and subsequently travel more often.

19.3 Part 2) Trends and Issues for Further Research

Having mapped the bulk of existing literature relating ICT and travel, the second part of this review combines that learned above with recent knowledge about how ICT is employed. The aim is to articulate future lines of inquiry and topics for further research. The difficulty of this task is compounded by the rapidly evolving nature of ICT, both the manner in which it is employed and its availability. For example, online spending reached all time highs in the second quarter of 2002, up 41% from the previous year to 17.5 billion. Some predictions go so far as to suggest that online consumer spending will increase to over 70 billion this year (Talarzyk and Widing 1994) –indeed a startling growth projection. On the contrary, some skeptics point to the still miniscule share of e-commerce (a mere 0.64 percent of all retail sales). There remains considerable uncertainty as to how this online spending will manifest itself, particularly as it relates to travel. Past failures of electronic home shopping have been documented (Talarzyk and Widing 1994). One need look no further than the experience of Kozmo.com (the now defunct online delivery service for sundries who closed operations after only three years) to learn of the relative uncertainty associated with this line of service.

Online users amount to an estimated 98 and 140 million people in the U.S. (between 34 and 50 percent of the U.S. population) (ePaynews 2002). This number is rising daily as Internet and other computer use becomes more deeply integrated into everyday patterns of behavior. In a similar growth phenomenon, there were over 128 million cellular phone subscribers by the end of 2001, up from 109 million in 2000 (Pastore 2002). But again, the mere availability of technology does not necessarily mean it will influence travel. For example, an estimated 66 million American internet users say they are on-line "just for fun," including sampling music, checking sports scores or electronic gaming (Horrigan and Rainie 2002). This category probably includes the gathering of information (e.g., reading about news events). Such use may enhance one's quality of life (by providing additional information or entertainment) but may have little role in affecting travel patterns.

The bottom line is that the research community is realizing that ICT affects different travel in different ways. A breakdown that analyzes substitution, modification, generation, or neutrality for one travel purpose is just the tip of the iceberg. We should not be surprised to see changes in one type of travel affect another type of travel. Some elements may substitute in one respect but enhance another. And, examining instances of subsistence, maintenance or discretionary travel in isolation oversimplifies issue. Past studies certainly point such issues of complexity and may identify such confounding issues as topics for future research. However, there is little writing that is available that suggests how to do it, much less a road map for framework for understanding such relationships. This part is admittedly more on the latter than the former but much needed nonetheless.

To more clearly articulate the complexities that pervade this research we provide Fig. 19.1. Our prism highlights three dimensions to represent how a comprehensive understanding of ICT and travel rests on knowledge from each leg. Absent of study of (or at least mention) one of these dimensions, a study falls short. The x-axis dimension–purpose of travel–is adequately defined in part 1 of this paper. But this dimension needs to be inextricably tied to the y-axis–the effect on travel. While described in previous literature (as well as above), the attention devoted to this topic is still relatively superficial. It is for this reason why further discussion is devoted below to the y-axis as well describing concepts introduced by the z-axis–the effect on sub-tasks of the activity.

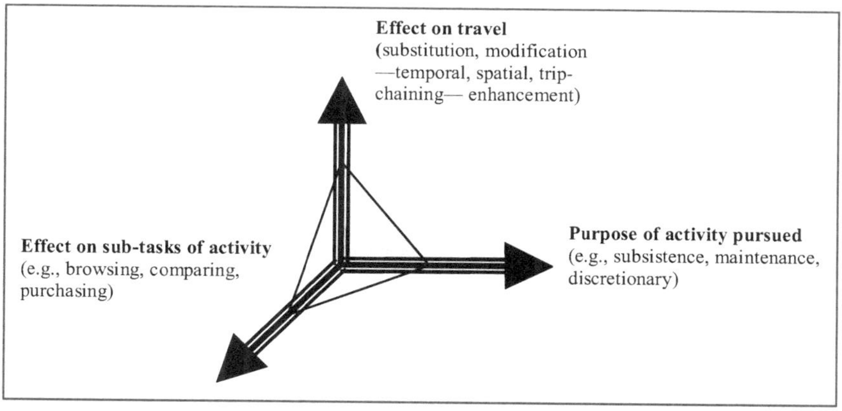

Fig. 19.1. Dimensions for further research of ICT and household travel

Effect on travel

A well recognized second dimension for inquiry relates to the effect ICT will have on travel. The principle effects–substitution, modification, generation, and neutrality–are described above. These four issues, however, comprise a limited range for this dimension. Travel is likely to be affected in ways broader and more detailed than just these four; or the travel may include more than one. It is important for us to understand the detailed behaviors that may be implied under each cover. Take for instance just one effect–modification. The three examples provided below describe some of the complexities.

- Imagine the case of the teleworker, who is home during the workday and picks up groceries in the morning when the crowds are less (rather than on their typical route home from work). In this case, the substitution of the subsistence trip provides the flexibility pursue a modification (i.e., temporal shift) for a maintenance trip.
- Imagine the role that internet information would have in affecting the geographic distribution of where residents shop. Here the knowledge provided by ICT affects the geographical distribution of where the individual shopped.
- Imagine how the time freed from on-line grocery shopping would allow increased time to sip coffee at the café. In this example we see how the substitution of maintenance travel increased the time spent in discretionary activities.

We quickly see the limits of any relatively simple substitution-modification-generation taxonomy. ICT may trigger changes mode of travel, the sequence of trips, the chaining of trips, and/or the time in which they are pursued. The issues are compounded when considered jointly. However, due attention is deserved.

Sub-tasks of the activity

The third piece of the ICT-travel puzzle is one that the research community is becoming increasingly aware of. Referenced above, it relates to the different ways in which ICT enters into sub-tasks associated with any given activity. Couclelis (forthcoming) provides greater detail on the general tasks outlined in Salomon and Koppelman (1988) that tend to be associated with ICT and shopping for any but the most trivial of goods. These tasks include: (a) becoming aware of need or want of a product, (b) gathering information about options, (c) searching and browsing, (d) seeking advise/expert help, (e) inspecting alternatives, (f) deciding on an item to be purchased, (g) deciding on a vendor, (h) purchasing a product, (i) tracking the status of an order, (j) getting an item to delivery point (e.g., home), (k) returning/exchanging an item, (l) seeking post-sales service. Only one of the tasks, purchasing the product, is commonly considered in analysis. It is, after all, the task in which the important transaction takes place and also the one that is instrumental to the livelihood of bricks and mortar establishments. While other tasks (for example, b, c, e, g, l) are recognized to be affected by ICT, a detailed and thorough understanding of the nature of these relationships is at the heart of internet shopping and currently unavailable.

For some endeavors, the availability of on-line information has already changed certain customs. The process of contacting governmental agencies or individuals, searching for housing, or pricing major purchases (Horrigan and Rainie 2002) are a few examples where internet use has started to eliminate the need for travel. Take for instance the purchase of a new car which typically involves stopping at several dealers to get the best price. It is now common practice to inspect the invoice price on-line prior to traveling to a single auto dealer to purchase the car. In this case "information gathering" has translated into travel substitution. But one must still be conscious of the fact that while ICT may help reduce travel associated with the acquisition of information it may not necessarily reduce travel associated with the purchase of an item. It would be interesting to identify these activities and thresholds that have been met to make such activities more mainstream.

When considering the role of ICT in completing subtasks a final matter stands out–differentiating between the population online buyers and online users. According to Jupiter Media of the 140 million online users, only 65 million (46 percent) are online buyers (ePaynews 2002). The most commonly cited reason for not purchasing on-line is the risk associated with relaying credit card information over the internet (Bhatnagar et al 2000). While this population is forecasted to increase in upcoming years, the division is an important issue for consideration because it implies a considerable population may be browsing for information.

Issues, Strategies and Hurdles

Much like any intervention that affects travel, the above text describes how issues relating ICT and travel are far from clear. The complexity demands continued methodological advancements and focused study. For example, many examples suggest tradeoffs exist between trip generation, mode split or other aspects of travel. The researcher is encouraged to bring methods, strategies, or techniques from other aspects of transportation research (or other fields for that matter) to tackle the problems. For example, few (if any) ICT studies closely examine these tradeoffs using econometric models designed for such purposes (e.g., simultaneous models). Frequently, such tradeoffs even fail to be mentioned. Alternatively, many of the tradeoffs may be best pursued using qualitative modes of inquiry, currently underused in transportation research. There remain seemingly endless modes of inquiry together with a burgeoning use of ICT

To help clarify examples research topics relating ICT and travel, we provide Fig. 19.2. Each box represents an example activity for investigation; a relatively comprehensive study would most likely shed light on multiple boxes. The manner in which the activity relates to two of the dimensions is represented by its placement in the box. The lighter shading (towards the right) is used to represent the degree to which ICT may be stimulating additional travel, much to the chagrin of many transportation planners. In future pursuits, the transportation researcher is encouraged to wrestle with a few pieces of the puzzle while respecting the overall picture of the puzzle. This is indeed a difficult line to toe.

Of course, myriad difficulties will exist. And, before such difficulties can be overcome, they need to be identified. Below, we identify some of these hurdles, many of which have been introduced in previous study (Salomon 1985; Hjorthol 2002; Gould 1998; Handy and Yantis 1997):

- Technologies that are widely promised for the future prove infeasible or are replaced by the next great technology before they have a chance to be adopted for mainstream use;
- The increasing familiarity of technology by children and other youth will likely have longer lasting impacts;
- There currently exists a dearth of information documenting all different purposes of travel (often just broken down by five different purposes) and modes (often failing to obtain reliable data for pedestrian trips);
- The need for uncovering and understanding the various ways in which individuals use different forms of technology (e.g., browsing versus purchasing);
- Separating subsistence from maintenance and/or discretionary travel–they are often times intricately related (for example, a decrease in subsistence travel will likely result in an increase in other travel (Salomon 1985)). Teasing out the effect of one is likely to tell on part of the picture;
- The interactions between different types of travel are likely to be different in various contexts. There are also methodological problems in measuring them (Salomon 1985);
- More extensive time use (and activity based travel) analysis is required to determine how time freed from using ICT might be used in other activities;
- The potential for cross-substitution between different types of activities (e.g., substitution of surfing the internet for watching television);
- There exists dramatic variation across households (access to educational and financial resources often determine the degree to which ICT influence household behavior).

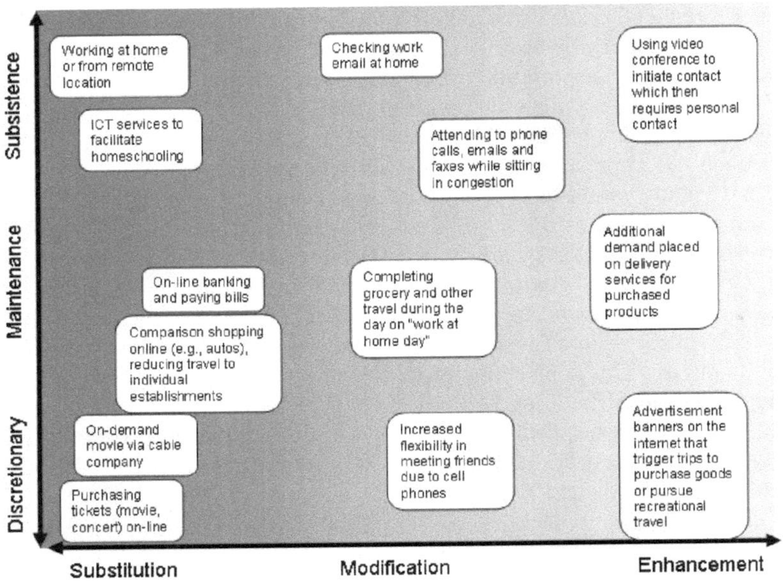

Fig. 19.2. Examples of the complexity in which ICT affects travel

Each box represents an example activity for investigation. The manner in which the activity relates to two of the dimensions is represented by its placement on the x and y axes (z axis not shown). Lighter shading (towards the right) represents the degree to which ICT may be stimulating additional travel

Implications for practicing planners and researchers

One purpose of this work is to stimulate additional research by providing a state of the literature and concrete examples of how this work is needed. This paper goes above and beyond past work but suggesting examples of the many different ways that ICT affects travel.

Strategies to expose the myriad of ways in which ICT affects household and personal travel can be better understood by pulling from other disciplines. For example, a stronger understanding of the spatial implications is especially important as the effect on efficient trip chaining and spatial-temporal components are central to understanding ICT and travel. A better understanding of the time and cost savings of ICT would perhaps increase the accuracy for econometric models. Finally, a deeper knowledge of the market segmentation of the different types of ICT uses would similarly enhance the ability to understand the rapid change.

Much of the ICT issue lies at the heart of land use and transportation planning. It has strong implications on crafting and revising the zoning codes in order to create more efficient land use patterns by using ICT to help off set peak period related problems. It is important to encourage development that will blend well together, i.e. blend ICT friendly and not-so-friendly developments together, blend substituters, enhancers together.

19.4 Summary

This paper serves two purposes to aid our understanding of how ICT and travel behavior relate. It first provides an up-to-date review of over fifty studies on the subject by mapping and discussing existing work across three dimensions. These three dimensions are the degree to which the study is (1) primarily conceptual or empirical in nature, (2) primarily addresses subsistence, maintenance, or discretionary activities, and (3) able to comment on the hypotheses of substitution, modification, generation or neutrality. Second, it identifies and describes a framework together with further issues to consider in future investigations relating ICT and travel. Examples are identified and there is a call for broader use of methodological advancements. The aim is that it will also serve as a springboard or a blueprint for more detailed lines of inquiry related to ICT and household travel.

The study of ICT and travel is complex and challenging–though one that provides several avenues for investigation. This task is one that has been best described by Mokhtarian (2000):

"against the slower moving demographic and organizational changes that may be occurring naturally, the highly volatile technological environment and attendant consumer response speed up some of these natural changes and bring about entirely new ones…Thus improving our understanding of these processes is a moving target, and no sooner do we think we have made progress in answering one question then we realize that the question has been rendered obsolete or unimportant in environmental shifts."

The work spotlighted in this review relates to only one piece of the ICT puzzle –that of household travel– which comprises an important consideration to burgeoning use of ICT. As congestion, auto-reliant travel, and centrifugal forces of development continue, researchers, modelers, and policy officials are likely to demand more detailed understanding of ICT's role in tackling such phenomena. Several avenues and courses of study are needed to help uncover such phenomena; this work helps in identifying the itinerary and providing a preliminary roadmap for doing so.

Acknowledgements

This work has been supported by the Intelligent Transportation Systems Institute at the University of Minnesota and the STAR21 Project as part of the State and Local Policy Program.

References

Batty, M (1997) The Retail Revolution. Environment and Planning B 29: 1-2.

Ben-Akiva M, Bowman JL (1998) Integration of an Activity-based Model System and a Residential Location Model. Urban Studies 35(7): 1131-1153.

Bernardino A, Ben-Akiva M (1996) Modelling the Process of Adoption of Telecommuting: Comprehensive Framework. Transportation Research Record 1552: 161-170.

Bhat C, Koppelman F (1993) A Conceptual Framework of Individual Activity Program Generation. Transportation Research 27A(6): 433-446.

Bhat CR, Misra R (1999) Discretionary Activity Time Allocation of Individuals Between In -Home and Out-of-Home and Weekdays and Weekends. Transportation 26: 193-209.

Bhat CR, Carini JP, Misra R (1999) Modeling the Generation and Organization of Household Activity Stops. Transportation Research Record 1676: 153-161.

Bhatnagar A, Misra S, Rao HR (2000) On Risk, Convenience, and Internet Shopping Behavior. Communications of the ACM 43(11).

Bowman JL et al (1998) Demonstration of an Activity-Based Model System for Portland. in 8th World Conference on Transport Research. Antwerp, Belgium.

Bradley Research and Consulting et al (1998) A System of Activity-Based Models for Portland.

Cairns S (1996) Delivering Alternatives: Successes and Failures of Home Delivery Services for Food Shopping. Transport Policy 3(4): 155-176.

Couclelis H (2002) Pizza over the Internet: E-commerce, the Fragmentation of Activity, and the Tyranny of the Region. Entrepreneurship and Regional Development, forthcoming.

Cox B (2002) E-commerce - Color it Green, in CyberAtlas.

ePaynews, Compiled Statistics (2002) http://www.epaynews.com/statistics/purchases.html#24.

Golob TF, Regan AC (2001) Impacts of Information Technology on Personal Travel and Commercial Vehicle Operations: research challenges and opportunities. Transportation Research C 9, 87-121.

Golob TF (2001) Travelbehaviour.com: Activity Approaches to Modeling the Effects of Information Technology on Personal Travel Behaviour. In: Travel Behavior Research, The Leading Edge, D. Hensher, Editor. Elsevier Science/ Pergamon: Kidlington, Oxford: 145-184.

Gould J, Golob TF (1997) Shopping without travel or travel without shopping? An investigation of electronic home shopping. Transport Reviews 17: 355-376.

Gould, J.: Driven to Shop? Role of Transportation in Future Home Shopping (1998) Transportation Research Record 1617: 149-156.

Guiliano G (1998) Information Technology, Work Patterns and Intra-metropolitan Location: A Case Study. Urban Studies 35(7): 1077-1095.

Hamer R, Kroes E, Oosterroom HV (1991) Teleworking in the Netherlands: An Evaluation of Changes in Travel Behaviour. Transportation 18: 365-382.

Hamer R et al (1992) Teleworking in the Netherlands: An Evaluation of Changes in Travel Behaviour - Further Results. Transportation Research Record 1357: 82-89.

Handy S, Mokhtarian P (1996) Forecasting Telecommuting: An Exploration of Methodologies and Research Needs. Transportation 23: 163-190.
Handy S, Yantis T (1997) The Impacts of Telecommunications Technologies on Nonwork Travel Behavior, Southwest Region University Transportation Center: Austin, TX: 51.
Handy SL, Mokhtarian PL (1995) Planning For Telecommuting. Journal of the American Planning Association 61(1): 99-111.
Hjorthol RJ (2002) The Relation Between Daily Travel and Use of the Home Computer. Transportation Research A 36: 437-452.
Horrigan JB, Rainie L (2002) Getting Serious Online. Pew Internet and American Life Project: Washington D.C. 22.
Jonnalagadda N et al (2001) Development Of Microsimulation Activity-Based Model For San Francisco: Destination And Mode Choice Models. Transportation Research Record 1777: 25-35.
Kilpala HK, Seneviratne PN, Pekkarinen SM (2000) Electronic Grocery Shopping and Its impact on Transportation and Logistics and Special Reference to Finland. in 79th Annual Meeting of the Transportation Research Board. Washington DC: Transportation Research Board.
Kitamura R (1988) An Evaluation of Activity-based Travel Analysis. Transportation 15: 9-34.
Kitamura R et al (1990) Telecommuting as a Transportation Planning Measure: Initial Results of California Pilot Project. Transportation Research Record 1285: 98-104.
Koppelman F, Salomon I, Proussaloglou K (1991) Teleshopping or Store Shopping? A Choice Model for Forecasting the Use of New Telecommunications-Based Services. Environment and Planning B 18(4): 473-489.
Kraut RE (1989) Telecommuting: The Trade-offs of Home Work. Journal of Communication 39(3): 19-47.
Lehman-Wilzig S (1981) Will Cities Become Obsolete? Telecommunications Policy 5: 326-328.
Lund JR, Mokhtarian PL (1994) Telecommuting and Residential Location: Theory and Implications for Commute Travel in Monocentric Metropolis. Transportation Research Record 1463: 10-14.
Ma J, Goulias KG (1997) A dynamic analysis of person and household activity and travel patterns using data from the first two waves in the Puget Sound Transportation Panel. Transportation 24(3): 309-331.
Marker JT, Goulias K (1999) A Framework for the Analysis of Grocery Teleshopping. in 79th Annual Transportation Research Board.
Misra R, Bhat CR (2000) Activity Travel Patterns of Non-Workers in the San Francisco Bay Area: Exploratory Analysis. Transportation Research Record 1718: 43-51.
Mitchell WJ (2002) Electronic Cottages, Wired Neighborhoods and Smart Cities. In: Smart Growth: Form and Consequences, T.S. Szold and A. Carbonel, Editors. Lincoln Instuitute of Land Policy: Cambridge, MA: 66-81.
Mokhtarian PL Salomon I (1994) Modeling the Choice of Telecommuting: Setting the Context. Environment and Planning A 26: 749-766.
Mokhtarian PL, Salomon I (1996a) Modeling the Choice of Telecommuting: 2. A Case of the Preferred Impossible Alternative. Environment and Planning A 28: 1859-1876.

Mokhtarian PL, Salomon I (1996b) Modeling the Choice of Telecommuting: 3. Identifying the Choice Set and Estimating Binary Choice Models for Technology-based Alternatives. Environment and Planning A 28: 1877-1894.

Mokhtarian PL, Salomon I (1997) Emerging Travel Patterns: Do Telecommunications Make a Difference. in Recent Developments in Travel Behavior Research. Austin, TX: Oxford.

Mokhtarian PL, Meenakshisundaram R (1999) Beyond Tele-substitution: Disaggregate Longitudinal Structural Equations Modeling of Communication Impacts. Transportation Research C 7(1): 330-352.

Mokhtarian PL (1998) A Synthetic Approach to Estimating the Impacts of Telecommuting on Travel. Urban Studies 35(2): 215-241.

Mokhtarian PL (1990) A Typology of Relationships Between Telecommunications and Transportation. Transportation Research A 24(3): 231-242.

Mokhtarian PL, Nagurney A, Dong J (2001) Teleshopping versus Shopping: A Multicriteria Network Equilibrium Framework. Mathematical and Computer Modelling 34: 783-798.

Mokhtarian PL (1991) Defining Telecommuting. Transportation Research Record 1305: 273-281.

Mokhtarian PL, Handy SL, Salomon I (1995) Methodological Issues in the Estimation of Travel, Energy, and Air Quality Impacts of Telecommuting. Transportation Research A 29(4): 283-302.

Mokhtarian PL (2000) Telecommunications and Travel, in Transportation and the New Millenium. Transportation Research Board: Washington DC.

Mokhtarian PL (1991) Telecommuting and Travel: State of the Practice, State of the Art. Transportation 18: 319-342.

Moss ML, Townsend A (2000) How Telecommunications Systems Are Transforming Urban Spaces. In: Cities in the Telecommunication Age: The Fracturing of Geographies, J.O. Wheeler, Y. Aoyama, and B. Warf, Editors. Routledge.

Niles J (1994) Beyond Telecommuting: A New Paradigm For The Effect of Telecommunications on Travel. Department of Energy: Washington DC.

Nilles J (1993) City of Los Angeles Telecommuting Project Final Report. JALA International Inc.: Los Angeles: 89.

Nilles JM (1991) Telecommuting and Urban Sprawl: Mitigator or Inciter?. Transportation 18: 411-432.

Nilles JM (1976) The Telecommunications-Transportation Tradeoff. Development of Policy. New York City: Wiley. 196.

Nilles JM (1988) Traffic Reduction by Telecommuting: A Status Review and Selected Bibliography. Transportation Research 22A: 301-317.

Parker EB (1976) Social Implications of Computer/Telecoms Systems. Telecommunications Policy 1: 3-21.

Pas E (1982) Analytically Derived Classifications of Daily Travel-Activity Behavior: Description, Evaluation, and Interpretation. Transportation Research Record 879: 9-15.

Pas E (1984) The effect of selected sociodemographic characteristics on daily travel-activity behavior. Environment and Planning A 16: 571-581.

Pastore M (2002) Wireless Voice Encroaching on Wireline Customers, in Cyber Atlas.

Pendyala RM, Goulias KG, Kitamura R (1991) Impact of Telecommuting on Spatial and Temporal Patterns of Household Travel. Transportation 18: 383-409.

Preece J (2001) Sociability and Usability in Online Communities: Determining and Measuring Success. Behaviour and Information Technology 20(5): 347-356.

Reichman S (1976) Travel adjustments and life styles: a behavioral approach. In: Behavioral Travel -Demand Models, P. R. Stopher and A. H. Meyburg, Editors. Lexington Books: Lexington, MA: 143-152.

Salomon I, Koppelman F (1988) A Framework For Studying Teleshopping Versus Store Shopping. Transportation Research A 22: 247-255.

Salomon I, Koppelman FS (1992) Teleshopping or going shopping? An Information Acquisition Perspective. Behaviour and Information Technology 11(4): 189-198.

Salomon I, Schneider HN, Schofer J (1991) Is Telecommuting Cheaper Than Travel? An Examination of Interaction Costs in a Business Setting. Transportation 18: 291-318.

Salomon, I (1986) Telecommunications and Travel Relationships: A Review. Transportation Research A 20(3): 223-238.

Salomon I (1985) Telecommunications and Travel. Journal of Transport Economics and Policy 19(3): 219-235.

Shen Q (1999) Transportation, Telecommunications and the Changing Geography or Opportunity. Urban Geography 20: 334-355.

Talarzyk W, Widing R (1994) Direct Marketing and Online Consumer Information Services: Implications and Challenges. Journal of Direct Marketing 8(4): 6-17.

Toffler A (1980) The Third Wave. New York: Bantam Books.

Underhill P (1999) Why We Buy: The Science of Shopping. New York: Simon and Schuster. 255.

Viswanathan K, Goulias KG (2001) Travel Behavior Implications of Information and Communications Technology in Puget Sound Region. Transportation Research Record 1752: 157-165.

Wells K et al (2001) Telecommuting Implications for Travel Behavior: Case Studies from Minnesota. Transportation Research Record 1752: 148-156.

Yen JR, Mahmassani HS, Herman R (1994) Employer Attitudes and Stated Preferences Toward Telecommuting: An Exploratory Analysis. Transportation Research Record 1463.

SPRINGER NATURE

GPSR Compliance

The European Union's (EU) General Product Safety Regulation (GPSR) is a set of rules that requires consumer products to be safe and our obligations to ensure this.

If you have any concerns about our products, you can contact us on ProductSafety@springernature.com

In case Publisher is established outside the EU, the EU authorized representative is:

Springer Nature Customer Service Center GmbH
Europaplatz 3
69115 Heidelberg, Germany

FSC
www.fsc.org
MIX
Papier | Fördert gute Waldnutzung
FSC® C083411

Kolibri 360 GmbH
Ferdinand-Jühlke-Straße 7
99095 Erfurt, Deutschland
produktsicherheit@kolibri360.de